D1538094

Data Warehouse

from Architecture to Implementation

Barry Devlin

 **ADDISON-WESLEY**

An imprint of Addison Wesley Longman, Inc.

Reading, Massachusetts • Harlow, England • Menlo Park, California • Berkeley, California
Don Mills, Ontario • Sydney • Bonn • Amsterdam • Tokyo • Mexico City

Executive Editor:	Lynne Doran Cote
Associate Editor:	Katherine Harutunian
Production Supervisor:	Patty Mahtani
Manufacturing Supervisor:	Charles Dutton
Cover Design and Illustrator:	Eileen Hoff
Copy Editor:	Susan Middleton
Proofreader:	Joyce Grandy

Library of Congress Cataloging-in-Publication Data

Devlin, Barry
    Data warehouse: from architecture to implementation / Barry
Devlin
    p.   cm.
    Includes index.
    ISBN 0-201-96425-2
    1. Database management. 2. Database design. I. Title.
    QA76.9.D3D473   1997
    005.74–dc20   96-27708
                                         CIP

This book represents the views of the author, and not necessarily the views of IBM or the publisher.

Copyright © 1997 Addison Wesley Longman, Inc.

All rights reserved. No part of this publication may be reproduced, stored in a retrieval system, or transmitted, in any form or by any means, electronic, mechanical, photocopying, recording, or otherwise, without prior written permission of the author.

Text printed on recycled and acid-free paper.

ISBN 0201964252

6 7 8 9 1011 MA 02 01 00

6th Printing   January 2000

For my father, Gerry

Preface

I first conceived of the idea of writing a book on data warehousing during a series of 2-day seminars known as the "Information Warehouse Master-Class" that I and a number of IBM colleagues had developed and presented around the world from 1992 to 1994. From the many companies that attended these seminars, one principal requirement was clear: they needed a common definition or architecture for a data warehouse, detailed enough to drive a consistent implementation within their organizations, yet concise enough to allow the whole company to understand and accept it. It was from the MasterClasses and the needs of these companies that I developed the representation and terminology of the data warehouse architecture used in this book.

In 1992, only a few real data warehouse implementations existed, each one hand-crafted and custom-built. Today, the vast majority of companies are planning to build or are actually building a data warehouse. While working with these companies over the years, I and other consultants saw the need to develop methodologies that cover the entire implementation process. This process continues to present major difficulties for many data warehouse implementations. I am convinced that companies today need a generalized and rational implementation approach to this complex process. The methodology described in this book is the result of crafting and proving the implementation approach over the years in real warehouse implementation projects.

Clearly, I have distilled the material covered here from interactions with many colleagues within IBM, with other consultants working in the field, and most especially from many hours of work with clients. Without their contributions, this book could not have been written. On the other hand, responsibility for any errors or misinterpretations is, of course, mine.

It would be impossible to acknowledge by name everybody who has contributed to this book. To name anybody is to run the risk of omitting some valuable contributions; to those people I apologize in advance. However, I would like to especially thank a number of people either individually or collectively, whose support, knowledge, or time made this book possible:

- the team who designed and built the original data warehouse in Dublin for IBM Europe

- the members of the Information Warehouse Solution Centre from 1991 to 1994

- the companies I've worked with over the years, especially those who have agreed to be directly referenced here: Martijn Bossenbroek (ABN AMRO), Børre Lunde and Solveig Øien Berg (Gjensidige), and Laura Sager (Whirlpool)

- the colleagues who have contributed to or reviewed the material: John Bair, Peter Cabena, Ciarán Ennis, Keith Holmes, Edwin Humphreys, Jim McGovern, Paul Murphy, Barry O'Brien, Pat O'Sullivan, Phil Teale, Michael Storey, and Feargal Supple

- the external reviewers who have added significantly to the book: David Christian, John Kneiling, Eric Rawlins, Richard Rist and Terry Moriarty

- John Holland and Dónal O'Shea, who introduced the book to Addison Wesley Longman

- the team at Addison Wesley Longman: Lynne Doran Cote, Katherine Harutunian, Patty Mahtani and especially my editor Susan Middleton

Last, but not least, a special word of thanks to my family, Lil, Katherine, Alan and Emma, who have become convinced over the past year that I can exist only in symbiosis with my PC.[1]

Barry Devlin

---

[1] The text of this book was produced entirely in Microsoft Word and the graphics were developed using Lotus Freelance Graphics.

Table of contents

Part IV Unlocking the data asset for end users

10 Designing business information warehouses   *223*

11 Populating business information warehouses   *247*

12 User access to information   *261*

13 Information—data in context   *275*

Table of figures and tables

Figures

Tables

Chapter 1

Introduction

Information is pivotal in today's business environment. Success is dependent on its early and decisive use. A lack of information is a sure recipe for failure. The rapidly changing environment in which businesses operate demands ever more immediate access to information. New management theories require its pervasive use as they restructure the way in which organizations operate internally.

Few businesses have more than a fraction of the information they need. They describe themselves as "drowning in data" but lacking even the most basic information. The distinction between data and information is fundamental to the problem businesses face. **Data** is what the information systems (IS) department creates, stores, and provides. **Information**—data in its business context—is what the business needs.

As businesses transform themselves to compete in an ever more rapidly changing world, the world of information as seen by managers and other decision makers is also undergoing extensive, fundamental change. Here, as in the real world, borders are being moved, removed, or rebuilt. Former hegemonies of information have collapsed, to be replaced with new approaches. Where once there was a need for order and structure, now the focus is dynamic, shifting, and changing.

Within all this change, one requirement takes on a new importance. The end user has always hoped that the information world is "round"; that any place on its surface can be reached from any other point by any path. The need now is to get there faster, more easily, and with more certainty than before, and to get there independently, unaided by the IS department.

The problem is that the IS department has always been too busy on its individual islands of data to look beyond their shores. Of course, IS managers know that the information world is round—it's just too big, too complex to tackle. However, the end user's need for information in this rapidly changing environment leaves IS organizations with little choice but to raise their sights and consider the wider world. Data warehousing provides the means to do this.

1.1 Why this book?

The changes outlined above are of enormous significance to business. In many cases, adapting to them will be the difference between survival and success. The IS department has a vital role to play in supporting the business through these changes. Unfortunately, they come at a bad time for IS. (End users have been known to ask when isn't a bad time for IS!) The IS department is under pressure to reduce costs yet still deliver ever more advanced function. Furthermore, the technology is changing more rapidly than ever.

The purpose of this book is to enable the IS department, by using data warehousing, to respond effectively to the business and technological changes that are taking place and, indeed, to support and promote these changes.

This book provides the means to understand, design, and build a data warehouse.

1.2 Audience

As is evident throughout this book, data warehousing bridges the gap between the end user and IS. To implement a warehouse, the IS shop needs a broad understanding of what the business needs for data are and how pervasive access to data can transform the business. To support its implementation, end users need to understand some of the problems associated with the current IS infrastructure and the reasons the warehouse cannot be built overnight.

The primary audience of this book is the group of people in the company who will be responsible for planning and implementing a data warehouse. This group will be composed of both IS staff and end users, but will most likely have a stronger IS content. Therefore, if you are the IS manager, designer, or architect of your company's warehouse project, this is your guidebook. It attempts to answer the two most common questions about a data warehouse: What *exactly* is it? and How can it *ever* be implemented?

End users who need to justify a data warehouse and are involved in planning its application to business problems are the other target audience. If you are such an end user, the book provides you with the basis for answering two of the most pervasive end-user questions about data warehousing you're like to face: Why do it? and, If this warehouse is so important, why can't we have it now?

1.3   Structure

A data warehouse implementation and a herd of elephants have much in common. Both are extremely difficult to get moving, but when they do, everything in their paths is subject to change. In either case, the manager who leads from behind is likely to get "dumped on"! The structure of this book is designed to allow the implementation to be managed from the fore but to reduce the risk of being trampled.

Part I, *"The evolution of data warehousing"*, provides an historical overview of how management information needs and approaches have evolved. It shows where we stand today, before starting to plan for a data warehouse. It also provides a brief explanation of what a data warehouse actually is and how it is structured. In other words, where is the herd of elephants, and what is it doing at the moment?

Part II, *"Principles of data warehousing"*, takes a first, deliberately silent, balloon ride over the elephant herd. The objectives are to:

- define the scope of data warehousing

- describe, at a high level, the architecture of the data warehouse

- introduce techniques and tools that are vital to its implementation

In ***Part III***, *"Creating the data asset"*, you are now running in the middle of the herd. This part gives you the IS viewpoint of the approach you need in order to manage and control data before giving it to users. Topics include:

- designing and modeling the data warehouse

- populating the warehouse from existing operational data

- managing the data warehouse environment

For a view of the landscape after the elephants have passed, turn to ***Part IV***, *"Unlocking the data asset for end users"*. This part describes how the warehouse supports end users—with information rather than data. It covers the following topics:

- designing and populating information warehouses

- providing user access to information

- using various tools to provide the business context for this information

By ***Part V***, *"Implementing the data warehouse"*, you are ready to step in front of this herd of elephants, to lead and direct it. (You could consider this book a virtual reality trainer before attempting the real implementation!) This part brings together the detailed information you will need to:

- enable overall structuring of the warehouse
- justify its implementation
- build it according to a clear methodology

The conclusion provides a brief look over the horizon to glimpse some future directions for data warehousing.

No attempt is made in this book to evaluate or recommend products with which to implement a data warehouse. This has been a deliberate choice, for two reasons: First, it encourages implementers to postpone making product choices until they understand and accept the rationale for the approach. Second, because products in this area are evolving rapidly, any judgments made in this text would be likely to become rapidly obsolete. However, the theory and practice described here should provide you with a firm foundation for evaluating data warehousing products.

Part I

The evolution of data warehousing

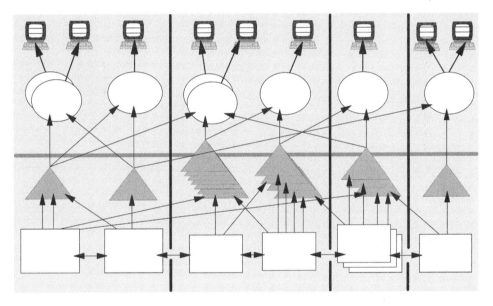

The historical context

Chapter 2

The data warehouse—a brief history

The concept of a data warehouse springs from the combination of two sets of needs—two sets that are not normally associated, but, which taken together, allow a new insight into the underlying problem and thus present a novel possibility of solution. These needs are:

- the business requirement for a company-wide view of information

- the need of the information systems (IS) department to manage company data in a better way

Taken alone, the business demand for a company-wide view of information can lead to solutions based on allowing any user to access any data wherever it resides. However, such solutions are simplistic because they ignore the fundamental distinction between data and information. In fact, what business users require is information—often defined as data within its business context. Because of the way applications have been and continue to be built, they not only contain data divorced from a business context, but are also seldom consistent across the breadth of the company. Such data is simply unsuitable for direct use by end users.

Similarly, the IS need for improved data management, when taken alone, seems to present no more than an IS cost-reduction or technology implementation project, albeit one of considerable size and complexity. Thus, on the basis of implementation cost and return on investment alone, this requirement sinks to the bottom of the priority list.

However, combining the two sets of needs gives a new perspective. If the IS needs for data management were addressed, the business need for a company-wide view of data would be far easier to meet. Similarly, the need for a company-wide view of data and the obvious business benefits it would bring are the justification required for solving the data management problem. It was from this juxtaposition of user and IS needs that the concept of a data warehouse evolved. The word "evolved" is particularly appropriate in this context. The data warehouse has been approached many times and from many directions in the last decade; many partial implementations exist today. But its full potential has not yet been realized because no comprehensive methodology exists and because software tools lack the necessary function.

In the mid-1990s, data warehousing has become one of the buzzwords of the computing industry. While those of us who have been preaching the value of the concept for almost a decade may see this development as a vindication, such popularity brings its own problems. One problem is that the underlying meaning of the term becomes diluted as vendors emphasize and adapt particular concepts to match the strengths of their products. It must be remembered that data warehousing was not, and indeed cannot be, vendor driven. It was invented by real companies to satisfy their known business needs. These needs will continue to exist and will even grow as the technological environment in which business operates becomes ever more complex. Data warehousing, whatever its current popularity, should not be seen as a passing fashion.

To trace the history of the data warehouse, shown in Figure 2-1, is to some extent to trace the history of computing itself. Many of the key developments in computing in general have directed the evolution of the data warehouse. The historical aspects themselves are only of peripheral interest. However, the progression of technical and business developments can be used as a yardstick against which to measure the current situation in any company or part of a company, in order to understand how best to proceed.

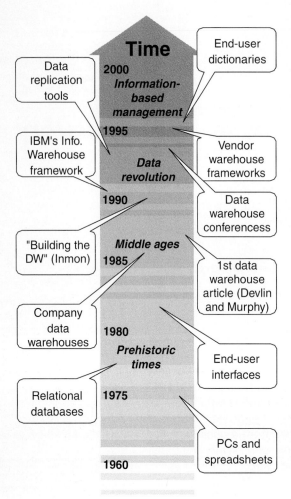

Figure 2-1: *Data warehouse evolution*

This chapter traces the historical evolution of data warehousing over the last 20 to 30 years and leads to a set of five key assertions of the information needs that companies must address. It also provides an initial definition of the structure and components of the data warehouse.

2.1 Prehistoric times—before the 1980s

The first appearance of the end user in the geological record can be traced to the period from the early to mid-1970s. Prior to this era, computing was solely the preserve of the IS shop, and data was distributed to the business on reams of green line-flow paper. Two technical developments—the PC and the relational database—during this period contributed to the emergence of the end user as a separate species.

The development of the microcomputer—or, as it later became known, the PC—along with the first data-oriented, end-user application, the spreadsheet, drove the emergence of the end user. With these first crude tools, end users began to stand on their own feet, taking control of their own data for the first time, and working beyond the shadow of the IS shop. While the data available was restricted and highly localized, the experience of independence was a major advance for end users, giving them the confidence and basic skills to take advantage of the later technical developments of that era. This new species of end user was characterized by its ability to prosper on the border between the empire of the businessperson and the land of the data-processing expert.

Up until the mid-1970s, because of the complexity of computer hardware and software, the end user was a rarity. Most businesspeople had little exposure to technology and looked to "someone else" to provide them with any information they needed as a basis for decision making. Data-processing people, on the other hand, were generally forced by the technology of the time to dedicate themselves to the physical aspects of manipulating bits and bytes in the machines they tended.

By the mid-1980s, the gulf between these two approaches had diminished significantly, and end users with the ability to deal with both the business and technical aspects of data became more common. Their growth in number was enabled by the simplification of data-processing technology, most evident in the PC, that occurred around that time.

It would be unfair to say that IS departments resisted the advent of the end user. From today's perspective, with the seemingly obvious advantages of the PC as an end-user platform, it is easy to assume that no other solution is possible. However, at that time, time-sharing systems, mainframe or minicomputer based, were seen as an obvious way to support and promote the end-user movement while retaining the necessary degree of control over it. Indeed, many of the issues identified by IS managers in the 1980s relating to the control and management of data and software in the PC environment are still not fully resolved, and are reemerging in the context of current debates on how to use the Internet and intranet within companies.

Distinguishing characteristics of end users

End users are:

- *familiar with business terms*

- *driven by real business needs to solve existing problems or to find new opportunities*

- *aware of the value of "real" information in decision making*

- *at ease using technology to meet their goals*

- *open to "do-it-yourself" solutions but keen to avoid repetition*

- *understand the meaning of data in current applications*

The second technical development of this era, which had profound effects on the evolution of the end user, was the definition and development of the *relational data model* [Codd (1970)] and its subsequent introduction into database products. It is true that both IS personnel and the vendors themselves saw the relational database simply as a new and improved database design to support traditional transaction processing. However, mediocre transaction-processing performance in the first products, combined with the recognition by end users that this new database model afforded greater flexibility, led to the adoption of the relational paradigm as the basic technology for providing data to end users.

In many respects, this was an era of experimentation in end-user computing. Most of the data provided was restricted in scope, and users were primarily interested in what could be done with the data on hand rather than in what other, better data was available. The first, primitive end-user tools grew in sophistication in this period, evolving into on-screen charting, report generation and formatting, as well as query management tools.

The IS reaction to this explosive growth in tools and functions was, quite naturally, to try to impose order on this seeming chaos. This was usually done through evaluation, approval, and certification processes aimed at choosing a relatively restricted number of end-user tools that would be supported by the IS organization. This process continues to some extent today, but it is more prevalent in those organizations where end-user function remains secondary in the business priorities or where the IS department still retains tight control of the data of the company.

Companies that survived and prospered beyond this era learned, in general, to promote and encourage this new and relatively untamed species of end users, and IS shops began to look for ways to feed them the data they needed. The application-oriented approach to delivering data to end users, described in Chapter 3, was the primary means of doing this.

The decline of data processing

Data

The computerized representation of business information.

As the end user was emerging, another trend became evident. This relates to the ways that computing can be justified and where it benefits the overall business.

Over the past 30 years, almost all of the data-related aspects of running a business have been automated. Business managers have generally justified these developments on a "do it cheaper" basis. Automation of manual and mainly repetitive processes can be subjected to time-and-motion types of analysis. Benefits such as increased speed of throughput and improved accuracy can then be measured in terms of cost reduction, and the savings can then be offset against the costs of the development and maintenance of the computer applications used. This justification model is widely understood today and widely used in successful data automation projects.

With the increasing power and sophistication of computer technology, more complex processes can be automated. Indeed, previously impossible processes can be implemented because of the computer power available. As an example, consider how the retail banking process has changed over the last few years by using new technology. Bookkeeping functions were automated at first to reduce the costs of the accounting processes. As the speed of applying transactions to the accounts increased, banking could begin to move toward a real-time environment. This

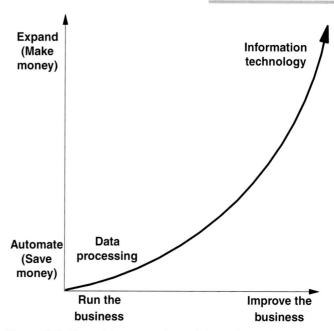

Figure 2-2: *From data processing to information technology*

further enabled the implementation of the now ubiquitous automated teller machines (ATMs), which are capable of many different banking functions and allow differentiation between banks by providing new services.

The outcome shown in this example, along with many similar examples from disparate industries, was that the justification for investment in computing moved from cost elimination to competitive advantage as a result of improved business function. This trend, shown in Figure 2-2, is often described as a move from a data-processing approach to a business-driven information-technology strategy.

Information

A representation of the business understood and used by end users.

In addition, it became apparent over time that the competitive advantage gained from data automation tends to be rather short-lived. This is because processes in the same industry segment are very similar. As a result, when one company finds an innovative way to change its process, its competitors can immediately begin to implement the same innovation in their own processes, and the playing field is rapidly leveled.

The challenge, therefore, has been to identify areas where computing could support activities beyond the day-to-day production processes. Support for decision-making processes became a prime target by the mid-1980s—at just the time end users were beginning to appear on the computing landscape in significant numbers. The combination of these two factors led to a new era in the evolution of management support systems.

2.2   The middle ages—mid- to late-1980s

If the previous era can be characterized by the technical innovations that led to the emergence of a new species of user, the identifying feature of the middle ages was an attempt to impose order on the world of the end user. The need for order was greatest among the larger companies with extensive production-computing facilities already in place. It was here, within the broader unstructured evolution of end-user computing, that outbreaks of architecture now occurred. Strategies and architectures are the preserve of IS organizations in large, successful companies, but it is often the case that such architecture groups are inward-looking and focus on purely IS concerns. In those cases where the IS architecture group had, in addition, a strong end-user input, the environment was right for the evolution of the next stage of warehousing—the adoption of a data warehouse architecture specific to the individual company.

The IS and user problems in informational computing will be described in some detail in Chapter 3, but one common thread runs through them: data used in different parts of the business is poorly integrated. The focus of these data warehouse architectures was thus data rather than function. Different companies approached the architecture from different directions but essentially ended up with similar solutions, each of which could be described as a subset of a complete architecture.

A key aspect of the solution, identified at an early stage, was the need for a common method for describing the data to be obtained from the operational systems and made available to the informational environment. The emergence of data modeling approaches [Chen (1976), Zachman (1987)] and tools at this time allowed IS personnel to begin the process of formally documenting the data needs of the users and the database structures required to satisfy those needs. While data modeling appeals strongly to the IS desire for law and order, unless it leads to the increased availability of data or significant improvements in quality, it is of less interest to end users. As a result, data modeling proposals are often met with some skepticism by management. However, when management realizes that the benefits of data modeling can best be achieved by implementing the modeled data in the end-user environment, it often takes a more positive view.

An early successful warehouse architecture and implementation dating to the mid-1980s at ABN AMRO Bank is described on page 13.

Another feature that occurs frequently in the records of this era, and that is also seen in the ABN AMRO example, is the provision by IS of a locally developed, improved user interface to data. In general, this approach resulted from the IS view that the end-user tools available in the traditional environments were not sufficiently user-friendly, especially in comparison with tools becoming available on PCs. Some organizations recognized that while PCs were the future end-user environment, the current inventory of dumb terminals and the lack of a manageable way of linking mainframes and PCs together drove the implementation focus toward upgrading the mainframe-based user interface.

An interesting aspect of the history of this era is the almost complete absence of major vendor initiatives in the fossil record. In the mainframe environment, the major database suppliers were concentrating on basic database function, often update-oriented, frequently performance-related. A few vendors, such as Teradata, did concentrate on end-user databases, but they were seen very much as niche players at the time. Query tools were aimed mainly at the data literate and were often seen as database accessories rather than tools in their own right. In the PC environment, the focus was on individual rather than corporate computing, and data on the PC was usually assumed to be personal, privately managed, and isolated from the company data, which resided on the mainframe.

Real-life example: ABN AMRO Bank (Netherlands)

ABN AMRO, one of Europe's largest banks, is a classic example of an early, successful data warehouse implementation. The initial work was undertaken from 1986 to 1989 in AMRO Bank, driven by the bank's IS shop. (AMRO and ABN Banks merged in 1990.)

A key feature of the implementation was the emphasis placed on end-user needs. However, the bank knew that end users could not definitively specify their long-term needs. As a result, these requirements were modeled rather broadly, and all available data was stored in the warehouse. This was implemented in a DB2 database. The reasoning was that the data warehouse should be as flexible as possible, and thus able to meet unanticipated user needs. This approach is quite different from the traditional development of management information systems, which tries to determine users' needs more precisely in advance.

Data was copied from the operational systems using COBOL programs. Such programs were developed because general data copying and manipulation tools were then rare. However, considerable maintenance was needed as the business environment changed.

A particularly innovative aspect of the implementation was a data-driven menu and query system, developed by the bank itself. Again the aim was to encourage users to find the data they needed themselves. The front end also provided a dictionary to the end users, so that they could understand the meaning and business context of the data they were using.

The success of this data warehouse implementation was seen in its initial uptake by users. In fact, in the first few years of general use, its usage grew at an annual rate of 50%, and by 1995 the warehouse supported some 3,000 end users and was still growing.

Data warehousing first emerged in this period between 1984 and 1988. It evolved in different ways in different companies. Significant steps were taken in understanding the need for a structure or architecture for making data available to end users. Companies recognized the importance of data modeling, and the value of the user interface became clear. A number of misconceptions also arose about the benefits to be gained and the size of company to which warehousing applied. These errors were cleared up later. But by the end of this period, those companies that had experimented in the area realized that warehousing was key to the expansion of end-user computing and were looking for ways to implement the concept.

Toward the end of this era, the first public definitions of a data warehouse architecture appeared. In 1988, for example, I collaborated on one of the first articles describing the architecture of a warehouse [Devlin and Murphy (1988)]. This article described work undertaken in 1985 and 1986 to design a data warehouse for internal use by IBM Europe. The almost universal reaction was agreement on the approach and functional needs but surprise that vendors were not providing product solutions.

Operational and informational systems

Early attempts to support decision making were based upon the automation of the traditional reporting approach. This led immediately to the concept of a partitioned view of the business data: one part dedicated to running the business at a detailed level and the second part focusing on managing the business at a summary level. By the end of the middle ages, a distinction had evolved between the *operational* (or production) systems and the *informational* (or decision support) systems, as shown in Figure 2-3. This distinction is fundamental and, although now widely known and accepted, is worth reviewing.

Operational systems have the following characteristics:

Operational systems

Run the business in real time, based on up-to-the-second data, and are primarily designed to rapidly and efficiently handle large numbers of simple read/write transactions.

- They run the business on a second-to-second basis.

- The data they contain is a current and largely real-time representation of the state of the business.

- Individual events (or transactions) in these systems are generally limited in scope, are rather simple, and often result in an update of the data.

- They are optimized for fast response time for predefined transactions, and have a special focus on the performance of update transactions.

- They are used by people who deal with customers or products on an individual level, for example, clerks, salespeople, and administrators.

- They are increasingly used by customers themselves.

The characteristics of **informational systems** are quite different:

- They are used to manage and control the business.

- The data is historical or point-in-time; that is, it represents a stable view of the business over a period of time or at a particular point in time.

- Optimization is for inquiry rather than update.

- The use of these systems is loosely defined and may be wholly unpredictable.

- They are used by managers and end users to understand the business and make judgments and decisions based on this knowledge.

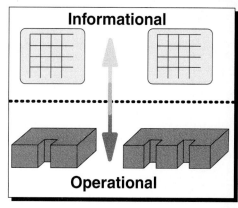

Figure 2-3: *The operational/informational split*

As shown in Figure 2-3, the boundary between the two categories is not crystal clear, but it is distinct enough to be useful. In fact, it provides a common starting point for all discussions of data warehousing. It should not be concluded from this division that an inventory of existing applications can be neatly categorized into two well-defined groups. Because of the way applications have developed, informational components may have been added to previously developed operational applications. This is most often the case where the informational function is report-oriented or performs a simple predefined inquiry. However, in many cases, it is fairly easy to identify which parts are operational and which are informational.

> *Informational systems*
>
> *Manage the business based on stable point-in-time or historical data, and are designed mainly for unplanned, complex, read-only query.*

2.3 The data revolution—the early 1990s

The majority of warehouse implementations in the middle ages were driven by enlightened IS organizations, which saw that the approaches then used for delivering data were not robust enough to support future growth and that the users' ability to use the data would be impaired by a lack of business meaning. The success of these implementations is a tribute to the persuasiveness of the IS managers who sold the concept to the business. They often convinced the users that the modest or even nonexistent immediate benefits of the warehouse implementation would be justified by future opportunities. These IS managers and architects were indeed the explorers and pioneers of a new territory.

Widespread acceptance of this new approach depended on the business community in general recognizing the need for and value of a broader view of business data than had been previously available. The first evidence of this recognition comes from the folklore of those early days of the data revolution. These tales usually illustrate the emergence of a new species of business manager, one who saw a new potential use for existing data, if only it could be readily accessed. Many of these tales don't use the phrase "data warehouse" to describe the approach taken, but the underlying principles are clear in hindsight.

Significantly, within these tales, there is a common theme—the use of data for marketing or competitive advantage.

At the beginning of this era, many industries were subjected to significant changes in their business environments. International recession cut profits, governments deregulated industries that were once closely controlled, competition increased in commodity markets, or political changes at a global level significantly altered the marketplace for certain types of goods.

In the airline industry, for example, deregulation has dramatically increased competition levels. One of the more successful airlines in this new environment achieved significant marketing advantage by integrating frequent flyer and ticketing data to drive a new and highly focused marketing approach. The relationship is obvious in retrospect—the most frequent travelers are businesspeople who often travel business class, book late, and need highly flexible tickets. Linking the data in the frequent flyer program to the ticket sales system allows new, targeted marketing campaigns offering special concessions to these travelers to ensure their loyalty to that airline. Furthermore, this combined data could allow both the prediction of the likely success of any campaign as well as the ability to track its progress. This marketing need clearly drives a warehousing requirement—the ability to join data from different sources and analyze it in new ways not envisaged when the original systems were designed.

The food industry offers a more dramatic example of the result of changing the ways in which data is used. A major manufacturer of snack foods was seeking to improve both the actual sales of the product as well as the efficacy of marketing campaigns. Point-of-sale data provided an obvious metric of sales in each store, but such data was voluminous and mostly inaccessible to marketing. Data on shelf space and location was also needed but was not automated. This information was generally known only to the manufacturer's delivery staff, which was the only contact point with the smaller retail stores. In the solution, the delivery staff's knowledge of product placement was automated and combined with a summarized set of point-of-sale data and information on local marketing campaigns. This process allowed the company to expand the role of the delivery staff to a combined sales and delivery role. Using known sales patterns, marketing campaigns, and proposed discount levels, they could now enter into negotiations with the store owners on product positioning and shelf space.

These two examples show the new business requirement that drove the data revolution. The business needed a new view of how the company operated—a view that covered previously separate aspects of the business. And taken to its logical conclusion, it became obvious that this view would eventually need to be enterprise-wide.

Toward benefit-based justification

The change of focus to business-driven warehouse implementation afforded an opportunity to reevaluate the types of benefits warehousing could provide. A feature of data warehousing in the middle ages, when IS was driving the implementation, was the assumption that the warehouse could be justified by cost savings or improved efficiency. This sprang from the traditional IS approach to cost justification, based firmly in an application-driven model of development. While such benefits do exist for a warehouse project, it is often quite difficult to justify a warehouse from this point of view alone. This is particularly the case when the initial implementation tries to resolve cross-departmental data inconsistencies. Many IS managers have discovered, to their cost, that trying to sell the warehouse with the message that it will resolve such inconsistencies is a dangerous approach. They meet with quizzical looks and some probing questions about who was responsible for introducing these very same inconsistencies.

> *In practice...*
>
> *Trying to justify a data warehouse solely on the basis that it will resolve current data consistency problems seldom succeeds.*

However, with a business-driven implementation, it became obvious that the prime benefits accruing from a warehouse related to its ability to allow for the use of the data in new and innovative ways. Thus, the warehouse became a vehicle for enterprise-wide business change and rejuvenation.

A 1996 study [IDC (1996)] of 62 data warehousing projects undertaken in this period shows an average return on investment of 321% for these enterprise-wide implementations in an average payback period of 2.73 years.

Also, whereas the initial warehouse implementations were limited to large companies with significant IS resources, the data revolution made it clear that the warehousing concept applied to any organization of sufficient size to warrant a division of labor, and consequently of data, between separate departments. Thus, warehousing does not apply to a company of, say, 50 people, but beyond that, potential benefits from the approach could arise.

Thus, the change from IS- to business-driven warehouse implementations led to a significant change in the perception of the approach. New areas of benefit led to new demands for data and new ways of using it.

Technological advances

From a technological point of view, advances in data modeling, databases, and application development methods began to make such demands feasible, if not immediately capable of complete implementation in all cases.

The main focus of vendors who entered the emerging data warehouse market during this period was on data replication and data access tools. It had long been recognized that the major technical difficulty in bringing data into the end-user environment was the fact that the data existed on a diverse set of platforms and that some form of automation was required to move the data efficiently and regularly from those platforms.

Over these years, operational applications have moved progressively away from extensive internal development toward the increasing use of purchased packages. Operational applications have been commoditized. This is simply a recognition that their incremental competitive value has so diminished that fully customized development is seldom viable. Informational applications, in contrast, promise significant opportunities for competitive advantage and return on investment. This promise, combined with the fact that data warehouses are built on top of a diverse legacy of operational applications, means that the informational environment will be the scene of most major application developments over the coming years.

The geological strata of this period are also littered with the advertising material of software and hardware vendors who began to realize the potential value of this market. Indeed, the popularization of the subject can be seen in the major data warehousing conferences that became prevalent at that time. While such popularization and vendor marketing activity gave rise to some cynicism, in truth, the convergence of business need and technical advances was a significant feature of the era, and brought the whole concept of warehousing to the forefront of executives' minds.

The data revolution, however, was not merely an era of popularization. It laid the foundations for an expansion of the warehousing concept beyond the types of data traditionally associated with decision support, and began to bring together all aspects of how end users perform their jobs.

In practice...
Informational application development will be the focus of investment over the next 5 years.

2.4 The era of information-based management—into the 21st century

Both the theory and the practical realization of warehousing have developed slowly over the last 10 years, with a peak in interest over the last year or two. The disadvantage of such a slow growth is that there exist a number of different definitions of what is meant by a data warehouse.

However, a number of key business needs, supported by clear technical directions, were defined as early as the 1980s, and these can still be seen as the key indicators today.

Today, we can look forward and dare to predict the future based on the history just outlined. Key to this prediction is the recognition that the need for competitive advantage (sometimes a polite term for survival!) is driving the support base for decision making from data toward information, as shown in Figure 2-4, and is expanding the audience for such support beyond the confines of the traditional management arena.

The direction can be characterized by the term ***information-based management*** (and abbreviated to IBM if that acronym were not already in use). It is transforming the way in which decision support is delivered to the end-user community. It can be summarized by the following five themes:

1. A single information source

The required raw data comes from many sources, both internal and external to the company, and exists in a variety of forms, from traditional structured data to such unstructured data types as documents or multimedia. Whatever the source or type of raw data, before being made available in the end-user environment, it must be cleansed and reconciled to ensure its quality and integrity. This reconciled information is the single, ultimate source for information-based management.

2. Distributed information availability

Information-based management is not solely a headquarters function, but will be highly distributed organizationally and geographically. These activities may need, and will often demand, independent but logically connected information stores to enhance mobility, performance, or confidentiality. Such stores are unlikely to map directly to individual sources of raw data.

3. Information in a business context

Users can best understand and handle information when it is placed in the context of the business activity they perform. Data definitions provided by business experts therefore become the norm, and information catalogs containing these definitions and aimed at

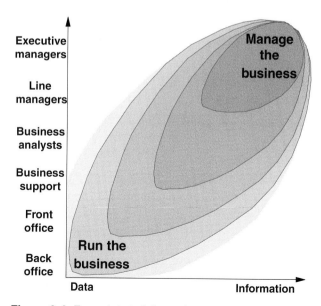

Figure 2-4: From data to information

the end user are likely to become sources for data definitions even for the IS department.

4. Automated information delivery

As data is transformed to information and moved through increasingly complex pathways within and between organizations, automated delivery mechanisms become a necessity. Automation is required not only in the actual delivery process but also in defining the required data transformations and movements. Especially in the area of distributed information, the usability of these automated delivery mechanisms must be assured.

5. Information quality and ownership

Information is a vital asset of any company, and, like any other asset, it must be managed and protected. Its quality must be ensured. Ownership of documented and traceable information is a prerequisite to realizing the value of this asset.

The remainder of this book describes the architectural and implementation consequences of these five themes.

2.5   What is a data warehouse?

Data warehouse

A single, complete, and consistent store of data obtained from a variety of sources and made available to end users in a way they can understand and use in a business context.

Based on this history of end-user computing, a first, high-level definition of what constitutes a data warehouse is appropriate.

A *data warehouse* is simply a single, complete, and consistent store of data obtained from a variety of sources and made available to end users in a way they can understand and use in a business context.

Achieving completeness and consistency of data in today's IS environment is, however, far from simple. The first problem is to discover how completeness and consistency can be defined. In the context of the business, this means understanding the business strategies and the data required to support and track their achievement. This process—called enterprise modeling—requires substantial involvement of business users and is traditionally a long-term process. In data warehousing projects, enterprise modeling is a vital input to the design and must progress in parallel with the actual implementation.

Knowing what data is required is but the first step. This data exists today in various sources on different platforms, and must be copied from these sources for use in the warehouse. It must be combined according to the enterprise model, even though it was not originally designed to support such integration. It must be cleansed of structural and content errors. This step—known as ***populating the data warehouse***—is recognized as one of the most difficult technical aspects of warehouse implementation.

The data thus copied and transformed according to the enterprise model is stored in the data warehouse. In order to be understood and used in a business context, this data must be transformed into information. The analysis needed to do this has already been performed in the modeling step above. What the end user needs is a ***catalog*** that describes the data in its business context and acts as a guide to the location and use of this information.

Finally, end users require a set of tools to analyze and manipulate the information thus made available. These tools provide the interface between the user and the information, and are the final step in this overall transformation of raw data into useful and usable information.

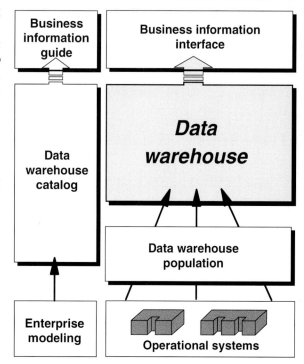

Figure 2-5: *The data warehouse*

These major components of the data warehouse are shown in Figure 2-5. They are expanded and defined in further detail throughout the remainder of this book.

2.6 Conclusions

The evolution of data usage just described has taken place against the background of technological change. Indeed, some of the strides made by end users were driven by the availability of new tools. This close synergy between usage and technology can be expected to continue, and is the reason why data warehousing cannot be solely the preserve of either IS or business departments.

Over the years, the focus for IS personnel has shifted from automating the day-to-day running of the business to enabling its growth and management. This shift is the fundamental driver of data warehousing—and the starting point for the architecture and implementation approach that is the subject of this book.

Some technical architectures make the assumption either that implementation will start from a green-fields situation or that the current structures can be demolished and rebuilt from the ground up. With data warehousing this cannot be the case. In fact, any approach to building a data warehouse that begins by insisting on redesigning existing operational applications is clearly doomed to failure because of the pervasive and disparate nature of these applications. Therefore, it is first necessary to put into context the technical environment from which most companies are starting today. That is the subject of the next chapter.

Chapter 3

Today's development environment

To understand where you are going, it is helpful to know your starting point. Our starting point is the existing IS environment. The approach to delivering IS function to the business has developed over the past 30 years and has many strengths. There are, however, a number of weaknesses that are particularly relevant when trying to meet the type of business needs described in Chapter 2. In particular, these limitations give rise to a variety of constraints on end users charged with managing the business. They also pose problems for the IS department when it is trying to implement a data warehouse in today's data processing environment.

This chapter describes:

- the origins of the current application development process

- how this development process has been applied to the operational environment

- how this development process has been applied in the informational environment

- the problems encountered by users and IS personnel as a result of this development process

3.1   Fragmented application development

All new tools and technologies are introduced into a business in a piece-meal fashion. This is a result of a number of factors. New tools are expensive and have to be applied in limited areas where the return on investment is greatest. New technologies are untried, and the risk of failure must be contained by the introduction of new approaches in a series of pilot projects. Data processing was no exception.

These factors, together with the normal human limitation on the size of task one can reasonably manage, have led to a fragmented implementation of data processing in all businesses. Departments or divisions, local or headquarters organizations, have all separately implemented operational applications to run those parts of the business for which they are responsible. This fragmentation can be seen in such examples as the following:

- Different order-entry applications are used for different (but closely related) product lines within the same company.

- A logically continuous process from order entry through dispatch to billing is split over a number of independent applications based on organizational responsibilities.

Of course, such fragmentation also has some benefits. With independent applications focused on separate areas of business function, projects can deliver application function to identified groups of users with well-defined needs. This focus enables more rapid deployment of functionality and leads to development projects of known scope and predictable size. These benefits are of significant value when developing operational applications.

3.2   Operational application development

The operational environment, by its very nature, is driven by the needs of the business to deliver goods or services. Thus it is defined primarily by the actions required rather than by the data used to accomplish this. Users' needs are described on the basis of short-term activities. Analysis can concentrate on what is needed to enter an order, schedule a delivery, and so on. IS can focus on the inputs and outputs needed for these well-bounded activities. Individual activities can lead to independent applications, each optimized for the needs of its related activity. The users' requirement here may be summarized as "automate this procedure". The success of the automation is judged on such simple measurements as increased throughput or reduced cost at the business level and on ease-of-use or response time at the level of the user.

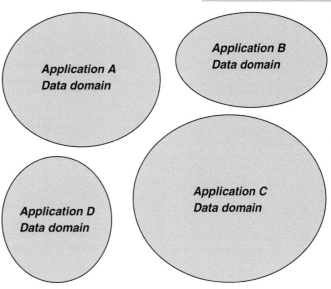

Data processing has been geared over the years to succeed using this model. Most business computing has been directed toward operational systems. IS personnel consequently have an application-oriented view. But what is an application? In this context, an **application** is simply a set of functions that the users perceive as related and have probably been developed in some integrated manner.

Figure 3-1: *User view—independent data domains*

However, the IS view of this integrated set of functions determines how the development is bounded, particularly the scope of data included in the application.

Figure 3-1 depicts the data scopes of operational applications in a traditional development environment. Here the IS department has defined a number of sets or **domains** of data, each of which corresponds to the application needs of a group of users. While this view is adequate for the users, IS personnel are burdened by the knowledge that, in reality, these sets of data are not truly independent. In some instances, data flows from one domain to the other, while in other cases, data is shared between domains. This is shown in Figure 3-2, where data is shared to varying extents between applications A, C, and D. In physical terms, this means that when these applications were built, they stored and accessed common data in one or more shared databases. This approach enables a high level of consistency between the data in these applications. This consistency is an important consideration when such data is copied for informational purposes, as described later in this chapter.

Figure 3-2 also shows data flowing between applications. In this case, a subset of the data in application A is passed at intervals to application B, which then uses that data as if it were its own. This process may introduce inconsistencies between these two sets of data. As an added complication, a further subset of data (either disjoint from or overlapping with the subset flowing in from application A) is now passed to application C at intervals. While this activity is driven by valid business needs, the net result may well be to decrease the level of consistency of the data among appli-

> ### Application
>
> *A set of functions that end users perceive as related and have probably been developed in some integrated manner.*

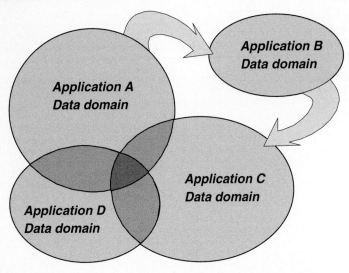

Figure 3-2: Reality—interlinked and overlapping data domains

cations A, C, and D, with unfortunate consequences for decisions based on the combined set of data.

As demonstrated here, application-oriented development is optimized to deliver function related to clearly defined but narrow goals. The effect on the data, however, is that the data used in the application is also focused on that same narrow goal. This can, and often does, lead to a situation where application design-ers build their own data definitions, based on their local application needs. Every IS organization can quote its own favorite examples of the inconsistency that ensues, but the most difficult problems arise when the key data is inconsistent. For example, if the customer number in one order-entry system is defined as an eight-digit field and in another as a seven-digit field, matching the data between the two applications becomes an immediate issue.

Where a strong data administration group exists within the IS organization, this type of problem can be reduced, but it is exceedingly difficult to elimi-nate entirely. Application developers and project managers are more strongly driven by the immediate needs of the business problem they are trying to address than by the concern that someone, somewhere in the organization, may at some future date encounter a problem because a previous project defined or used data in a nonstandard way.

The inconsistencies that exist and will continue to exist in the operational data mandate that a single source of informational data be defined. This would prevent operational inconsistencies from being reflected into the informational world. While many organizations continue to tackle the data consistency problems in the operational environment through programs entitled "application reengineering", this structure is widespread and can at best be changed only gradually.

It may also be assumed that these operational data consistency problems are solely historical, caused by immature approaches to application devel-opment. It then follows that widespread use of modern computer-aided software engineering (CASE) tools will eliminate these problems in future applications. While IS departments in some companies are employing these CASE tools with increasing success, a new breed of application de-velopers, empowered by PCs and client-server innovations to develop their own operational applications, is emerging in departments and local groups. In general, these developers have less understanding of the need for data consistency than do traditional IS developers. To further complicate matters, these new application developers work on an increasingly diverse set of hardware and software platforms, and with relatively primitive methods of coordinating their design decisions.

The reality is that the development of operational applications is function driven rather than data driven and is likely to remain that way for the foreseeable future. As a consequence, data in the operational environment will continue to lack the required level of consistency to enable true cross-enterprise data use.

3.3 Application-driven decision support

Since IS departments were familiar with application-driven development for operational systems, it was only natural that they would deploy the same approach when the first demands for informational applications emerged in the 1970s. It is instructive to chart this development and its problems by using an example. Although this example is based on the development of decision support in a multinational manufacturing company, an almost identical evolution has been described for most large companies in all industries worldwide.

Decision support systems (DSS) and management information systems (MIS)

Departmental DSS

Figure 3-3 shows the development of the initial **decision support systems** (DSS) for this company. Data is copied from various operational systems such as order-entry, accounts payable, and so on, within the different divisions. This data feeds DSS systems based on a variety of tools using relational databases (DB2, Oracle and SQL/DS) and file-based systems (APL/DI) aimed at specific end-user functions and running on different platforms such as Teradata, mainframes, and PCs. One of the first departments to need decision support was sales administration, which was responsible for planning and managing the sales of custom-built products. To support these needs, starting in the late 1970s, data was copied from the order-entry database, cleansed and transformed, and made available in APL/DI. Technically and organizationally, this process was eased because both operational and informational applications had broadly similar user bases, and were within the same part of the organization.

Traditional informational systems, often limited in scope or flexibility, providing end-user access to data.

The success of this system and similar needs in other departments led to similar departmental informational systems in such areas as finance and service among others. These systems were based on databases local to those departments, used locally developed copy programs, and fed into

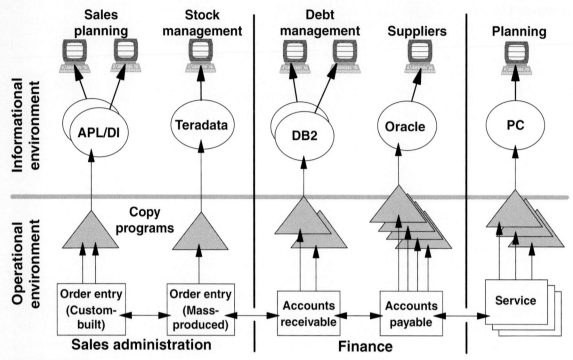

Figure 3-3: Departmental decision support systems—initial implementation

informational systems appropriate to the department's needs. This structure led to one of the first problem areas for users. Some departments wanted to take advantage of the relational databases then appearing, in order to provide better tools or improved ease-of-use for their users. In general, although this is clearly advantageous for users of these newer systems, it increases the complexity of the informational environment for users who must use multiple systems with conflicting user interfaces.

Such vertical fragmentation of informational systems is typical in many companies. This fragmentation is clearly business driven because the majority of the decision support needs in a department are related to data originating within that department. The span of these applications is very similar to the traditional operational applications that IS shops have previously developed. Also driving this fragmentation is the way end users express their requirements. Users' management information derives primarily from printed reports generated at intervals by operational applications. For this reason, users tend to express their needs for informational applications in terms of automating the delivery of familiar reports.

As end users' familiarity with the data available to them increases, so does the sophistication of their requirements. They are no longer satisfied with simple copies and summaries, and request more complex selections and combinations of data. Such requirements drive substantial amounts of selection and conditional logic (if-then-else statements) into the **copy programs**. In the copy programs shown in our example, new data provided in the informational environment was in some cases based on the combination and analysis of data over five different coded fields, each of which contained one of up to seven different values. For example, as the business changed in the early 1980s, sales analysis codes were invented and changed with some frequency. These codes consisted of combinations of information about the type of product, the industry sector of the customer, the terms and conditions of the sale, and so on. In general, this type of processing, common in many copy programs, leads to highly convoluted conditional logic. As the analysis needs of the business change, these constructs become increasingly complex, often littered with redundant code segments, and maintenance becomes a major problem.

> **Copy program**
>
> *A program written by the IS department to copy data from an operational system and customize that data according to specific end-user requirements.*

The complexity of copy programs increases for another reason, related to end users' familiarity with their data. Users gradually begin to realize there are errors or inconsistencies in the data they receive. While these problems may well originate in the operational applications which are the sources for these copy programs, solving them at the source is often too expensive or too slow. In these cases, the copy programs may include corrections, thereby further increasing their complexity and thus their maintenance costs. Given these factors, copy programs have a tendency to become classical "spaghetti code" over time.

In spite of these difficulties, in our example, these narrowly focused decision support applications were considered a success both by the IS shop, who provided the data, and by their end users, who benefited from them.

Departmental DSS in larger departments

However, even within individual departments, users soon needed data from more than one operational application and to combine the results. This stage of development is illustrated in Figure 3-4. For instance, in the sales administration department, separate operational applications had been implemented for different types of product. Orders for traditional products were handled by a large common IMS application. Orders for mass-produced products were handled through a separate minicomputer-based application. Spare parts were often tracked through local applications on a variety of hardware and software platforms. To answer the most basic questions, like how much business is obtained from a particular customer, data from all these systems had to be combined. In order to do this, the scope of the copy programs was enhanced to take data from a number of systems and combine it in the DSS environment.

As will be evident to any IS department that has attempted it, this step immediately brings to light any inconsistencies in data between the source applications. These inconsistencies can exist at two levels.

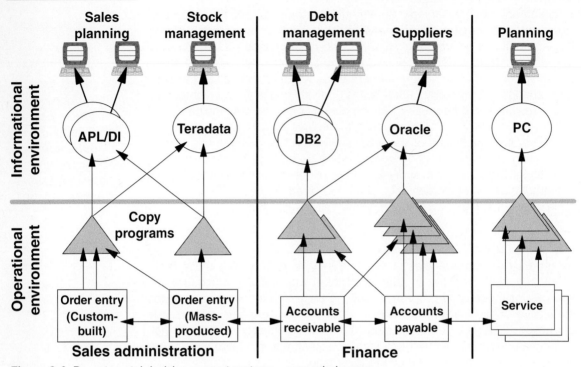

Figure 3-4: Departmental decision support systems—expanded scope

The first, and more fundamental level, is in the data definitions, as previously mentioned. Inconsistencies in data definitions are important because they can identify interpretations of the business that differ fundamentally from one application to the next. Consider the case of an order for a ship and an order for a box of rubber grommets. It is likely that once an order for grommets is in the database, it is considered legally binding, whereas the order for a ship may appear in the system in a conditional mode prior to legal or contractual commitment. Thus, when trying to ascertain the current value of business outstanding, these two orders in their respective databases should be treated differently, even though their data definitions are unlikely to reflect this. Resolving this type of inconsistency in the copy program generally requires a detailed analysis of the business processes supported by each of the operational applications. This is followed by the inclusion of conditional logic in the copy program to deal with the different cases. If sufficient differentiation has not already been made in the operational databases between the opposing business meanings, it may be necessary to modify the operational applications themselves to allow meaningful informational comparisons.

The second level of inconsistency is in the data itself where data usage conventions differ across applications. For example, in one application a contact name field may be described as "Last-name, First-name", while in another it is described as "First-name Last-name". Resolution of this type of inconsistency is less expensive than for the previous case, because detailed analysis of the operational applications is unlikely to be required. However, implementing a solution in the copy program is risky if the conventions for data usage are not rigorously enforced in the operational application and if they vary over time.

In addition to these data-related problems, the technical difficulties of obtaining data from different hardware and software platforms prior to its combination and reconciliation are also a significant obstacle to overcome.

However, within the departmentally oriented informational applications described earlier, these types of problems can be overcome, and in this example company they were broadly known and understood by the IS organization in the early 1980s. The end users were thus generally satisfied with the data made available to them from within their own departments. However, it was becoming apparent at this time that there was an additional need—most departments needed data that could only be obtained from the operational databases of other departments.

Cross-departmental DSS

The development of cross-departmental DSS in our example company is shown in Figure 3-5. The main consequence of this development was a large increase in the number of data flows between the operational and informational environments. In addition, the sources and targets of these data flows were owned by different departments.

Designing and building copy programs that spanned departmental boundaries presented IS developers with a larger set of problems. Of course, the inconsistencies in data definition and content encountered previously within departments recurred, but in more fundamental ways. But new problems also arose. One was organizational—how to balance the needs of the organizations involved. When end users in finance needed data from an operational application in sales administration, the operational order entry application had to be modified in such a way that was not required by sales administration. IS personnel were left to resolve this conflict without any obvious mediator.

In general, another aspect of the data inconsistency problem is often encountered at this stage. It is a significant and potentially lethal inconsistency, but one that is often overlooked by the IS department in the design stages. It frequently becomes evident only when the end users have become thoroughly familiar with the data they are receiving. This problem is temporal inconsistency in the data. Once again, the source of the problem can be traced back to the application architecture of the operational systems. Although the data domains of the operational applications are sepa-

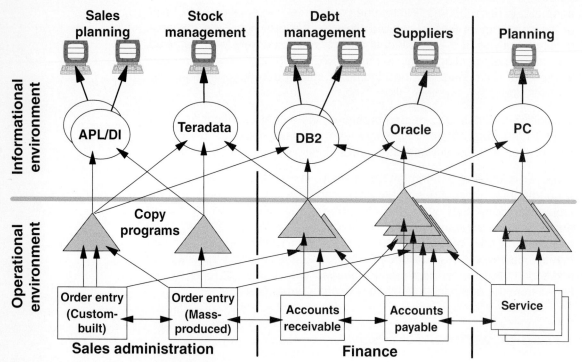

Figure 3-5: *Cross-departmental decision support systems*

rate and broadly independent, data is passed between them when needed, as described earlier. And the phrase "when needed" is the key to the temporal inconsistency problem that ensues.

Again, our example illustrates the problem. The finance department operated on a monthly cycle, and its operational applications were designed to gather data at month-end to prepare the financial status reports. This data then remained stable throughout the following month. Sales administration tracked the business on a weekly basis, while marketing required a daily business-management scenario. The operational applications in each area were designed around these business cycle times, as was the frequency of data transfer between them. As a consequence, data in different applications had different time spans of validity, and so could not be directly combined except at certain times.

In general, expanding the scope of the copy programs to handle the movements of data across departmental boundaries and to combine data from different operational applications results in a considerable growth in complexity. In particular, the logic needed to cleanse data is duplicated now in a number of different copy programs, and any future changes in the structure of the base operational data cause substantial duplication of maintenance effort on the related copy programs. This problem could be avoided by architecting the copy programs to ensure code reuse. However, the organizational structure tends to prevent this from happening, because ownership of the copy programs often lies with the target informational applications, so the duplication goes unrecognized.

3.4 The Info Center

The implementation described in the previous section was typical of the *Info Center* approach, a concept which was popular in the mid-1980s [Hammond (1982), Brancheau *et al.* (1985)]. The focus of the Info Center was the end users. It enabled them to touch and manipulate the data required for any task, and it provided tools end users could easily use to do this. There is no doubt that for many companies this was a radical step forward at that time. PCs were becoming widely available, and users were beginning to see, often for the first time, that they could work with the data themselves. The Info Center, although still mainframe oriented, contributed to and supported end users in this new mode of working. For many IS organizations, this first focus on end-user computing needs was a significant challenge, forcing them to step up to the task of evaluating user tools, supporting users who were not computer-literate, and dealing with a different type of user requirements [White and Christy (1987)].

However, the Info Center concept did not address the need to develop methods of delivering data from the operational environment to the emerging informational environment, nor did it address problems related to matching data from different systems. In essence, the Info Center promoted *ad hoc* data copying to the informational environment, where, as end users defined each new need for data, the IS shop responded with a specific copy program.

The Info Center concept, because it encouraged making data available to end users without providing any structure to deliver this data, led inevitably to one of the most well-known problems encountered in IS shops today—daisy chains of data, shown in Figure 3-6.

Daisy chains of data

Depending on the variety, a daisy may be a flower or a weed. Unfortunately, the daisy chains that grow in data are definitely pests. With each new request for data, IS personnel are faced with the question of where to find the required data. For the early decision support applications, data sourcing was simple. Even for the first informational applications based on data from multiple operational databases, the choice was relatively clear. The original operational databases were the only available data sources. However, as the number of sets of copied data grew, a new source of data

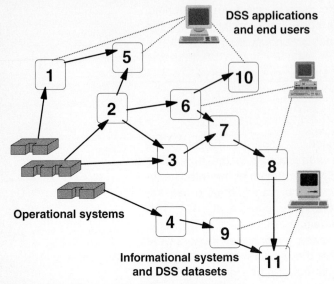

DSS applications and end users

Operational systems

Informational systems and DSS datasets

Figure 3-6: *The growth of daisy chains of data*

to satisfy informational needs became available—the existing informational applications (or copies) themselves.

These copies are especially useful for satisfying urgent decision support needs, because the data there is already cleansed or transformed in some way. But over the years, daisy chains of data are built of copies based on copies derived from copies of the original operational databases. These chains are joined together into complex networks of data flowing from the operational applications to the eventual end users. As shown in Figure 3-6, even when the original use for an intermediate copy (for example, datasets 2, 3, 4, and 6) has disappeared, the copy must be retained because it is an essential link in one or more chains of data.

The IS department is not alone in contributing to this hidden duplication of data. End users themselves manually copy data from screens and reports (processes colorfully known as "screen scraping" and "report scraping") and enter it into their own informational applications.

In this environment, hidden duplication of data rapidly becomes widespread, but is seldom recognized as an issue. This is because the organizations that implement the copy programs are largely dispersed.

In addition to the obviously wasteful duplication of data, the interlinking of data chains provides an ideal environment for the growth of data inconsistency. The data paths shown between datasets 2, 3, 6, and 7 can very easily lead to corrupted data in dataset 7 if related data elements are copied from dataset 2 but transformed according to different rules in datasets 3 and 6. When they are then reunited in dataset 7, the original relationship is likely to have been lost.

It should also be remembered that these networks must operate in a specific order, often on a nightly basis, to move data to the Info Center. As a consequence, a relatively minor problem, such as a lack of temporary disk space, at an early stage of the chain not only affects that step but can cause all subsequent copy programs to fail.

The ensuing computing environment is a complex and fragile creation. Data is duplicated many times, often in hidden or forgotten ways. Any change in the contents or structure of the original operational systems ripples through the copying environment into the informational systems, frequently in unpredictable ways. A change in one copy program causes a domino effect on the downstream programs. Dataset 2 in Figure 3-6 has a pivotal role in supplying data to five datasets (5, 6, 8, 10, and 11) accessed directly by end users. A change in any data item in dataset 2 can affect any or all of these users.

This effect can be particularly damaging in companies where the IS function has been decentralized or where departmental IS organizations exist. In these cases, the developer of the first copy programs is usually unaware that another developer has based a second copy program on the output of the first. If any link in the chain fails, subsequent links are no longer valid—either data is not updated or, where data comes from multiple paths, updated and outdated data are combined to produce erroneous results.

The maintenance of these copy programs can be politely described as challenging. Because the input data comes from multiple applications, often on different software platforms and sometimes on disparate hardware platforms, the developers need to understand the structure and contents of a number of databases and the changes in these databases driven by operational needs. As the operational applications go through their development and maintenance cycles, any required changes in the copy programs must be designed and developed in a short period of time late in the development cycle of the operational systems, when the changes to those databases are finalized. Once the IS department has made the new version of the informational database available to users, any subsequent problems or changes in end-user needs that arise must be addressed in the copy program, as the operational system is no longer open to further modification.

In such situations, almost all of the resources applied to the copy programs are tied up in the maintenance of existing code. This situation effectively prevents any further expansion of these systems to include data from other areas of the business.

3.5 Conclusions

Businesses have made widespread use of an application-driven approach to the delivery of informational systems. This has led to the widespread availability of decision support applications and to associated business successes. However, a number of technological limitations are apparent, which become increasingly significant as the size and complexity of the informational environment increases. They affect the end users as well as the IS organization, as summarized next.

User constraints

Users of decision support systems developed using the traditional application-driven approach commonly complain of the following difficulties, all of which can be traced directly back to the method of development:

1. "I can't find the data I need."

    - Data is scattered over a variety of systems with different interfaces and tools, causing users to spend time switching between systems.

    - There may be many potential sources for the required data, but these may differ in subtle ways, and it is not clear which version, if any, is the correct one.

2. "I can't get the data I need."

    - Expert help is often required, which must be scheduled as part of the already unacceptable backlog of IS work.

    - Some types of information are unobtainable without extensive reworking of existing operational applications.

3. "I can't understand the data I found."

    - The data available is poorly documented, often in terms not well related to the business view of the user.

4. "I can't use the data I found."

    - The results are often not as expected because the data is mismatched either in meaning or in timing.

    - Data must be manually transferred into the environment in which the user is working.

All of these constraints add up to some rather unhappy end users, who blame the IS department for their problems. The impact on the business is that end users take longer to make poorer decisions than should be the case. The end result is higher costs and/or lost opportunities.

IS problems

In this environment, IS personnel also complain of a variety of problems:

1. "Developing copy programs isn't simple."

    - Duplicate function is required in many of these programs, but recognizing existing function and reusing it are difficult in most companies because of organizational barriers or technical limitations.

- The logic to transform data from its operational form into information that is suitable for end users is complex and volatile.

2. "Maintaining copy programs presents serious problems."

   - A change in a single source application impacts a large number of interrelated and dependent copy programs, each of which must be separately analyzed and changed.

   - In many cases, interdependencies between copy programs are undocumented or unknown.

   - Because of the complexity of the transformation logic and the overall maintenance approach, copy programs rapidly turn into "spaghetti code".

3. "Data storage volumes grow rapidly."

   - Uncontrolled data duplication exists within the data copying and informational environments, leading to excessive volumes of data.

4. "Data administration is complex."

   - Lack of standardized data definitions leads to a loss of control in the informational environment.

   - Multiple sources exist for each data element.

IS managers can thus point to significant maintenance and data management problems resulting from this approach to providing decision support. These problems lead to excessive costs associated with decision support, slow turnaround times for business-driven updates of the systems, significant levels of error in these updates, and an increasing inability to expand management information support from existing to new areas.

The one, overwhelming consequence of all of these limitations is that IS personnel can have little or no confidence in the quality of data being provided to end users. In this respect, the IS department is failing to fulfill its obligations to the business, and indeed may be contributing to the ultimate failure of the company if wrong decisions result from this false data.

The solution is, of course, the implementation of a data warehouse. Part II describes the structure of the warehouse and its underlying principles, and shows how the data warehouse addresses the issues outlined here.

Part II

Principles of
data warehousing

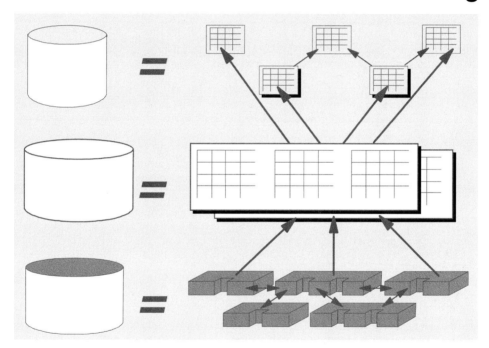

Architecture and design techniques

Chapter 4

Types of data and their uses

There are many varieties of data stored in computers today. Some types of data are particularly appropriate for storage and management in a data warehouse. Others are not.

The purpose of this chapter is to distinguish among the different **types of data**, and to identify those appropriate for data warehousing. This analysis sets the **data scope of the warehouse** and forms the subject of the remainder of this book.

The chapter then further categorizes the types of data to which warehousing can be applied according to their usage. In particular, **business data** and the **metadata** that describes it are each divided into three distinct categories. This categorization allows underlying structures for control and management of the data to be deduced. Such structures form the basis of a data architecture, which we first define at a high level and then further refine throughout the course Part II.

The chapter ends with a description of data that formally lies beyond the scope of the data warehouse. Such data does interact with warehouse data, and these interactions have important implications for the structure of the warehouse.

It may be argued that the classification of data in this chapter is self-evident. However, a number of terms introduced in this classification are key to understanding why it is important to structure the data warehouse as described in this book. In addition, although the definitions of the types and uses of data are relatively simple, deciding in which category to place any existing data is sometimes more difficult than might be expected.

4.1 Types of data

For the purposes of this book, *data* is defined as a computerized representation of business information. At the highest level, data can be partitioned in many ways. Three axes are particularly useful when determining the scope of a data warehouse:

1. **Meaning**

    Data may have intrinsic meaning or may be a representation of something that has meaning. This distinction is the most fundamental and perhaps the most difficult to understand.

    Computer-based data has long been used to run and manage a business. Such data, called **business data**, represents the state of the business, and its value lies in the meaning it represents.

    Another type of data is growing rapidly in importance. This data has its own intrinsic meaning, and its value lies in its content rather than in what it represents. Thus, it is termed **data as a product**, because it is produced, bought, and sold in the same way as any physical product. Examples are digitally stored movies or books.

    Finally, at the other end of the scale, there is **metadata**, which describes the meaning of data. Such metadata exists only to define or describe business data or data as a product.

2. **Structure**

    Data may be highly structured, consisting of many well-defined inter-related fields or records, or unstructured, where the internal structure is very variable, or it may fall anywhere between these two extremes.

3. **Scope**

    Data may be personal, where its owner can change it as he or she pleases, or public, where its use is shared among a number of people and any changes require careful management.

Figure 4-1 apportions data according to the three axes listed above. The three major types of data identified according to meaning appear across the figure. Each is subdivided into structured and unstructured data, and within business data and metadata, there is a further division[1] between public and personal scope. The sizes of the different boxes give an impression of the relative volumes of the different types of data.

---

[1] Note that the public/personal axis is mirrored for structured and unstructured data for ease of drawing the scope of the data warehouse.

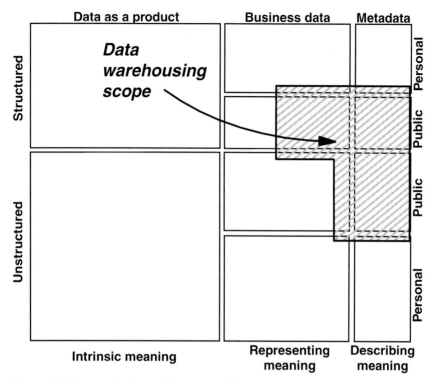

Figure 4-1: *Types of data and the scope of the warehouse*

The scope of data warehousing

With the current popularity of data warehousing, vendors and consultants are promoting a variety of meanings for the term. From some definitions, you might conclude that data warehousing covers all the data in the enterprise (or even the universe!); other definitions lead to the conclusion that a data warehouse is a technical solution based on a particular tool.

The scope of data warehousing used as the basis of this book is represented by the shaded areas in Figure 4-1. This scope has been chosen for a number of reasons:

- It meets the business and IS needs shown in Part I and focuses only on those needs, without trying to solve all the data problems of the enterprise.

- It covers the business, organizational, and technical elements needed.

- It is achievable within a reasonable timeframe using a level of resources most businesses can afford to invest.

- It starts from a realistic view of the IS environment today and of its limitations imposed by past evolution.

**Data
warehousing**

*Provides the self-
consistent and
well-understood
data needed to
manage the
business both as
a whole and in its
individual parts.*

These considerations narrow the scope of the warehouse to the data used
to manage the business. Data warehousing therefore:

- supports the need to manage the business in its entirety and in its
  constituent parts in a fully self-consistent manner

- is based on business data that its users understand

From Figure 4-1 it can be seen that the warehouse (1) focuses on business data and metadata that are mainly public in scope and (2) covers
both structured and unstructured components of business data and
metadata. The rationale for this boundary is described in the following
sections.

The potential future growth in this scope is described in Chapter 20.

4.2 Business data

Business data

*The data required
to run and
manage an
organization,
typically a
business
organization.*

Business data is that data required to run and manage the business or
other organization. It represents the activities that the business undertakes and the objects in the real world—customers, locations, and products—with which it deals. It is created and used through transaction
processing systems and decision support systems (DSS).

Within business data, different types of data must be handled. The categorization shown in this section was first defined in the Information Warehouse architecture [IBM (1993)]. The distinctions are based on an
assessment of how businesses use data. Other criteria include consideration of the technical processes and the requirements for timeliness that are
applied to it. The choice of these criteria is based not on any theoretical
consideration but rather on experience of what has worked in many management information implementations. The types of data that emerge
based on these criteria are then used to determine the placement of the
data, its level of duplication, and the rules for managing it.

Criteria for data-typing business data

There are four criteria used to determine types of business data. These
are (1) its use in the business, (2) its scope, (3) whether it is read/write or
read-only, and (4) its currency. Let us consider each of them in turn:

1. **Usage in the business**

   Data is used in the business to accomplish two broad objectives:

   - *Operational data* is used to run the business and is related to
     short-term actions or decisions.

- **Informational data** is used to manage the business in the longer term.

Operational data is the primary business data within the organization and is the source of all informational data, as shown in Figure 4-2. Both operational and informational data are structured according to their access and usage needs.

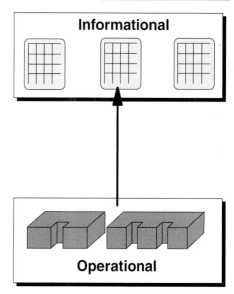

Figure 4-2: *Operational and informational data*

2. Scope of the data

Data may represent a single item or transaction, or it may be a summary of the net effect of a set of items or transactions:

- **Detailed** or **atomic data** is critical to running the business, but it is also used in some of the simpler business management tasks. It often focuses on basic objects or transactions such as individual products, orders, or customers.

- **Summary data** is used in managing the business and showing a broad view of the way the business is operating.

3. Read/write versus read-only data

Read/write data has fundamentally different usage and management characteristics from read-only data:

- **Read/write data** requires careful design of the update process to ensure that business integrity rules are obeyed. Its structure is optimized for writing to databases or files.

- **Read-only data** (a misnomer, since it is, of course, written at least once) is usually designed with unplanned inquiry in mind and provides a stable base for repeated reading.

4. Data currency

The currency of data reflects where it is positioned on the timeline of the business, as shown in Figure 4-3:

- **Current data** is a view of the business at the present time. It is up to the second and is subject to change over time based on business activities. It presents an accurate representation of the current performance of the business.

- **Point-in-time data** is a stable snapshot of the business data at a particular moment in time and reflects the status of the business at that moment. A daily close-of-business view of data and a month-

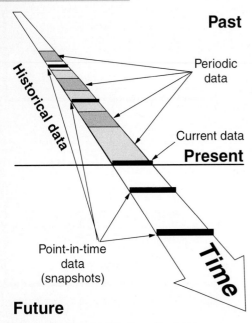

Past

Periodic
data

Current data

Present

Point-in-time
data
(snapshots)

Time

Future

Figure 4-3: Types of data on the business
timeline

end set of data, used for the following day
or month, are examples of point-in-time
data. Point-in-time data can represent
views of the past or may be predictive, representing planned or predicted future
events.

*   *Periodic data* is an important further class
    of data. It provides a definitive record of the
    business as it changes over a period of
    time. Such periods of time are of varying
    duration, but the time period covering a
    number of years is of particular interest in
    data warehousing.

These concepts form the basis for the proper treatment of historical data (including periodic data and
past snapshots) in the warehouse, and are further
expanded in Chapter 6.

The three types of business data

The criteria defined in the previous section allow us to identify three types
of business data. Initially, we focus on structured rather than unstructured
data. This is because structured data is usually implemented first in a data
warehouse, and also because the distinctions among the three types of
structured data are clearer.

Because the above criteria are subjective to varying extents, it may not
always be obvious how to decide the data type of real business data in
some instances. This does not invalidate the categorization. It merely
confirms that the real world is not always neat and orderly. And the reality
is that in some circumstances, the same piece of data may be used for two
or more different purposes. However, the identification of this multipur-
pose data is useful in itself. The business should examine such items to
ensure that the current usage is valid.

Real-time data

*Up-to-the-second,
detailed data
used to run the
business and
accessed in
read/write mode,
usually through
predefined
transactions.*

Real-time data

Real-time data is current or up-to-the-second data representing the current status of the business and is used to run the business. It occurs at a
detailed level and is accessed in read/write mode.

In general, real-time data is the data created, manipulated, and used by
operational or production applications. Such data is traditionally found in
files and databases in the mainframe environment, and is controlled and
managed by the IS department. Although the newer databases may be

relational, even today the majority of this type of data still exists outside the relational database world. In older systems, such data is often poorly structured or contains highly complex structures as a result of repeated maintenance.

Real-time data is not confined to mainframes or legacy applications. A new category of client/server applications creates real-time data on workstations and servers. This real-time data is now distributed throughout the enterprise and is seldom under the direct control of the IS department. Increasingly, real-time data originates outside the company entirely. This occurs when inter-enterprise processes, such as orders or invoices, are passed between organizations using electronic data interchange (EDI), and the incoming data is used as the basis for the receiving company's activities.

Table 4-1 shows some common examples of real-time data. Such data exists in a variety of formats and locations. Its size varies enormously. The common factor is the use that is made of the data—it is used to run the business at a detailed level.

Given that the data warehousing scope has been defined as management of the business, real-time data falls outside that scope. However, because real-time data is the ultimate source of all other business data, its influence on the data warehouse is very strong.

Table 4-1: Examples of real-time data

Data	Industry	Usage	Technology	Volumes
Customer file	All	Track customer details	Legacy application, flat files, mainframe	Small–medium
Account balance	Finance	Control account activities, e.g., withdrawals	Legacy application, hierarchical database, mainframe	Large
Point-of-sale data	Retail	Generate bills, manage stock	Client/server, relational database, UNIX system	Very large
Call record	Telecommunications	Billing	Legacy application, hierarchical database, mainframe	Very large
Production record	Manufacturing	Control production	New application, relational database, AS/400	Medium

Derived data

Derived data

Point-in-time or periodic data, at a detailed or summary level, derived by some process from real-time data and used to manage the business.

Derived data is simply data that is derived, through some process, from real-time data. It is used to manage the business, in a read-only mode, rather than in the day-to-day operation of the business. It may be at a detailed or summary level. Because it is derived from real-time data, it is either point-in-time in nature, representing a view of the business at that time, or periodic in nature, preserving an historical record of the business over a period in time.

Derived data is that set of data that has been traditionally used for decision support. It is found throughout the organization today, from relational databases on mainframes, to specialized spreadsheet packages on PCs, and everything in between. Although it is the ideal that the data derivation step should be automated, in some cases the process can still be manual, with the contents of printed reports being typed back into management information tools. Examples of derived data are shown in Table 4-2.

The extent to which derived data differs from its source depends on the business requirements. In the simplest cases, derived data can be a snapshot or point-in-time copy of the real-time data and thus exists at a detailed level. In Table 4-2, for example, derived claims analysis data is very similar to the real-time claims data from which it was derived. Another important type of derivation is summarization, where detailed data is brought to a higher level of aggregation. Both detailed and summary data may be subsetted by selecting only some of the fields (vertical subsetting) or some of the instances of the data (horizontal subsetting). Sales sum-

Table 4-2: Examples of derived data

Data	Industry	Usage	Technology	Volumes
Sales summary	All	Historical sales patterns by month and year	Spreadsheet, PC-based, individually based	Small, summary
Market analysis	Retail	Analysis of campaigns by area and demographics	Multidimensional database, parallel computing	Very large, detailed
Claims analysis data	Insurance	Pattern analysis, detection of fraud	Relational database, mainframe	Large, detailed
Key indicators	All	Executive information with drill-down	Executive info. system, client/server, relational database, and files	Small–medium

maries, for example, may contain only net-profit figures and be calculated only for specific regions.

Finally, new data can be derived from a combination of existing fields or records. This type of derivation, often called enrichment, is one of the most important types of derivation for providing new and original views of the business. However, it is also different in one significant respect from the other types of derivation processes. While the other processes are inherently self-consistent, enrichment is consistent only if the data being combined is logically related to one another. Many of the problems that users, and indeed IS departments, experience with derived data are a result of combining data that is not logically related. It is the recognition of this problem area that leads to the next category of data, reconciled data.

Reconciled data

Reconciled data is generated by a process designed to ensure internal consistency of the resulting data. This process operates on real-time data at a detailed level. A second key aspect of the process of generation is that it maintains or creates an historical set of data. Reconciled data is thus seen to be a special category of derived data.

In traditional decision support environments, reconciled data is seldom explicitly defined. In many cases, it does not exist at all. Where it does exist, it is seldom physically stored, being only the logical result of some operations that take place in the derivation process. In other cases, it exists only in temporary files. It is thus not recognized as having any business consequence. In fact, reconciled data is the pivotal element of the data warehouse. As a result of the widespread use of the application-driven development approach, real-time data is not self-consistent over the entire scope of the enterprise. This makes data reconciliation a necessity.

> *Reconciled data*
>
> *A special type of derived data that occurs at an historical, detailed level and is designed and used to ensure consistency of data across the entire enterprise.*

Thus, whenever data from multiple sources has to be combined, developers must first analyze the structure and content of the sources in order to define combination rules. Then they need to develop a process to enforce these rules. Typically, such processes include functions such as matching and manipulation of fields, conversion of field contents into consistent forms, and, in extreme situations, various types of error correction. A few examples can best illustrate the concept of reconciliation.

Unique identification keys for entities such as customer or product often differ from application to application. In some cases, a direct relationship may exist between the two structures. For example, an old application uses a six-digit code as a key to customer, while a newer application has extended this field to eight digits, but uses the older six-digit format as a subset of the newer definition. Combining these two fields is a simple matter of extending the field received from the older application. A more complex problem arises when there is no direct relationship between the two keys. Here it may be necessary to manually construct a cross-reference table in order to reconcile these two sets of data.

Coded fields often require reconciliation. Two classic examples are the codes "m/f" or "1/2" to represent male and female in different applications, and the variety of country coding systems used by different departments. Reconciliation in this case requires the definition of a common value set and translations from the different base values.

A far more complex type of reconciliation relates to the time dependence of data in different applications. Financial applications produce data that is based on the month-end position. If such data is to be combined with sales data keyed to the daily close-of-business, then a reconciliation step is required that rolls the financial data into time consistency with the sales data. This reconciliation process will differ depending on the day of the month, varying from no action at all at month-end to the application of a full month's changes on the day before month-end.

Unstructured business data

Unstructured business data

Business data with minimal field or record structure, such as image, audio, and video data.

Management information systems have traditionally focused on well-structured data. Such data commonly has the following characteristics:

- A significant proportion of the data is numerical.
- There are multiple attributes for each entity (expressed as multiple fields per record or multiple columns per table).
- Multiple relationships exist between different entities.
- Most of the individual attributes are small in size.

At the other end of the scale is unstructured data, the characteristics of which are opposite to those listed above. Image, audio, and video are examples of highly unstructured data. Textual data such as notes and documents fall between the two extremes. The importance of less structured types of data is rapidly increasing in all businesses and consequently in informational systems.

Unstructured data is less readily classified according to the three types of data defined earlier than unstructured data. Nonetheless, it is far more appropriate to classify unstructured data according to the data categories that have already been defined than it is to use a totally different scheme. The rationale for this approach is founded on the recognition that both structured and unstructured data are used together in the same processes by users and must be managed to the same extent by the IS department.

Therefore, it is better architecturally to concentrate on the similarities rather than the differences between structured and unstructured data.

Real-time unstructured data corresponds to electronic images of business transactions that cannot be easily decomposed into many discrete data fields. Production image-processing systems are prime examples of operational applications that create and manage such data. Thus, an image of an insurance claim form, a stored copy of a printed bank account statement, or an image of a driving license with signature and photograph are all real-time unstructured data. Notes in an electronic mail system are a further example of this kind of data.

Derived unstructured data can be considered as summarizations or abstractions of the real-time data, as for structured data. However, the process of summarizing is much less mechanical for unstructured data than it is for structured data. Sales figures (structured data) can be summarized by marketing territory simply by adding up the individual detailed entries; summarizing customer satisfaction comments by product type requires a product manager to read the detailed data and compose a summary report.

Any required reconciliation of unstructured data occurs through its associated structured data. Thus, a textual account of a traffic accident stored in a text-processing system could be reconciled with a video of the accident scene stored in an image database. Both of these are clearly unstructured data. However, the reconciliation occurs through the claim number, which is structured data. Therefore, one can conclude that reconciled unstructured data has no physical existence.

The application of the four data-typing criteria to unstructured data is therefore qualified by the following considerations:

1. **Usage in the business**

   Running the business versus managing the business can be distinguished as for structured data.

2. **Scope of the data**

   Summary and detailed levels of data can be distinguished for textual and audio data, but the relationship between the two levels is generally not derivable by algorithm. In image data, some summarization of specialized image types is possible (for example, geographical data can be summarized by moving to lower resolution levels), but in general the distinction is not viable.

3. **Read/write versus read-only data**

   This distinction is valid for both structured and unstructured data.

4. **Data currency**

   Unstructured data is generally less time-sensitive than structured data.

In practice...

**Unstructured
data should be
included in the
warehouse, but
only after
structured data is
well supported.**

The conclusion is that unstructured data can and should be included in the data warehouse. This approach facilitates the use of such data in conjunction with the more traditional structured data. Such joint usage becomes more likely as the ability of DBMSs to store and handle unstructured data improves. However, unstructured data is more voluminous than structured data, more difficult to manipulate, and today not as well supported by databases and other tools. Therefore, although unstructured data is of considerable business value, the effort in realizing this value is proportionately higher than for structured data. Unstructured data is thus not a good candidate for an initial data warehouse implementation.

4.3 Metadata

Metadata

*Data that
describes the
meaning and
structure of
business data,
as well as how it
is created,
accessed, and
used.*

As the variety of data stored and used in a business increases, and as the diversity of uses to which it is put expands, there arises a compelling need to formalize a way of describing both the data and the uses made of it, in order to ensure that full and consistent use is made of the business data. *Metadata* satisfies this need, being most simply defined as "data about data" [Dolk and Kirsch (1987), Burk and Horton (1988)].

However, this simple definition of metadata implies that the subject of metadata is only data. In reality, business data does not exist in a vacuum. It is created, maintained, and accessed through business processes that are implemented through applications. Therefore, the business needs a full description of its business data and the processes by which to maintain and use it. Metadata thus describes a number of aspects of the business and of the corresponding application functions.

Metadata is also required to describe data as a product. However, since such data is outside the scope of data warehousing, we will not consider the corresponding metadata further here.

Criteria for data-typing metadata

In a similar manner to business data, metadata can be classified according to some basic criteria. In contrast to business data, however, the criteria for metadata are simpler and more definite in their interpretation. This is mainly a result of the narrower scope and more restricted purpose of metadata as compared with business data. There are two basic criteria—where it is used in the application life cycle, and whether it is used actively or passively. Let us consider these two criteria more closely:

1. **Alignment to the application life cycle**

   The use of metadata in the process of defining and building business applications and their associated databases differs from its use when these applications and databases are in production. This leads to a distinction between:

- **Build-time metadata**, designed to facilitate consistency of use, as well as re-use of both data and function by application and database designers

- **Production-time metadata**, designed to facilitate finding, understanding, and using the required data in the business

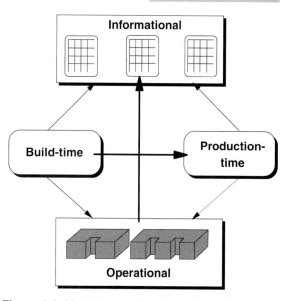

This classification of metadata is analogous to the division of business data into operational and informational categories. Both characterizations focus on how the data is used and what this implies about its structure. Moreover, just as operational data is the basic source for informational data, build-time metadata is the primary source

Figure 4-4: *Metadata and its relationship to business*

(although not the only source) of production-time metadata. This sourcing of both data and metadata is shown by the heavy arrows in Figure 4-4.

This analogy does *not* imply that build-time metadata describes operational business data and that production-time metadata describes informational business data. Build-time metadata is used in the design of both operational and informational systems, whereas production-time metadata supports the use of both environments. These relationships are illustrated by the lighter arrows in Figure 4-4. However, it is important to note that the *ad hoc* use of the informational environment does mean that production-time metadata is far more important in the informational environment than in the more structured world of operational applications. While the users of operational applications seldom need metadata to support their use of these systems, end users of informational systems can gain full benefit from these systems only if they are well supported by production-time metadata.

2. Active or passive use

This characteristic describes the technical use made of production-time metadata:

- Metadata that is used to control the action or function of some application or other piece of software has an active role.

- Metadata used in look-up mode, generally by a person, to find some business data or to understand some characteristic of that business data is being used in a passive mode.

The database catalog in a relational database is an example of a basic form of metadata. This catalog often exists in two forms, supporting these two different types of use. The catalog tables exist in the database as a permanent record of the structure of the database; they are used passively by users in order to locate and understand items in the database. However, another copy of this metadata is often stored in memory for active use by the database manager. This split ensures that the catalog is not a performance bottleneck in the system.

The three types of metadata

Applying these criteria to metadata leads to defining three types of metadata: build-time, control, and usage metadata. (By coincidence, this is the same number of types as for business data. However, the characteristics of these three types differ from those of business data.)

Build-time metadata

Build-time metadata

The metadata created and used in the process of application and database design and construction.

The original source of metadata used in the warehouse (and indeed elsewhere) is the process by which business applications and data are described and defined. Metadata created and used during this phase is build-time metadata.

According to the definition of data warehousing scope, build-time metadata is outside the scope of the warehouse. However, as for real-time business data, build-time metadata cannot be ignored because it is the source of the metadata that does fall within the scope of the warehouse. Today, build-time metadata is generated and stored in data modeling and application design tools such as CASE tools. For older, existing applications, build-time metadata often exists only implicitly in the database or file designs of the application, or in the design or user documentation.

Build-time metadata is stable in comparison with the business data it describes. In general, such metadata changes only when the overall structure of the business or its implementation in applications changes. Metadata that was defined during the design of an application will be unchanged from the first introduction of that application until a new version is introduced, and will then remain stable between version upgrades. In comparison to changes in the business data itself, version changes are relatively infrequent. For operational applications, upgrades often occur only once or twice a year. For informational applications, they may occur more frequently, perhaps as often as monthly in some cases.

Even when an application is upgraded, only a small proportion of the metadata is likely to change. Metadata describing business meaning may be stable over a period of years, depending on the market in which the company operates.

Control metadata

Control metadata is actively used by the warehouse infrastructure as a mechanism to manage and control the operation of the infrastructure itself. It is therefore part of the production-time metadata. It has two sources.

Detailed physical structure information is ultimately sourced from the build-time metadata. Because it is designed for active use by the warehouse infrastructure, this metadata is unsuitable for end users.

The second source of control metadata is the warehouse infrastructure itself. Such metadata describes the ongoing activities to which warehouse data is subject. This metadata is important both to the users and the administrators of the data warehouse. There are two types:

1. **Currency metadata**

   Currency metadata describes the actual information about the currency or timeliness of the business data. Examples are the time of last update of a table in a database, or the first time a particular application is run on any day. Such information can be supplied only by the tool or application that supplies the business data or runs the application.

   Among the different types of metadata, currency metadata is unique in the level of detail, and thus volume, that it can attain. Such metadata exists as timestamps, often at the level of individual records in the business data.

   Currency metadata is also far more volatile than other metadata, changing at a rate similar to that of the business data itself. Whenever a change in data takes place that needs to be tracked, metadata is generated. Typical examples of such changes are business events, where the timing may often be a part of the substance of the event, and movements of data from the operational to informational level, where the metadata is required to add context to the data as it is stored in the warehouse.

   As a consequence of both of these differences, currency metadata often requires special treatment, rather than consideration as simply another type of metadata.

2. **Utilization metadata**

   Utilization metadata is most closely associated with the security and authorization functionality used to control access to the warehouse. In addition, this kind of metadata provides the means for tracking how data or functions are used in the warehouse, and thus for ascertaining its usefulness or value to the end users.

   Utilization metadata is subject to frequent change, and depending on the level of detail required, can attain significant volumes.

Control metadata

Metadata actively used to control the operation of the warehouse, of which currency and utilization metadata are most important in managing and using the warehouse.

Usage metadata

Usage metadata

Metadata
structured to
support end
users' use and
understanding of
business data.

Usage metadata is the most important type of metadata for the user of business data, particularly in the informational environment. This is where the end user gains business benefit and IS personnel achieve improvements in productivity.

Usage metadata is sourced from build-time metadata and is similar in content. The distinction lies in the way metadata at this level needs to be structured in order to enable end users to productively search and explore it. The structure required by end users is significantly different from that needed by application and database designers.

Usage metadata describes the following aspects of the data or application:

- **Meaning in the business**

    This category of metadata describes the business activity in a formal and structured way. This characteristic allows users to relate data elements or application function to their purpose in the business. Allowed value sets and their business implications are also described.

    When data and application meaning are known, the user can relate these back to the real business, and IS personnel and the user community can communicate on the same terms.

- **Ownership and stewardship**

    Ownership expresses the relationship between the data or application and the organization, and denotes who takes responsibility for particular aspects of maintaining them. Ownership may be partitioned such that, for example, one person may be responsible for the accuracy of a file's contents, while another person takes responsibility for its on-time delivery. Data ownership may be assigned to business executives. In this case, a subsidiary function—data stewardship—is usually defined to indicate the day-to-day responsibility for the data.

    In the warehouse environment, ownership of data is more important than ownership of application function, but paradoxically data ownership is more difficult to determine or assign. Once it is defined and tracked, end users can take responsibility for the quality of the data.

- **Data structure**

    Structural metadata describes the technical shape of the data. There are many different types of structure that may need to be stored. For example, a data element may be described in terms of where it is physically stored, what database structure is used, whether it is character or numeric, what its size is, and what application manages it.

- **Application aspects**

Similarly, the metadata must include descriptions of application functionality, what language it is written in, what data it uses and produces, and what prerequisites, if any, are required when using it. In this context, applications may be those used directly by end users or those responsible for the maintenance of the contents of the warehouse, such as the population applications. Thus, the relationship between operational source and informational data linked by a particular extract application is documented here.

For such maintenance applications, scheduled operation time is an important part of the metadata. In general, scheduling metadata is used with currency metadata. For example, while it may be interesting to know that a particular piece of business data was last updated at the end of last month, unless the planned update schedule is also known, it is impossible to determine whether this data is really current.

> *In practice...*
>
> *Many end users relate meaning in the business to the original operational source of the data. This practice is dangerous, because data sourcing will probably change. However, the metadata must recognize and support the mental link between the two.*

Structured and unstructured metadata

While the distinction between structured and unstructured is strong for business data, this is not so for metadata. Unstructured metadata may play a significant role throughout the implementation of the warehouse. Such metadata consists mainly of free-form textual descriptions of data and processes in the business, and it exists side by side with more structured metadata such as table names or relationship definitions.

4.4 Data beyond the scope of the warehouse

The previous sections described the major types of data included in the scope of data warehousing. Now it is appropriate to outline the types of data excluded from that scope, and the reasons for so doing.

Data as a product

Some companies collect, manipulate, or produce information in electronic form as a business. This class of data is growing rapidly in importance and value but falls outside the scope of data warehousing as defined here, and indeed outside the scope of traditional data-processing systems. Data as a product is produced and stored for its own intrinsic value and not as a means of running or managing a business. It is a product of a business activity, can be bought and sold, and must be managed and controlled like any physical product.

*Data as a
product*

*Data with intrinsic
meaning and
value that is
designed to be
bought and sold,
as with any
physical product.*

There are many examples of data that fall into this category. For example, this book's value lies in its information content. As a product, it is today produced on paper. However, for most of its production process, it existed as textual and image data in a computer. In the future, it may be considered worthwhile to produce an electronic version of the book that can be bought and sold. In a similar manner, video and audio products such as movies and music recordings are increasingly produced, stored, and eventually sold as digital data.

Clearly, data such as those just described is significantly different in structure and content from that which IS staff are used to handling. However, it is not its lack of structure that separates data as a product from traditional business data. The difference is rather in the way such data is used in the business. The value of traditional business data lies in how well it reflects the reality of the business activities. With data as a product, its value is intrinsic to its content, and therefore it can be, and indeed must be, managed in a different way from business data. Business data changes incrementally, and the changes that take place within the data are of great significance to running and managing the business. Data as a product, on the other hand, must be structured in such a way that it can be bought and sold. This requirement implies that such data exists in discrete versions, rather than containing incremental changes.

Although the majority of data as a product is unstructured, it should not be assumed that all of it is. One particular example of structured data as a product illustrates very neatly the difference between such data and business data, and the relationship between the two.

Consider market research companies that analyze market trends and produce and sell the data output from these analyses. This data is structured and in content is very similar to the data that companies use to run and manage their businesses. Furthermore, when this data is purchased, it does in fact become a part of the management information of the purchasing company. In this way, it is transformed from data as a product into business data.

From the point of view of the market research company, this data is its product. This company must, of course, maintain a separate set of business data in its application systems to run and manage its business of producing and selling this product.

In a similar vein, some of the business data of a company may have intrinsic value, allowing it to be sold. This is a transformation of business data into data as a product. For example, the customer database of a telecommunications company or the sales of a product line in a retailer may be marketable assets. However, before such data can be sold, it must be separated (usually copied) from its business data source and turned into a product such that different subsets and versions can be sold and tracked separately.

Data as a product is outside the scope of the data warehouse as defined here. However, the tools and techniques that are used to build and manage a data warehouse can also be used in a similar manner to build and manage data as a product.

Personal business data and metadata

Personal data is defined simply as data that is under the control of a single individual. It is created, used, and deleted by that person as required in that part of the business process for which he or she is responsible. Such data has always existed, from the salesperson's scribbled notes on a potential order to the executive's Filofax containing names, addresses, and birthdays of key customer contacts; from handwritten forecasts of next year's sales to "to-do" lists of tomorrow's tasks. As PC usage grew, much of this data was computerized in spreadsheets, personal information managers, and so on.

Prior to the 1990s, personal data was of limited importance in the IS world. It existed, of course, and its existence was recognized by the IS shop. But its volumes were fairly limited, and it was relatively isolated from the mainstream of business data. Both of these factors have changed dramatically since then. End users now have desktop data storage in the order of hundreds of megabytes and even gigabytes. Improvements in LAN and client/server technology have led to a vast increase in the movement of data between the desktop and the corporate IS environment. As personal data is copied onto servers and linked to networks, it becomes attractive to consider sharing it. Conversely, as corporate data is copied to the desktop, it becomes subject to personal manipulation and control.

This new freedom of movement of data between the personal and public domains does lead to some uncertainty in drawing the boundary between the domains. The key distinction is the level of control and management that can and should be applied to personal data in this environment. Clearly, personal data cannot be controlled or managed by the IS shop. As a result, the IS department cannot stand over its quality or its integrity— and should not be asked to do so.

Consequently, personal data is generally outside the scope of the data warehouse, unless its relationship to public data is particularly close.

> **Personal data**
>
> *Data under the control of one person, which he or she can delete or change as needed, without having to consult anybody else in the organization.*

4.5 Internal and external data

In the past, the majority of data of interest to an organization originated within that organization. Even where data originated externally, the number of sources was small enough and the volumes of data low enough that the impacts of external data on the overall architecture were relatively in-significant. This is no longer valid. For example, it is reported that there are now more than 10,000 on-line consumer data sources in the United States, covering 1,500 variables about 150 million people. The extraordi-nary growth of the Internet over the past few years has also caused an exponential growth in the volumes of data electronically entering and leaving all organizations.

Architecturally, external data can be divided into the same categories shown in Figure 4-1 on page 43, with the exception that personal data can essentially be ignored. This is because personal data, once it has crossed an organizational boundary, is no longer personal data.

Given the defined scope of data warehousing, the following inter-nal/external interactions must be considered, as shown in Figure 4-5:

- **Structured business data**

  Because of the ease with which it can be combined with existing inter-nal data, external structured business data must be handled with great care. Inbound data must undergo a reconciliation process with internal data as it enters the organization in order to ensure its consistency with existing internal data. This implies that the associated external metadata must also be made available to the receiving organization.

  With outbound structured business data, the associated metadata must also be made available. Care is also required in this case, as le-gal liability issues may arise from supplying incorrect data.

- **Unstructured business data**

  Similar considerations apply to unstructured business data. However, because it is harder to embed unstructured data automatically in the decision-making process, the dangers associated with it are corre-spondingly smaller.

- **Data as a product**

  External data as a product enters the data warehouse as business data, and therefore is subject to the same reconciliation needs as ex-ternal business data. Outbound business data may also be trans-formed into data as a product as previously mentioned.

- **Metadata**

  Metadata seldom leaves or enters the organization as an end in itself. Rather, it accompanies business data across the organizational boundary. This movement is needed to allow such business data to be understood in context and reconciled as required.

In practice...

Free access to external data such as Internet resources must be regulated by organizational procedures to maintain internal data quality and consistency.

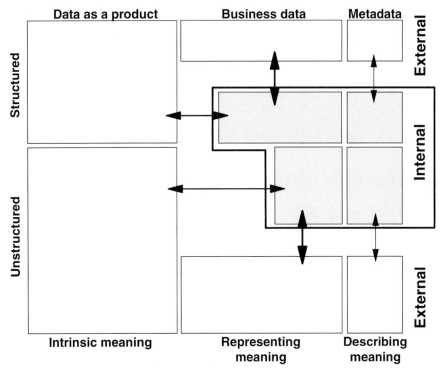

Figure 4-5: *Relationships between internal and external data*

The implications of this analysis are of some significance when planning to link the organization to the Internet. While formal relationships can be established with the traditional suppliers of electronic data, use of the Internet is far more informal. Organizational and personnel procedures will therefore be needed to ensure the internal consistency of data in the organization, as users begin to gather data from these sources.

4.6 Conclusions

The scope of data warehousing is always difficult to define. This is especially true given the popularity of the subject and given attempts by vendors to benefit from this popularity by continually expanding the scope to include as much of their product line as possible. However, this chapter defines the scope of data warehousing in terms of the types of data it supports.

Data is divided, on the basis of its usage, into business data and metadata, which are included in the warehouse, and data as a product, which is not. Personal business data and metadata are also largely excluded from the warehousing scope.

Business data and metadata are further categorized according to usage and structural characteristics. Within business data, this allows the identification of real-time data (used to run the business on a second-by-second basis) and derived data (used to manage the business). Real-time data lies outside the scope of the warehouse. The key to data warehousing, however, lies in the third type of business data. Reconciled data, a special category of derived data, provides the means to ensure data consistency within the historical record of the business.

There are three types of metadata. Of particular interest to data warehousing is usage metadata, which is structured for use by end users, and currency metadata, which describes the timeliness of business data. Build-time metadata, used in application development, lies beyond the scope of the data warehouse.

The relationships between internal and external data are defined. Where data crosses the organizational boundary, special measures are usually necessary to ensure its quality.

These further sub-categorizations allow a further bounding of the data warehousing scope, but more importantly, they form the basis of the conceptual architecture described in the next chapter.

Chapter 5

Conceptual data architecture

One of the first steps in designing any data processing system is to establish an overall architecture for the system and to gain widespread acceptance of that architecture. The design of a data warehouse is no exception.

Traditionally, the design of operational systems begins with the application architecture. This results from the emphasis operational applications place on the functionality that users require, and indeed, specify most readily. This approach is further supported by the relatively narrow data scope that such applications address. However, because of the overriding importance of data coherence in the data warehouse, it becomes clear that data—both business data and metadata—must be the starting point in architecting the warehouse.

This chapter examines, in order of increasing complexity, three alternative **data architectures** for business data. Each has its own advantages and disadvantages. The criteria that are important in evaluating these three architectures vary across implementations. The flexibility with which data may be accessed and used has already been identified as a critical success factor for end users. Data quality management is a prime concern for IS personnel. Other factors will be more or less important in specific situations. While there is thus no single architecture that is most appropriate to every situation, one particular approach will be the clear winner in the majority of cases.

For metadata, the situation is simpler. A single data architecture, presented here, supports all three alternatives of the business data architecture.

5.1 Business data architectures

The three architectural models described in the following sections have one thing in common: they are all based on real, practical experience. Because they grew from the reality of implementation, they are less pure than theoretical architectures, but the types of data already discussed form a sound basis for defining them.

The three architectures are named according to how many layers of data they encompass. These data layers are conceptual rather than physical. Thus, in any implementation, a layer can be identified by its types of data, not by its physical placement. Although one can decide where to place data directly by noting the characteristics of the types of data, the three data architectures give a more understandable basis for data placement.

In a similar vein, we describe each architectural approach from an enterprise-wide view. There are, of course, significant advantages to taking a consistent approach to data architecture across the organization. However, different areas of the business may adopt different approaches based on differing business needs. This leads to the application of the data architecture at departmental or divisional level.

In all three architectures, the term **enterprise asset data** is used to describe the set of all data that is considered to be useful in running and managing the business. The scope of this data is enterprise-wide in preference, but it may be restricted to a department or division if needed.

5.2 The single-layer data architecture

The key, underlying principle in the single-layer architecture is that any data element is stored once and once only. While this goal may be difficult or impossible to achieve, the structure of this architecture encourages and enables this goal. In a single-layer architecture, no essential distinction is made between any of the types of data previously described—all data is treated equally. (This is a highly democratic architecture!) As shown in Figure 5-1, both principal data usage needs, represented by operational and informational applications, act on the same set of data without restriction beyond normal security limitations.

Although not a strictly correct description, this architecture essentially treats all data as if it were real-time. Derived data may exist within this architecture but it is not treated any differently from the real-time data from which it originated.

The strengths of the single-layer architecture derive from its goal of storing each data element only once. Because of this, it clearly minimizes data storage requirements and avoids data management problems associated with maintaining multiple copies of data in synchronization. The weaknesses of the approach are also obvious. The main one is the contention that can occur between the operational and informational applications, leading either to data being unavailable to the informational applications or degraded response times for operational applications. Another weakness of the approach is that it provides no help in defining how distributed data can be implemented, nor how geographically distributed users can access the single copy of the company's data.

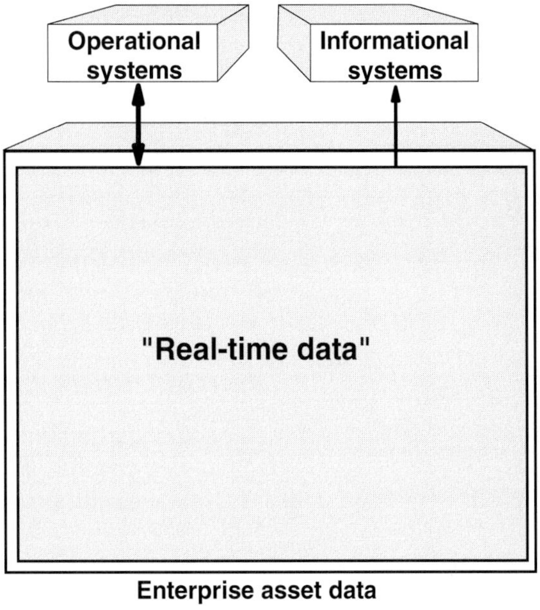

The types of businesses (or business processes) to which this architectural approach is well suited are therefore clear. If data volumes are particularly large and there is limited need to analyze the data at a summary level, the strength of the approach (requiring minimum data storage) is maximized while its weakness (poor support for informational uses) becomes less important. These aspects will often also be reflected in the overall approach the company has adopted to data storage in general, namely, centralized or mainframe oriented.

Figure 5-1: The single-layer data architecture

An example of the type of data that is well suited to this particular approach is geographical or geophysical data used by oil exploration companies. Typically, the data volumes are enormous and the required analysis is detailed-level pattern searching. In this environment, a key requirement is to minimize the volumes of data stored, while supporting user access to it from a variety of user environments.

Warehousing within a limited scope

Excepting the rather specialized circumstances above, this architectural approach is best limited to specific application areas within an organization that has adopted a two- or three-layer architecture (see Sections 5.3 and 5.4). The following circumstances are particularly suited to this:

- One application (or a small number of tightly coupled applications) is generating very large amounts of real-time data.

- The data is well modeled, and thus is internally consistent.

In practice...

Development of a warehouse aimed at storing historical data from a single source is usually faster than development of a warehouse of similar size from multiple sources.

- Updates are done by adding records rather than updating existing ones, thus reducing conflict between write and read operations.

In these cases, the data can be restricted to a single copy used for both operational and informational purposes. Prime examples of this type of data are detailed point-of-sale and telephone-call data, which form the basis of many large-scale data warehouses used today for analysis of customer behavior. Note that such warehouses focus on extending the data in the historical dimension, but they do not address the key business need of providing consistency across the breadth of the enterprise.

Virtual data warehouse

Virtual data warehouse

A logical warehouse where the user is given direct access to multiple sources of operational data through middleware tools.

Using today's terminology for data warehousing, vendors or consultants sometimes propose a *virtual data warehouse* as a way to rapidly implement a data warehouse without the need to store multiple copies of the data. The virtual warehouse uses advanced networking capabilities to allow any user tool, anywhere in the network, direct access to any of the real-time data and existing derived data (subject to security constraints).

This approach is also driven by a desire to reduce data redundancy and volumes and thus simplify data management. It essentially tries to keep as few copies as possible of each piece of data. This approach is yet another flavor of the single-layer architecture. It thus has a number of drawbacks arising directly from the underlying rationale for that approach:

1. In operational systems, data is designed to support fundamentally different processes from those needed in informational systems. Thus, it is distributed and duplicated in optimal ways for the operational process, but when an end user tries to access this data, he or she cannot know which copy of the data is correct or where it is located.

2. No prior reconciliation of operational data is attempted so this approach does not promote data quality or consistency.

3. Users can develop and maintain their own data derivations from raw operational data, which further compromises data consistency.

4. Historical views of the data may be impossible to obtain because of the limited amount of such data stored by operational systems.

5. End-user access times are unpredictable, depending on table joins, translations between different database formats, network load (which is likely to be high in this approach), and so on.

6. Users can easily construct meaningless queries, or the "query from hell" (or database scan), because they potentially have access to all data at a detailed operational level.

The virtual warehouse and other flavors of the single-layer architecture thus provide little or no support for the five principles stated at the end of Chapter 2, and will not be considered further.

5.3 The two-layer data architecture

An improvement on the single-layer architecture is to recognize the two different data usage—operational and informational—needs and to split the data into two layers as shown in Figure 5-2. The lower layer, used by the operational applications in read/write mode, is true real-time data. The upper layer, used by informational applications, is derived data. The derived data may be as simple as a direct copy of the real-time data, or it may be derived from the real-time data by some computation.

This approach immediately solves one of the main problems of the single-layer architecture—the contention between the two types of data usage when operating on a single data source. A second benefit is that it explicitly addresses end users' needs for data different from that stored as real-time data. Such needs are satisfied by allowing many different derivations from the same real-time data, where each derivation, at detailed or summary level, is aligned to specific users' needs.

However, one of the problems this architecture introduces is a high level of data duplication, often in a very uncoordinated manner, in the derived data layer. This duplication leads to an explosion in data storage requirements, but more importantly to significant data management and administration problems. The extent of the business and IS problems encountered in the two-layer architecture has already been outlined in Part I. The principal reason for these problems can be easily seen by redrawing this figure to emphasize that each of the two layers is, in reality, composed of multiple, overlapping sets of data. Furthermore, there is not a simple one-to-one relationship between the sets of data in the real-time and derived layers. This is shown in Figure 5-3.

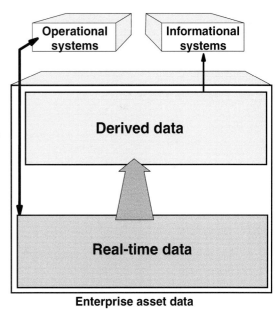

Figure 5-2: *The two-layer data architecture*

Although these problems are significant, you should not conclude that the two-layer architecture does not work. This architecture, which traces its origin to the Info Center approach of the early to mid-1980s, is by far the most common implementation approach used today. Increas-

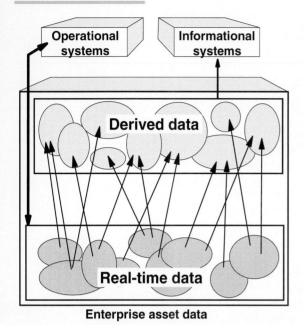

Figure 5-3: *The hidden complexity of the two-layer architecture*

ingly, efforts are being made to architect this type of implementation both academically [Kaula (1994)] and in practice [Orr (1995)].

We can relate the environments in which this approach is successful to its strengths. Although it can handle reasonably large data volumes, it is better suited to implementations in which the computing environment is fairly homogeneous and that are limited to a small number of hardware and software platforms. There are two reasons for this. First, data management is simpler when the data is stored in the more centralized manner that a homogeneous environment often entails. Second, the derivation processes are easier to control in this type of environment.

The two-layer architecture also works in companies where decision support requires mainly summary-level data, derived primarily from single data sources. Again, we can relate this success to the fact that this type of derivation avoids the main problems inherent in this architecture.

Examples of two-layer implementations are widespread and are not confined to any particular industry. In medium-sized companies, they can meet the majority of localized end-user needs. In larger companies, they are less capable of meeting these needs because of the quantities of data or variety of computing platforms involved. In general, the two-layer architecture is characteristic of companies in the early and middle stages of decision support implementation. In the later stages, the need to include larger volumes of data or data from a wider variety of sources generally leads to problems in maintaining data quality and managing the data extraction processes. Today, the increasing decentralization of end-user data to a variety of PC and local area network (LAN) platforms also works against the two-layer architecture. These problems lead to the three-layer data architecture discussed in Section 5.4.

Data marts

Data mart

A localized, single-purpose data warehouse implementation.

The term *data mart* is a current buzzword in data warehousing. It is used to describe an approach in which each individual department implements its own management information system (MIS), often based on a large, parallel, relational database or on a smaller multidimensional or spreadsheet-like system. This approach is essentially a traditional two-layer approach, delivering specific data to groups of users as required.

The main impetus for data marts is the use of automated data replication tools to populate these new databases, rather than the manual processes and specially developed programs previously used. However, these systems, once in production, are difficult to extend for use by other departments, for two reasons: first, there are inherent design limitations in building for a single set of business needs; and second, any expansion of scope entails disruption of existing users.

Data marts in themselves are therefore not recommended as a strategic approach. However, while the strategic approach is being implemented, a data mart may provide an opportunity to improve some of the current data sourcing. This solution could have short-term productivity benefits, but does not address the larger and more serious issue of data integrity and consistency.

5.4 The three-layer data architecture

The key to the three-layer architecture lies in recognizing that in the two-layer approach the transformation of real-time data to derived data really requires two steps rather than the one step that the two-layer architecture implies [Devlin (1991)]. The two steps are:

1. *Reconcile* the data from the diverse data-sets in the real-time layer.

2. *Derive* the data required by the users from the data thus reconciled.

This leads to the architecture depicted in Figure 5-4. In this approach, the lower layer is pure real-time data, the upper layer is pure derived data, and the middle layer is a **reconciled data layer** [IBM (1993)]. Reconciling data between the different sets of data in the real-time layer requires an understanding of how these sets of data relate to one another, and what their role is in the business. In practice, this understanding is defined through a data modeling process, carried out at an enterprise level rather than at the level of individual applications. The relationship between the reconciled data layer and the enterprise data model is vital to understanding how the three-layer architecture works.

You can understand the concept by considering how one might rationalize data from any two

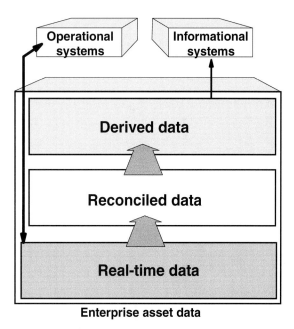

Figure 5-4: *The three-layer architecture*

existing applications and what the consequences would be. As an example of this kind of reconciliation[1], assume that an order-entry application manages a database containing a customer file, a product file, and an orders file. An invoicing application manages a database containing a customer table and an invoices table. When data from these two systems is required in the management information arena, parts of this data must be combined and rationalized. The customer file from the order-entry system and the customer table from the invoicing system must be combined to form a single customer table in the warehouse. Therefore, a more generalized customer entity must be defined, satisfying the needs of both business areas, as shown in Figure 5-5.

In addition, in the management information environment, data from these two application areas must be associated with other data in ways not originally envisaged in the operational applications. For example, there may be a need to analyze how invoices relate to the original customer orders to find what percentage of orders is shipped as a single batch. However, the operational application generates invoices based on shipments that comprise partial orders (due to non-availability of products). In order to meet the management information need, the relationship between these two entities must be more fully defined.

Thus, even though each of the operational applications may be modeled, a new level of model is required to describe the composite database. This model must take into account not only the known requirements for the use of this data, but also any anticipated, possible future uses.

Reconciled data layer

A physical realization of the enterprise data model, and thus a normalized database.

Expanding these considerations to three, four, and eventually all applications, you can see that a warehouse containing reconciled data from the whole company must represent the data model of the whole company—the **enterprise data model**. The physical representation closest to this data model is a normalized relational database. The reconciled data layer is therefore envisaged as normalized (or as close to normalized as other constraints allow) and implemented in a relational environment. These aspects are dealt with more fully in Chapters 6 and 8.

In addition to resolving the semantic differences described above, a second important aim of the reconciliation step is to address the different time dependencies of the underlying operational systems. Unfortunately, this second aim is not supported by any theoretical approach such as data modeling and is thus more difficult to achieve. Time dependence must be seen from two view points:

---

[1] Here, reconciliation occurs between sets of data within the real-time layer and not between a set of data in the real-time layer and the resultant set in the reconciled layer, as you might assume from the accounting usage of the term.

1. Business time dependence is a business requirement and is most clearly seen in accounting where the profit or other key indicators are measured at set intervals, such as monthly. It is logically inconsistent to compare such month-end figures with other information that is measured on a daily or even real-time basis. The reconciled data layer handles this aspect by clearly defining the different time dependencies of the data contained therein.

2. Application time dependence is an artifact of the way operational applications have been designed to interact. While each operational application maintains internal time consistency in its own data, compromises are often made when data created or updated in one application is made available to others. For time-critical data, such as the simultaneous debit and credit of a large financial transaction to two databases, the data transfer is real-time. At the other extreme, changes in a customer reference database may be distributed to the order-entry or invoicing customer tables only after close-of-business, to balance network load. In these cases, the sequence in which data is added to the reconciled layer needs careful planning.

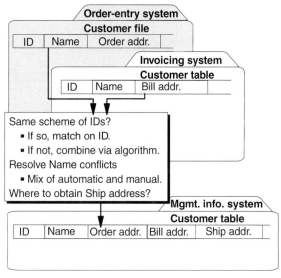

Figure 5-5: *An example of reconciliation*

The purpose of the reconciled data layer

The reconciliation step therefore takes data from diverse, heterogeneous, geographically distributed operational systems and combines and enhances it into a single, logical image of the enterprise data model. The purpose of the reconciled data layer is to be the single, definitive, authoritative source for all data required by end users of management information or decision support systems. From this layer can be derived any combination of data that users may require, today or in the future.

If we take Figure 5-3, and draw its equivalent in the three-layer architecture, we can clearly see the two distinct steps—reconciliation and derivation—in Figure 5-6.

Sets of data in the real-time data layer are reconciled with one another as part of the process of being copied to the reconciled data layer. This step is driven by the need for cleansing the real-time data to eliminate its inconsistencies and irregularities. No new data is created in this step; the value added comes from the reconciliation itself.

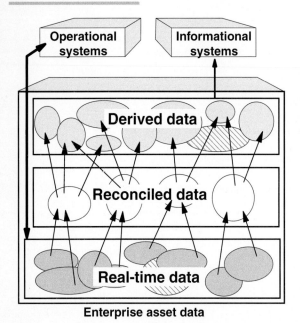

Figure 5-6: *Reconciliation and derivation in the three layers*

In the second step, the derived data that end users need to satisfy business requirements is obtained by combination, transformation, and other processes carried out on the reconciled data. This step is driven by end-user needs for information based on a single, reliable source. New information of value to the business is produced only in this step.

End users seldom, if ever, access the reconciled data layer directly. The principal reason for this is that the modeled and normalized structure of that layer is generally unsuitable for end users. The vast majority of decision support processes require data combined from a number of different entities (or normalized tables). This joining process is one with which end users are uncomfortable, because it requires a very formal approach to ensure its validity. Moreover, the data in this layer spans the complete organization and, as such, is of a broader scope than most users would ever require. These business reasons limit the widespread direct use of the reconciled data layer for management information purposes. Also, the required functions—joining tables and selecting small subsets of data—are expensive in terms of computer usage. End-user access to the reconciled data layer, if allowed at all, is therefore confined to a small number of technically skilled business analysts who need to view the business as a whole. The vast majority of end users pursue their business needs through the derived data layer.

The derivation step in the three-layer data architecture is conceptually and technically simpler than the equivalent step in the two-layer approach. This is a direct result of the fact that the data serving as the source of the derivation step is aligned to the business model and is internally consistent. In addition, if the data in the derived layer is also modeled, then the relationship, or mapping, of the data between the two layers can be automatically derived from the two models. This is an important consideration in the later population of the warehouse.

In practice...

On-line query performance is not a design consideration for the reconciled layer.

The relationship between the data in the reconciled layer and that in the derived layer is analogous to the role of *ad hoc* and predefined queries. The reconciled layer corresponds to the *ad hoc* query requirement, in that any question may be phrased but the effort required to obtain the answer cannot be determined in advance. The derived layer corresponds to predefined queries where the questions that users can ask are limited but the effort needed to get the answer is better defined. The derived layer may thus be considered as being composed of the stored results of a set of common predefined queries.

Thus, the derived data layer consists of sets of data that have been optimized for the needs of particular departments, groups of users, or even individuals. Within each smaller, and often less formally structured, set of data, end users can run their regular reports or develop the queries they need. One reason for the success of a data warehouse that separates reconciled from derived data is that that many management information needs are largely predefined and repetitive. The technical implication of this simple observation is a dramatic reduction in the computing resources needed to support the warehouse. The computationally intensive activities already identified—joining and subsetting the reconciled data—are normally only performed when moving the data, usually on a daily basis, from the reconciled layer to the derived layer, rather than every time an end user makes a query.

As an example, consider the scenario where marketing branch managers have been assigned different geographical territories. Within each territory, the products being sold are the same and the business measurements are also broadly similar. Each manager therefore requires only a small subset of the reconciled data to analyze and plan his or her business. As shown in Figure 5-7, this data consists of a subset of the rows and columns in a subset of the normalized tables, combined according to a particular set of rules. Thus, for each branch manager, three subsets of the data in the reconciled data tables are joined (represented as heavy,

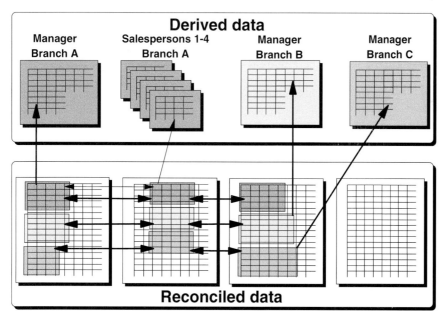

Figure 5-7: An example of the relationship between reconciled and derived data

In practice...

The cost of storing data in both reconciled and derived layers is offset by the reduction in CPU power that would be needed to support the same users from a single set of data. In addition, CPU cost is both distributed (for end-user queries) and moved to off-peak times (for populating the derived layer).

double-headed arrows) and copied (shown as heavy, single-headed arrows) into the derived layer.

As you can see in the figure, if each manager had to go to the reconciled data for each query, then each query would contain a common part which joins the required tables and extracts a subset based on territory identifier. Unfortunately, this common part is computationally challenging! The alternative approach—which performs the join only once and stores a branch-oriented subset of the combined data as derived data—is obviously more reasonable. In addition to reducing the level of computing power required, this method allows more organizational control on the scope and type of data provided to the branch managers. In support of reporting integrity, all branch managers are given a single view of the data as a basis for reporting. In addition, however, they can define new views of the data for their own planning purposes.

Examples like this show the full power of the three-layer architecture. Branch managers have direct, immediate, and inexpensive access to the data they need regularly and use in predefined ways. When they need to go to another view of the data, be it a more detailed view of the data they normally use or a different set of data, they have the ability to request it from the reconciled layer.

Furthermore, within each branch, the individual salespeople also need to manage their own territories in a similar manner. Depending on the circumstances, the data stored could be subsets at an individual level or a single subset for the whole department, within which each salesperson has his or her own view. This decision revolves around a tradeoff between data storage volumes and performance considerations. In the example shown in Figure 5-7, data sets are stored at an individual level.

The source for these sets of data is the reconciled data layer, represented in the figure by the lighter arrows. From the point of view of performance and computing cost, one might argue that these subsets could be better sourced from the derived data already supplied to the branch manager. However, consider what happens in this case if the subset being provided to branch managers is changed to reflect new business needs. This change may have the unanticipated side effect of altering the salespeople's view of the data, and thus can potentially invalidate their decision making. In this particular instance, the likely impact of this is insignificant, because the branch managers and salespeople share a close relationship (organizationally, at least!), so sourcing a salesperson's data from his or her manager may be a valid option.

In a more general sense, such an approach poses real dangers of reverting to the daisy chains of data dismissed in Chapter 3. In order to avoid this data quality problem, the IS shop must specially identify and manage derived data serving as the source for further sets of derived data. This point is further clarified in the logical data architecture in Chapter 7.

The need for a physical implementation of the reconciled data layer

If most or all of the use of the data takes place in the derived data layer, we may pose the question Why physically realize the middle layer at all? Is it not sufficient that the reconciled data exist only temporarily while the derived layer is being populated? Although this approach is superficially attractive, it has a number of significant drawbacks. Five reasons for physically realizing the reconciled layer are discussed below.

Support for new informational uses of data

The most important role of the reconciled data layer is to support new, previously unanticipated end-user needs. When such a new requirement arises, the user needs a single, definitive place to look in order to satisfy it. If the reconciled data layer does not physically exist, the options available to the user are to:

- Go back to the operational data.

  This approach requires IS support to build a new reconciliation process, or it may entail reinventing a particular reconciliation of that data.

- Go to existing derived data sets and use these as a base.

  This option is particularly dangerous, leading to daisy chains of data.

If the reconciled data layer is physically available, users can be directed to this layer as the place to satisfy their new needs. Given its normalized structure, not all end users are likely to be able to use it directly to derive the required data. However, because of its relationship to the enterprise data model, the more adept users could perform this task, avoiding the need to involve IS personnel.

Support for the implementation of data modeling

The importance to the IS department of the reconciled layer as a physical implementation of the enterprise data model should not be underestimated. Enterprise modeling is often criticized because it is difficult to ensure its use in future application development and because it produces a description of the business (at some considerable expense) that is rapidly overtaken by changes in the business. The reconciled data layer provides a method whereby the enterprise data model can directly influence future application developments. This layer can ensure the continuing relevance of the model to a changing business because of its central role.

In addition, a physically realized reconciled layer centralizes the responsibility for maintaining data quality on an ongoing basis.

Support for reengineering of operational applications

In the longer term, the existence of the reconciled layer will support the reengineering of operational applications to better satisfy changing business needs. Upgrading an existing operational application is easier, because there is only one source of data in the informational environment—the reconciled layer. Superseded operational function can be removed as long as the required data continues to be fed into the reconciled layer.

Today, some data is stored in operational systems simply because the company had nowhere else to keep it at the time it was first needed. Historical data often falls into this category. This data can be removed when the reconciled layer provides a better place to store it. This allows a simplification of the operational environment.

Reduced volumes of management information data

The volume of data in the informational environment is always a cause of some concern. One area of concern is the amounts of data required for data mining and similar activities where the aim is to seek unusual or significant patterns in increasingly large sets of data. While this is a valid concern, such data volumes are driven by a genuine business requirement, and to that extent may be considered unavoidable. However, a more worrisome aspect of data volumes relates to unjustified or hidden duplication of data in the informational environment. This duplication has a number of causes, all addressed by the three-layer architecture:

- Attempting to satisfy similar business requirements independently leads to building a similar or identical database a number of times.

- Data stored multiple times in staging files for reconciliation or derivation purposes becomes the base for further enhancement processes and thus becomes permanent.

- Business changes may make some data redundant, but because that data serves as the source for further derivations, it cannot be deleted.

Because the business recognizes the reconciled data layer as the single, modeled, definitive source for all information, these problems can be reduced or eliminated altogether.

There is a popular, if simplistic, misconception that in moving from a two-layer to a three-layer architecture, the number of copies of data increases from two to three, implying a 50% increase in data storage requirements. However, the reality is somewhat different. Looking at each layer in turn, we can observe the following:

- Real-time data—industry estimates suggest that operational data is duplicated over 10 times [Scheer and Hars (1992)].

- Derived data—the number of copies of data is large and increasing on LAN servers and PCs. So let's take 100 copies as an estimate.

- Reconciled data—because this is normalized and based on the enterprise model, there is only one copy of data in this layer.

Thus, even if there were no staging files in the two-layer architecture, the addition of another single reconciled copy of the enterprise data would increase the required storage by an insignificant percentage. However, examining the existing staging files may reveal some of them to be redundant. The implementation of the three-layer architecture may thus lead to a reduction in the storage requirements for current management information needs. Note the hatched sets of data in the real-time and derived data layers in Figure 5-6 on page 72. Because they lack arrowed connections, they are redundant.

However, the implementation of the three-layer data architecture *will* lead to a long-term increase in data storage volumes. A successful implementation will release the pent-up demand for data, particularly historical data that was previously either discarded or archived to tape. The strength of the three-layer architecture is that this increased storage is used in a controlled and understood way to satisfy new and unpredicted business requirements.

Reduced duplication of informational systems data

One of the most important benefits of a physical reconciled layer is the support it provides for simplifying the informational environment. This is a result of the reduction in data duplication that derives from its implementation. The ongoing management and maintenance costs of the single reconciled layer are significantly lower than those experienced where no reconciled layer exists.

5.5 A data architecture for metadata

As is the case for business data, the categories of metadata defined in Chapter 4 also lead to a structure or data architecture for metadata. For business data, the categorization led eventually to the preferred three-layer architecture. For metadata, the structure consists also of three parts. However, the parts are not layered, but, as shown in Figure 5-8, are interrelated so as to allow build-time metadata to feed both control and usage metadata directly.

While there are conditions under which the logical three-layer structure of business data may be collapsed to two or even one layer, the structure for metadata is more constant. This constancy results from the more limited

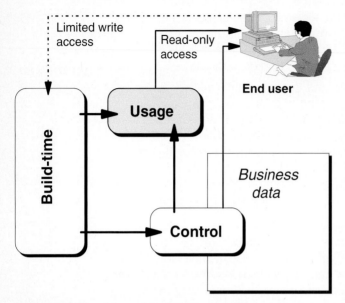

Figure 5-8: *The data architecture for metadata*

scope and use of metadata as compared with business data. In addition, metadata is a more recent concept. In the implementation of a data warehouse, therefore, it is simpler to align the metadata with the structure shown in Figure 5-8 than is the case for implementing the three-layer architecture for business data.

Build-time and control metadata exist today in a variety of places and are created and managed through many components. Indeed, the practical reality of locating and using such metadata in today's environment is not quite straightforward. Usage metadata, on the other hand, is seldom explicitly realized today, and, because its target audience is end-users, it is the key metadata component in the warehouse.

Metadata relationships and sources

We can best see the relationships among the three types of metadata and the importance of usage metadata by examining where each type of metadata resides today and how it is created and managed.

Build-time metadata

Tools that capture business meaning and logic, and represent this information in a meaningful way, all create and manage build-time metadata. Examples include data modeling and CASE tools [McFadden and Hoffer (1994)]. This business-level metadata is complemented by physical structure, storage, and timing information, which are also captured through CASE tools and therefore follow from the underlying business meaning. Build-time metadata is used in application development.

The sources of build-time metadata for older systems are more varied. Requirements and design documentation, where they still exist, may be the only written sources of business-level metadata. At the physical level, reverse engineering from database, file, and application designs is often required. In such cases, the relationship to the business meaning may have to be retrofitted based on the current usage of the system.

Creating ownership metadata is a particular problem. While directories and organization charts document the organization structure, the link between this structure and the data—representing ownership—is limited. Few organizations have a formal process by which business units assume ownership of data. Ownership, where it exists, is of applications rather than data. Furthermore, ownership of data at a personal level seldom, if ever, occurs. It is possible to effectively tackle data quality issues only if both organizational and personal ownership is defined and the company instigates processes to maintain valid and current ownership metadata.

Build-time metadata structures reflect the needs of the designers and developers of applications and databases, and therefore are unsuitable for use in production. Active use of this metadata in controlling the run-time actions of the system is generally ruled out for performance reasons, and the build-time metadata is therefore copied into the production environment as control data. The structure of this control data is optimized for run-time performance.

Similarly, the ability of end users to productively use build-time metadata is also limited. Build-time metadata and the CASE tools used to manipulate it have been designed for use by IS professionals who often need to update the metadata. End users have different skills, and their need to update metadata is limited and must be carefully controlled. As a result, build-time metadata is also copied into the warehouse as usage metadata.

> *In practice...*
>
> *Assigning organizational ownership of data can be done at design time, but personal ownership must be seen as part of an end user's job definition, and maintaining up-to-date personal ownership information should be a high-priority personal objective.*

Control metadata

The control metadata of interest in the warehouse is that which describes the currency and utilization of the business data. The source of such metadata is not the build-time metadata. For currency metadata, it is the applications or tools that physically create and update the business data. For utilization metadata, the source is the tools through which the end user accesses the data warehouse.

Currency metadata exists at a number of levels of detail. At the least detailed level, the currency information about data is stored at the table or file level. In this case, the metadata describes the validity in time of the entire set of data—for example, a customer list valid as of January 31, 1996. At an intermediate level of detail, currency metadata describes the time validity of each individual occurrence of the data. In physical terms, each record or row in the file or table has its own period of validity. Finally, validity can be tracked at the level of the individual fields within each record. This level of detail is virtually unknown; indeed, if implemented, the volume of metadata would exceed that of the business data itself.

At the two realistic levels of detail—file/table and record/row—different approaches are needed to store the metadata:

- At the file/table level, currency metadata is stored in the physical structures underlying the files or tables. It is thus separate from the business data. In order to make such metadata readily accessible to end users, it must be copied into the usage metadata.

- At the record/row level, currency metadata is almost always stored as timestamps. It resides with the business data it describes, rather than separately as is the case for all other types of metadata. There are also significantly greater volumes of this type of metadata. Therefore, currency metadata at the record/row level is not copied into the usage metadata, but is accessed directly by users *in situ*. As a result, end users seldom distinguish such control metadata from business data.

Currency metadata is seldom maintained in any formal way in most environments today. IS managers take responsibility for ensuring that data in management information systems is created on time and informally let users know when problems have arisen. The data warehouse environment demands a much more formal approach to maintaining this metadata, because of the number of users and breadth of data involved. This formalization requires that the tools that populate and maintain the warehouse create and maintain currency metadata automatically.

A similar set of considerations applies to utilization metadata. One can envisage a variety of levels of detail for utilization metadata. The realistic levels are file/table/view, row/record, and column. Except for the largest and most sensitive tables in the warehouse, it is likely that file/table/view-level tracking of utilization is appropriate. As tables increase in size, utilization tracking at the row/record and column levels supports archiving of seldom-used data.

Creating and maintaining utilization metadata are the responsibility of the tools used on the access path to the data. Such function could therefore be incorporated in any one of the end user tools, data access tools, or security functions of the database.

Usage metadata

The importance of usage metadata has only been recognized with the emergence of the data warehouse and the variety and volume of data it makes available to end users. This recent arrival presents both an advantage and a disadvantage. The advantage lies in the fact that the structure and physical storage can be defined to best suit the needs of the data warehouse. However, the novelty of usage metadata also means that few tools exist today to manage and use this metadata. The structure and storage of usage metadata are the subject of Sections 7.4 and 7.5.

In the early stages of a data warehouse implementation, the absence of tool support for usage metadata is not a significant issue, because the early stages of the warehouse usually contain a limited variety of data. However, with the growth in size and the expanded use of the data warehouse throughout the organization, such tools are a necessity.

Historical aspects of metadata

Over time, all businesses change, and such changes are represented in the business data and metadata. As is the case for business data, it is not sufficient to store only the current metadata of the business. The history of the metadata must also be maintained. The reason it is needed is to allow later reinterpretation of historical business data that has been saved according to the business model of the time, in the context of the current business model.

Unlike business data where change in content over time is incremental, changes in the content of metadata over time occur only in fairly large steps. This is because changes in the structure of the business data, which metadata describes, are reflected in the applications and data in a planned, staged manner through the application development process. While the rate of change is increasing, it is still far slower than that of the business data content.

Different types of metadata change at different rates, and some generalizations are possible:

- The enterprise model at the highest level changes only in response to major changes in business direction and can be expected to change only rarely. This stability is reflected in the metadata that describes the reconciled layer. There is one exception to this observation. During the initial construction of the enterprise model—a task that may be spread over a number of years—more frequent changes are the norm. These changes require careful handling during this period.

- For real-time data, change in the metadata is dictated by the IS-driven application development process, which is generally managed in a staged approach. The frequency of change in the past has tended to be yearly, but current application development approaches tend to reduce this to a 3- to 6-month cycle.

- For derived data, change in the metadata is more rapid, tending towards monthly or even more frequently. However, the data here ranges from transitory structures that support short-term business needs, to longer-term sets of data subject to regular maintenance. In the former case, where change is more rapid and unplanned, historical metadata is likely to be of less interest. In the latter case, there is a stronger need for historical metadata, but it is likely to change in a manner and at a frequency similar to operational applications.

- Currency and utilization metadata require special consideration. They change rapidly, and the historical record often needs to be preserved. The treatment of the history of such metadata therefore differs from that of other metadata and is similar to business data in terms of volumes and frequency of change.

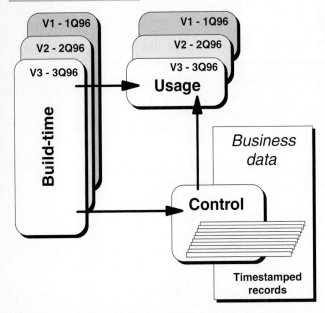

Figure 5-9: *Incorporating historical metadata in the architecture*

These considerations lead to two conclusions on the structures needed to include historical metadata in the architecture, as shown in Figure 5-9.

1. Build-time and usage metadata are versioned.

Because the changes in build-time and usage metadata are generally infrequent and well planned, the historical aspect of most metadata is best captured by a versioning approach.   This allows complete sets or logical subsets of the build-time and usage metadata to be stored and archived as appropriate.   Each version is likely to have a lifetime of 3 to 6 months.

One might consider a staggered versioning approach, where the metadata derived from the enterprise model is versioned on a yearly basis, operational metadata on a quarterly basis, and metadata related to derived business data on a monthly basis. While this would reduce the volumes being stored, it would also increase the complexity of managing the metadata. Given the importance of consistency in the metadata and also its relatively small volumes, this approach is unlikely to be worthwhile.

2. Control metadata is stored with the business data.

Currency and utilization metadata at the row/record level are directly related to the actual business data and are thus similar to business data in volumes and frequency of change. As a result, the history for such metadata is maintained along with the business data history. File/table level currency metadata is stored with usage metadata and is thus versioned.

Key aspects of the metadata architecture

The data architecture for metadata is significantly different in structure from the data architecture for business data. These differences derive from the uses to which metadata is put, and they drive differences in the subsequent physical implementation of metadata databases and tools. We can see these differences in use and their implications in three distinct areas:

- **Separation of creation from use**

  The creation (or build phase) of business data takes place in operational applications, and is placed in the real-time data layer. The use of this data in running the business occurs in the same layer, while its use in managing the business occurs in the derived data layer.

  Creation and operational use are generally placed together because they are closely related in the business process. For example, in the order-entry process, the creation of an order is highly dependent on existing data in the system, such as customer details and perhaps stock levels, which must be used in a real-time approach. Business data can be created in one company and used operationally in another. However, both sets of data remain in the real-time data layer.

  In metadata, the build (or creation) phase remains almost entirely separate from the usage phase. This is because the build phase occurs during application development and the usage phase occurs some time later when the application goes into production. This leads to a strong distinction between the audiences for the different types of metadata. The users of build-time metadata are in the IS shop—application designers and developers, and data and database administrators—while the subsequent use is in the business departments.

- **The boundary between business data and metadata**

  As with all other categorizations in the data warehouse, the split between business data and metadata is somewhat vague in some areas.

  Lookup tables can be considered as business data or metadata. In fact, they have both uses. A lookup table of country codes and names is used in a business application to print full addresses. It is also used by end users to clarify the results of an inquiry. As a result, lookup tables often exist both in the business data and in the metadata, and so must of course be kept in synchronization.

  At the extreme, metadata and business data are indistinguishable. Currency metadata at a record level, as already described, usually exists as timestamps within the business data. It can thus be treated as business data or metadata. Because of its volume and volatility, there is no way, and indeed no reason, to maintain two copies of the currency metadata.

- **The lack of layering in metadata**

  While it is vital to distinguish between the reconciled and derived layers in business data, the characteristics of metadata are different, and do not demand this layering. The basic reason is that metadata has to be reconciled in the build phase through enterprise modeling.

In addition metadata is inherently more stable over time than business data and therefore has less need for a structure that supports the concepts of current data, point-in-time data, and so on.   Although metadata is diverse in format and dispersed among many physical locations, its underlying structure is considerably less complex than that of business data.   Also, its creation and update are confined to a small group of people such as data administrators, who typically understand the importance of consistency.   All these factors contribute to the absence of layering within metadata.[2]

While the differences described above are significant, they do not imply that the two data architectures are incompatible.   Rather, they reflect the different levels of stability and requirements for use of the two types of data.   However, there is a resulting need to carefully place the metadata architecture in the context of the business data architecture in order to ensure a viable solution to the end users' need for data in a business context. We will see this unification of the business data and metadata architectures in the logical architecture described in Chapter 7.

5.6 Conclusions

Defining the conceptual architecture is the first step toward a successful data warehouse implementation.   The approach shown in this chapter derives from a combination of theoretical considerations and practical experiences.

The architecture for business data is based on a data-layering concept, and we can identify three distinct structures. The single-layer architecture rarely occurs because it produces contention among users over access to the single pool of business data.   The two-layer architecture is more common, often seen in smaller organizations or in the early stages of the implementation of an enterprise-wide data warehouse.   However, it suffers from long-term maintenance and control problems. This is a result of its *ad hoc* copying of data into the informational environment.

The three-layer architecture is by far the most powerful approach.   It is recommended in all situations where the business requires an enterprise-wide view of its data.   The power and success of the three-layer architec-

---

[2] It is important to carefully distinguish between possible metadata layers, under discussion here, and the metadata used to describe the different layers of business data.   Thus, although there is no need for separate reconciled and derived metadata layers, metadata describing the reconciled and derived business data layers is vital.

ture stem from its recognition of the pivotal role of the enterprise data model and its physical realization in the reconciled data layer.

All of these three architectures for business data can be implemented, and examples of each type do exist.

The choice of a conceptual structure for metadata is more limited because of the more restricted usage of metadata. Metadata has three components that do not operate in a layered fashion. The relationship between them effectively separates different uses of the metadata and avoids trying to build a single, unified repository for all metadata within the warehouse.

The conceptual three-layer business data architecture, together with the metadata architecture, provide the broadest support for both the data management needs of the IS department and the data access needs of end users.

Chapter 6

Design techniques

Designing a data warehouse requires the use of a number of techniques that are seldom used in developing operational applications or traditional informational applications. The need for these techniques springs from three characteristics of the warehouse:

1. The scope of the data warehouse eventually encompasses the whole enterprise.

2. The data warehouse contains the historical record of the business.

3. The source for all data in the warehouse is existing data, which may be dispersed, changing in both structure and content, and of variable quality.

These characteristics lead directly to the specialized design techniques described in this chapter.

Enterprise data modeling is a design technique that defines the contents of the warehouse and allows the entire scope of the business to be included in the data warehouse. This process cannot be achieved in a single step, but rather must be addressed in stages. This chapter first shows one approach to enterprise data modeling that supports a staged implementation.

The chapter then describes the **representation of time** in business data and a structure of **historical data** used to build and maintain a complete record of the business. A common structure is needed throughout the business data to allow end users flexible access to the data and to allow for its combination in the formats they require.

We conclude this chapter with a discussion of the underlying principles behind populating the warehouse. These principles, embodied in **data replication** functionality, enable the business to buy or construct tools that will ease the ongoing maintenance problems of obtaining data from multiple, variable sources.

6.1 Enterprise data modeling

The importance of a data model in the warehouse has already been mentioned. This section discusses how modeling techniques apply to the informational environment in general, and particularly to the three-layer data architecture for business data described in Chapter 5.

We start with an overview of modeling aims and terminology, although this text cannot provide a comprehensive explanation of modeling in general. Many existing textbooks, for example, Teorey (1990) and McFadden and Hoffer (1994), cover this topic in depth. However, it is important to understand the principles which can be applied in the context of data warehousing.

Basic terminology

The purpose of modeling

The purpose of modeling is rather simple—it is to provide an accurate record of some aspect of the real world in some particular context. This provides the user of the model with a clearer understanding of how the modeled objects behave, with the ability to predict the consequences of any action within the environment and the impacts of any change to it.

Business data modeling provides a view of the business that focuses on the data used, allowing the design of computer systems that support the way the business operates. Business data modeling therefore aims to provide:

- a record of accurate and meaningful business data definitions

- identification of valid, consistent business data structures that contain sufficient information to run and manage the business

- an indication of the similarities and differences between data from different sources and the relationships between them

Business process modeling focuses on business activities, providing:

- a record of accurate and meaningful business process definitions

- identification of the relationships between and within business processes

These models are closely related because any process will use certain data. Identifying which data is created or modified in particular processes is a particularly important aspect of that relationship.

The information contained in the combined model can be used at a number of levels in the business. At the highest levels, the model allows managers to plan the implementation of business strategies and to estimate the impact of business changes on the data needed to run the business. The model further provides the basis for planning systems development, allowing a clear separation between the logical requirements and the physical design details.

In the operational environment, the data and process models are equally important inputs to the systems design and development process. On the other hand, in the informational sphere, the data model is of far greater significance than the process model. The principal reason for this is that informational tasks and processes are, by their nature, less structured and less rigid than their operational counterparts. As a result, understanding the meaning of the data and its interrelationships is the key to designing the warehouse and enabling the unpredictable usage that end users require. Furthermore, the greater stability of the data model in comparison with the process model tends to reduce the impact of normal business change on the structure of the warehouse.

Entities, attributes, and relationships

The most common forms of business data modeling use the **entity relationship** approach [Chen (1976)]. In this approach, shown in Figure 6-1, an entity is any category of object in which the business is interested. Each entity has a corresponding business definition, which is used to define the boundaries of the entity—allowing one to decide whether a particular object belongs to that category or entity. The figure shows an entity called *"Product"*. *"Product"* is defined as any physical item that may be stocked in one or more of the retail stores in the company. Whether this definition is appropriate or not depends on the use to which the model is put. In this sense, an entity may be quite specific at one extreme, or very generic at the other extreme. Each entity has a number of attributes associated with it. An attribute is any characteristic of the entity that describes the entity and that is of interest to the business. The figure shows some typical attributes.

The second major element of the ER model is the relationship. A relationship exists between the entities in a model and describes how the entities interact. This interaction is usually expressed as a verb. In our example, the relationship between *"Product"* and *"Retail shop"* is defined as *"Retail shop stocks Product"*.

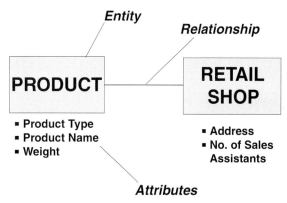

Figure 6-1: An example of an entity relationship model

Over the past 20 years, this basic model has been enhanced—Teorey *et al.* (1986) describe the types of extension—and has remained the basis for all practical data modeling approaches. Other semantic data models have been proposed, but with little success [Batra and Marakas (1995)].

Application and enterprise modeling

Application-level modeling

Application-level modeling

Data and process modeling aimed at developing specific business function within the scope of a single application.

The spectrum of generality in defining entities, mentioned above, is an important indication of how the model may be used. Traditionally, modeling has been used in the development of business applications with well-defined boundaries and roles. As a consequence, the entities are generalized only to the extent required within these boundaries. In the context of application development, this characteristic should not be taken as a criticism. In fact, it is a strength of the approach, because it allows both the potential users of the application and its developers to focus only on the data required and to do so in a structured manner.

Application-level modeling provides a logical view of the data required by the application, driven and defined by users' needs. This view is the basis for the logical and physical database design. This design, together with the process model, drives the application logic. A number of methodological approaches exist, using different notations and tools, and application development has been generally improved using these approaches.

However, application-level modeling provides no significant support for integrating applications or for combining data from different sources. This latter aspect is vital in the informational environment. Supporting this combination of data from different sources requires a broader type of modeling, known as enterprise modeling.

The role of enterprise modeling

Enterprise modeling

Modeling whose focus is a complete and integrated view of all the data and processes in the business.

Enterprise modeling [Goodhue *et al.* (1992), Scheer and Hars (1992)] attempts to treat the data entities at the most general level, so that all commonality in the business data is made visible and usable. While an application-level model's purpose is the design of an individual application, the enterprise model has broader aims. These include:

1. providing a single systems-development base and promoting the integration of existing applications where this is appropriate

2. supporting the sharing of data between different areas of the business

3. enabling effective management of data resources by providing a single set of consistent data definitions

4. supporting the creation and maintenance of company-wide management information

5. providing a structured methodology that involves business users in the implementation of business strategies that affect the information needs of the company

Many enterprise modeling efforts focus on the first and to some extent the second of the aims listed above. Traditionally, enterprise modeling is used in the operational environment to attempt to re-architect a set of existing and diverse applications that were never designed to work with one another in the first place. Unfortunately, the implementation of these aims can impact the running of the business. Changes in the existing operational application base are usually expensive and technically difficult. In many cases, these efforts are unsuccessful as a result of such impacts.

Because of these unsuccessful attempts to use enterprise modeling, this topic can be strikingly unpopular in many organizations today [Batra and Marakas (1995)]. Managers view it as something that has been tried before, that has cost a considerable amount of effort, and whose only result has been to produce a document that is never used and is becoming increasingly irrelevant as the business changes.

However, focusing the enterprise modeling effort on aims 3 to 5—which directly support the data warehouse—can lead to an implementation with a greater possibility of success and more relevance to the business in the short to medium term. One reason for this is that a warehouse implementation has technical and operational impacts on the business that, although still significant, are less than those caused by enterprise-wide reengineering of operational applications. In addition, the emphasis on consistency of data definitions driven by structured user input provides a sound basis for enhanced teamwork between IS personnel and end users.

Nonetheless, enterprise modeling for the warehouse still provides a considerable challenge to most companies. Because the scope covers the whole enterprise, the size of the project will require careful management to ensure that it delivers results in a reasonable time period. All parts of the organization must be involved in order to deliver a model of value to the business as a whole.

Involving the required business skills in itself presents a problem. The people needed are those with both a broad understanding of how the business works and a detailed knowledge of a particular area of the business. They should also possess a vision of how the business should work—because modeling is as much about the ideal as about the reality of the business. Unfortunately, because these are precisely the users considered most vital to running and managing the business, they are therefore the most difficult to enlist in the modeling work.

The approach, therefore, is to adopt a structure that allows for tackling the problem piece by piece, rather than as one large effort. We thus adopt a layered structure for the enterprise model, which can then be subsetted into different areas as the model becomes more detailed. The upper layers of the model take a cross-enterprise view that leads to a generic view of the enterprise data. This view can then be subdivided into business areas as we "progress down" the model.

An enterprise data model structure

Enterprise data model

A consistent definition of all of the data common to the business, from a high-level business view to a generic logical data design, that includes links to the physical data designs of individual applications.

A number of approaches to a methodology for enterprise data modeling have been proposed. Information engineering [Martin (1990)] is a well-known approach. Kerr (1991) describes a four-tiered methodology, while Scheer and Hars (1992) propose three different model types. Figure 6-2 shows the typical structure of an *enterprise data model (EDM)*. As you can see, the model is layered, and the triangular shape shows that the amount of information in the model is minimal at the top level but increases significantly the lower you go. Because the upper layers of the model are summary in nature, they are quite generic and are almost identical for all companies in the same type of business. As a consequence, vendors offer generic industry models that each individual company can then customize to its own needs. The structure shown in the figure is based on the Financial Services Data Model (FSDM) marketed by IBM [IBM (1994), Evernden (1996)]. Other industry models are available from a number of vendors.

At the top of the model, the *scope and architecture* layer provides a highly consolidated view of the business. It identifies a small number, usually between 10 and 20, of business concepts that are the primary subject areas about which the business must maintain information. These concepts, sometimes also called super-entities, are described completely in business terminology that is understood by, and used in common across, the whole enterprise. In order to achieve this, the business concepts are generalized as far as they possibly can be without becoming totally meaningless. The purpose of this layer is to provide a single, comprehensive, and comprehensible view of the business to which all of the lower, more detailed levels can be related.

The *business data classifications* layer provides a means of further defining the contents of the different concepts and categorizing them according to various business rules. This layer allows the different parts of the organization to verify the business concepts in more detail. It can be understood in purely business terms by business people who have no training in modeling techniques. As a generic description of the types of data used in the industry, it gives a comprehensive and complete starting point for customizing of the model.

In the finance industry model, for example, two of the concepts defined are *"Product"* and *"Involved Party"*. *"Product"* is self-explanatory—it is any offering that the financial institution sells. *"Involved Party"* is a generalization of the people or organizations with which the company has some legally binding interaction. This definition recognizes that both people and organizations have some qualities in common. This commonality must be recognized at a high level in the business to ensure that data at lower levels in the model are correctly interrelated. As a result, at this level of enterprise modeling, it is more important to recognize the commonality than the differences.

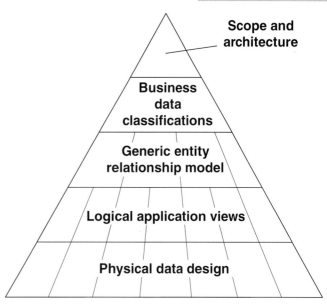

Figure 6-2: The layered enterprise data model (EDM)

Figure 6-3 shows the business data classification applied to *"Product"* and *"Involved Party"*. Classification schemes, shown in uppercase, allow the characteristics of the business concepts to be categorized in a structured way. Each classification scheme results in a number of classification values, shown in lowercase, each of which in turn may be subjected to another level of classification. At this level of the model, business rules can be defined between different classification values. For example, a *"Loan Product"* of type *"Line of Credit"* is offered only to *"Involved Parties"* that are *"Organizations"* of type *"Business"* and whose *"Financial Viability Type"* is *"Solvent"*.

Finally, the business data classifications layer provides a link from the concepts to the **generic entity relationship (ERM)** which is the pivotal layer of the EDM (see Figure 6-2).

While the two upper layers of the architecture are defined in a hierarchical structure, the generic ERM is structured as a classical entity-relationship diagram. At this level, the model is still completely enterprise-wide in its scope and is generic to all of the application views defined below it and indeed based on it. A typical generic ERM may consist of 200 to 300 entities, each described in the overall context of the enterprise as a whole. Like the two layers above it, this layer of the model is completely common to the whole enterprise; however, given the number of entities it contains, it also provides a first view of the organizational divisions of the company. This partitioning becomes evident with the observation that some of the entities are used almost exclusively by one part of the organization. Such an observation leads to the obvious possibility that these more localized

Generic entity relationship model (ERM)

The single, generic data model that describes all data commonly used throughout the business.

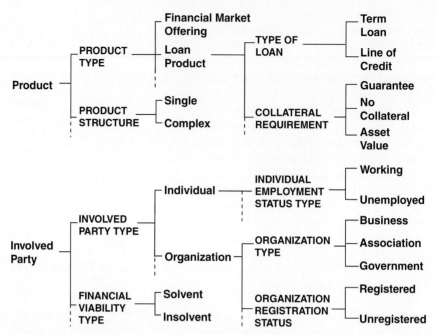

Figure 6-3: *An example of a business data classification*

entities can be defined separately from the overall company-wide aspects of the model. This compartmentalization provides a practical approach to implementation, allowing the model to be defined in stages.

The generic ERM is a complete model that identifies and describes in detail all entities, attributes, and relationships used throughout the business. It therefore represents a comprehensive, definitive, and enterprise-wide view of the company data. To construct such a model from scratch involves considerable effort. Fortunately, because of its generic nature, it is largely common to all companies in a particular line of business, and a starter set can therefore be obtained from model vendors for many types of industry.

The fourth layer of the model consists of the *logical application views*. These views are closely related to the generic ERM in content, but are partitioned into views that are the basis for specific applications. A single entity in the generic ERM can appear a number of times in the logical application views, with its attributes subsetted in different ways, in order to meet the needs of different business applications. It is the relationship between multiple entities in this layer and a single entity in the layer above that ensures that the resulting applications use data consistently. It may also indicate possibilities for data sharing between applications.

The final layer of the model, the *physical data design*, applies the physical implementation constraints, such as performance, data sourcing, physical distribution of the data between a number of locations, etc. These constraints are applied separately from the business usage considerations to ensure that technology changes can be accommodated without impacting the logical model.

A structure that covers the entire enterprise, from a summary-level view to the gory detail of the physical database models, must be both robust and amenable to change. As Figure 6-4 shows, the model can accommodate different types of changes, by localizing their effects to different parts of the model.

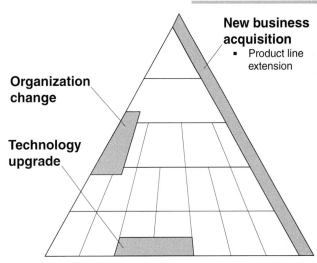

New business acquisition
- Product line extension

Organization change

Technology upgrade

Figure 6-4: A dynamic enterprise data model

One kind of fundamental business change is the acquisition of another company which may, for example, involve extending the parent company's product line. We can symbolize this type of change by adding a new vertical stripe of information to the model, and reworking the links between related areas. An organizational change within the existing framework, on the other hand, affects mainly the generic ERM as the processes that manipulate data are modified to reflect new organizational needs. These changes in the generic ERM also have some effect on the layers immediately above and below it. The effects of a technology change are confined entirely to the bottom layer of the model.

While this type of model structure is useful for application reengineering in general, it is particularly appropriate in the context of data warehousing. We can closely correlate it with the layers identified in the three-layer data architecture, as shown in the following section.

Enterprise data modeling and the three-layer architecture

When we compare the relative data scopes of the EDM and the three layers of the business data architecture defined in Section 5.4, a number of correlations become clear (Figure 6-5):

- Because the reconciled data layer spans the entire scope of the business, it corresponds to the generic ERM, which has the same scope.

- Real-time data, created and managed by operational applications of limited scope, is modeled through the logical application views.

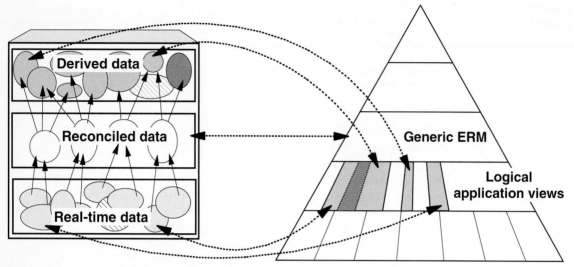

Figure 6-5: *The relationship between the three-layer data architecture and the EDM*

- Derived data, whose scope is restricted to the needs of single users or groups of users, is also modeled through logical application views.

- Logical application views for real-time and derived data may overlap or be quite distinct, depending on business needs.

In practice...

Support for model supersets, subsets, and versions is a high-priority requirement for modeling tools for warehousing.

Models for reconciled, derived, and real-time data must, of course, be taken to the physical data design level at the appropriate scope. The outcome is that at the physical level, entities may occur in three or more physical models—once in the model of the reconciled data layer, and once for every occurrence in the real-time and derived data levels. The common starting point for all of these models is the generic ERM. The existence of many logical- and physical-level models presents some difficulties in model management. Unfortunately, many traditional modeling tools do not easily support the management of multiple subsets and versions related back to a single master model. In this case, model management is a manual activity.

The value to end users

The previous sections have focused on the use of enterprise modeling to support the definition of the data warehouse. This aspect is highly valuable to the IS department. However, the work done in enterprise modeling can also be of value to end users. Because end users gain such value over the entire usage period of the warehouse (a far longer time period than for its development) and because they are far greater in number than IS personnel, the overall business value is considerably higher. Today, users do not gain the full benefit from the model because of the formal way in which it is presented. The data warehouse can help to improve this situation.

The business process and data definitions created as part of enterprise modeling form part of the metadata in the warehouse. By providing an efficient and user-friendly means of accessing and using this metadata, the data warehouse ensures that end users can benefit from the work done during the enterprise modeling phase. The business information guide, described in Chapter 13, provides the means of doing this. Given the amount of effort required of end users during the modeling phase, it is only reasonable that they should be a major beneficiary of this work.

6.2 Representing time in business data

Because a business changes over time, the business data must represent that change. However, traditional data modeling and application design approaches focus almost exclusively on a static view of the world [Tauzovich (1991)].

Tracking the use of time

Putting time into the data model

Figure 6-6 shows a very simple relationship between two entities, and the cardinalities of the relationship between these entities. Simply stated, a department may have zero to many employees, and an employee belongs to one and only one department. *Cardinality*—the number of instances of an entity that may be involved in a relationship—is important as one moves from the logical model to a physical implementation of the database, allowing decisions to be made on table structures and their keys.

However, there is an implicit assumption in the construction and reading of this diagram. The statement "an employee belongs to one and only one department" is true only at one point in time. Clearly, over his or her term of employment, an employee may belong to different departments at different times. The temporal aspect of this relationship is thus effectively ignored in a traditional ER diagram. Tauzovich (1991) thus proposed the introduction of *snapshot* and *lifetime* cardinalities to represent the static (or traditional entity relationship) view and the temporal view, respectively.

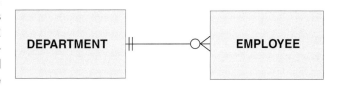

Figure 6-6: Cardinalities in the ER model

From a more fundamental perspective, the reason the snapshot and lifetime cardinalities differ is because **events** take place that affect the relationship between a particular employee and his or her department. Unfortunately, there is no obvious place to represent an event in a traditional data model. Thus, a number of attempts have been made to extend this model to include events [Dey *et al.* (1995)].

However, today's modeling tools incorporate little or none of this functionality and databases provide no explicit support for time dependency. The result is that designers usually add time dependency of data to application designs largely as an afterthought. This approach is often adequate in operational applications because they manage only real-time data and take a view mainly of the current state of the business.

A data warehouse, however, must explicitly consider the temporal aspects of the data it contains, because it must, by definition, provide an historical view of the business. And in the absence of formal support of these temporal issues from either modeling tools or databases, data warehouse designers have generally taken a pragmatic approach to the topic.

Timestamps

Timestamp

A specially defined field, in date-and-time format, that tracks when a data record has been created, deleted, or changed in any way.

One important pragmatic approach that is widely used is the application of **timestamps** to the data. Because data fundamentally changes at the field level, it is possible to represent time at that level, or at any of the higher levels in the structure, such as records/rows or file/table, depending on the granularity (detail) required. This is shown in Figure 6-7.

1. Tracking time at the field level

At the greatest level of detail, representing time at a field level involves applying a timestamp to each field, represented in Figure 6-7 by a "**t1**" field associated with each business data field. In this case, changes in the business can be tracked in great detail. However, the business need to go to this level of tracking is questionable in most cases. In addition, the volume of timestamp data generated is comparable with the volume of the actual data, making this an expensive option in terms of storage.

2. Tracking time at the record/row level

The technical problems of the first approach can be simplified greatly by timestamping at a record/row level, where the record timestamp[1] is updated whenever any field in that record is changed. From a business viewpoint, this approach meets all but the most exacting needs for tracking time and is very common today.

---

[1] There may be a need for more than one timestamp in some cases. For simplicity, we will postpone the question of multiple timestamps until Chapter 8.

3. Tracking time at the file/table level

Finally, one can timestamp the entire file or table, and update the timestamp whenever any field changes. This approach is not appropriate for controlling and auditing the data. However, it is often the level at which end users wish to track the currency of their data.

Snapshots, which represent a view of the business at some point in time, are implicitly or explicitly time-stamped at a file/table level. For technical reasons, highly unstructured data may also be timestamped this way.

Because between them they meet the vast majority of business needs, and because of their favorable technical characteristics, options 2 and 3 listed above are the preferred approaches. For the remainder of this book, we assume that tracking of time is performed at the record/row level where a complete record of changes is needed, and at a file/table level where snapshots are involved. Of course, some cases may require a combination of these approaches.

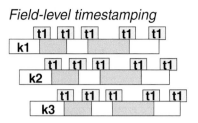

Field-level timestamping

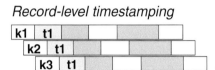

Record-level timestamping

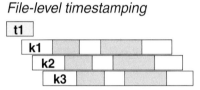

File-level timestamping

Figure 6-7: *Levels of timestamping*

How data changes

The ability described above to represent time in a database is not, on its own, sufficient to allow for the recording of historical data. In addition, one needs an understanding of how changes in data are captured and represented over time.

At a business level, data is changed through **business transactions**. Such transactions create, change, and delete records in real-time business data. A single business transaction may affect more than one data record, so that one business transaction may cause a number of events in the database. For the moment, we will focus on individual events that occur in the database.

In the majority of operational applications, it is the outcome of the event, rather than the event itself, that is stored. This is because most business activities are more intuitively understood and tracked by their **status** at a given time, rather than by the events that have occurred. However, it is possible to store either events or statuses [Soukeras and King (1994)], and the informational environment may require both approaches. It is therefore vital to recognize the differences between the two approaches, and their relationship to one another.

> **Business transaction**
>
> *The fundamental and smallest change in the business that is meaningful and complete in business terms, and that may cause one or more events at a database level.*

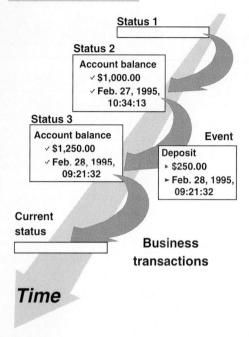

A view of temporal data based on status

A status-based view of time-dependent data, or ***status database***, consists of a series of timestamped records, each showing the state of an entity at a point in time. Typically, the points in time chosen in an operational application are the instants immediately after the events that update the database.

For example, as Figure 6-8 shows, in an application that manages bank accounts, each record that is written shows the amount of money in the account after applying the transaction. Each of these records is a status record. Each status record is, of course, related to the previous one by the event that takes place, in this case, equivalent to the business transaction on the account. The data in the transaction—a deposit of $250—is event data. Figure 6-8 also shows the temporal relationship between status and event data. The timestamp on status 3 is equal to the time at which the event took place. Similarly, the timestamp on status 2 is the time that the previous event took place.

Figure 6-8: Status records in real-time data

While status data is the normal day-to-day data stored in databases and files for many operational and informational applications, event data is often not stored for business purposes at all. Event data is stored in database logs for recovery purposes, although for most business purposes the data structure in such logs is too complex for general use. An important use to which event data may be put is to support data replication.

Status database

A database containing point-in-time records showing the state of an entity after the occurrence of an event.

Although business transactions are responsible for changes in business data, there is not necessarily a one-to-one relationship between business transactions and statuses, for two reasons:

1. In real-time data, a business transaction may cause events in a number of different records, spread over a number of different files or tables. For example, a transfer of money requires at least the source and target accounts to be updated by the one business transaction. This aspect is discussed further in Chapter 8.

2. As the data moves into the reconciled layer and on into the derived layer, many events may occur between two status records in the target layer. The number and kind of these events depend on the timing of the data movement and how often changes are captured. In addition, the timestamps on the status data may reflect the time the data was moved rather than the time the business transaction occurred. These differences are reflected in Figure 6-9, and the implications discussed in Chapter 9.

A view of temporal data based on events

The relationship between status and event data leads to the second representation of time in the data store. This alternative and far less common approach is to store only the events that occur. This is depicted on the right side of Figure 6-10, in comparison with the status approach shown to the left. The result is an **event database**.

Comparing the two approaches, we can see that the status approach stores larger volumes of data. This is because, in any change (except the initial one that creates the first record of the time series), most of the fields in the record remain unchanged but are duplicated anyway. In the event approach, only the primary record key and the identity and contents of the changed fields need to be stored at each change. The amount of data here is likely to be less than the complete record. It will be clear that as the lengths of the status data record decrease, as may be expected if the data structure is normalized, the difference in storage volumes required by the two approaches decreases.

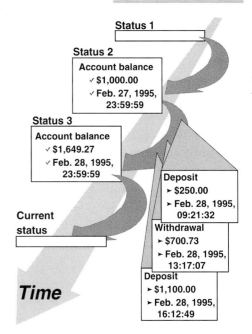

Figure 6-9: *Status records in informational data*

The event approach offers more flexibility than the status approach [Soukeras and King (1994)], unless the status after each event is recorded. This is particularly the case where retroactive events can take place. In the previous example shown in Figure 6-8, if it were later discovered that the deposit amount had been entered incorrectly, all subsequent status records would have to be recomputed

Whichever storage approach is chosen, significant processing is needed to translate that storage view into the other if business purposes require this. However, converting stored statuses into events rather than the reverse is generally simpler and more efficient, and offers greater data integrity. To convert from statuses to events requires taking records in pairs over the required time span and calculating the differences. In contrast, to convert from events to statuses means applying all events in sequence from the initial one until the required time, which may stretch over a considerable time period.

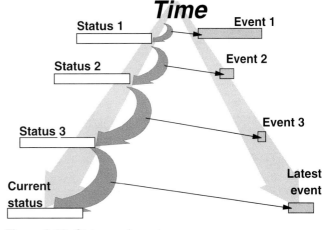

Figure 6-10: *Status and events*

Event database

A database containing a record of the events that cause the values of an entity to change.

This technical consideration, combined with the enterprise's requirement for a view of the status of the business, leads to the predominance of the status approach as a method for storing both operational data in the real-time data layer and historical data in the derived data layer.

In the reconciled data layer, however, the flexibility offered by the event approach, combined with its more natural fit to some types of data, may result in both approaches being used. For example, customer data would be stored as status records because it changes only infrequently and is less subject to retroactive change. On the other hand, the choice between the two approaches when storing bank account data is less clear. Storing the individual transactions—events—provides the maximum flexibility in later taking different views of the data. Storing account balances—the status records—allows the most efficient access to a status-oriented view. In practice, a combination of the two approaches may be employed.

Temporal data structures

Timestamps, together with the concepts of status or event representations, allow the maintenance of temporal data. However, we must address one final aspect of temporal data to understand how history is reflected in a database. This relates to the structure of the data and how new events affect existing data.

As shown in Figure 6-11, there are two basic ways in which this can happen, leading directly to the definition of transient data and periodic data. Each record is shown containing a key field **k** and a timestamp **t**. While the key field, being the unique identifier of the record, is mandatory in both types of data, the timestamp is optional in transient data.

Finally, we consider a third method of maintaining history—snapshots.

Transient data

Real-time data in which changes to existing records overwrite the previous data, and deletions physically erase records, leading to a loss of the historical record of the changes that data has undergone.

Transient data

The key characteristic of *transient data* is that alterations to and deletions of existing records physically destroy the previous data content.

Records can be added (for example, record **k6** at time **t2** in Figure 6-11) and deleted (record **k3** at time **t3**). However, there is no evidence in the data after time **t3** of the previous contents of record **k3**, or indeed that it ever existed. Records can also be changed. Thus at time **t2**, records **k2** and **k4** have been altered, and record **k4** is further altered at time **t3**. As in the case of deletion, previous states of changed records are lost.

It is also impossible to know how long any particular record will exist in the system. A record may change several times in a day or remain static for months. Because the details of each transaction on an existing record re-

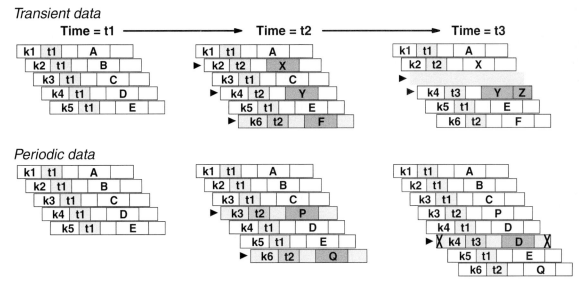

Figure 6-11: *Transient and periodic data*

place the previous details, the data relating to each record is available only until the next transaction that changes that record occurs.

This type of data is found exclusively in the real-time data of the operational environment. As a general rule, only statuses are stored as transient data. An event database that was transient would always contain only the latest event and would thus be of little or no value in any business process. A record of latest statuses, on the other hand, is a common and valuable way of tracking the business.

Periodic data

In *periodic data*, once a record is added to the store, it is never physically deleted, nor is its business content ever physically modified. Rather, new records are always added, even for updates to or deletions of existing records. Thus, at time **t2** in Figure 6-11, record **k3** is updated, but rather than the previous value **C** being overwritten with a new value **P**, a complete new record with the same key **k3**, but with a different timestamp **t2** is added. As a result, the timestamp is an integral part of the key to the record. Instead of deleting a record, this fact is handled by the addition of a specially marked record. In the figure, record **k4** is "deleted" at time **t3** by the addition of a record indicating this key value is no longer valid. Addition of new records is identical to that shown earlier.

Periodic data thus contains a complete record of the changes that have occurred in the data. Periodic data is *persistent* in nature because it provides a permanent record of the data and its changes. Either statuses or events can form the basis for this complete record.

Periodic data

Data recording the history of the business over a period of time by maintaining a complete record either of all statuses or of all events that have occurred.

Periodic data is found in the real-time data of operational systems where a record of the previous states of the data is important. Thus, bank account systems and insurance premiums systems often use this approach. Order-entry systems, on the other hand, are usually based on transient data. This choice reflects different business needs for tracking and auditability. However, in almost all operational systems the duration for which this persistent data is held is relatively short, due to performance and/or storage volume constraints. This may be termed **semi-periodic data**.

Periodic data is found in the derived data layer where it is used to support trend analysis of historical data.

The reconciled data layer consists entirely of periodic data because of its role as the historical record of the business.

Snapshot data

Snapshot data

A point-in-time view of the business data showing its status at a particular time, which is then kept as a (potentially) permanent record of that state of the data.

Snapshot data is a stable view of the data as it exists at some point in time. It does not contain any record of changes in the data that resulted in its arrival at this state. If it is updated, it may be totally replaced, or at a detailed level, records may be changed similarly to how transient data is changed.

This type of data occurs most often in the derived data layer. Snapshots usually represent the business data at some time in the past, and a series of snapshots can provide a view of the history of the business. However, predictive or planned business states are also snapshots, in this case representing the future.

Like periodic data, snapshot data is also persistent in nature because it provides a potentially permanent record of the data at a point in time. Note that a view of the current business position of an enterprise is not a snapshot because it is not stable over time. However, the current business position can be *captured* as a snapshot and preserved, as long as we understand that, as of the following instant, it no longer represents the current position.

6.3 Historical data

The need to access historical data is one of the primary incentives for adopting the warehousing approach. In particular, historical data plays a significant role in warehouses used for trend analysis of buying and usage patterns, which focus on particular areas of the business data. Historical data also constitutes a large and increasingly important component of enterprise asset data, where it provides the definitive record of the business.

The need for historical data

Requirements for maintaining an historical record of the business fall into two broad areas:

1. **A view of the business at a given time**

    In general, end users need to see views of the business as it exists at different times. Some times have particular business significance. Closing of accounting or taxation periods, and major business events such as reorganizations or acquisitions are times that require such a view. These views must be stable, allowing the same inquiry at different times to produce the same results. Such needs are met by snapshot data.

    The need for some of these views of the business is known in advance, so the IS department can therefore pre-store the required data. Other needs are not predictable, either in timing or in data content. In such cases, the data cannot be stored in advance, so end users need an approach that enables the generation of such retrospective data.

2. **Business trend analysis**

    The analysis of trends in the business can be expressed in terms of understanding the differences between a series of point-in-time views. For example, managers calculate profitability at the end of each monthly accounting period and store it as part of the reporting data for each month. The trend can thus be analyzed from month to month. However, this approach is rather limited because of its restriction to a monthly period. In times of rapid change, the same managers might need to analyze the trend on a daily basis, in which case, daily reporting data would be required.

    It is therefore appropriate to set the fundamental level of business change—the business transaction—as a basis for trend analysis. Data that contains a record of business transactions over a period of time has already been identified as periodic data. Based on this periodic data users can undertake trend analyses at any level of granularity. An added bonus is that one can generate a view of the business at any point in time.

Positioning historical data in the warehouse architecture

In the context of the three-layer conceptual data architecture, historical data is a mix of different types of data and potentially resides in any or all of the three layers.

In practice...

If historical data is extensively used in operational systems, some common use of real-time and reconciled data may be possible, but only if the real-time data is modeled at an enterprise level.

By definition, operational processes use real-time data, representing the current status of the business. However, a view of the events leading to this up-to-the-minute status is also needed. The time span of this historical data depends on the business in which the company is involved.

In the financial industry, for example, both extremes occur. Operational applications dealing with personal bank accounts may handle data pertaining only to the current month, which is sufficient for any transactions that may need to be handled. At the other extreme, operational insurance applications need access to data spanning the entire client involvement with the company to verify his or her entitlement to a particular claim. In this instance, the time span of the current data is such that it encompasses virtually all the historical data of the enterprise.

Informational processes, on the other hand, are largely based on historical data. Both derived and reconciled data are therefore historical in nature.

Derived data is used to analyze and manage the business, and may consist of snapshots of the business—for example, the quarterly profit-and-loss statement for each of the last 12 quarters—or of periodic data such as the record of all transactions on an account over the last year. The type and volume of historical data required in each set of derived data is therefore dependent solely on the business need of the users of that derived data.

Reconciled data

Reconciled data covers a time period at least equal to the longest required to manage the business.

Reconciled data is driven by the need to support enterprise-wide consistency and usage of data at the derived level. Historical data in the reconciled layer must therefore be as detailed and generic as possible. In addition, the previously stated characteristic of periodic data—the potential to generate any point-in-time view from it—means that reconciled data must be periodic and span a time period long enough to derive any required derived-layer data sets.

Historical business data therefore exists in all three data layers, but for different reasons in each layer. The source of historical data is the real-time data layer. In most cases, historical data is stored and used to some extent in this layer. The main usage of historical data is in managing the business, and thus occurs in the derived data layer. However, the role of historical data in the reconciled data layer is vital, because it is from here that all derived data is sourced.

Historical data volumes

Probably the most obvious characteristic of historical data is its potential volume and the associated costs of storing it. However, the volume of historical data that should be retained must be considered in terms of its potential business benefits.

At the extreme, it is clear that if all data is stored at the highest level of granularity and is never deleted, then all possible future queries and analyses can be supported. However, this approach can be difficult to justify by a cost-benefit analysis. In analyzing the costs and benefits of storing historical data, a number of general considerations arise.

Figure 6-12 shows typical usage versus data age curves based on a number of different criteria, from which we can draw the following conclusions:

- Summary data is used over a longer time span than detailed data.

- Managers and executives focus primarily on summary data for decision making, whereas operational usage of data is short-term and occurs at a detailed level. When building a business case, summary data therefore is far more valuable to the company in the longer term.

- Marketing functions tend to require longer-term access to detailed data than administrative and financial functions do. However, marketing use of summary data is also longer-term. It may be the case that the marketing requirement for older detailed data is as a result of the IS

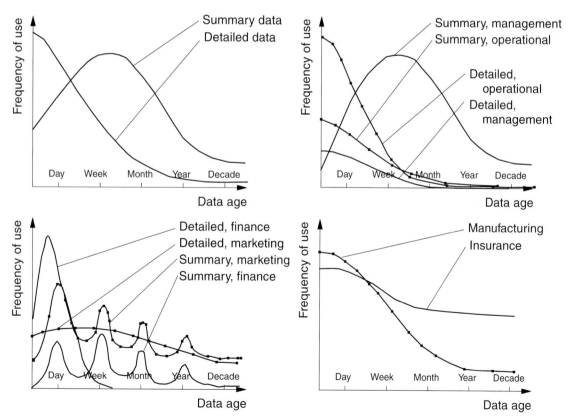

Figure 6-12: *The frequency of data use as a function of age*

In practice...

When defining the time span of historical data to be stored in the reconciled layer, it is better to err on the side of storing too much than too little, and defining an active archival strategy to manage the ensuing data volumes.

failure to store the correct summary-level data, or it may be due to the marketing department having more unpredictable needs than finance personnel.

- The length of the business cycle from conception to death of the product has a strong influence on the duration of use of detailed data but less of an influence on summary data. We can see this effect by comparing different industries with different business cycle times.

Such an analysis of the need for and use of historical data is carried out at the derived data level. From the maximum time span needed at the derived data level one can deduce the time span of data required for the reconciled data layer. Remember that the consequence of not storing all detailed-level historical data is that some future historical analysis requirements will be impossible to meet, because some required data will no longer be available. The likelihood of such needs arising, as well as the business consequence of not being able to meet them, must be weighed against the cost of storing and managing all historical data.

In addition, the physical implementation of the reconciled data layer must be considered. In particular, the archiving of data reduces the on-line storage volumes required, but is useful only if retrieval is straightforward. Archive and retrieval are covered in Chapter 8.

6.4 Data replication

Copying data might be described as the oldest profession in the data processing world! Copies of data have been created and used from the earliest times. Depending on the purpose of the copied data, the copy might have been identical to its source or might have been changed in some specified way. However, data replication goes beyond copying. Traditionally, copying has been an activity driven by immediate needs for data, initiated and designed without regard for the wider consequences. Data replication is copying under control.

The need to replicate data in data warehousing should, by now, be evident. The needs being satisfied are:

- population of the reconciled business data layer

- population of the derived business data layer

- population of usage metadata

While there are significant differences among these three needs, some underlying aspects are common to all three, which this section covers. Parts III and IV describe the specific details of each type of population.

This section introduces the technical functionality that underlies data replication, starting with a view of why the traditional approach to copying data is inappropriate in the data warehouse environment. This leads to a definition of data replication. This section concludes with a comparison of data replication in the warehouse and the other use of data replication—the synchronization of distributed databases.

While the data architecture and modeling activities constitute a significant challenge in the design phase of the warehouse, the implementation of the population function often comprises the most costly and time-consuming part of the entire implementation. The choice of approaches and their capabilities can influence the physical implementation of the EDM in the reconciled layer. Conversely, the physical locations of source and target data can significantly limit the available choice of tools for implementing the chosen replication strategy.

As a consequence of these considerations, data replication is the area of warehouse implementation where most tradeoffs are made—balancing depth of function, breadth of platforms supported, ease of maintenance, flexibility to support changing business and data needs, ease of use, and performance.

Application-level data copying

In this traditional approach, the requirements for copying data are determined solely within the scope of the application under development. A data copying program is then designed and built to extract the data from the source, enhance it as required, and deliver it to the target environment. This approach, called *application-level copying*, has grown from and is supported by a number of factors.

In all organizations, it is common to identify and satisfy decision support needs in advance of creating any formal strategy or framework to provide a common approach. As a result, the initial data copying programs are built independently in support of specific decision support requirements. In this way, the data copying and transformation is provided in discrete application programs, each with a narrow and well-defined scope.

In addition, project owners and managers favor this approach for valid reasons. Applications developed within the bounds of a single project are easier to manage and are more likely to deliver on time and within budget than those with significant external dependencies. Such applications can also be better tuned to perform to well-defined requirements.

However, the approach has significant drawbacks, and these are best understood in the context of the evolution of these copy programs, described in the following scenario.

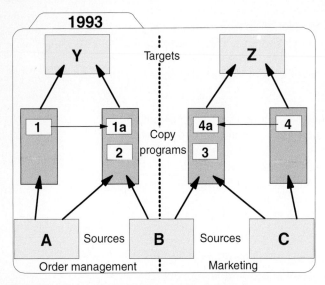

Figure 6-13: *Application-level copying (stage 1)*

A sample scenario

Figure 6-13 shows the environment at an early stage of development. Two different parts of the organization are copying data from the operational sources A, B, and C, and making it available to the informational applications Y and Z, each in support of its own set of end users.[2] Each group is well organized within the bounds of its own responsibility—as shown by the reuse of data transformation modules 1 and 4 in two different copy programs. However, there is little coordination between the two groups—as shown by the development of two different modules, 2 and 3, which perform basically the same extract function on source B.

It should be recognized that all of the problems with this scenario cannot be ascribed directly to the application-level data copying approach. Some relate to the data architecture and the lack of an identified source for each data element. These problems have already been addressed. Other problems mentioned here spring from the organizational divisions described in the scenario. However, the adoption of a controlled and managed approach to the technical aspects of data copying is an integral step in solving the overall problem.

Figure 6-14 introduces two new requirements. The first is the need to change source dataset A as a result of a change in the business. The changes required for modules 1 and 1a can be specified only after finalizing the redesign of source A. In a traditional application development approach, this implies the need to design, develop, and deploy modules 1 and 1a in the latter stages of the development cycle of source A. Not only must the developers of modules 1 and 1a design and develop the changes to these modules, but they must also test them in two different copy programs. This task is often a significant challenge.

The second requirement is the need for marketing to have a copy of some of the data in source A. There are two basic ways to achieve this.

---

[2] This example describes the organization as having independent IS groups within both the marketing and order management functions. However, the problems shown can also arise in an organization with a single IS department, because of the way in which support responsibilities are divided even within the bounds of this single organization.

1. Marketing can ask order management to provide a copy of the required data.

2. Marketing can develop a new copy program that extracts the required data from source A.

Both approaches have drawbacks. However, in this example, marketing decides to ask their colleagues in order management to provide the needed data. This approach is attractive to the marketing function because the structure and content of the source data is understood by the order management developers, thus avoiding learning costs. The outcome is that module 1a is further modified to take into account dataset Z as a new target for this data in source A. This has an unde-

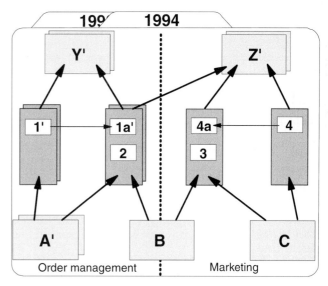

Figure 6-14: Application-level copying (stage 2)

sirable side effect: modules 1' and 1a' are no longer direct copies of each other and require separate maintenance whenever source A changes in the future.

The next stage of evolution is illustrated in Figure 6-15. Order management discovers a need to have access to data originating in source C. In this case, order management needs some specific changes to the data coming from source C and wants to maintain control of those changes. As a result, module 4a is provided by the marketing function, and order management uses this as the basis for developing a new module 4b to be incorporated into order management's own copy program. Over time, this module will diverge in structure and function from its original version.

Also illustrated in Figure 6-15 is the effect of a change in source database B, which is being used by the two separately developed copy modules 2 and 3. It is clear that both order management and marketing have to separately duplicate this change in their own copy programs. In this case, these changes may well introduce inconsistencies into the extracted data.

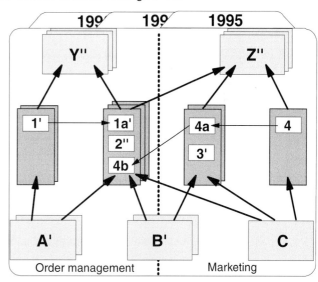

Figure 6-15: Application-level copying (stage 3)

The problems of application-level copying

The problems illustrated in the previous example can be summarized:

In practice...

The best starting point for an initial data warehouse implementation may use a subset of existing application-level copying programs in spite of the problems identified here with their use. This is true when the logic involved in transforming operational data for use in the informational environment is particularly complex, or when the operational environment is likely to change significantly in the near future.

- **Maintenance of individual copy programs is a challenge.**

  As the source operational databases change in structure or content in line with business changes, the copy programs must also be updated. Such maintenance is often complex because of the amount of data enhancement logic in these programs. In addition, there is often a significant time constraint: the copy programs must be updated in the time period between when the design changes in the source databases are completed and when they are put into production.

- **Consistency of copy programs is difficult to maintain.**

  Each operational database becomes, over time, the source for many copy programs. All parts of the organization must consistently understand the structure and meaning of this source data, as well as all changes made to it, in order to ensure consistent operation of the multiple copy programs based on it. In the absence of such consistency, significant conflict arises over how to interpret the data.

- **Overall cost grows exponentially.**

  As a result of the above factors, there is considerable duplication of effort across the organization in the development and maintenance of copy programs. As the number of copy programs increases, the effort involved in ensuring consistency within and between these programs increases very rapidly, and maintenance soon consumes all available resources designated to support the end-user environment.

Data replication—a definition

The problems outlined in the previous section lead to the need for a better approach to data copying, known as data replication.

Data replication, as it relates to the data warehouse, exhibits the following key characteristics:

- Control—data replication ensures consistency of results, irrespective of when or how the data is copied or manipulated.

- Management—it provides the ability to build and reuse function.

- Flexibility—it allows mixing and matching of functions and techniques where needed.

- Ease of maintenance—it enables a rapid, cost-effective response to changes in the structure or location of the source or target datasets.

- Integration of metadata—it provides links to the metadata of both source and target data, using or producing the metadata as required.

- Performance—it provides ways to support large data sources at a variety of levels of synchronization.

- Variety of sources—it supports the wide variety of data sources characteristic of today's IS environment through a single approach or through a consistent and interlinked set of approaches.

- Ease of use—users whose technical skill ranges from ordinary end user to database administrator can use this tool.

- Business context—it preserves the relationships imposed by the business processes when data is replicated.

The characteristics in the above list have been ordered according to their relative importance, based on the kinds of difficulties one encounters when copying and manipulating data in the warehouse with the traditional application-level approach.

> *Data replication*
>
> *A set of techniques that provides comprehensive support for copying and transforming data from source to target location in a managed, consistent, repeatable, and well-understood manner.*

The data replication process

In order to replicate data in a manner consistent with the characteristics outlined above, the steps in the process must be well defined. In a logical sequence, these steps are:

1. **Identify the source data.**

   In data warehousing, the source data is at a minimum defined and, in general, usually exists prior to any attempt to replicate it. Therefore, the process of data replication must first focus on obtaining this definition from wherever it already exists, rather than enabling the creation of a new definition.

2. **Identify or define the target data.**

   In contrast, the target data often does not exist in advance of defining the replication process. Ideally, the structure of the target data should be defined through the data modeling process as previously described. However, in some instances, particularly when the replication process is used to populate some types of derived data, the definition of the target data structure may form part of the definition of the replication process. This step, therefore, must equally support both acquiring an existing target data definition and creating such a definition if required.

3. **Create the mapping between source and target.**

   When the definitions of both source and target data are available, the next task is to define how the source data is transformed into the target data. This mapping definition is required to handle a variety of different types of transformation. These range from relatively simple physical types, such as EBCDIC (extended binary-coded decimal interchange code) to ASCII (American standard code for information interchange), to rather complex processes that combine a number of pieces of source data to generate new data in the target environment.

4. **Define the replication mode.**

   There are two basic modes of data replication: refresh and update. Refresh mode involves a bulk transfer of data from source to target. Update mode, on the other hand, identifies and transfers only changed data from the source to the target environment. It is often necessary to define in advance the mode of replication to be used. However, in some circumstances, this decision can be made at runtime. The choice of mode is based on the time dependencies found in the source data and required in the target.

5. **Schedule the process of replication.**

   The actual replication of data is usually scheduled to occur separately from the definition process (steps 1 to 5). In addition, the replication itself is often a repeated process, taking place at defined intervals, such as daily, weekly, monthly, and so on. The scheduling process should be capable of triggering immediate replication, but the mandatory requirement is for later and repeated triggering.

6. **Capture the required data from the source.**

   This is the first step in the actual replication process itself. The capture step, in common with the following steps, is expected to take place according to the defined schedule, and without further human intervention. The underlying method for extracting the data is dependent on the technology of the source data store and the chosen mode of replication. In terms of its timeliness, capture can range from real-time (or synchronous), through near real-time, to batch (both asynchronous).

7. **Transfer the captured data between source and target.**

   The transfer process must support a fully heterogeneous environment, where the source and target may reside on different types of machine, in different formats, and in different locations, connected by links of varying capability.

8. **Transform the captured data based on the defined mapping.**

   The transformation step may take place in the source environment or the target environment, or it may be distributed over both. Different types of transformation operate at different levels: changing one or more fields within a single record, combining records from different sources, aggregating records, and so on.

9. **Apply the captured data to the target.**

    Data can be applied to the target in two basic ways:

    *   Incoming data replaces existing data.

    *   Incoming data is appended to existing data.

    The rationale and approach used depends on several factors: the required replication mode, the ways in which the data was captured, and the time dependencies of the source and target data.

10. **Confirm the success or failure of the replication.**

    Any of the above steps in the replication process may fail. Within the overall process, fall-back mechanisms should exist to overcome specific failures. However, if the process cannot be completed, this information must be made available to the appropriate person.

11. **Document the outcome of the replication in the metadata.**

    The replication tool documents the success or failure of each step in the metadata. This provides the end user with information on the data currency in the target system.

12. **Maintain the definitions of source, target, and mapping.**

    As business needs change, there is a need to update the definition of the replication process to reflect changes in the source data, new requirements for the target data, new data transformations, and so on.

These steps, categorized into six areas (shown in the left column of Table 6-1) form the basis of the functional components of data replication.

Enterprise modeling and data replication

Few people today would design a new application without first modeling its data requirements. In many ways, data replication is just another application, albeit a rather specialized one, whose requirements are often more heavily influenced by technological than by business needs. However, the need for modeling as the first design step in data replication is often ignored.

In fact, data modeling is vital. Establishing a link from the EDM through to the definition of the source-to-target mapping is mandatory in order to create a replication process that is viable in the long term.

Table 6-1: *Categorizing the steps in data replication*

Function	Process step	Frequency
Administration	1. Identify the source data.	Once
Administration	2. Identify or define the target data.	Once
Administration	3. Create the mapping between source and target.	Once
Administration	4. Define the replication mode.	Once
Administration	5. Schedule the process of replication.	Once
Capture	6. Capture the required data from the source.	Frequently
Data transfer	7. Transfer the captured data between source and target.	Frequently
Transformation	8. Transform the captured data based on the defined mapping.	Frequently
Apply	9. Apply the captured data to the target.	Frequently
Process management	10. Confirm the success or failure of the replication.	Frequently
Process management	11. Document the outcome of the replication in the metadata.	Frequently
Administration	12. Maintain the definitions of source, target, and mapping.	As needed

The role of the enterprise data model

Establishing the relationship or mapping between the source and target data is the first and most important requirement in replication. The warehouse is driven by end users' needs to relate data to the reality of the business. It therefore follows that the EDM, being the theoretical foundation for the relationship between data and business meaning, is the fundamental basis for the source/target relationship.

Consider the following rather simple example. In one company, the business requirement is to provide a meaningful currency name in the management information view of the orders file, although in the operational system file this is represented by a one-character code. Therefore it is necessary to replicate the code representing currency type in the source to a meaningful currency name in the target. It is clearly possible to relate the source and target structures at a physical level. The mapping is described by a rule such as:

> **Source field**
> **maps to Target table, column**
> **according to Conversion Rule**

In this case, the source field may be defined in terms of an offset, length, and data type in the source record related to a variable name in a particular application program. The target table and column may be named according to some naming rules dictated by the data management needs of the IS department and the limitations of the DBMS used. Add the data location information, and the previously simple rule then becomes:

> **Source field**
>
> | | |
> |---|---|
> | Location: | MVSMKT12 |
> | Filename: | MKT.UST.0001 |
> | Offset: | 24 |
> | Length: | 1 |
> | Data type: | CHAR(1) |
> | Owning application: | MKT_SEGMNT |
> | Variable: | CURR_TYP |
>
> **maps to Target table, column**
>
> | | |
> |---|---|
> | Location: | UNIXACC1 |
> | Database: | ACCNTS01 |
> | Table name: | AC_T_CST |
> | Column name: | AC_C_CUR |
>
> **according to Conversion Rule**
>
> | | |
> |---|---|
> | Location: | UNIXACC1 |
> | Conversion program: | CURCONV |

Although all of the above data is clearly needed to effect the replication, the approach shown mixes data meanings, structures, and locations in a way that is both confusing and difficult to maintain. Although well disguised here, the business meaning and relationship between the source and target is essentially defined by the information about the owning application of the source and the conversion program that generates the target. Unfortunately, from the information shown, there is no way of determining, *a priori*, the meaning and relationship. It is based on a background knowledge of the systems that the designer of the mapping must possess.

The difficulty with this mapping definition is that it is not at all clear how or why this particular source field maps to this target table and column.

Describing the same replication requirement in terms of the EDM leads to a more logical approach, as shown in Figure 6-16. Currency code and currency name in this case are clearly related to one another as attributes

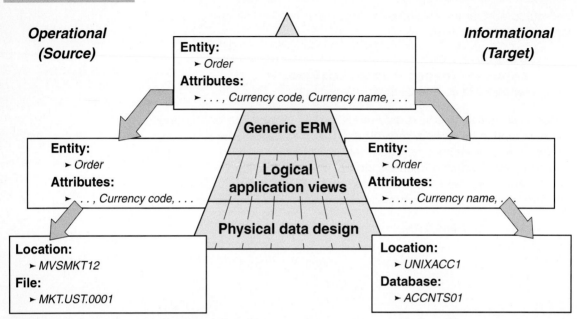

Figure 6-16: A model-driven definition of replication

of the order entity in the generic ERM. This entity is then further reflected in two logical application views—one for the operational system and the other for the informational environment. With the attributes now clearly related in a business sense, it is time to proceed to the physical level of the two models. This physical level still needs all of the location information that appeared previously, but there is now a clear separation between the logical and the physical information.

Model-driven replication

The preceding example illustrates some of the goals in *model-driven replication*. This section discusses them in more detail. They are:

- **Simplify the definition process.**

  Understanding the true relationship between the source and target data is critical to the success of data replication as a whole, and can only be based on the underlying EDM. Once this relationship is understood, the physical aspects of locations and structure of data can be addressed. The separation of logical and physical levels leads to a simplification of the definition process.

- **Reduce the development time and effort.**

  Moving away from the development of individual copy programs, each designed to copy a specific set of data, and toward a rules-driven approach leads to a significant reduction in development time and effort.

- **Reduce the maintenance overhead.**

  Changes in business needs must be isolated from changes in the physical structure of the data. While both types of change must be accommodated in the maintenance process, separation of the two types leads to a more easily managed environment.

- **Provide a common base of data and mapping definitions, irrespective of the mode (refresh or update) of replication.**

  As described later in Chapter 9, both modes of replication can apply at different times to the same data. It is therefore vital to use the same data and mapping definitions, or metadata, in both modes.

- **Make the replication metadata available to end users.**

  When end users analyze data they often question its sources and the rules applied in transforming it between source and target datasets. This leads to a strong requirement that the mapping information be available to, and understandable by, end users.

Supporting these goals places a number of requirements on the administration process that makes these definitions. The most obvious is the need for a common enterprise-wide model that spans both source and target requirements. This model provides the requisite separation between logical and physical definitions. A consequence of this requirement is the need for all the metadata relating to replication to reside in a logically single store. This ensures reuse and provides a single source of information required by end users.

Unfortunately, these needs are difficult to satisfy. The current environments for modeling and for administering replication are fragmented and disparate in most IS shops. The scale of this fragmentation is such that tackling it is a major challenge for vendors. However, it is worthwhile to set these goals at the outset, because the implications of tackling data replication in a piecemeal way are so serious. These include the potential for introducing significant data inconsistencies as well as the long-term maintenance issues described earlier.

Data replication—an alternative use

"Data replication" is a phrase commonly used in the computer industry today. As a consequence, it means different things to different people. In this book, data replication is defined in terms of the needs of data warehousing to build and maintain the data structures of the reconciled and derived data layers and of the metadata store. An alternative use of the term focuses on the need for synchronizing distributed databases, irrespective of the business use to which these databases are put [Goldring

Model-driven replication

An approach to replication in which the data and mapping definitions start from a business viewpoint and lead to logical- and physical-level definitions based on a layered enterprise modeling approach.

(1995)]. This definition leads to different principles for data replication and drives a different technical implementation.

It is not the intention of this text to describe the use of data replication for database synchronization in detail. However, a brief comparison with replication for data warehousing is in order, and shows the basis on which one may differentiate between the two types of replication:

- **Sources and targets**

    A large percentage of the operational data required as a source for the warehouse resides in legacy, or non-relational, data stores, both files and databases. The structure for the warehouse data is primarily relational. Replication for warehousing therefore needs a variety of sources, with a particular need for non-relational support when populating the reconciled data layer. Target support is mainly relational, but in the case of replication to the derived data layer extends to other types of target, such as spreadsheets or multidimensional databases.

    Replication for synchronization is almost exclusively concerned with the relational environment for both sources and targets. Support for non-relational sources and targets is generally seen as a secondary need.

- **Source/target relationships**

    When defining the data sources, targets, and the relationship between them, the process in data warehousing is driven by the business meanings of the sources and targets. Ideally, this business meaning is expressed through the EDM. In the context of populating the reconciled data layer, the source data often does not conform to the current data model of the business, and the transformation required when moving the data is often complex. The transformation required when moving data between the reconciled and derived data layers is generally far simpler in nature.

    In replication for database synchronization, the business meaning is often less important than an understanding of the underlying physical data. The relationship between sources and targets is usually easily defined based solely on the database schemas. The resulting transformations are generally simple subsets that can be expressed in terms of straightforward set operations.

- **Data movement**

    Replication for database synchronization is often described as the realistic alternative to distributed two-phase commit, which permits the complete synchronization of multiple databases.   Replication allows two or more databases to remain almost synchronized, which is sufficient in many cases. The requirement is thus to support two-way data

In practice...

When selecting tools to support data replication in a warehouse environment, the highest-priority requirements are flexibility and extensibility of data sources and transformations supported— rather than for near real-time or two-way replication, which are emphasized by tools designed for database synchronization.

movement with any needed contention management, and to be able to move the data at any frequency, including close to real-time.

In warehousing, the requirement is technically simpler. Data always flows from the operational to the informational environment. This leads to a one-way movement of data. And, as previously described, the requirement is to be able to view the data in defined time slices, typically of a duration of a day or longer, rather than having the target environment reflect the source status minute by minute.

Table 6-2: Comparison of the uses of data replication

Replication in data warehousing	Replication in database synchronization
Multiple source structures	Relational sources
Relational targets	Relational targets
Driven by the data model	Driven by the database schema
Complex transformations	Less complex transformations
One-way	Two-way
Point-in-time	Near real-time
Automated	Automated

These disparate needs are summarized in Table 6-2. While both types of replication strongly support automation of replication function, there are significant differences. Notice that replication for database synchronization requires a more robust approach to data synchronization but is largely confined to the relational environment. Replication in support of data warehousing, on the other hand, must allow for more complex transformations of data between a greater variety of sources and targets.

Functional components of data replication

In describing data replication in the warehouse, in whatever context it appears, we can perceive a common structure. This structure is based on the six categories of function identified in Table 6-1. Figure 6-17 shows the relationships among the functional components of data replication. These components form the basis for all subsequent descriptions of data replication in Parts III and IV.

Administration is the entry point for all use of the data replication function. In order to obtain the maximum benefit from existing definitions of data sources and targets, administration uses the metadata describing the source and target to locate and understand their structures and to build relationships between them.

The output of administration is the information needed to enable process management and the individual run-time components (capture, apply, transformation, and data transfer) to perform their respective tasks.

Depending on the variety of source data types and on the replication modes in use, one or more **capture** components are required. Based on the data needs defined through the administration component, capture reads from all of, or a subset of, the source data and makes it available to the data transfer or transformation components. Completion of the capture process and any errors that occur are notified to process management.

After the required data has been captured, the next process may be either transformation or data transfer. Which process is invoked depends on whether the source and the target are in the same environment or in different ones, and where the transformation is best performed. **Transformation**, as the name implies, converts data as received from the source into the structure best suited to the needs of the target environment. A number of different types of transformation are useful in data warehousing.

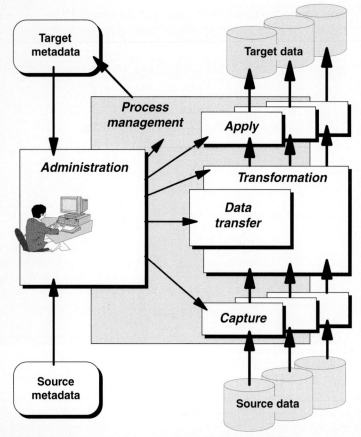

Figure 6-17: *Functional components of data replication*

Finally, there are one or more **apply** components depending on the variety of target environments and replication modes in use. Apply writes the incoming data to the target database in one of a number of ways, from a simple unconditional insertion of the new data, to a more complex approach that preserves existing data and allows for the generation of historical data.

Data transfer is responsible for the physical transfer of data within and between different systems and platforms. Scheduling and control of the run-time components is the responsibility of **process management**. Required schedules are defined through administration. However, process management may take environmental factors and error conditions into account when scheduling actions. Both process management and data transfer are complex components that operate in and across all of the different physical environments, both the operating system and the network, within which data replication occurs.

From replication to population

Data replication is the underlying technology that supports the population of the data warehouse with both business data and metadata.

Three of the six components identified above—capture, transformation, and apply—provide functions central to the act of replicating data. However, the functionality required in all three components varies, depending on which type of population is occurring. Details can be found in later chapters, as follows:

- Capture, transformation, and apply of business data from the real-time layer to the reconciled layer—see Chapter 9.

- Capture, transformation, and apply of business data from the reconciled layer to the derived layer—see Chapter 11.

- Capture, transformation, and apply of metadata from the build-time component to the usage component—see Chapter 13.

The administration component supporting data replication, and the two remaining components—process management and data transfer—are described under the topic of data warehouse management in Chapter 19.

6.5 Conclusions

The techniques identified in this chapter are key to successfully implementing a data warehouse. Each addresses a vital need in the overall design:

- Enterprise data modeling supports the definition of a common and agreed view of the data required to understand, run, and manage the business, both today and into the future. Without such a view, a data warehouse implementation can be no more than traditional development of discrete informational applications.

- The techniques for representing the time dimension of data lead to the ability to store historical data in a way that supports its use for many business purposes throughout the organization. The provision of a definitive record of the business' performance over a long period of time is a key requirement of data warehousing.

- Populating the data warehouse is an area of considerable technical difficulty. The IS department requires a powerful set of closely integrated data replication functions to build and maintain the volume of constantly changing data that constitutes the data warehouse. Without such a tool set, IS shops do not have the productivity to deliver the level of data quality required by the users.

Although none of these techniques is completely unique to data warehousing, their use in the warehouse environment does lead to some special considerations. In particular, the combination of techniques provides a new set of tools with which any intending warehouse implementer must be familiar.

Chapter 7

Introduction to the logical architecture

Types of data and the concepts of business data layers and metadata components provide the basic theory of the data warehouse structure. The previous chapter described the basic tools with which to design the data warehouse. The time has arrived to begin the design process in earnest. While Parts III and IV show the detailed design, this chapter provides an overview of the logical architecture of the warehouse.

In the move from conceptual to logical architecture, this discussion covers a number of factors:

- high-level constraints due to technology as seen today and predicted over the next few years

- the organizational aspects of ownership and development

- the geographical distribution of data and function

From the point of view of the data structure, we introduce the ***business data warehouse*** and ***business information warehouses*** which are the logical (and eventually physical) implementations of the reconciled and derived data layers, respectively. We also introduce the ***data warehouse catalog***, which comprises the metadata of interest in the warehouse.

Finally, this chapter provides an overview of the functional components that support this data structure. They are positioned relative to the data structures and also in relation to one another.

7.1 Business data in the data warehouse

As stated in Chapter 5, the real-time, reconciled, and derived data layers are conceptual. As we move toward a physical implementation of the data warehouse, it becomes clear that each of these layers has a physical counterpart. However, none resides in one physical location, and all are implemented in a variety of ways. Figure 7-1 introduces the high-level logical data architecture that is used throughout the remainder of this book, and maps its components on the right to the three data layers on the left. The figure also shows the relationship between the logical architecture and that commonly misused term "data warehouse", shown as a dashed box. The confusion about what precisely a data warehouse is stems from the fact, evident in the figure, that it maps onto both the reconciled and the derived layers of data.

Operational systems

Operational systems

Applications that run the business on a day-to-day basis using real-time data.

Operational systems are the applications used to run the business, and the data they use, in files and databases, is real-time data. Such applications exist today in a variety of formats and locations, and are thus both heterogeneous and distributed. New applications continue to be built and are even more heterogeneous and distributed than in the past, today being implemented in a variety of client/server environments.

While reengineering projects try to simplify this environment in order to reduce heterogeneity, a number of factors negate this effort. The increasing trend toward distributed systems favors technological diversity, as newer systems are built on newer platforms. The increasing autonomy of departments and computer awareness of users reduces the control a central IS department can exercise. The need to develop applications more rapidly also mitigates against standardizing operational systems. Therefore, it is difficult to envisage any significant rationalization of this physical environment, and in some instances the diversity may grow.

Operational systems are often equated to legacy systems, but they differ in one important aspect. Legacy systems often contain reporting functionality, which is used to manage the business as opposed to running it. Such function, although only a small part of the legacy application, must be distinguished from the truly operational functionality. Its proper place is in the derived layer, and over time it should be moved there.

Because operational systems interact with one another, passing data back and forth and modifying it as needed, it is always necessary to identify definitively and as early as possible the "correct" source of any particular data item needed in the warehouse. Data modeling—in particular, the re-analysis of existing data in the context of the EDM—has a key role to play here.

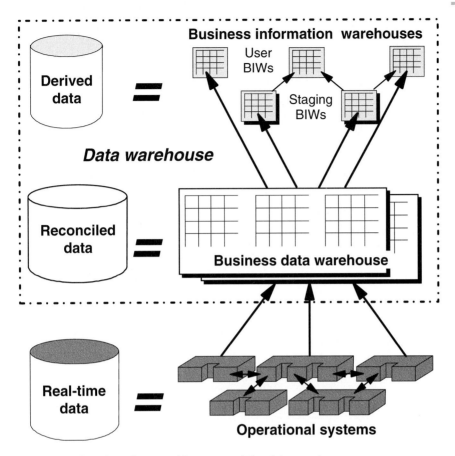

Figure 7-1: *The three-layer architecture and the data warehouse*

Operational systems are the source, and indeed the sole source, of all data in the warehouse. This statement is self-evident when considering internal data describing the day-to-day activities of the business. Such data is created through transaction-processing systems within the business itself. However, this statement does require some clarification when dealing with external data, predictive data, corrections, adjustments, data re-use, and personal data. These types of data enter the warehouse from operational systems or from systems that interact with the warehouse as operational systems, as shown in subsequent sections.

The business data warehouse

The **business data warehouse (BDW)** is the physical realization of the reconciled data layer. The characteristics of this reconciled data layer, which have already been described in Section 5.4, apply equally to the BDW. It is, therefore:

Business data warehouse

The physical implementation, in a largely centralized manner, of reconciled data, designed to be the control point and single source for all data made available to end users.

- detailed
- historical
- consistent
- modeled
- normalized

The BDW is implemented in a fully relational environment, as the environment that best represents its modeled and normalized nature. While in theory the BDW can be distributed, the reconciliation process requires that large amounts of data be matched and interrelated, a process that is more suited to a non-distributed implementation. In addition, today's relational databases and networks provide somewhat limited support for fully distributed processing. Therefore, it is likely that, for the foreseeable future, the reconciled data layer will continue to be implemented on a small number of large servers, such as traditional mainframes or database machines.

Organizational aspects also drive the BDW toward a centralized implementation. This is because the BDW is intended to be the control point where the quality and integrity of data are assured before making it available to the wider audience of end users. Such a control point is likely to be the responsibility of a single part of the organization, probably a central IS department, and is more easily managed in one place.

Security of the BDW is an important consideration, since it contains all of the data of the business in an integrated form. Physical security alone also warrants a centralized approach to storing this company asset.

Given the large size of the BDW—as a result of its historical nature—only a portion of it, and perhaps only a small portion of it, may be physically on-line at any one time. The remainder thus exists in an archived form.

The BDW is seldom, if ever, used directly by end users. Rather, it is the source for all data in the business information warehouses. The implication is, therefore, that performance issues for the BDW revolve around the largely off-line or batch processes of populating it from the operational systems and extracting data from it for downstream use.

Business information warehouses

A ***business information warehouse (BIW)*** is the generic name for any system used in the reporting, analysis, or prediction of the business. This includes management information reporting, decision support, and executive information systems as well as marketing analysis systems, data mining applications, and so on.

This environment is highly distributed, mainly found today on client/server and workstation-based implementations. While this environment will continue to be highly distributed, it is less heterogeneous than the real-time data layer. Most BIWs exist in a relational-like structure based on rows and columns. Relational-like environments include truly relational databases as well as spreadsheets and multidimensional analysis tools.

BIWs, containing derived data, are designed to support the business needs of end users, whether individually or in groups, departments, or divisions. They may contain detailed or summary-level data, periodic data over some historical time span, or snapshots. The structure of BIWs is optimized for on-line query performance, either *ad hoc* or predefined.

Business information warehouses are populated either directly from the BDW or indirectly through other BIWs. Direct sourcing from the BDW is to be expected, based on the relationship between derived and reconciled data defined as by the conceptual architecture. The need to source BIWs from existing BIWs is based on the fact that many BIWs are very similar in content and that the derivation of each BIW directly from the business data warehouse is not the best use of computing resources. However, the advantages of sourcing BIWs from other BIWs needs to be balanced against the risk of creating daisy chains of data, as described in Chapter 3.

This leads to two types of business information warehouse: **staging BIWs**, which are authorized as sources of other BIWs, and **user BIWs**, which are not so authorized. Staging BIWs require special management (rather like the BDW) to ensure consistency and integrity of the data stored there.

> *Business information warehouses*
>
> *Applications used by end users to manage the business, and their related periodic or snapshot data, at either a summary or detailed level.*

A note on terminology

The term *data warehouse* has many common meanings. In its earliest usage, it was applied to all publicly available data in the end-user environment stored in the relational format, without any further distinction between different types of data contained therein. Inmon (1992) and Inmon and Hackathorn (1994) use the term *data warehouse* in a similar fashion, but they further qualify it as subject-oriented, integrated, time-variant, and non-volatile. IBM's *Information Warehouse (IW)* [IBM (1991)] covers all data that is considered an asset to the enterprise, including both operational and informational data, but again focuses on informational needs. White (1995a) gives a good overview of the types of implementation that are commonly described as data warehouses.

In this text, the term *business data warehouse (BDW)* is used only to mean the physical implementation of the reconciled data layer of the three-layer data architecture, and the term *business information warehouses (BIWs)* to mean the physical implementations of sets of derived data satisfying particular informational needs.

7.2 Business data—other considerations

Special data needs

In the conceptual architecture, and in the logical architecture described thus far, all data flows in a single direction: from real-time to reconciled to derived in the conceptual view, and from operational systems to the BDW and on to BIWs in the logical view. However, a number of valid business requirements imply the need for data to flow In the opposite direction:

- **Corrections**

  When end users discover errors of fact in their BIWs, they usually correct their own data and will often, quite rightly, want this correction reflected back into the source data in order to ensure a consistent view of the business. These corrections are needed in the operational systems, the BDW, and the BIWs.

- **Adjustments**

  Similar in effect to corrections, adjustments reflect a change in the categorization of data in the business due to changing circumstances. The data was correct originally, but the users later need to use or analyze it differently. This leads to the need to change data in the BDW and may sometimes also affect the operational systems.

- **Data reuse**

  Data that was originally considered to be derived may become the input for further operational processes. For example, in the analysis of customer buying patterns, end users (such as sales managers) may require combinations of basic customer classifications. These new categories are created as part of the derivation process, and are stored in BIWs. These same categories are later used as the basis for a new commission system for the sales force. This is operational process requires data from the BIWs.

- **Predictive data**

  Data used to forecast trends and set future operational states also starts from a BIW and is used to set up data in the operational systems. For example, an analysis of raw material costs in the derived data layer allows calculation of new selling prices. This can be input to the operational systems with an effective date of the next month.

All of the above tends to suggest that there is a need to allow data to flow back through the layers of the architecture. This approach, however, presents some substantial problems.

The rationale for unidirectional data flow

The rationale for a unidirectional flow of data is based on the underlying definition of the types of data and stems from basic data management principles. It is widely accepted that data should be created and maintained in a carefully controlled and managed environment, so that it can be verified and validated during input through one consistently defined set of input-checking routines. Operational systems meet such conditions.

Allowing data to flow back from the BDW to the operational systems would bypass these validation processes and create the opportunity for inconsistency to arise. At the very least, these routines would have to be duplicated for data reentering the operational environment. At best, validation would be common between data entry and data reentry from the BDW.

Data flowing backwards from the BIWs to the BDW is even more problematic. At least in the case of the BDW and operational systems, both are under the control of the IS department, allowing some level of confidence that the data is consistent between the two layers. In the case of the BIWs, however, such data is generally outside of IS control and therefore its consistency and integrity are extremely difficult to verify. In addition, data entering the BDW from the operational systems is subject to reconciliation and cleansing and is assumed to have been subjected to basic validation and verification in the operational systems. Therefore, the BDW does not contain such function, and data entering it from the BIWs would essentially bypass all of these checks. For both of these reasons, data reentry from the BIWs to the BDW is not recommended.

Nonetheless, the business requirement for some type of "reverse" data flow is clear and must be addressed by the data warehouse.

Supporting "reverse" data flows

The solution to each of these needs is based on the recognition that, in each case, new data is being created. The fact that this new data is closely based on existing data is, to a large extent, irrelevant. The principle is that new data is created and maintained in the real-time data layer by operational systems. And a key responsibility of operational systems is to verify and validate the data they receive—from whatever source.

Traditionally, human operators input data manually into operational systems. Increasingly, data is crossing company boundaries electronically, via electronic data interchange (EDI), for example. Corrections, adjustments, reused data and predictive data are no different, except that their sources are internal data used by end users within the organization. Figure 7-2 shows that such data is returned, by a pathway outside the scope of the warehouse, to the verification and validation processes of the operational systems. From there, it reenters the BDW in the normal way.

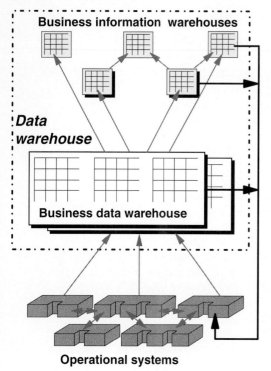

Figure 7-2: *"Reverse" data flows*

One aspect of this solution may cause problems. This relates to timing aspects. Corrections and adjustments fed around the reverse loop are not immediately available in the BDW or the BIWs. Typically, there will be a delay of at least a day between detection and correction of the error or change in the first BIW, on the one hand, and its availability in the BDW and other BIWs. If this is a problem, a special mechanism may be needed to immediately propagate such data.

The timing problem may be more serious in the case of data reuse. This is because the data being fed back is itself being used in real-time processes. In the example introduced earlier regarding customer buying patterns, if the BIW creating the customer categories is updated on a weekly basis, there is a significant opportunity for confusion and error to arise when calculating salespersons' commissions on a monthly basis. While the "reverse" data-flow solution may be acceptable in the short term, it actually indicates that a fundamental data element required for running the business is missing from the operational systems.

On the other hand, recall that the distinction between operational and informational processes is a generalization that is true most of the time but in some cases turns out to be incorrect. The distinction is based not on any theoretical principle but rather on pragmatism and thus can be ignored in some circumstances. However, broad experience has shown that it is far more useful, and produces more usable systems, to maintain the distinction as far as possible.

In short, if data is being fed back into the operational systems, it must go through the same validation as any other data entering the operational systems. In addition, time-related aspects require special attention to ensure that the reverse loop does not introduce temporal inconsistencies.

Personal data

When the boundaries of data warehousing were defined in Chapter 4, personal data largely fell outside its scope. This was a result of the level of control and management that could be exercised over such data in comparison with public data. However, where personal data does fall within the scope of the data warehouse, its positioning in the architecture should be defined.

In practice...

Data reuse is not necessarily good; significant reuse of derived data in operational systems often indicates a need to review the function of the operational systems.

The three-layer architecture allows personal data to exist in both the real-time and derived data layers. At the conceptual level, no distinction is made between personal and public data in either of these layers. Personal data can be centralized or distributed. It can be reconciled with public data or derived from it. Personal data does not exist in the reconciled data layer, simply because that layer is the logically single representation of the enterprise data model (EDM), and thus the exact opposite of personal data.

At the logical level, however, one distinction between public and personal data is necessary in the derived data layer. Staging BIWs, already defined as BIWs that are available as the basis for further derivation, are therefore subject to special control and management constraints. Personal BIWs cannot be staging BIWs, because personal data, by definition, is controlled and managed only by the owner. Note, however, that the architecture allows personal BIWs to be sourced either directly from the BDW or from staging BIWs. This mapping of public and personal data onto the logical architecture is shown in Figure 7-3.

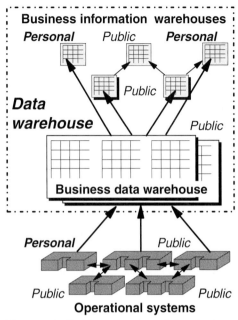

Figure 7-3: Public and personal data in the three-layer architecture

Another, more traditional approach to dealing with personal data in the warehouse is shown in Figure 7-4, based on Inmon's architecture [Inmon (1992)]. This scheme makes a distinction between departmental and individual data by placing them in distinct layers. (In the three-layer architecture, both are part of derived data.) However, this distinction is somewhat arbitrary given the flexible organizational structures toward which companies are moving, where transitory groups of users come together for a set task and then disperse. Moreover, there is a mandatory cascade of data through the four layers[1] as shown in Figure 7-4. The three-layer architecture, as depicted in Figure 7-3, provides more flexibility and the potential for better performance in populating personal BIWs.

The implications of applying the three-layer architecture to personal data are clear. Real-time data in the personal domain must be reconciled before being included in the public BDW. A step in this reconciliation is matching the real-time

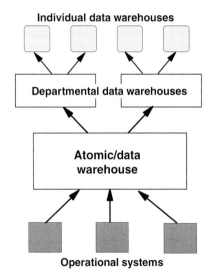

Figure 7-4: A traditional approach to personal data

---

[1] Regarding the other layers, the atomic/data warehouse in Figure 7-4 is roughly equivalent to the BDW, although Inmon allows some summary data at this level, while the BDW does not. Operational systems are identical in both approaches.

data to the EDM and establishing a mapping between the two layers. The long-term validity of this mapping is dependent on the stability of the structure of the source data. Therefore, the owner of the real-time personal data must relinquish a degree of control over that data. Data administration in this environment must address how to agree on and maintain this distribution of control.

Applying this concept to an example such as an executive's personal contacts database is instructive. If the executive decided to share the contents of this database with a wider audience, the recommended data warehousing approach would be to analyze its structure in the context of the EDM, carry out the reconciliation step, and then place the data in the BDW, where it becomes generally available.

The technically simpler approach is, of course, to use a shared database on the LAN, and allow the other users access to the data as defined by the original owner. This latter approach is usually the preferred choice, because it can be deployed more rapidly and at less initial cost. This simplicity is bought at the risk of compromising the longer-term integrity of the company's data and possible future duplicate development of similar databases elsewhere in the company. Cases where the value of sharing real-time personal data (such as the contents of planning spreadsheets) is higher require careful consideration of which approach to sharing data is better in the long term.

7.3 External data

There are two broad categories of **external data** that arrive in ever increasing quantities in today's business. The more obvious is external management information that directly impacts the decision-making processes of the business. The second source, more operational in nature, is data that arrives via EDI. The volumes of both types are rapidly increasing. We next consider both of these in some detail.

External management information

Analyzing and understanding the performance of a company requires access to the total operational data of that company in a structured way. However, to comprehend the company's prospects in the marketplace and to plan for its future success, access to data from the market in general is a strong requirement. As a result, strategic planners and executive management usually need a significant amount of external data. In the past, this external data was gathered informally and was seldom automated. It was thus effectively ignored by the IS shop.

With the increasing computer literacy of executives, the development of more powerful executive information systems (EIS), and the widespread availability of external data in a computerized form, external data has become an important consideration in the warehouse. The pervasive nature of the Internet today is causing an explosive growth in the amount and variety of such information.

In addition, the financial implications of decisions at this level in the organization are significant. When such decisions are based in part on external information, external data imported into the business should be managed and controlled as carefully as internal data.

In most organizations today, external data is generally obtained at the discretion and under the control of individual end users. This situation is yet another consequence of the growth of PC use among end users and management. Suppliers of market trend data and general economic indices such as stock exchange prices have seen a market opportunity in these PCs and have made their data available via modem connections, either directly or through the Internet. As a result, most external data enters companies through end users' PCs. This approach creates opportunities for several kinds of inconsistencies and errors:

- The end user's interpretation of the meaning of the data and particularly its relationship to internal company data may be erroneous.

- Errors in interpretation are difficult to discover and correct.

- Different users may choose different, and conflicting, sources for external information, which, when fed into the decision-making process, leads to confusion, re-investigation, and postponed decisions.

These observations lead to an inevitable conclusion: external data that is of significance to the decision-making processes of a company must be subject to an acceptance process. This process chooses the most appropriate source, aligns it to the appropriate internal data, and ensures common availability throughout the company. External data must be reconciled with internal data and other external data through the EDM before it is used as a basis for decision making. These actions align precisely to the actions taken as data enters the reconciled data layer.

The conclusion, shown in Figure 7-5, is that a source of external management information can be treated as an operational system: it feeds data directly into the BDW as any internal operational system would, and the data is subjected to the same modeling and reconciling actions as internal data. This reconciliation occurs while populating the BDW, as represented by the inbound arrow. This process can be undertaken only if a comprehensive set of metadata describing both the meaning and structure of the external data accompanies the data.

External data

Business data (and its associated metadata), originating from one business, that may be used as part of either the operational or the informational processes of another business.

In practice...

External data must be subject to a formal acceptance process before being used within the company.

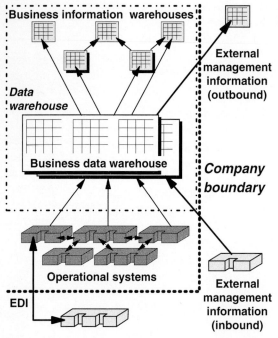

Figure 7-5: The data warehouse and external data

However, external management information differs from the internal operational systems in one respect. The receiving company usually has less control over the structure or content of the data received than it has over the structure and content of its own real-time data. This difference is less significant than you might at first assume. Even with internal operational data sources, one principle in designing a data warehouse is to minimize the impact on the existing real-time data, and in many instances, the BDW developer has only minimal influence on the operational system.

The real challenge in handling external management information is, however, not technical. It is primarily an organizational issue where end users must be willing to sacrifice some freedom of choice in obtaining external data in order to ensure the overall consistency of such data within the company. The expansion of the Internet and current thinking on its future pervasive role both suggest that access to the Internet will be the norm for most end users. It is therefore impossible to prevent the entry of external data into the organization at the BIW level by technical means. End users need to understand the consequences of arbitrarily including such data.

For outbound external management information, such as reports to regulatory bodies, the situation is simpler. Since this information must come from a verifiable and trustworthy source, the most obvious choice, as Figure 7-5 shows, is the business data warehouse.

Electronic data interchange

The other common means by which increasing volumes of data are transferred between organizations is electronic data interchange (EDI) [Kalakota and Whinston (1996)]. EDI is essentially an operational process and is the means by which operational applications in two companies exchange information. The type of data involved is thus real-time data.

As with any other data input into operational applications, EDI data must be subject to verification and other checks as part of the process by which the operational application accepts it. As a consequence, by the time the informational environment sees this data, it has already been assimilated into the internal real-time data. As shown in Figure 7-5, therefore, EDI data has no direct interaction with the data warehouse.

In practice...

The minimum criteria for accepting entry of external data into the BDW are: (1) the availability of comprehensive metadata, and (2) a binding agreement that the supplier will notify the company in advance of any changes in this metadata.

7.4 Metadata in the data warehouse

Metadata is obviously required in all three layers of the architecture. However, not all of the metadata is required in every layer, and the three components of metadata, described in Chapter 4, assume differing levels of importance in the different layers of business data.

As shown in Figure 7-6, the architecture requires a common base of build-time metadata, containing the definitions of all three layers, in order to express the relationships between them. It is possible to use different modeling tools for the different environments, and in such instances, the definitional metadata must subsequently be reconciled. It is generally better to use the same modeling tool for all three layers in order to avoid this remapping. Unfortunately, for historical and technical reasons, build-time metadata has usually been defined through a variety of means, with various levels of integration possible.

Like build-time metadata, control and usage metadata are also required in all three layers, but the actual content of these metadata stores varies according to the needs of the layers.

Because the BDW contains the complete reconciled data of the enterprise, it also holds the most comprehensive usage and control metadata. The BDW records the main currency metadata at a detailed level of the history of the individual BDW records, while currency metadata at a more summary level may be stored in the usage component of the metadata.

The derived and real-time data layers need to store only that metadata required in each layer. In logical terms, this is represented as the sum of the control and usage metadata for the applications at each level. This metadata is likely to be physically subsetted and distributed within these layers as appropriate. In BIWs, where new data is derived by aggregating or combining detailed data, the appropriate usage metadata is also stored for use at this level.

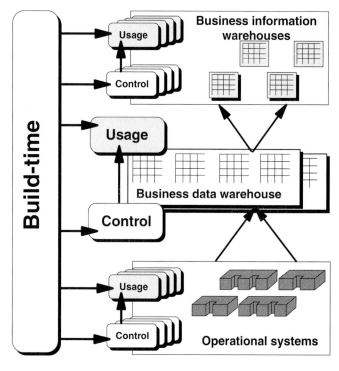

Figure 7-6: *The placement of metadata in the three-layer architecture*

Figure 7-6 also shows the correct master source for metadata in the BIWs. It is a mistake to assume that, because the BDW is the single source for all business data, the usage metadata describing the reconciled layer is the source for further usage metadata describing the derived layer. Usage metadata for BIWs is sourced directly from build-time metadata and from the control metadata for the BIWs.

Figure 7-6 emphasizes the essential unity of the enterprise's metadata in the build phase—a unity that is mandatory in order to reflect the consistency and interdependence of the EDM. Such unity can only truly be achieved with the support of a comprehensive and consistent set of tools for the build phase. Principal among these tools is a data modeling tool used with a good EDM.

We can relate the sources of metadata back to the aspects of control and usage metadata described in Section 4.3. In the ideal view, an IS architecture such as the ones described in Zachman (1987) or Evernden (1996) provides the framework for sourcing all metadata. The EDM is the most important source of metadata and operates in two ways. First, it describes the business in a self-consistent way and creates a relationship between the logical data structures and processes. Second, the physical level of the EDM provides the link to the real implementation of the data and applications as described in database catalogs. Other aspects of the IS architecture allow one to derive ownership and process information from organization charts, systems management tools, and so on, as shown in Table 7-1.

Today's reality is less neat and might be more honestly described as a mess! Metadata is generally captured only partially and, when it is captured, is stored in diverse places. In this respect, it can be compared to operational data. But for metadata there is an additional problem. Maintaining operational data as it changes over time is absolutely essential for running the business. The maintenance of metadata, on the other hand, is almost nonexistent in most companies, even in those cases where it has been initially captured. This is because the business can usually get away with using the group memory of the users to figure out what data really means.

Thus, business meaning is partially documented in user manuals and systems documentation, but this information must always be supplemented by the knowledge of the actual users of the systems. Data and application metadata are more formally maintained but often fragmented between design documentation, system catalogs among other sources.

The establishment of data ownership is often a major task in itself. However, once defined, it should be maintained logically in conjunction with the personnel and organization directory of the company. This requires specific, and mainly new, functionality. Similarly, the sources of currency and

---

In practice...

Plan for significant effort in the capture and maintenance of metadata, because the processes needed to track data ownership, utilization, and other metadata are often non-existent.

scheduling metadata are logically part of the processes that create and maintain the business data, but special actions are often required to capture metadata from these sources. Utilization metadata is also likely to require custom solutions to be built on existing user tools.

A further barrier to populating the usage metadata components of the warehouse is the current lack of compatibility among metadata stored in different tools. As a result, the initial set of metadata to support a first data warehouse implementation is usually built using a tactical approach. These compromises do not, however, detract from the importance of metadata in the data warehouse, nor from the need to define a strategic approach for incorporating metadata into the data warehouse architecture. This approach is known as the data warehouse catalog.

Table 7-1: *Metadata sources*

Metadata aspect	Optimal source	Likely sources today
Meaning in the business	EDM—generic ERM and logical application levels	Design documents, user manuals, informal conventions between end users, and personal knowledge
Ownership and stewardship	Personnel directory, including organization charts, plus specific, personally-managed ownership information	Seldom found, requiring both organizational and technical solutions
Data structure	EDM (logical and physical levels) and specific application data models	Database catalogs, data descriptions in programs, design documentation, and users' knowledge
Application aspects	Enterprise process model (logical and physical levels) and specific application function models	Design and user documentation, and users' personal knowledge
Currency	Operational applications, data replication, and systems management tools	Uncommon, and likely to require custom solutions
Utilization	End-user tools and data access tools	Uncommon, and likely to require custom solutions

7.5 The data warehouse catalog

Data warehouse catalog

The physical store of all usage and some control metadata in the data warehouse, partitioned and distributed among the BDW and multiple BIWs.

Within the complete set of metadata now defined, it is possible to identify a particular subset that is vital to the use and management of the data warehouse. This subset is known by many names, such as "business data directory", "business information dictionary", "information directory" among others [White (1995b)]. Many of these terms imply only a portion of the uses to which this set of metadata is put in the data warehouse.

We therefore focus on the content of the metadata itself, and use the term *"data warehouse catalog (DWC)"* to describe this subset. The DWC contains all the metadata required to use and manage the data warehouse. It thus contains all the usage metadata and a part of the control metadata associated with the BDW and BIWs, as well as part of the usage metadata associated with the operational systems. This subset is shown in Figure 7-7.

Build-time metadata is not included in the DWC because the process of building the warehouse is logically separate from the process of using and managing it. However, the majority of build-time metadata is duplicated in the control and usage components. Some control metadata in the informational environment is also excluded from the DWC because this metadata exists solely to support the infrastructure. The portions of the control metadata that are included relate to the scheduling and currency of the data. The DWC also includes a portion of the usage metadata of the operational systems. This portion describes the specific use of data in the operational environment which may differ from that in the informational environment, but is likely to be of value to users needing to understand the ultimate source of their data.

The DWC and the means by which end users access and use it are key components in any data warehouse implementation. Together they provide the user with the ability to effectively use the business data stored in the warehouse.

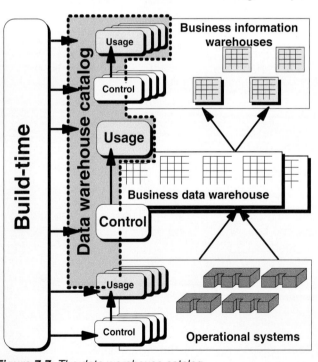

Figure 7-7: The data warehouse catalog

7.6 Operational systems

Although outside the scope of a data warehouse, the operational systems are the major source of data in the warehouse. The structure and architecture of the operational systems are thus key factors in determining the difficulty of implementing a data warehouse.

One of the principles of data warehousing is that operational systems should not require reengineering to any significant extent in order to build a data warehouse. Nonetheless, some aspects of the architecture of operational systems' often come to the fore when designing the data warehouse itself; these are discussed in this section.

Reference data

In many instances, a company decides to implement a data warehouse as part of a larger review of the data architecture. Such a review addresses both the operational and informational environments, often focusing on the operational area where there are known problems and shortcomings in the existing structure.

A common outcome of these reviews is that sets of data common to a number of operational application areas are identified. Tried and trusted data management principles prompt the IS shop to reduce duplication of data between these areas. This leads to the consideration of a **reference data** approach, whereby one (or a small number) of applications control and manage each reference database and a larger number of applications use this data for reference (read-only) purposes. Customer or product databases are common candidates for reference databases.

Data modeling of reference databases involves synthesizing the models of the contributing applications and often leads to a highly normalized and generic database structure. As a result, reference databases are often similar or even identical in structure to the normalized databases in the BDW. The question thus arises: Is it necessary to copy the reference data into the reconciled data layer, or can one set of data serve both operational and informational needs?

Based on the definitions of real-time and reconciled data, the conceptual architecture states that the two sets of data serve different purposes, and should thus be kept separate. The key difference between them relates to the timeliness of their data. Real-time data is by definition up to the second, whereas reconciled data is a periodic view, in which any time dependencies have been reconciled. In practice, therefore, reference data can be used jointly by operational systems and as part of the BDW if, and only if, that reference data has been designed as periodic data and includes the current data. If this condition is met, the question then reduces to considerations of physical design, such as performance and access.

In some cases, the reference datasets may have minimal time dependency (such as in the case of product reference data for products with long life cycles), or the implementation is such that time dependency has been eliminated (for example, by restricting update to times when the dependent applications are off-line). In such cases, the architectural differences between real-time and reconciled data are minimal, and one need only consider the practical physical implications. These include:

- **Hardware and software compatibility between environments**

    The hardware and software platform of the reference data must be equally accessible from the informational environment and from the potentially diverse operational systems. The BDW is implemented in a relational database. The operational environment is usually heterogeneous. Therefore, the question is whether the disparate operational systems can readily access a relational database of reference data.

- **Geographical location issues**

    The operational environment may be widely distributed physically. Therefore, it is important to know how readily distributed applications can use reference data located in the BDW and what the performance implications are.

- **Access contention**

    In general, one of the biggest issues with reference databases is contention for access to this common data. Bottlenecks in this area adversely affect all the operational systems dependent on this reference data. Using the reference data also within the BDW can increase the risk of impacting the performance of the operational systems.

In practice...

Reference data, although often structured identically to reconciled data, should not be shared between the real-time and reconciled layers.

Any conclusion about how to handle reference data must be based on a balance of benefits and risks. The main benefit in using reference data in common between the BDW and the operational applications is the reduced maintenance cost associated with multiple copies of data. The data replication load is reduced, but this effect is largely offset by an increase in the processing required to maintain and access the reference data. The risks of sharing reference data center mainly on the potential performance impacts on the operational applications, which, between the design tradeoffs and physical contention issues, are significant. Thus, the common use of reference data between the operational systems and the BDW is generally not recommended.

Operational data stores

The **operational data store (ODS)** is one of the more recent concepts in data warehousing. Its purpose is to address the need of users, particularly clerical and operational managers, for an integrated view of current data. This need is difficult to satisfy when the business has a variety of legacy operational applications that were not designed to work together.

> *Operational data store*
>
> *A modeled store of detailed operational data designed and structured to allow better integration among such data when it is used for immediate inquiry.*

A full description of the ODS concept is given in Inmon and Hackathorn (1994), from which the definition of the ODS used here was taken. This section attempts to position the ODS within the three-layer architecture. While the need addressed by the ODS is valid, it fits only partly within the scope of the data warehouse, and the part that does belong in the scope can be satisfied without introducing a new architectural component. Thus, the role of the ODS in the three-layer approach is not very clear.

An analysis of the type of data that is contained in an operational data store and the uses made of it reveals a number of problems when mapped back to the types of data defined in Chapter 4. Data in the ODS is:

- subject-oriented
- integrated
- volatile (that is, updatable)
- current or near-current

In terms of the data typing criteria used here, "subject-oriented" and "integrated" correspond to "modeled" and "reconciled", while "volatile" and "current or near-current" correspond to "read/write", "transient and current". The data usage in the ODS is described as mainly informational (although focusing on the current time), but may also include update (that is, operational) processes.

From the above discussion, it is clear that the data proposed for the ODS is a mixture of real-time and reconciled, which can potentially be used in either an operational or an informational mode. Such a mixture of types of data contradicts the layering principles of the three-layer architecture. Consequently, a reanalysis of the business requirement is indicated, and leads to an alternative approach, as the text will show.

The initial rationale for the ODS is to improve consistency and integration in the operational use of real-time data. A clerk, for example, should be able to inquire about the total amount of money owed by a particular customer of a bank, even though the customer may have several accounts, managed by different operational applications. This purely operational need can be addressed by reengineering the operational applications and the developing reference datasets as described earlier. In fact, such an approach is the only way to fully address the underlying data quality issues associated with such an environment.

The second rationale for the ODS is that it addresses more general reporting needs limited to current or near-current data. In the three-layer approach, this need can be satisfied from the data warehouse itself by allowing more frequent population of the BDW and BIWs where required. As the functionality of replication tools improves, it is possible to move toward populating the BDW at near real-time frequencies, thus enabling quite sophisticated informational use of the BDW or, preferably, of data sourced from it. Using this approach to populating the BDW can also satisfy operational queries, without resorting to a transient data structure such as the ODS.

In summary, within the three-layer approach to data warehousing described here, there is little justification for introducing the concept of an operational data store, because the needs it addresses are already adequately covered by the architecture.

The great operational/informational divide

The debate over operational data stores leads back to one of the initial generalizations made in data warehousing—the distinction between operational and informational processing, and the need to have two distinct sets of data. As previously stated, this generalization is valid and useful in the vast majority of cases, and is supported by identification of the three fundamental types of business data: real-time, reconciled, and derived. However, as with all good generalizations, there are exceptions.

In some applications it is difficult to make the distinction between operational and informational components. This is especially the case where the time scale of the decision process is very short and the results of the analysis are fed back directly into the operational processes of the business. In such cases, a single set of data would probably best handle the business needs.

As shown in the discussion of the ODS concept in the previous section, the three-layer architecture is capable of handling these situations, albeit with difficulty as feedback cycle times approach real-time frequencies. However, the alternative is more radical. It demands a significant restructuring of the data architecture to allow substantial *ad hoc* inquiry on the real-time data. Technical limitations of database management systems limit the usefulness of this option for the foreseeable future. In addition, the design and development of such systems are notoriously difficult.

The conclusion, therefore, is that such mixed operational/informational applications, while attractive in some cases, are best implemented on separate operational and informational lines in the short to medium term.

7.7 Data warehouse functionality

In examining the logical architecture the discussion in this chapter thus far focused exclusively on the aspects relating to data. This emphasis is driven by the overriding importance of coherence, consistency, and integration of data in the warehouse. There is, of course, a significant level of function needed to support the data architecture as described. This section introduces and positions that functionality.

Figure 7-8 shows the structure of the three-layer architecture for business data, expanded to include metadata. Some simplifications have been made to enhance its clarity (and to leave space for the inclusion of the functional components).

This figure immediately implies functionality through its use of arrows to represent the processes of populating various parts of the data warehouse with data. Population components are based on the data replication technology previously introduced in Section 6.4.

There are underlying similarities among the processes of populating the various targets, and these allow the use of a common set of data replication tools. However, there are also significant differences between the different types of population. For example, populating the BDW requires significantly more complex enhancement of the data during the replication phase than population of the BIWs does. Similarly, population of the DWC has far less demanding time dependencies than population of either the BDW or the BIWs. This gives rise to three distinct population functions—**BDW population**, **BIW population**, and **DWC population**—as shown in Figure 7-9, which are dealt with in detail in Parts III and IV.

The second broad area of functionality provides for the access to and use of the business data and metadata in the warehouse. End users of the warehouse use business data and metadata in different ways. While business data is both explored and analyzed as an end in itself, metadata is explored (but not analyzed), only in order to understand the business data. (Analysis involves searching for the underlying reality behind the data,

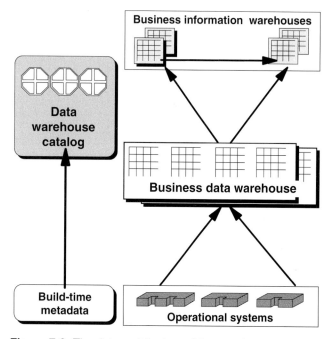

Figure 7-8: *The data architecture of the warehouse*

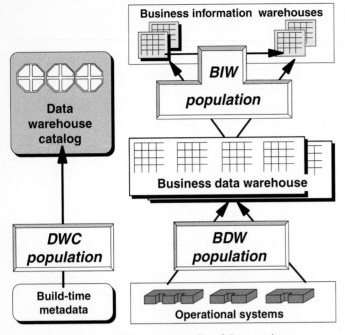

Figure 7-9: *The population functionality of the warehouse*

whereas exploration restricts itself to a search for the relationship between the different aspects of the data.) These different uses lead to two functional components. The business information interface (BII) provides the function required for business data, while the business information guide (BIG) provides the function needed for metadata— as shown in Figure 7-10. The broad arrows introduced here do *not* indicate further replication of data, but rather the access to and use of a set of data from a particular component.

Access to business data is provided through the **business information interface (BII)**. As previously discussed, the primary sources of business data for end users are the BIWs of the derived data layer. However, there may be occasions when there is a need to access the BDW directly. Direct access to the operational data may also occasionally be a requirement, especially in support of business situations in which the immediacy of the data is more important than its consistency. The relative importance of these three access needs is indicated by the varying thickness of the arrows. Note that direct access by end users to the operational systems is outside the scope of the data warehouse.

The second end-user directed component is the **business information guide (BIG)**. This provides the function needed to use the data warehouse catalog in a variety of ways to find relevant business data, to understand its significance, and to benefit from its previous use. This function requires more than simple access to the DWC; it implies a strongly interrelated structure for the catalog itself. As Figure 7-10 also shows, there is a close link between the BII and the BIG, which allows the end user to move easily and transparently from one to the other. These two components are dealt with in Chapters 12 and 13.

Last, but not least, Figure 7-10 adds **data warehouse management** to the data warehouse. This is not a component in the sense that the previously discussed functions are. Rather, it consists of a number of functions that underlie the operation and management of the total data warehouse environment and the principal components already defined. The data warehouse management functions include:

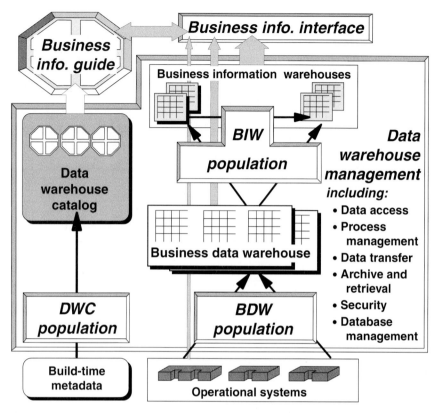

Figure 7-10: *The complete logical architecture of the warehouse*

- **Data access**

  The variety of physical formats and locations in which data may reside requires a data access component. This component, described in Chapter 12, isolates the business-related function of the end-user components from the technical function of accessing the physical data and transforming it into a format usable by the BII.

- **Process management**

  There is a need to coordinate actions among the components of the warehouse, which often operate on different platforms. For example, BIW population should only take place if and when BDW population has been successfully completed. Such interdependencies are defined and managed through process management.

- **Data transfer**

  Data transfer function is required to physically move data into and within the data warehouse. It provides the transport layer beneath the population functions, supporting both bulk and record-level transfer.

- **Security**

  Given that the data warehouse contains the entire data asset of the organization, security is required to control access to and use of the data it contains.

- **Database management**

  Because the data warehouse is physically realized as a set of databases, both centralized and distributed, the normal set of management functions for databases is required.

These last four items are addressed in Chapter 19.

As Figure 7-10 shows, this is a rather complex architecture, where each component contains significant functionality, and where there are substantial interdependencies among the components.

7.8 Conclusions

Exploration of the logical architecture of the data warehouse leads to identifying the building blocks—of both data and function—needed to implement a warehouse.

The business data warehouse is seen as the pivotal element for the control and management of a quality data asset. In many senses it is a shunting yard (for those of us who remember railway technology!) where data from operational systems is brought, split up, and rejoined in a variety of new ways before feeding into the business information warehouses, which are the usage points for end users.

The data warehouse catalog is the prime store of metadata required by users of the data warehouse, who access it through the business information guide. Between these two components, the business meaning of data, first defined through the EDM, is made available to end users.

Finally, the three population components, particularly BDW population and BIW population, are vital tools for filling the warehouse with data in a way that is achievable and productive. It is on these components that the ability of the IS department to deliver data to end users rests.

Part III

Creating the data asset

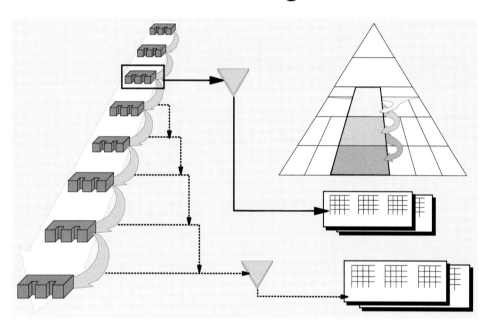

Business data warehouse design

Chapter 8

Business data warehouse design

Principles are all very well, I hear you say, but what about the practicalities? In the end, both must be combined to build a data warehouse. The starting point for this is in the design of the business data warehouse (BDW).

Part III of this book is devoted to the BDW. It has been stated that the BDW is like a shunting yard for data and, like all such yards, is generally not a place where users are allowed. Indeed, there is little reason for them to be there—data in the BDW is of limited use to the users for reasons of design and technology, as previous chapters have already described.

What takes place in the BDW is the creation of the data asset of the business. This phrase benefits from a little explanation. Data is *not* created in the business data warehouse. Existing data is used to create an asset—an asset that must be managed and protected. The creation, management, and protection of the business' data asset is the *raison d'être* of the BDW.

This chapter addresses the **design** of the business data warehouse. It starts with an expansion of the **enterprise modeling** approach and describes its application to this layer of the data architecture.

The chapter then explains the way in which **periodic data** is represented in the BDW. This leads to a consideration of the volumes of data that must be stored and ways to manage them. It particularly indicates the need for **archive and retrieval** of the data in the BDW.

Finally, the chapter ends at a more physical level, with the possible use of **parallel database** technology for implementing the BDW.

8.1   Modeling the BDW—general design

Chapter 6 showed that the model for the reconciled layer is the generic entity relationship model (ERM). Because the reconciled layer is implemented through the business data warehouse, the generic ERM represents the common, enterprise-wide view of the data required in the BDW. However, defining such a model is not an insignificant task. To have any hope of success, and indeed to be confident of completing this model at all, we must divide the process into a number of stages.

The high-level enterprise model

High-level enterprise model

A formal, high-level description in business terms of the information needed and used to manage the entire business, understood by business users and IS personnel.

Figure 8-1 shows the first step in modeling the warehouse using the layered enterprise data model (EDM) introduced in Chapter 6. Because the warehouse takes an enterprise-wide view of the business, modeling starts at the top of the triangle. The objective of this step is to obtain a unified view of the data required to run and manage the company. This must begin at a sufficiently generic level that all sections of the business can accept it, but go into sufficient detail to allow reasonably independent subsets to be identified as the basis for further work. Judging what is a sufficient level of detail is specific to each organization. However, it basically requires taking the generic ERM to a level of detail that identifies with certainty the key entities commonly used across the enterprise, that provides the more localized key entities with an initial definition, and that identifies the important relationships. Only minimal attribute information is needed at this stage. The result, shown in Figure 8-1, is that the **high-level enterprise model** covers the top two layers of the EDM and some portion of the generic ERM.

If a generic industry model already exists, this first step is reasonably straightforward, involving the initial customization of the industry model to the individual company environment. In this case, the initial piece of work could take less than 4 to 6 weeks.

Where no industry model is available, the effort involved will be larger. There exist two approaches in this case:

1. **Use the generic model of another industry sector as a base.**

   At the highest levels, there is some obvious similarity among different industries—all of them deal with customers, products, agreements, and so on. This approach exploits such similarity. However, greater customization than in the previous case is clearly required to take a generic model from another industry and apply it to the business.

This is probably the only feasible approach where no generic industry model exists for the business in question and where data modeling has not previously been used to any significant extent in developing existing applications. Where a base set of data models exists, companies may use an alternative approach.

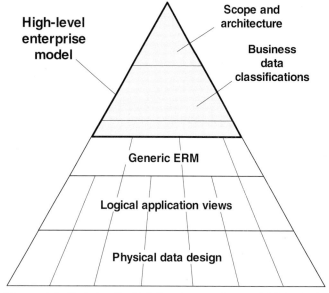

2. **Use existing models developed to support specific applications or business areas.**

This approach develops the EDM by combining existing models for individual parts of the company. Where explicitly defined models for certain areas of the business do not exist, it may be necessary to ab-

Figure 8-1: Defining the high-level enterprise model (shaded)

stract models from existing, unmodeled applications. A key danger in this reengineering approach, and one that must be rigorously avoided, is that the resulting model may simply reflect how the application systems look today, rather than providing a true view of the data needs and structures of the business.

The first approach—of looking at the higher levels of a generic data model taken from a different industry—avoids this problem. Combining that generic approach with the use of existing models allows for benchmarking the model against an enterprise model for completeness, and also allows reuse of certain sections of the existing models.

The additional effort involved here will depend on two factors: the extent to which individual parts of the organization have already adopted modeling as an application development approach, and the ability of the overall organization to harness this effort to bring it together in a consistent way at a cross-enterprise level.

The value of this piece of work is twofold. At a business level, it allows the strategic requirements for information to be analyzed (or verified, if they already exist). At a technical level, it provides a basis for later subsetting the model along theoretically correct lines. Gjensidige Insurance provides an example, shown next, of the benefits and difficulties of this approach.

The aim is to keep the time span required for this effort short, ideally under 2 months. Investing more time at this stage of the process is unlikely to be justified by the minimal additional benefits.

> *In practice...*
>
> *The elapsed time for high-level enterprise modeling should be limited to a maximum of 2 months—the return on further effort is minimal.*

Real-life example: Gjensidige Insurance (Norway)

Gjensidige Insurance is the second largest insurance company in Norway, employing ap-proximately 4,000 people in both headquarters and 240 branch offices throughout the coun-try. It operates in all segments of the insurance market.

By early 1995, its IS department had delivered a number of discrete MIS applications, which were well received by the users. However, it was clear that this approach could not meet the increasing needs of end users for more information and, indeed, for more integrated informa-tion. They adopted a data warehousing approach and the need to model the BDW.

During their first project, Gjensidige were able to compare two approaches to building a data model. They began developing their own data model but soon adopted a generic insurance industry model—the Insurance Application Architecture (IAA) from IBM. Their conclusions were:

- *The generic approach presents a steep learning curve at first.*

- *A key benefit of the generic approach is that it allows the designers to step back and view the business as a whole.*

- *The generic model also allows a more strategic view of the business and supports better communication between the data warehouse development team and both current and potential future end users.*

- *In comparison, when using an internally developed data model, it is exceedingly difficult to get away from the design assumptions inherent in the source operational applications.*

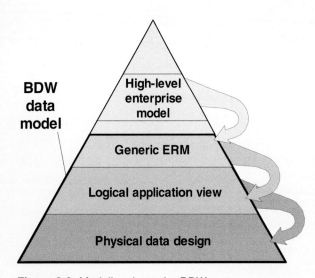

BDW data model

Figure 8-2: Modeling the entire BDW

Modeling the full BDW

One might theoretically consider modeling the BDW in its entirety. Figure 8-2 shows this process of taking the EDM through the layers of increasing detail from the initial high-level enterprise model, through the ge-neric ERM for the full BDW, and on to the logical application view and finally to the physical data design.

The most important aspect of this progres-sion is that the scope remains enterprise-wide at each layer (represented by shading the full width of each layer in Figure 8-2). Because each layer goes to a greater level of detail than the one above it, this progres-sion implies a series of steps of increasing effort. In fact, the work in each step is at least an order of magnitude larger than in the previous one. Clearly, the design of the complete BDW cannot be undertaken in one step. It can only be achieved in a staged approach.

However, whether the process is carried out in a single leap or in small steps, its ultimate goal of remains—to define a physical data design for the complete business data warehouse.

8.2   Modeling the BDW—a segmented approach

In fact, it transpires that even defining the generic ERM at an enterprise-wide level is too large a task to undertake in a single step in an acceptable time scale. Therefore, the approach is to model in a number of vertical segments. Figure 8-3 shows the segment defined during the first phase of BDW development. The segmenting starts by modeling of a chosen sub-set of the high-level enterprise model and leads eventually to the definition of the physical structure of version 1 of the BDW.

Each vertical model segment corresponds to an area of the model that covers a set of strongly related entities, some of which are common to the entire enterprise and the remainder of which are fairly localized in their usage. It is important that the entities in each segment be strongly inter-related and that there be a weaker relationship between these entities and those outside the chosen segment. In these circumstances, it is possible to model the entities within the segment at a detailed level while reducing the risk that the detailed modeling of the surrounding segments (at a later stage) will impact the work already done in the first segment. Of course, given the iterative nature of the modeling process, the risk cannot be entirely eliminated, but this approach is a good compromise.

While a variety of different segmentation patterns may be visible in the high-level model, the most useful ones correspond broadly to the key concepts or super-entities of the business and often relate to the functional divisions in the company,

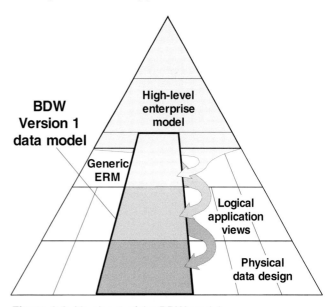

Figure 8-3: Version 1 of the BDW model

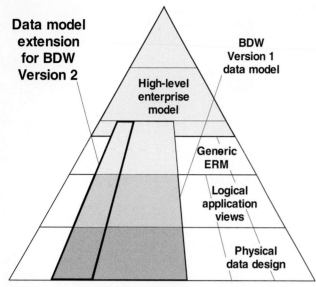

Data model extension for BDW Version 2

BDW Version 1 data model

High-level enterprise model

Generic ERM

Logical application views

Physical data design

Figure 8-4: Extending the model of the BDW

such as marketing, finance, etc. The choice of which segment of the high-level model to take first, and subsequently, to the level of the fully detailed generic ERM is driven by business and organizational needs and is dealt with in Chapter 15.

Figure 8-4 shows the additional modeling needed for version 2 of the BDW. Note that a segment adjoining the first has been chosen. In general, this approach leads to the maximum synergy between the efforts in two phases of the implementation.

Although the effort involved in defining the high-level enterprise model is relatively small, a question that often arises is, can this initial piece of work be skipped?

The answer is yes, but there is likely to be a price to pay later. The high-level enterprise model is of value to the IS department in defining the boundaries for the segmented modeling approach described above. Well-defined boundaries minimize the overlaps between the different segments of the model, and thus reduce the need to rework the model as additional segments are added at later stages in the development process. Such rework cannot be entirely eliminated, of course, but experience suggests that the up-front effort invested in the high-level model is later repaid by reduced levels of rework at the segment boundaries.

Steps in modeling the BDW

Figure 8-5 shows the process involved in moving from the high-level enterprise model to the physical data design, depicting two major iterations: (1) scoping the generic ERM and (2) designing the physical structure of the BDW database.

In practice...

In many companies, the first and most important model segment is centered on the customer entity of the high-level enterprise model.

Scoping the generic ERM

The main emphasis of the first iteration shown in Figure 8-5 is scoping the generic ERM to those aspects of the model that apply particularly to informational systems. Within this step, the time-related aspects that allow for the maintenance of periodic data are an important consideration. In the early versions of the warehouse, another way to set the scope is to focus on a particular segment of the model. The result is a logical application view of a part of the BDW.

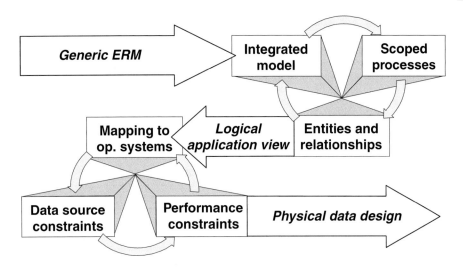

Figure 8-5: *BDW design as an iterative process*

Designing the physical BDW database

The design of the physical BDW database is the second iteration shown in Figure 8-5. This database should be as close a representation as possible of the logical application view. The underlying reason for this is to minimize the number of model translations necessary when moving data into or out of the BDW. Data coming from the operational systems must be reconciled in the context of the overall EDM. The definition of the reconciliation process is more complex if the physical design of the BDW has been compromised. Similar arguments apply to the derivation step. In addition, it is likely that any physical design compromises made to improve reconciliation may impact the performance of derivation. Similarly, any compromises made to improve the performance of data reconciliation from one set of operational sources may degrade the performance of reconciliation from other sources.

While it is clear from these arguments that the physical data design of the BDW should aim to be identical to the logical application view, this ideal is seldom achieved. In reality, as Figure 8-5 shows, a number of significant compromises are made in this second iterative step of the modeling process. This step is often one of the most technically difficult parts of the process. The reason for this lies primarily in the sources of data that feed the BDW—the real-time data handled by operational systems. In addition, some recognition must be given to the need to feed the data from the BDW into a variety of BIWs.

We can identify three distinct areas in the design process where substantial compromise is required:

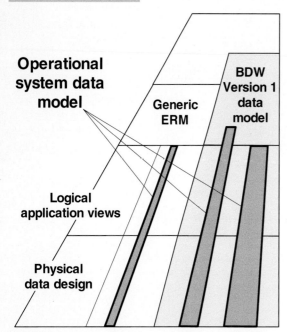

Figure 8-6: *Relationship between the operational system data model and that of the BDW*

1. Mapping to operational systems

Real-time data is either entirely unmodeled or modeled within a very narrow scope. As a result, defining the mapping or relationship between the real-time data and the reconciled data in the BDW is not straightforward. For unmodeled data it is first necessary to reverse-engineer a model from the physical data structure. Whether defined from business needs or reverse-engineered, the **operational system data model** is likely to be significantly different from the EDM.

Figure 8-6 represents a relationship commonly found between these models. The lighter, broader stripe represents the modeling carried out for version 1 of the BDW. The narrower, darker stripes, together representing the data model of an operational system, are an imperfect match to the BDW data model. Because of the way the operational system was originally designed, some of the data contained in it falls beyond the bounds of any logical segment of the BDW model. Thus, some data in the operational system will not be brought into the BDW, although it is important to understand the relationship between the excluded data and the data that will be imported. In addition, the operational model covers only a subset of the BDW data model. As a result, data required in the BDW but not found in this operational system (those parts of the BDW model in Figure 8-6 which are not overlapped by the operational model) must be sourced from other operational systems or omitted from this version of the BDW.

The warehouse designer is thus faced with the choice of reengineering the operational applications or compromising the physical design of the BDW, at least in the short term.

2. Data sourcing constraints

These constraints relate to the physical availability of data in the operational environment. Typical examples include cases where the required data elements exist only in physically separate machines and are not available as input to the BDW, and cases where data is stored in a transitory manner in the operational databases and so is not available when the BDW is updated.

3. Performance constraints

In addition to compromises above are the normal tradeoffs between performance and data volumes. However, these tradeoffs are influenced by two factors unique to the BDW:

- BDW population operates on fixed sources and with significant operating constraints. Because the operational systems are fixed, the needed transformations may be substantial. The process is usually required to work within a small, contracting batch window.

- BIW population has similar operating constraints. In contrast, the BIW targets may be only partially defined at this stage, adding to the risks involved in BDW design.

The design goal is that the business data warehouse be a physical representation of the EDM. In the early versions of a data warehouse, this aim is seldom if ever achieved. It is compromised in a number of ways. The segmentation of the EDM at the generic ERM level (driven by project doability) leads to some discrepancies near the segment edges in the evolving logical application view. At the physical data design level, there are the compromises due to model mapping, data sourcing, and performance problems. It is clear, however, that these inconsistencies have to be addressed over time as additional segments are added to the generic ERM and as operational applications move through their normal maintenance releases or are completely replaced. It is therefore vital to ensure that the compromises are fully documented within the modeling tools in use.

In practice...

For first-time BDW designers, there is usually a rather substantial learning curve. The physical design of the BDW is significantly different from that found in operational database design. The sourcing constraints common in BDW design seldom apply to operational data.

Evolution of the BDW data model

Some theoretical approaches to modeling assume that the modeling takes place in a "green-fields" environment. This expression implies that there is no existing data, or at worst that the existing environment will be rapidly converted to a new structure based on the model. This assumption is not valid for warehousing. The basic tenet of warehousing is that legacy operational applications are likely to continue to exist for the foreseeable future. Therefore, the model that describes them, whether that model has been explicitly expressed or not, will also continue to exist. The enterprise business model is realized through the implementation in the BDW. This will become a permanent representation of the business model. Thus, a number of models exist and will continue to exist in support of the informational and operational environments.

In order to see the relationships between these models, consider first the simple case—when the segment of the generic ERM being implemented corresponds to a set of real-time data that has not been automated previously or is undergoing complete reengineering at the same time version 1

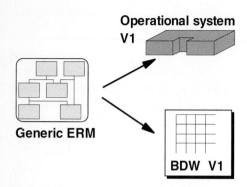

Figure 8-7: *Common design for operational and informational systems*

of the warehouse (BDW V1) is being designed. As Figure 8-7 shows, the generic ERM is the common base from which to derive logical application views for both the operational and informational layers. The logical application view of the BDW has a broader scope than that of the operational system, but in the common areas they will match closely. In the physical data design, these two views lead to the design for the BDW, on the one hand, and to the design for the operational application, on the other.

These two physical designs differ, particularly because of the performance constraints caused by the real-time data access and update operations of the operational system. However, because the operational system design must also support feeding data into the BDW, these two physical designs must relate back easily to the common generic ERM.

From a modeling viewpoint, this approach has many advantages, and provides the opportunity for defining and confirming a common model between the operational and informational environments, which can be expected to remain relatively stable over time. There is one drawback to this situation that relates to the scope of the projects being undertaken. Essentially, the projects address the implementation of two interconnected databases with some overlapping and some conflicting requirements. This is a complex relationship that requires careful management of development priorities and design change procedures.

The more common situation is where the source operational systems already exist and are in maintenance mode. As Figure 8-8 shows, the design of version 1 of the BDW is still based on the EDM. However, there is little or no opportunity to adapt the existing operational system to the EDM at this stage. Additional compromises are thus needed in the design of the BDW, driven by the existing model of the operational system.

In addition, this is not a stable state. As described earlier, the aim is for the physical model of the BDW to approach the logical model described by the generic ERM. In order to achieve this, the physical model of the operational data must also change to align more closely with the EDM. Compromises made in the original BDW design to sup-

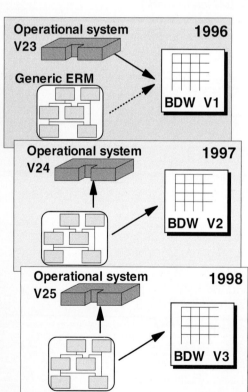

Figure 8-8: *Model evolution*

port data sourcing can be relaxed, so the BDW design approaches the ideal. Because the operational system is in maintenance mode, such changes in the physical model of the operational data are accommodated in the maintenance cycle. This leads to an evolving BDW data model, as shown in Figure 8-8.

Ideally, in such an incremental evolution of both models, the modeling tools should support versioning of the models. In reality, few modeling tools provide significant support in this area. The process is thus essentially manual, and the number of steps should be minimized by applying the necessary resource to quickly upgrade the operational system.

8.3 Modeling the BDW—practical results

The process described in Section 8.2 provides a number of benefits in the initial design of the BDW and in its subsequent evolution:

1. **A generic data view of the business**

   Starting from the enterprise-wide view leads to a BDW design that is capable of supporting a wide variety of end-user needs. The resulting structure is generic to the business and largely independent of the processes that create and use the data it contains. This data structure is commonly known as **subject-oriented**.

2. **Extensibility**

   The use of an EDM ensures the maximum flexibility at the earliest stage of design. This reduces later changes in the BDW structure when new users or needs require new and different BIWs.

3. **Timely delivery of business function**

   Segmentation of the model allows the IS department to address different business needs at different times. This allows a staged delivery of business function and an early deliverable from the data warehouse development without compromising its overall design.

This process, based on an enterprise-wide data modeling approach, carries with it all of the difficulties of enterprise modeling [Aggarwal and Rollier (1994)]. It therefore requires an initial investment in resources and skill to build and possibly purchase a generic industry model.

Nonetheless, it is a worthwhile investment. It results in a data warehouse that is normalized around the important data entities of the business. Typically these entities include customer, product, location, organization, and their interrelationships—all key aspects of managing the business.

Subject-oriented data

Data structured around the major entities in an enterprise data model and largely independent of the creation and usage processes.

8.4   The structure of periodic data in the BDW

The data in the BDW is periodic in nature, representing the history of the changes in the business data over a prolonged period of time. As mentioned earlier, the normal approach to storing this periodic data is to use timestamped status and event records. Within this guideline, however, there are a variety of schemes to maximize the efficiency of the timestamps. This is especially the case for periodic data in the BDW, because the data record structures in the other two layers are largely dictated by other considerations, such as business requirements or the limitations of existing applications.

Each instance of a business entity, such as an order or a customer, is represented in these schemes by a set of records, each of which has the same business key but is differentiated by the timestamp(s) used as part of the key. These timestamps show the period of validity of a particular record. For the moment, we assume that the period of validity is based on event timings from a business point of view rather than from a technical or database view. We will return to this assumption later.

Timestamping approaches

Using a single timestamp

The simplest approach, shown in Figure 8-9, is to implement a single timestamp field, **start time**, identifying the time at which a record became valid. A record is then deemed to be invalid when there exists another record with the same business key and a later timestamp.

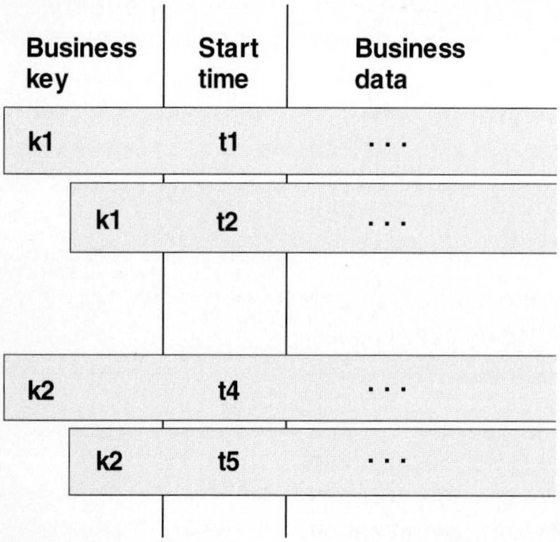

Business key	Start time	Business data
k1	t1	. . .
k1	t2	. . .
k2	t4	. . .
k2	t5	. . .

Figure 8-9: Periodic data using start times

This structure is ideal for event data, described in Section 6.2, for which the timestamp represents the time at which the event took place. Account transaction data in a bank is a good example of event data.

However, when looking at status data, it presents a number of problems in returning the results of two types of query. These queries are relatively common when populating BIWs, and must therefore perform reasonably efficiently

1.   A very common class of query is based on the current value of the records, but in this scheme the only way to identify these records is to find the latest timestamp of the periodic set. This is clearly an inefficient process.

2. Another common type of query is to establish a view of the data as of a particular time in the past. To support this, the period of validity of each record must be known, in order to compare it with the required time. However, with this scheme, the end of the period of validity of one record can only be found from the next record in the periodic sequence. Because the BDW is stored in relational technology, the process of finding this next record requires accessing and sorting all records with the identified business key.

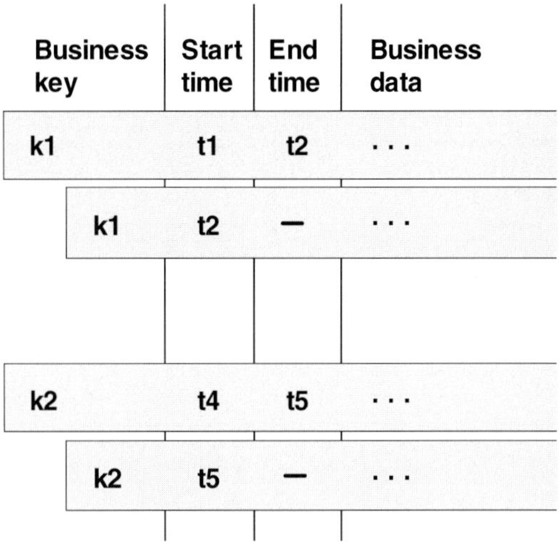

Business key	Start time	End time	Business data
k1	t1	t2	. . .
k1	t2	—	. . .
k2	t4	t5	. . .
k2	t5	—	. . .

Figure 8-10: Periodic data using end times

Using two timestamps

To address these problems, a second timestamp is added to each record, as shown in Figure 8-10. This second timestamp, **end time**, identifies the end of the period of validity of the record. In this scheme, the current record is identified by a special value, which may be the null or other special value, in the end time field.

This scheme matches the business needs for the analysis of status data. For event data, an end time is a somewhat artificial concept in business terms. However, it is useful in technical terms, because it allows more efficient location of the latest transaction.

Setting the end time for a record takes place when the record superseding it is written. The need to find and update the superseded record thus introduces some overhead into the update process. For example, in Figure 8-10, when record **k1,t2** is added to the BDW, the update process must locate record **k1** with a null value for end time and replace the value of end time in that record with **t2**. However, the performance improvements in retrieving data compensate for this added update overhead.

Using additional fields

In a perfect world, a scheme using two timestamps would be sufficient. However, other problems may arise. Operational applications, the original source of periodic data, are often designed without consideration for the consequences of storing history. One important consequence of this omission can be seen in the use of business keys. In some businesses, key values are reused over time. An example of this is the use of order numbers in a business with a short selling cycle. These are generated within a fixed range, which is then recycled after some period of time. In this case, carrying these order numbers into a periodic warehouse does not allow a distinction between sets of related records for different orders.

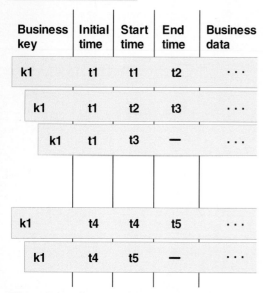

Business key	Initial time	Start time	End time	Business data
k1	t1	t1	t2	. . .
k1	t1	t2	t3	. . .
k1	t1	t3	—	. . .
k1	t4	t4	t5	. . .
k1	t4	t5	—	. . .

Figure 8-11: *Periodic data using initial times*

This problem can be addressed without impact on the operational application by introducing another timestamp, *initial time*, on each record. Initial time identifies the time at which the sequence of related business events began and is therefore equal to the start time of the first record of the sequence. Within the periodic data, the new business key is a composite of the operational business key and the initial time. The use of initial time is shown in Figure 8-11.

Like the previous scheme, this one also entails copying some information between the existing record and the record that is superseding it. For end time, the requirement is to take the start time of the new record and copy it into the end time of the old record. For initial time, the need is to copy initial time from the old record into the new one. Unfortunately, depending on the replication approach used, this type of update may be difficult.

At this stage, one might be tempted to ask if more than three timestamps could possibly be required. However, one final problem remains with these schemes—the difficulty in recognizing what action has caused a particular record to be created. This is particularly needed for records that represent the completion of a sequence of records, in other words, the deletion of a particular instance of a data entity. In periodic data, no record is ever physically deleted, but is instead marked as no longer current in the business.

Business key	Initial time	Start time	End time	Action flag	Business data
k1	t1	t1	t2	A	. . .
k1	t1	t2	t3	C	. . .
k1	t1	t3	—	D	. . .
k1	t4	t4	t5	A	. . .
k1	t4	t5	—	C	. . .

Figure 8-12: *Periodic data using status flags*

One approach is to designate a special value of end time to represent this state. A more general approach is to introduce one final field—not a timestamp, but a flag—the *action flag*, to indicate the action in the operational system that created each of the records. As Figure 8-12 shows, this flag can take one of three values:

- A—representing the *addition* of a new data instance (the first record in the sequence)

- C—a *change* or update of an existing data instance

- D—the *deletion* of a data instance (the last record in the sequence)

This approach represents probably the most functionally rich solution, catering to all possible data access and technical requirements. In many specific instances, some of these fields may be unnecessary.

Choosing the appropriate structure

The structures described above represent a variety of possible approaches to representing history in the BDW. Except for the start time timestamp, each is optional. Their use depends mainly on the abilities of the BDW and BIW population functions. End time and initial time can both present difficulties in populating the BDW. The use of start time alone can cause performance difficulties in selecting particular subsets of data in populating the BIW.

In summary, a combination of start time and end time, supported by an action flag, generally provides an efficient structure for status data in the BDW. Event data can generally be managed using a start time and either an end time or an action flag.

Time representations in the BDW

As previously mentioned, the question of how a period of validity is defined requires further discussion. The previous section focused on the business view of time. While this clearly meets the business need, it is important to consider another factor—the temporal integrity of the data. This is vital in the data warehouse environment, where data is copied through a number of layers. As a result, the relative timings of events in the operational applications and in the population of the warehouse are vital to maintaining the temporal integrity of the periodic data.

To understand these implications, it is useful to construct a number of timelines or axes, along which events can be placed, such that these time axes are mutually independent. There are four main time axes to be consider in this context:

1. **Valid business time**

   This is the time when a business event occurs in the real world.

2. **Business transaction time**

   This is the time when a business event enters the operational system. The business transaction time for an event can never be earlier than its valid business time, but it can be the same or later. For example, if you make a cash withdrawal from an automated teller machine, the operational application debits your account as the cash is paid out. On the other hand, if you make a deposit in the same machine, the bank will not credit your account until the cash has been manually counted and a bank clerk has entered the information into the system. In the first case, valid business time and business transaction time are the same. In the latter case, the valid business time of the deposit depends on whether it is seen from the viewpoint of the customer or the bank, but the business transaction time is clearly later than the valid business time.

3. Operational database time

This is the time when the data relating to a business event is written to the operational database by the business transaction. In most cases, the business transaction time and operational database time are equal, or as close as makes no difference. The difference between these times is relevant only when the business transaction updates multiple databases, and some of the updates are asynchronous for some reason, such as geographical distribution of the databases.

4. BDW database time

This is the time when the business event is written into the warehouse. With very rare exceptions, this time is later—often considerably later—than the business transaction time.

Of these four times, all are system generated with the notable exception of valid business time, which must be input by a user.

There is another category of time that often confuses discussion of the above timelines. We may term this category "user-defined time". This is any time that is recorded in the business data itself and has no relationship to any of the above times. As an example, consider a personnel planning application. This system stores dates when promotions are planned. These dates may be in the past or in the future and are part of the business data of that application. The business time axis measures the times the planned dates are entered or changed and not the planned dates themselves [Bair (1996)].

When analyzing and tracking business performance, valid business time should clearly form the basis for measuring time and assigning periods of validity to business events or statuses of interest. In some cases, however, the valid business time is not recorded in the operational system, and an alternative such as business transaction time must be used. However, maintaining the temporal integrity of data may require the use of additional timelines. This is due to the fact that valid business times, because they are not system generated, are subject to input error.

The result is that the decision on which timelines to use in any particular data warehouse implementation depends not only on the business needs, but also on the technical implementation of the population step as well as on the way time is managed in the operational environment.

Complexities in capturing time—an example

Figure 8-13 shows some of the complexities that may be involved. In this example, a business event—signing an order for an aircraft—takes place at time **t0**, the valid business time. After the legal and contractual aspects are agreed, the order is entered into the manufacturer's operational systems via a business transaction taking place at time **t1**. Because the time of the initial order, **t0**, is important for scheduling the priority of manufacture, it is stored as part of the business data for this transaction.

The business transaction updates two databases, the headquarters' order management database at time **t2** and the manufacturing facility's work-scheduling database at time **t3**. Because the order management database and the business transaction are part of the same application, **t1** and **t2** are identical. However, the work-scheduling database is on a remote system and updated overnight, and therefore **t3** is greater than **t1**. For historical development reasons, the initial order time **t0** is stored in the work-scheduling database in the operational environment, not in the order-management database.

Moving data from the operational databases into the data warehouse involves using a staging file. Ideally, the company might have written the business transaction so that it updated the staging file as well as the two databases, as this would have eliminated some of the complexity of updating the warehouse. Unfortunately, this would have involved substantially changing the way this application worked. As a result, the company chose an alternative approach, involving the separate capture of changes to both operational databases. The various ways of moving data from the operational to the informational environment are discussed in Chapter 9.

Two tables in the reconciled layer are affected by this business transaction at time **t1**: the orders table and the planes table. Modeling the orders table shows that it obtains most of its fields from the order management database in the operational environment, but also requires the initial order time **t0**, which was stored in the work-scheduling database. The planes table is fed only from the work-scheduling database.

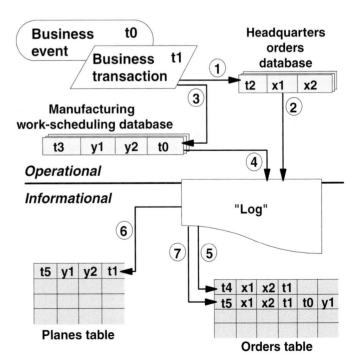

Figure 8-13: Timing in the population of the BDW

This situation leads to difficulties in synchronizing the update of data in the warehouse.

The orders table is updated at time **t4** with the information from the order management database. **t4** occurs on the night following **t1**, because the order management database is updated synchronously with the business transaction. However, because the work-scheduling database is also updated only on the night following **t1**, the data from this database is not available to the warehouse until **t5**, which is 24 hours later than **t4**.

In practice...

Incomplete data must be clearly marked in the BDW to prevent further replication.

The overall result of this in the BDW is that two updates are applied to the orders table, at **t4** and **t5**, both of which originated from the transaction that occurred at **t1**. The planes table is updated at **t5**, also originating from the transaction at **t1**. Clearly, a link must be stored in the warehouse to relate the data of these two tables together. Figure 8-13 shows this link as being composed of the time **t1** and the key field **y1**.

While this example has been designed to illustrate a number of different problems that can arise in this area, it is representative of real-life situations and shows that generating periodic data from operational data can be rather complex. It also illustrates that data in the BDW can remain in an incomplete state for a period of time. Subsequent steps, such as the capture step in BIW population, must know which data is incomplete in order to avoid presenting it to the end users.

Practical choices of timestamps

When a periodic view of data is being generated from real-time data stored and managed by operational systems, the previous example and general experience lead to the following considerations:

*   Valid business time, when stored in the operational systems, is the obvious choice as the basis for timestamps in the BDW, because it provides a true representation of the history of the business. However, this must be used with care because such fields are subject to input error, and indeed, to future changes in business meaning.

*   The time when a business transaction occurs, as timestamped by the operational application, provides the most reliable guide to the historical sequence of events. It is thus useful for reconciling database changes that are related to one another in a business sense but have been separated in time for technical reasons.

*   Where valid business time has not been stored or is known to be unreliable, business transaction time is a candidate for use as the Start, End, and Initial timestamps, although the variety of potential sources tends to mitigate against its use.

- In those cases where business transaction time is not captured (as is often the case in legacy operational systems), the BDW needs a mechanism for temporal reconciliation based on the business data content.

- In such cases, an alternative source for timestamps is also required. This is normally the BDW database time, which is preferred to the operational database time because of the variety of potential sources of operational database time.

8.5   Archive and retrieval

As with most aspects of business life, creating and updating the data warehouse receive far more attention than the processes that eventually remove data from it. However, anticipated data volumes in the warehouse and potential annual growth dictate the need for a strategy to determine which data should be retained indefinitely in the warehouse and which should have a defined life span. The categorization of data in these terms is clearly business driven and must therefore be incorporated into the enterprise modeling activities.

Archive and retrieval

A function providing managed and efficient storage and retrieval of data between the different levels of a storage hierarchy.

It is a basic principle that any data stored in the warehouse, whatever its age or frequency of use, should be readily available to end users. However, the fact that the data should be readily available does not imply that all data should be immediately retrievable. Archiving seldom-used data provides considerable cost savings by moving it to cheaper storage media, but, as a consequence, that data is less immediately retrievable. This should not pose a problem. If the warehouse design logically includes archived data, end users can see all the data that it is available, both immediately and with some delay. The warehouse therefore requires an *archive and retrieval* function that moves data transparently and efficiently between a set—or *storage hierarchy*—of physical storage devices with different storage costs and access speeds.

Considering the archived data as an integral part of the total set of data in the warehouse leads immediately to the following design aspects:

- Enterprise data modeling is the foundation for data warehouse design. Archived data should be in a form that is easily related to the model.

- The warehouse consists of a hierarchy of storage media, from magnetic disks for frequently used data, to optical disk and tape media for seldom-used data.

- Data should automatically migrate between the levels of storage based on the frequency of use. As an alternative, archiving could be based

In practice...

Because of anticipated data volumes, the first data warehouse design should consider archive and retrieval needs.

on data classes related to the EDM and automatically triggered by the age of the data.

- The retrieval mechanisms must be able to handle requests for subsets of the archived data based on a wide variety of selection criteria. These criteria include not only to the age of the data required but other factors such as geographical region, product categories, and any classifications that are meaningful in business terms. Retrieval should therefore also be based on the EDM.

- Archived data must continue to correspond to the model that describes it. When the EDM changes to reflect new ways of running the business, the old model must be archived to allow future retrieval of data based on the old model.

- The need to support retrieval of data for immediate use requires archiving not only the data itself, but also its structure and context—the metadata maintained in the DWC.

The considerations just listed apply to the whole warehouse environment. However, archive and retrieval must satisfy different needs for data in different layers of the three-layer architecture. The varying temporal structures of data in these layers (discussed in Chapter 6) are the most important factor in determining how data is archived:

- **Transient data**

   Transient data occurs in the operational environment. Because of its volatility, transient data must be archived at a record level at creation time to capture all occurrences. Archive and retrieval of operational data is outside the scope of this book.

- **Snapshot data**

   Snapshot data, found in BIWs, is already a logically complete set of data referring to a particular time period. Complete sets of data are therefore archived in this layer. We discuss archive and retrieval for BIWs in Chapter 10.

- **Periodic data**

   Periodic data, characteristically in the BDW or in historical BIWs, is generally thought of as being archived in batches that relate to a particular time period. For example, at the end of each month, all data relating to the same month in the previous year may be archived. However, we must consider some additional factors (covered in the next section).

Archive and retrieval in the BDW

Traditionally, data has been archived when it is no longer needed on-line. As a result, archiving and deleting data are often seen as being closely related. However, data can also be archived when it is created. Archiving data at creation time has a number of advantages:

- Data recovery (in the event of accidental loss) and data retrieval become synonymous, eliminating the need for a separate backup-and-recovery mechanism.

- The action required when users no longer need data on-line is reduced to a simple deletion. This allows for a simpler process and more dynamic decision making about when deletion should occur.

- Synchronization of metadata and data is easier to support.

In the case of the BDW, where the data is persistent, the possibility exists to archive either at creation time or at deletion time.

Because of these advantages, it is preferable to archive data during population of the BDW, especially if a comprehensive set of replication functions facilitates this approach. The initial warehouse design can and should include this approach. Considering archive and retrieval of data during the earliest design phase allows greatest flexibility in choosing the physical placement of data, which is not the case when considering the topic only when the budget for disk space runs out.

> *In practice...*
>
> *Archiving data in the BDW is best performed as part of the population step, and should be considered in the initial design phase of the complete data warehouse and implemented as soon as practicable.*

A structure for archive and retrieval

The structure depicted in Figure 8-14 shows archive and retrieval in the data warehouse. Off-line storage consists of a number of levels, of which two are shown. Each level contains images of data archived from one or more areas of the data warehouse—metadata and business data from the BDW and BIW layers. The archival of BIW data is addressed in Chapter 10. The physical location and structure of the different levels of this store can be centralized or distributed as required.

Data in the BDW can be archived either at creation or deletion time. The figure shows both approaches, but the preferred approach is to archive at creation time because this provides the maximum flexibility in deciding how long the data needs to be kept on-line, as well as supporting recovery considerations. As a result, BDW population feeds the archive, in addition to populating the business data warehouse.

The metadata in the data warehouse catalog is archived at creation time to ensure that the current version is always available in the archive. An archive index stores the metadata required to support the archival and re-

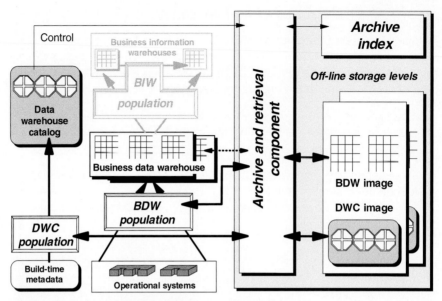

Figure 8-14: *A structure for archive and retrieval*

trieval components. This is used to locate the required data, and in conjunction with the DWC, both on-line and in the archive, supports the structuring of retrieved data.

The structure is thus similar to a traditional hierarchical storage management (HSM) approach. However, storing an additional copy of the on-line BDW in the archive allows recovery of the BDW in the event of a disaster without the need for a separate backup-and-recovery function.

8.6   The role of parallel databases

The underlying purpose of *parallel databases* is to enable multiple processors to each handle separate parts of any activity on the database. This allows parallel databases to handle larger volumes of data more quickly than traditional databases do; they are also potentially more scalable. The disadvantages are that this requires breaking activities into parts that can operate independently, and arranging data accordingly—an often complex procedure. See Bontempo and Saracco (1995) and other works for a more complete description of the principles and practice.

From this general concept we might conclude that, given the large volumes of data a warehouse must handle, a parallel database is an obvious choice of technology for a warehouse implementation. While basically sound, this conclusion must be treated with a degree of caution. In particular, the different ways in which the BDW and BIWs are used has a significant influence on the applicability of parallel database technology in each layer. Chapter 10 covers the use of parallel databases in BIWs.

When considering the use of a parallel database for the implementation of the BDW, the following aspects of the design and usage of the BDW are particularly important:

- The BDW is large—hundreds of gigabytes is now commonplace—and substantially normalized.

- The BDW physical data design may undergo significant changes over the period in which it is being built up. This time period may extend over 2 or 3 years.

- The data in the BDW is updated regularly by adding records. There is a significant level of work involved in this population step, making up-date performance a vital design consideration.

- The data in the BDW is further used to populate the BIWs. As many BIWs become relatively standardized, extracting data from the BDW can be optimized for these BIWs by using "batch" queries.

- *Ad hoc* direct inquiry on the BDW is rare or nonexistent, and *ad hoc* indirect usage for the construction of new BIWs is relatively infrequent and seldom requires rapid response times.

These factors lead to some conclusions about the types of parallel data-base likely to be useful for the BDW.

Parallel databases that have been optimized for read-only access, with special emphasis on speeding up operations that rely on a full table-scan of the database, provide less benefit than we might expect in the BDW. This is because the processes that output data to the BIWs—which are, in fact, the most common queries—are largely predefined and the database can therefore be suitably optimized to support these processes.

Shared-nothing or shared-memory parallel approaches (based on arrays of processors, each with a dedicated disk for data storage) may present difficulties during the initial 2- to 3-year growth phase of the BDW. This is because optimizing the performance of databases in these environments is dependent on the way data is distributed across the different disks. In the physical database design, the criteria for partitioning the data across the different disks, which must be decided in advance of loading the data, depend on a knowledge of both the contents and the usage of the data. This very close coupling between the physical database design and the assumptions in the logical model about the distribution of data values leads to database structures that are rather rigid and inflexible to changes in overall data content. These considerations tend to mitigate against the use of such databases in the BDW during the growth phase, when such factors are poorly understood and subject to change. However, once the BDW design is stable, these factors can usually be safely ignored.

All optimizations come at a price. And a database that is well optimized for *ad hoc* inquiry may thus be optimized at the expense of update capabilities or performance. Any such tradeoff should be closely examined, because in the BDW, the function and speed of the input and output processes are usually more important than *ad hoc* inquiry performance. As the warehouse grows in both data volumes and types of use, any improvement in the data throughput of the BDW depends on the ability of the IS shop to balance input and output performance and to flexibly modify the physical database structure as needed.

The traditional, general-purpose relational databases that have been enhanced to support parallel processing are likely to provide a good basis for the BDW. This conclusion stems from the fact that such databases are broadly optimized so that all aspects of database operations benefit from the performance gains of parallel processing. Thus loading, indexing, indexed searches, and table scans all benefit by allowing both inbound and outbound processes in the BDW to run faster.

> **In practice...**
>
> *While factors such as storage volumes and performance are important, the difficulty of tuning a parallel database is a good reason for choosing a traditional database for the initial BDW implementation.*

The conclusion, therefore, is that parallel databases can provide significant performance advantages and scalability to the BDW. As the size of the BDW increases, they may become a necessity in order to provide sufficient performance. The improved scalability of massively parallel processing (MPP) designs over symmetric multiprocessing (SMP) systems tends to favor their use in the data warehousing environment. However, this statement, like all hardware-dependent statements, is subject to revision as the technologies mature.

The introduction of parallel databases during the initial growth phase of the data warehouse can lead to administrative overheads of distributing and redistributing data over the disks in the parallel machine. It may therefore be more appropriate to begin construction of the BDW in a more "traditional" relational environment, and later migrate to a parallel database. The compatibility of the two database environments—both the database itself and the tools and utilities that surround it—is, of course, a major consideration.

8.7 Conclusions

As the central component in the data warehouse, the BDW must be designed with considerable care. The design phase is, however, subject to a number of unusual pressures.

It should be recognized from the outset that the design will take place in stages, spread over 2 to 3 years. The design will be put into production in the data warehouse in the same stages, so the level of rework from stage to stage must be minimized. The layered, segmented modeling approach is designed to do this, while promoting the early delivery of usable sections of the BDW. However, controlling the modeling and initial implementation projects, and in particular the approach to change management, are vital to the success of the undertaking.

BDW design is subject to many more constraints and outside influences than the majority of application development projects in the operational environment.

In order to support the periodic nature of the data in the BDW, designers must define the structure of the record timestamps. This will enable any required temporal subset of data to be extracted from the BDW for use in the BIWs in the future. It is also vital for the reconciliation for temporal inconsistencies between different operational systems.

Archive and retrieval of the data in the BDW should also be taken into account at an early stage of the design, in order to cope with the anticipated data volumes. At the physical level, designers need to evaluate parallel databases for possible use, for the same reasons.

One key physical design issue—centralization versus decentralization of the BDW—has not been discussed in this chapter. This is because these decisions have a strong dependency on BIW design aspects as well as on organizational factors covered later in the text. This issue is dealt with in Chapter 18.

Finally, the strengths and limitations of the replication approaches used both to populate the BDW and to distribute data to the BIWs add a further twist to the complexity of the design phase. This topic is the subject of the next chapter and is further addressed in Chapter 11.

Chapter 9

Populating the business data warehouse

Populating the business data warehouse (BDW) has always been considered to be the most technically challenging part of building a data warehouse. Historically, it is the part of warehousing where tools were first developed to try to reduce the effort involved. And experience shows that it still tends to be one of the most costly and time-consuming aspects of a data warehouse implementation.

Chapter 6 introduced the functionality of data replication. This generic function is designed to reduce the effort involved in populating the various parts of the data warehouse and, in particular, to reduce the complexity of populating the BDW.

This chapter describes the process of getting data to flow smoothly and reliably from the operational systems into the BDW. This discussion is structured in terms of the three key runtime components of data replication previously identified—capture, transformation, and apply.

First, a number of key characteristics of real-time data in operational systems and reconciled data in the BDW, as well as their relationship, are restated. This leads to a discussion of the following topics:

- *Capture* of data from operational systems

- *Apply* of the captured data to the BDW

- *Transformation* of data between the two environments

The definition of which data to capture, how to transform it, and where to apply it is the responsibility of the administration component of data replication, which is discussed in Chapter 19.

9.1   BDW population—initial considerations

When considering the use of replication functions in BDW population, the key factors to be consider are as follows:

- Operational systems seldom maintain a complete historical record of events—thus the source data is usually transient or semi-periodic.

- The source data in the operational systems is likely to be heterogeneous and may be poorly structured.

- The BDW must contain a complete historical record of the business—thus the target data is periodic.

- The target data in the BDW is in relational format, well-structured, and likely to be largely centralized.

- Because these two environments—the operational systems and the BDW—are so divergent, the relationships between the two sets of data are particularly complex.

The characteristics of the operational source data determine the functionality required of capture. The transience of the operational data limits the types of capture that can be used when a complete record of the changes in that data is required in the BDW. In addition, the number, variety, and indeed the age of operational systems that are common sources of data for the warehouse further complicate the problem.

Similarly, the characteristics of the target BDW environment dictate how apply must behave. Because the BDW contains periodic data, apply must be nondestructive—it must not overwrite existing records. However, restricting BDW to the relational environment and using a data model for its design simplify the apply component relative to the capture function.

Finally, the relationship between the source data and the target data drives transformation. The complex relationship between these two sets of data leads to a need for sophisticated transformation function at this level. In some cases the relationship is so specific to one company that there is no possibility of providing generic function in this area.

Capture

A component of data replication that interacts with a source data store to obtain a copy of some or all of the data contained therein, or a record of changes that have occurred there.

9.2   Capture—an introduction

Chapter 6 introduced the capture component of data replication. It is that component of a data replication tool or application that obtains data from the database or file containing the source data. In general, not all of the data contained in the source is required. Although all of the data could be captured and the unwanted data then discarded, it is more efficient to capture only the required subset. The capture of such a subset, without reference to any time dependency of the source, is called *static capture*.

In addition, where databases change with time, we may need to capture the history of these changes. In some cases, performing a static capture on a repeated basis is sufficient. However, in many cases we must capture the actual changes that have occurred in the source. Both performance considerations and the need to transform transient or semi-periodic data into periodic data drive this requirement. This type of capture is called *incremental capture*.

Static capture

Static capture essentially takes a snapshot of the source data at a point in time. This snapshot may contain all of the data found in the source, but usually it contains only a subset of the data.

Static capture

A method of capturing a time-independent or static view of all or a subset of the data in a source data set.

Static capture occurs in a number of cases, although it is not as common as the more complex incremental capture. Examples are:

- the first time a set of data from a particular operational system is to be added to the BDW

- where the operational system maintains a complete history of the data and the volume of data is small

In such cases, it is seldom necessary to move all data from a particular source to the BDW target environment. Many fields in the operational databases exist solely for technical reasons related to maintaining integrity or improving performance. In legacy systems, there may be redundant and/or obsolete data. Such data is irrelevant to the task of managing the business and need not be captured.

Incremental capture

Incremental capture recognizes that most data has a time dependency, and thus requires an approach to efficiently handle this. The volume of changes in a set of data is almost always some orders of magnitude smaller than the total volumes. Therefore, an incremental capture of the changes in the data rather than a static capture of the full resulting data set is more efficient. Incremental capture must collect the changes in such a way that applying these changes to the target builds a valid representation of the data in that environment.

Incremental capture

A method of capturing a record of the changes that take place in a source dataset.

However, incremental capture is substantially more complex than static capture. It has a strong dependency on the way changes in the source data are made and stored. Nonetheless, the periodic data of the BDW is normally maintained in this way.

Because of the different ways time dependency is represented in operational data and in the BDW, and because of the different technologies used, incremental capture has a number of "flavors". Before describing these approaches, however, we must examine how such data is stored and the strategies for conversion between these types of data.

9.3   From operational data to the BDW

Chapter 6 introduced the key concepts describing the temporal structure of data. There are the three categories of time-dependent data—transient data, periodic data, and snapshots. In addition, we noted that temporal data may be stored either as status or event databases. This section shows the use of these concepts in operational data and in the BDW.

Data in operational systems

The majority of real-time data managed by operational systems is transient. In some cases it is periodic, but we need to distinguish between true periodic data, where the history of changes is maintained for a significant and known period, and semi-periodic data, where the history of changes is maintained for only a short or undetermined time. Operational data is largely status data, because this is the view of interest to the business. The event view is rare and can be stored only when the data is periodic.

We can be simplify these different aspects into two broad categories of operational data with which the capture function must work.

1. **Transient or semi-periodic status data**

    This category represents the majority of data in operational systems. Examples include:

    *   orders and sales databases
    *   bank accounts
    *   customer files

    From the point of view of capturing it, the key characteristic of such data is that it is impossible to know how long any particular record will exist in the system. A record may change several times in a day or remain static for months.

If it is transient data, the details of each transaction replace those of the previous one. Therefore, each record is available for capture only until the next transaction that changes that record occurs.

For semi-periodic data, records are not overwritten, but superseded records may be discarded at any time. For example, the operational system may retain only the last five statuses for each record. As in the case of transient data, it is impossible to predict how long any record will remain in the operational database.

2. Periodic status or event data

This category of data is much less common than the previous one. It is found in industries where the operational systems must deal with historical data on a daily basis. The most common examples are from the insurance industry, where policy information is often stored as periodic status data and claims information as periodic event data.

For periodic data in the operational systems, whether status or event data, a complete record of changes is available, and capture is therefore less complex than in the previous case.

> *In practice...*
>
> *An operational system must be treated as transient unless the record of relevant changes in the data is preserved for a period of time guaranteed to be longer than that between capture runs.*

Data in the BDW

Turning our attention to the BDW, we see that the data here is, by definition, periodic and persistent over a time period determined by the business need for historical data. The data may be stored as statuses or events depending on the outcome of enterprise modeling of the BDW.

The business requirement in moving from the operational environment to the BDW is to maintain a complete and continuous history of the changes to the operational data in the BDW. If the source data already contains such a history (category 2 above), then the capture step is rather simple, because all the required data will exist no matter when capture runs.

On the other hand, in the more common situation (category 1 above), there is no guarantee that all of the required data will be maintained in the operational system. In this case, the technical requirement is to capture transient and semi-periodic data in such a way that:

- All required records, no matter how short their life span, are captured.

- Overwritten records (deleted or changed by a business transaction) are captured before their demise.

Once the changed data is stored in a safe place, where it can be accessed by the other replication components, the task of the capture component is complete. The construction of the record of changes lies beyond the capture component and is handled by the apply component.

9.4   Six data capture techniques

Section 9.2 distinguished between static and incremental capture.

1.   Static capture—the simplest technique, its basic functionality is in sub-setting the captured data.

This functionality is also used in incremental capture. However, incremental capture is not a single topic. On closer examination, it can be divided into five different techniques, each with its own strengths and weaknesses. The first three of these are types of ***immediate capture***—changes in the source data are captured immediately after the event causing the change happens. Immediate capture guarantees the capture of all changes made to the operational system, irrespective of whether the operational data is transient, semi-periodic, or periodic.

Immediate capture

Capture of changes at the time they occur, ensuring a complete record of changes in transient, semi-periodic, and periodic data.

2.   ***Application-assisted capture***—depends on the application that changes the operational data to also store the changed data in a more permanent manner.

3.   ***Triggered capture***—depends on the database manager to store the changed data in a more permanent manner.

4.   ***Log capture***—depends on the database manager's log to store the changed data.

Because of their ability to capture a complete record of the changes in the source data, these three techniques are usually favored for incremental data capture. However, in some environments, technical limitations prevent their use. In such cases, either of the two ***delayed capture*** strategies can be used if the business requirements allow:

Delayed capture

Capture of changes at specified times, producing a complete record of changes only in periodic data.

5.   ***Timestamp-based capture***—selects data that has changed based on timestamps provided by the application that maintains the data.

6.   ***File comparison***—compares versions of the data to detect changes.

Delayed capture occurs at predefined times, rather than with the occurrence of each change. In periodic data, this behavior produces a complete record of the changes in the source. In transient and semi-periodic data, however, the result in certain circumstances may be an incomplete record of the changes that have occurred. These problems arise in the case of deletions and multiple updates in transient and semi-periodic data and are discussed later in the context of timestamp-based capture.

The remainder of the section describes each of these techniques in detail.

Static capture

The basic functionality of static capture is to take a snapshot of the source data. As shown in Figure 9-1, static capture operates directly on the operational data, whether that data is in status or event form and whether it resides in a file system or database.

The variety of sources that exists in most companies presents the main problem for capture. Operational systems store data in sequential and indexed files, as well as in hierarchical, relational, and other databases. In addition, there is the variety of physical storage formats and data representations to handle. The expectation of the capture component is that it produce its output—the subset of data that has been captured—in a common, simple format.

Subsetting dimensions

There are three dimensions of subsetting data for capture.

- **Entity dimension**

  The simplest way to subset the data for capture is by entity. In this case, all information pertaining to a particular subject is selected for capture. The output is an image of the total contents of the entity, often in a simpler structure than in the source. In structured query language (SQL), selecting along the entity dimension equates to:

  ```
  SELECT      *
  FROM        CUSTOMER_FILE
  ```

- **Attribute dimension**

  In the attribute dimension, some attributes, but not all of them, are selected from all occurrences of the data for a selected entity. In SQL, selecting along the entity dimension equates to:

  ```
  SELECT      NAME, PHONE_NO, CITY
  FROM        CUSTOMER_FILE
  ```

- **Occurrence dimension**

  In the occurrence dimension, all of the data about a selected set of occurrences is selected. In general, occurrences are selected based on the contents of one or more fields in each record. In SQL, selecting along the entity dimension equates to:

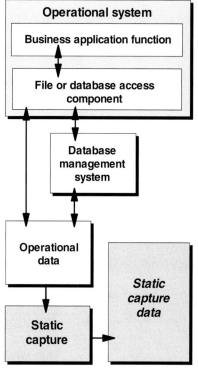

Figure 9-1: Static capture

Application-assisted capture

A method, built into the source application, that preserves its data for immediate capture of incremental changes in that source.

```
SELECT      *
FROM        CUSTOMER_FILE
WHERE       CITY = 'Paris'
```

And, of course, all of these dimensions can be combined to select some of the attributes in a subset of the occurrences or, at the extreme, to select one field from one record of one file.

Note that these subsetting approaches are also used in the five incremental capture techniques described next.

Application-assisted capture

The first approach to incremental change capture that an application developer might consider is to design (or modify) the operational application to provide a continuous, nonvolatile record of changed data in parallel with its primary task of maintaining the operational data. This type of capture is clearly immediate. In addition, there is no single, physically identifiable capture component; capture function is embedded in the operational application, as shown in Figure 9-2.

This approach, while undoubtedly providing high flexibility and control of the data captured, is extremely complex for existing systems. The main reason is that legacy systems are usually poorly designed and documented. Often, the skills needed to analyze and change them no longer exist in the organization.

However, in designing new operational systems, developers could apply this approach for two very powerful effects: to separate the business logic from the database access, as shown Figure 9-3, and to create a common component used by all operational systems in the company. In this approach, each business application reads and writes data to a common, defined application programming interface (API) rather than directly to the database. A common component is then responsible for database access, as well as for capturing all changed data. This design has a number of advantages:

- Developers of business applications are insulated from the complexities of database access and can focus on the business logic.

- If it is decided to replace the database management system (DBMS), all changes affect only one component, rather than all the applications.

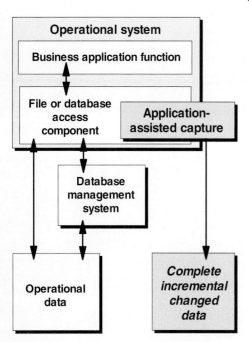

Figure 9-2: Application-assisted capture

- Similarly, application-assisted capture takes place only within this one component and is thus transparent to application developers. It can, therefore, be modified within the bounds of this component.

This approach also underlies replication schemes based on message-queuing technology. Such advanced replication technologies are particularly useful in highly distributed environments, and represent a significant step forward on most of the approaches that are more widely available today.

The detailed design of application-assisted capture is beyond the scope of this text, but one aspect can be used to illustrate some of the underlying complexity of BDW population. This kind of complexity must be considered in all types of incremental capture.

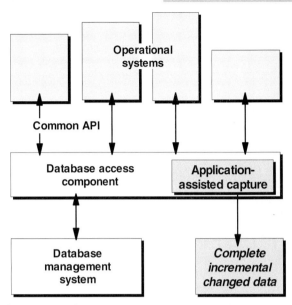

Figure 9-3: *Common application-assisted capture*

When populating a periodic status table in the BDW from an operational system storing transient or semi-periodic status data, the data of interest is the record as it appears immediately after a change to it has been made. An example of updating a record in the operational data is shown in Figure 9-4. The data immediately available to application-assisted capture is the data included in the event or transaction. Looking at that data, we can see that, on its own, it is not enough to specify the afterimage. This method has two problems:

1. Fields (other than the key) that are not changed by the transaction do not appear in the event itself.

2. Some data in the event may represent the way in which an existing field is to be changed, rather than the result of the change.

In the first case, if the application is to capture the unchanged fields (*"abcdef"* in this example), the capture code has to go back and read the record from the operational system's file or database. In the second case, the application must read the before image along with the event data and do the calculation. The resulting status is then available to the application during the transaction. However, there may be cases where the DBMS is responsible for the calculation. In the example shown in Figure 9-4, the

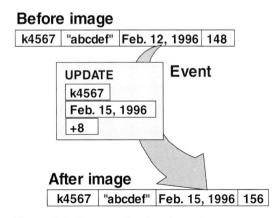

Figure 9-4: *An example of update*

Triggered capture

A method for immediate capture of incremental data changes, dependent on the use of trigger technology in the source DBMS.

transaction might simply specify "Today" rather than "Feb. 15, 1996", allowing the DBMS to do the work. The result is a need to return and read the afterimage within the application.

A similar situation occurs in the case of delete. At the operational level, all of the data is physically deleted in transient data, but in the periodic data of the BDW—and therefore in the captured data—the requirement is to retain the data but to mark it as no longer valid. The usual representation is the record key plus a code to indicate a deletion. Such a record must be generated by the capture component in the captured data each time a delete occurs in the operational system.

When the operational data is periodic status or event data, these situations do not arise. In such cases, application-assisted capture, as well as the other types of incremental capture, is substantially simpler.

Triggered capture

This approach moves the responsibility for immediate change capture from the application to the DBMS, as shown in Figure 9-5. Of course, this method assumes the DBMS in the operational environment is suitably equipped. Therefore, this approach is not appropriate for use in systems that store the operational data in files rather than databases.

We can think of triggers in databases as specialized stored procedures that are activated under certain conditions or when certain events happen. In simple terms, triggered capture is based on defining triggers for all database events for which changed data should be captured. These triggers cause a subsequent transaction that places the event or changed record in a side file or some other suitable store for future processing. The implementation of triggers varies from one DBMS to another.

For performance reasons, it should be possible to trigger capture when specific columns change, so that events affecting data used only in the operational system will not cause data capture. In such cases, the approach allows particularly specific selection criteria for capture to be set. This method is therefore appropriate in cases where only a small subset of all the events occurring in the source needs to be captured. However, as the percentage of changes to be

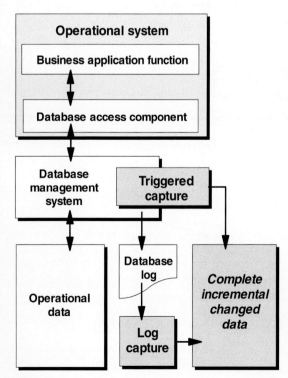

Figure 9-5: Triggered and log capture

captured increases, performance is likely to become a concern, because each database update transaction on the operational data triggers a second transaction to capture the change.

To support the capture of status data, the trigger mechanism should be able to specify that the capture procedure executes after a row has changed, in order to capture the afterimage of an insert or update. For deletes, the procedure may run before or after the delete, provided the key of the record is made available to the procedure.

For event data, it is the event rather than its outcome that is critical. In certain cases, this may cause problems. For example, the operational source data may be in status format, as in the case of bank account balances. However, in the BDW, a record of account transactions may be deemed a more appropriate way of storing the basic historical data. A triggered approach is unlikely to be useful in this case because the actual event data may not be available to the DBMS when capture is triggered.

Log capture

This final approach to immediate incremental capture, like triggered capture, takes the function out of the application and places it in the DBMS, as shown in Figure 9-5. Consequently, data from sequential or indexed files cannot be captured by this method, because there is no DBMS.[1]

Changes to operational data are usually maintained in a log for backup and recovery purposes. This log can also be used as the source from which to capture changes. This assumes that the DBMS maintains a log containing sufficient information to support replication, and that the log is preserved long enough for the capture component to access it. For example, if the requirement is to capture status data, the log must store in a usable format the afterimages of the data changed by the database transactions. For event data capture, of course, the log must store the transactions themselves.

In capturing changes from the log, the log capture tool must take particular care to correctly handle commit points and rollbacks. Only changes committed in the source database are required. Once the process has captured the required changes, any subsetting of fields (the attribute dimension) can then take place in the same way as for static capture.

> **Log capture**
>
> *A method for immediate capture of incremental data changes that uses the log maintained by the source DBMS.*

---

[1] Alternatively, this function can reside in a transaction manager. This is rather rare in practice, so for simplicity we focus on the DBMS for this function. Similar considerations apply in both cases, except that a transaction manager allows the possibility of using log capture with file-based as well as DBMS-based sources.

Timestamp-based capture

A method, dependent on the existence of timestamps in the source data, that can capture a possibly incomplete set of changed data from the source.

Log capture is usually a very efficient approach to incremental capture. Log writing is a basic and well-optimized activity for all industrial-strength DBMSs and is required to enable recovery and rollback. The analysis of log records needed to capture the changes takes place outside the main processing sequence, so it can be relegated to off-peak periods or to a machine other than the one running the operational system. Thus, log capture can be optimized to protect the performance of the operational update process: the only activity that has to take place when the update transaction occurs is required anyway for database integrity.

Because of the proprietary nature of DBMS logs, it is generally the developer of the DBMS itself who should develop and provide the log capture mechanism. Although it may be possible to reverse-engineer the required data from the logs, this approach can never be guaranteed to support all possible cases or to upgrade from version to version of the DBMS.

Timestamp-based capture

Timestamp-based capture is a special case of static capture on the occurrence dimension. In this case, the source records must contain one or more fields of timestamp information, which can be used as the basis for the record selection. The records of interest are those that have changed since the last run of the capture component. These records have a timestamp later than the time of the previous capture. Timestamp-based capture is, therefore, clearly a delayed-capture approach.

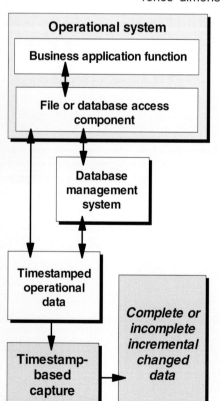

Capture has no role in creating or maintaining the timestamp information. The applications creating and updating the operational data must therefore manage these timestamps. As shown in Figure 9-6, the capture component operates against timestamped operational data, stored in either a file or a database. The output is shown as complete or incomplete incremental changed data. Where the operational data is periodic, the output is complete incremental changed data. Transient and semi-periodic data require closer examination.

If the operational data is transient or semi-periodic, timestamp-based selection cannot capture intermediate states of data records that have changed more than once in the period of time since the previous capture. In the transient data example shown in Figure 9-7, an order for 100 items is placed at 9:30 AM on Monday. The state of this order is captured on Monday night and saved in the BDW. On Tuesday at 11:15 AM, the purchaser decides to increase the order quantity from 100 to 200, and the operational

Figure 9-6: Timestamp-based capture

system reflects this, overwriting the previous quantity of 100. In the afternoon, the seller discovers that there is a shortage of these items and informs the buyer, who decides at 4:10 PM that she will accept 125 items, and go elsewhere for the remaining 75. The operational system is then updated to reflect that 125 items are required, overwriting the previous quantity of 200. The state of the order is captured again on Tuesday night, and the quantity of 125 saved in the BDW.

You might wonder whether the information that the buyer had an order in for 200 items at one stage during the day is significant. This is a business decision. If it is neither significant nor likely to be, the historical record being captured is an adequate approximation of the real business. However, if it is significant, then the BDW has lost historical information of interest. In the latter case, if the operational environment does not support one of the complete incremental capture approaches described previously, the only remaining option is to upgrade the operational system to store periodic or semi-periodic data instead of transient data.

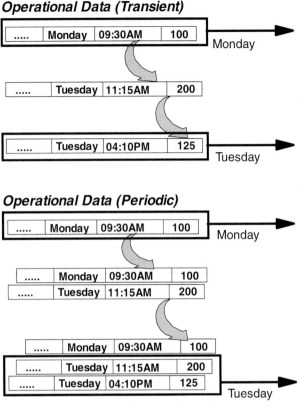

Figure 9-7: *Examples of timestamp-based capture*

Figure 9-7 also shows the case for periodic data. Here, changes in the operational data do not overwrite the previous record. On Tuesday night, then, both records (the first at 11:15 AM and the second at 4:10 PM) are available for capture. Once they are captured and the operational system no longer requires these records, they may be deleted.

In the case of semi-periodic operational data, the deletion strategy affects the level of approximation that the BDW periodic data can reach. A deletion strategy that deletes multiply updated records only after they have been captured does, of course, ensure completeness of the BDW. An approach that stores only a fixed number of occurrences of each record is always open to the potential problem that a greater number of changes may occur between two capture runs.

There is another potential problem affecting the completeness of the output from timestamp-based capture. This relates to how the operational system treats records when the business state they represent no longer exists.

> *In practice...*
>
> *Delayed incremental capture is useful for transient data sources only if the business does not need to see every change occurring in the operational system reflected in the BDW.*

In practice...

Timestamp-based capture requires special treatment of deletes in the operational system in order to capture them.

In the example shown in Figure 9-7, let's assume the order is sent out on Wednesday. This is no longer an order, and traditionally, in the transient environment, the record would be deleted. Timestamp-based capture cannot detect this change because the record no longer exists in the system. Therefore, the record from Tuesday will always remain in the BDW. Such a representation of history would not be acceptable in the BDW. As a result, to support this type of capture, the operational system must treat deletes in transient data as it would in periodic data—the record must be marked as invalid rather than physically deleting it—at least until the capture component has run.

File comparison

As a method for capturing operational data, file comparison is usually considered to be the last resort. It requires keeping a copy of the data as it existed before updating has begun (say, last night's data) and using this together with the current copy of the data (say, tonight's data) as input to a standard file comparison program. This is shown in Figure 9-8. The output is the set of changes that have occurred in the given time period. As for the previous method, this is a delayed-capture approach, and whether the set of changes is complete or not depends on the persistence or transience of the source. The factors discussed in the previous section apply equally here, except that this method detects deletes.

There are two main drawbacks to using this method of capture: it requires (1) keeping both before and after copies of the operational file or database, and (2) sorting and comparing a large number of records for a potentially small number of changes. The performance of this method thus depends strongly on the size of the source and the power of the sort and compare programs.

However, this type of capture has the advantage of working under conditions in which none of the other approaches are usable. It is particularly useful where the operational system is file based rather than in a database, and an approach dependent on the DBMS such as log or triggered capture is thus unavailable. It also works even when timestamps do not exist in the source, because any change anywhere in a record is sufficient to cause detection of the updates to the source.

Finally, file comparison requires no changes to the applications that maintain the source data, nor to the structure or content of the source data itself. It is therefore particularly suitable for use with legacy systems.

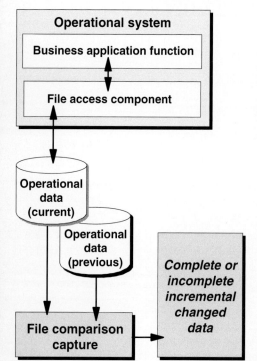

Figure 9-8: File comparison-based capture

In a variant of this approach, it is possible to reduce the sizes of the files to be compared by using a static capture approach to first select only those parts of the previous and current files that are of interest.

A final point on timing, applicable to both timestamp-based and file comparison capture, is of interest. Both approaches allow the gathering of changed data at intervals the business defines—for example, daily, weekly, or monthly. However, these two techniques require a period when the data is stable in order to capture the data. This may pose some problems as businesses move toward continuous 24-hour operation. Such problems are effectively tackled only by using the immediate incremental capture methods described previously.

File comparison

A method for capturing a possibly incomplete set of changed data by comparing two versions of the source data.

A comparison of the approaches

Static capture is required at least once in all situations, in order to initially populate the BDW. One or more incremental capture approaches will usually be required in order to capture or generate history in the BDW or to improve overall performance. Each of the five approaches to incremental data capture has its strengths and weaknesses. Unfortunately, none is a clear winner in all circumstances, and in most organizations where there is a mix of environments, it may be impossible to limit the choice to static capture and a single variety of incremental capture.

This section describes the various strengths and weaknesses, which are summarized in Tables 9-1 and 9-2. For ease of comparison, Table 9-2 groups together the three immediate incremental capture methods, while static capture and the two delayed capture methods are treated together in Table 9-1.

The three approaches shown in Table 9-1 show a high degree of similarity in the areas compared. The most significant difference is the applicability to legacy systems. The difficulty in applying the timestamp-based method to legacy systems in comparison to the other two methods results from its dependency on timestamps provided by the operational applications—a relatively rare occurrence.

Neither of the delayed-capture approaches can completely support the generation of periodic data from transient or semi-periodic data in the operational systems. On the other hand, all three immediate capture methods in Table 9-2 allow the capture of a complete record of the changes in the operational environment, and therefore support the construction of periodic data representing an historical view of the business. However, there is a reasonably strong assumption that the operational data is stored in a database rather than being file based. Only application-assisted capture handles file-based data.

Table 9-1: Comparison of static and delayed incremental capture methods

Advantage / disadvantage	Static capture	Timestamp-based capture	File comparison
Capture of data changes over time	N/A	Partial	Partial
Build history from transient or semi-periodic data source	N/A	Incomplete	Incomplete
Support for file-based operational data	Yes	Yes	Yes
Product based or internally developed	Product	Both	Product
Internal development cost	None	Medium	None
Applicability to legacy systems	Yes	Unlikely	Yes
Modification of existing applications	None	Likely high	None
Impact of changing database vendor	Confined	Confined	Confined
Impact on performance of operational systems	None	None	None
Processing within peak times	No	No	No
Effort in defining each capture	Small	Small	Small
Flexibility in defining each capture	High	High	High
Maintenance of associations between business transactions in the source	N/A	No	No

From a development and maintenance viewpoint, application-assisted capture is the most expensive to implement, because it has a great impact on existing applications and because its development will probably have to be undertaken internally. Both triggered and log capture are product based and therefore cheaper to implement.

The openness of the approaches, judged on how changing database vendor impacts each method, is quite varied. Neither static capture nor the two delayed incremental capture approaches suffer significantly provided that the tools chosen support multiple database formats. In spite of the fact that log capture is intimately related to the internal processing of the DBMS, one could argue that this approach is the most open of the imme-

Table 9-2: *Comparison of immediate incremental capture methods*

Application-assisted capture	Triggered capture	Log capture	Advantage / disadvantage
Complete	Complete	Complete	*Capture of data changes over time*
Yes	Yes	Yes	*Build history from transient or semi-periodic data source*
Yes	No	Rarely	*Support for file-based operational data*
Internal	Product	Product	*Product based or internally developed*
High	None	None	*Internal development cost*
Unlikely	Unlikely	Yes	*Applicability to legacy systems*
High	None	None	*Modification of existing applications*
Variable	Widespread	Confined	*Impact of changing database vendor*
Medium	Medium	None	*Impact on performance of operational systems*
Significant	Significant	Small	*Processing within peak times*
High	Medium	Small	*Effort in defining each capture*
High	Medium	Medium	*Flexibility in defining each capture*
Yes	Yes	No	*Maintenance of associations between business transactions in the source*

diate capture approaches. This is because, provided the new database has a log capture function, modification of the environment is confined to accommodating the new output structure. On the other hand, triggered capture varies significantly from one DBMS to another, so a change in database supplier could entail extensive and widespread rewriting of trigger procedures.

The impact on the performance of the operational systems is clearly minimal for the static and delayed approaches, because they operate largely separately from the source. Performance considerations favor log capture among the immediate capture approaches because it does not require any additional database reads. Also, the majority of the required processing can be performed outside the main transaction-handling process, and thus can be relegated to off-peak times in many cases.

The effort involved in defining each instance of capture and the flexibility in defining the conditions for each capture are quite varied. It is worth noting that the flexibility of application-assisted capture is paid for in the added effort required for definition.

A final difference among these three immediate-capture approaches is of interest. When a business event causes an update to more than one table in the operational database, being able to reflect the association between the changes into the target environment may be useful. The example of the aircraft manufacturer in Section 8.4 shows the complexities arising when this association is not maintained. When using the triggered or application-assisted capture approaches, this relationship can be maintained relatively easily. However, with log capture, it is lost, because the DBMS is only aware of the changes as they relate to individual tables.

A final point on the delayed-capture approaches is appropriate. They can only build an approximation to a full historical record if the operational data is transient or semi-periodic. In essence, they assume that there exists a time interval within which it is not necessary to track multiple changes. For many business processes, this time interval is a business day. To phrase this another way, if the business needs to keep an historical record of its affairs at fixed times only, such as the close of business each day, then delayed-capture approaches are adequate. In addition, both approaches directly access the operational data. They therefore need a time when the operational data is not being updated, sufficient to allow the capture procedure to obtain a consistent set of data. They further assume that this period of inactivity in the operational system happens regularly enough to meet the need of the business for an historical view of the data.

In practice...

Log capture is usually the preferred approach to complete incremental capture.

In summary, few companies use application-assisted capture due to its cost and complexity. Of the two product-based approaches, both depend on the operational data being in a database rather than a file. Log capture tends to give better performance, and because it can support non-relational databases, has better applicability to legacy systems. Where log capture is not applicable, one must rely on the delayed capture approaches. Of these, file comparison is more common simply because it has no prerequisites, although timestamp-based capture is more powerful.

9.5   Output data structures from capture

Two key requirements determine the structure of the data output from the capture component:

1. Data should be stored in a format that the apply, transformation, or data transfer components can easily use.

2. Data content and characteristics should be documented.

The data output should satisfy these conditions irrespective of how capture works internally, although the capture approach can influence to some extent the structure of such output data. The main difference in structure lies in whether the output is generated at a record level or at a file level.

Output generated at a record level allows more flexibility in handling of the output data. Data can be moved from the operational environment to the BDW in small batches—if needed, record by record in a near real-time approach. This facility can be a distinct advantage when operating in conditions where the nighttime batch window is narrow. There is a disadvantage, however, in this approach to data transfer: it requires more rigorous controls to ensure the integrity of the data transfer and to take account of potential missing records and records out of sequence.

Given that the capture component operates independently of the other replication components—an approach that provides the most flexibility in implementation—an appropriate structure for the output data is a ***self-documenting format***. In such a format, the characteristics and content definitions are always available with the data itself, allowing the receiving component to apply the appropriate processing. Such self-documenting formats are common in the area of text document processing, although the completeness and complexity of such schemes are usually unnecessary here because of the structured and repetitive nature of the output records.

In addition, this descriptive information should be recorded in the data warehouse catalog (DWC), since it is metadata. Both end users and administrators of the warehouse require such information.

Using a common store for data replication control metadata is an attractive option in the data warehouse. Such a store provides a single repository for use by all components of data replication. It also ensures the integrity of the transferred data irrespective of the source, target, or means of replication. However, two factors inhibit the provision of such a store:

- the variety of data environments, both hardware and software

- the number of existing programs or tools, each of which adopts its own approach to storing and managing metadata

These inhibitors are part of the real heritage of IS development over the years and are unlikely to be easily overcome in a generic way. Within a single company, the IS department may take an approach involving the judicious choice of tools and some amount of in-house development which together address these needs. However, in general, this area is likely to remain one in which full integration is difficult to achieve.

9.6 Apply—an introduction

Apply

A component of data replication that applies the captured and transformed data to the target data store.

The apply component of data replication takes the output of the capture component (either directly or via transformation and/or data transfer) and applies this data to the target system. Apply operates in one of four modes, which, in order of increasing technical complexity, are as follows:

1. **Load**

    In load, apply loads or reloads the target dataset, so that any existing target data is completely replaced by the incoming captured data.

2. **Append**

    In append, apply unconditionally appends the incoming captured data to the existing target data. The existing data is preserved, but, depending on the contents of the captured data and on the DBMS of the target, new records may duplicate existing ones or may be rejected.

3. **Destructive merge**

    In this mode, apply merges the incoming captured data into the existing target data. Where the keys of the existing and incoming data match, the existing data is updated accordingly; where they do not match, new records are added.

4. **Constructive merge**

    This mode is similar to destructive merge but with one important difference. Where the keys of existing and incoming data match, apply marks existing data as superseded but does not overwrite it. Incoming records are therefore always added to the target.

The choice of which mode to use in any particular circumstance depends on the type of time dependency required in the target data:

*   Snapshot data

    A snapshot, being a static view of the data at a point in time, is created through the load mode. After the initial load, append can expand the snapshot using incoming data from a different source, under certain conditions described later.

    A snapshot remains static and at some stage is either deleted or replaced by a set of data for another point in time. This replacement could result from a second load process, or a set of changes could be merged into the existing snapshot. This is a destructive merge because a snapshot does not preserve any historical view of data.

- Transient data

  Transient data is also created through a load and optional append, and maintained via destructive merge. From the viewpoint of the apply component, transient and snapshot data are virtually indistinguishable. The only difference is the update frequency: transient data is updated on an ongoing basis, while a snapshot is updated at intervals.

- Periodic data

  Periodic data—an historical view of the business—is also created by a load. After the initial load, append can expand the data using incoming data from a different source, under certain conditions.

  Constructive merge is the most effective mode for maintaining periodic data, because records must never be deleted from periodic data. Append can also update periodic data, but only if a mechanism exists to mark superseded records after the captured data has been appended.

9.7 Apply during BDW creation

Captured data is applied to the business data warehouse in two sets of circumstances. Initially, data is applied as part of the process of creating the BDW. Later, it is applied as part of ongoing maintenance of the periodic data in the BDW. Each circumstance uses different apply modes.

Creating the BDW consists of a number of discrete activities. First, there is the design and creation of the tables. Table design is covered in Chapter 8. Translation of the design into physical table schema and subsequent creation of the tables occurs in one of two ways:

1. as an output of the modeling, through the use of CASE tools that generate data definition language (DDL) for the required database

2. as an output of the replication administration component, described in Chapter 19, which generates DDL but may implement it as part of the load step that initially populates the table

The creation phase is followed by the initial population of those tables. This population may be repeated a number of times in the development environment, although hopefully only once in the production environment! As the BDW is populated, or immediately afterward, any required indexes are generated.

The initial population step may also consist of a number of stages, where data is brought together from a number of non-overlapping operational systems. In many warehouse implementations, data from such opera-

Load

**A complete load
of the captured
data into the
target dataset,
irrespective of
any existing data.**

tional systems is included in the BDW in a staged manner. Each additional set of data for inclusion in the BDW goes through a process similar to the first set.

Two of the four apply modes—load and append—support BDW creation.

Load

Load is the simplest and broadest type of apply. This mode of apply simply loads captured data in the format required by the target database, in this case, the relational database where the BDW resides. As shown in Figure 9-9, three options exist:

1. If the table to be loaded does not already exist, load first creates it and then loads in the data.

2. If the table already exists, the data is loaded into it.

3. If the target data already exists, the incoming captured data replaces it in its entirety. This may be achieved either by dropping and re-creating the entire table, or by deleting all existing data and writing the incoming records to the target.

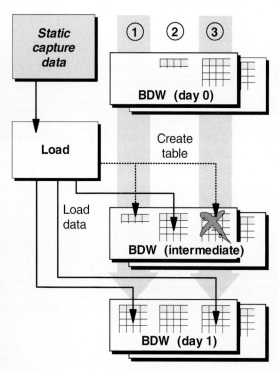

Load uses the output from static capture as its input in BDW creation. This sets an initial state for all BDW records being created. Technically, load could use incremental changed data as its input. However, in this case, load could set some of the initial states to be updates or deletes, which would be unlikely to make sense in business terms.

The load component has only a minimal need to know about the structure of the incoming data. However, load obviously needs the names of the target tables. If table creation is to occur as part of this step, the names of the columns and types of data in each are required. Otherwise, the process needs a method of matching input data fields to existing columns. This may be based on the order of the input fields and columns or on column names.

Load components are often optimized for particular DBMSs, sometimes by handling data load and index generation through parallel processes.

Figure 9-9: Load mode of apply

Append

We can think of append as an adaptation of load where, if the target data already exists, the initial deletion step is not carried out, and all incoming records are written to the target. Append meets the need, mentioned earlier, to expand a previously created BDW with data from additional sources. As we can see in Figure 9-10, append simply adds more records (or occurrences) to a previously existing BDW table. Like load, and for the same reasons, append takes its input from static capture.

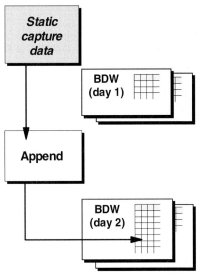

Figure 9-10: *Append mode of apply*

The limitations of append must be clearly understood. Because append mode, by definition, does not examine existing records before adding the incoming captured data, problems can arise where existing and incoming records have the same key. The approach of the append component in this situation is either to create a second record with the same key or to refuse to insert the new record and give an error message. Both approaches have some implications for the ongoing integrity of business data where record keys play a vital role. Therefore, append must be used with great care where there is a possibility of duplicate keys between the existing data in the BDW table and the incoming data.

This restriction is best illustrated by an example. Consider the initial creation of the customer table in the BDW of an international company. This table is quite large and is sourced from a number of different operational systems. Therefore, it is built in a staged manner. The first stage includes, say, only German customers.[2] This portion of the customer table is created using the load mode of apply. Three months later, the French customers are included. This next portion of the customer table is created using the append mode of apply. All works well because the operational systems ensure, by design, that there is no overlap of German and French customer keys—at least, until the European Union removes all borders!

If the operational systems are designed differently, problems can arise. Let's assume stage 3 in the BDW population adds customers of a subsidiary of the French operation. Customers of this subsidiary who reside in France have been tracked in the operational system of the subsidiary using the customer numbering system of the parent company. However, the subsidiary also operates in Belgium and Switzerland. For these customers, the operational system assigns new customer records. A static cap-

> **Append**
>
> *A complete load of the captured data into the target dataset, adding to any data that may already exist there.*

---

[2] For simplicity in this example, we deal only with individuals as customers and so do not have to worry about companies as customers, which would require some careful modeling to take account of international operations.

ture of the data from this system clearly produces a set of captured records that partially overlaps with the existing BDW.

The use of append in this case results either in duplicate records for French customers or a number of error messages (and a possible program abend) during apply processing, depending on the characteristics of the BDW database and the apply program. One possible way to preserve data integrity is to instruct the append component to simply not write duplicate entries without error messages. Another solution is also rather obvious. Simply capturing only those customer records for non-French customers (selection along the occurrence dimension) will eliminate the append problem.

However, other types of overlap are impossible to detect in advance. For example, consider the case where the operational systems are product centered, and the stages of   BDW creation are aligned to the operational systems. In the initial stage of BDW creation, the customer table receives the names of all customers who bought product A. Apply is in load mode. In the second stage, data from the operational system handling product B is to be included in the BDW. Some customers from this system have also bought product A, and so their names already exist in the BDW. Others are new and must be added. Append has similar problems as before, but excluding from the new captured data the customers who bought product A is more difficult to accomplish in such a situation.

Examples such as this second one are particularly common where legacy systems have grown around product areas and the product set has expanded over time, either by expansion of the business or by takeover or acquisition. In this case, the append component must be told to ignore record key conflicts and simply not apply such records to the existing data. More modern operational system designs avoid such problems by using a single database of customers—this is the reference data approach described in Section 7.6.

In practice...

Instructing append to ignore expected conflicts may mask the existence of conflicts that indicate underlying problems in the data design.

Note also that, so far, we have assumed that the conflict in record keys does not indicate an inherent problem in the quality of the captured data; simply that it comes from sources operating independently of one another. In this instance, the data model or design is fine, but its implementation is uncoordinated. A more serious data quality problem occurs when the data design is in error. This is addressed through transformation function, as Section 9.11 describes.

Append therefore introduces the need to make some decisions based on the contents of the captured data. Two questions to answer are:

• Are conflicts possible between the existing BDW and captured data?

   In certain circumstances, it is possible to know that the captured data contains records whose set of keys does not overlap at all with that of the BDW. In this case, no conflict will occur, and append is both a simple and efficient means of applying the incoming data.

- When such conflicts occur, what should be done?

  If the data involved indicates a likelihood of conflicts, then appropriate subsetting in capture may avoid them or append may be instructed to ignore them. Unexpected conflicts may point to a design flaw.

9.8 Apply during BDW maintenance

Ongoing maintenance of the data in the BDW requires a method that supports the periodic nature of this data. Any apply method, therefore, that physically deletes or overwrites data cannot be used.

A second aspect that requires careful consideration is the maintenance of the timestamp information that is so important in defining the historical nature of the BDW. In the previous section, when discussing the keys of records, it was sufficient for us to consider the business key on its own. In the maintenance of the BDW data, however, we must always consider both the business and the timestamp parts of the key.

As shown in Section 8.4, the important timestamps are start time and end time. As previously stated, the business key and both of these timestamps are concatenated to form the key of a BDW table containing status data. For event data, only the business key and start time need to be concatenated. This section focuses on how to maintain a status table, because it is the more complex and because we can easily derive the situation for an event table from that for a status table.

The most important apply mode for maintaining the BDW contents is constructive merge. This mode is designed to maintain periodic data by protecting the existing contents of the data records and adding all new records representing the new state of the business. Append can also have a role in maintaining the BDW contents, although this is confined to particular circumstances.

Constructive merge

A method of applying captured changed data to a periodic dataset, which builds and maintains the historical record of changes to the source data.

Constructive merge

The objective in constructive merge is to build a periodic dataset in the BDW from the changed data records received from the capture component and that reflects previous and current states of the operational source.

In this apply method, there are logically two steps. The first step adds all changed data to the BDW. The second step depends on the nature of the changed data itself. We can best understand this approach by taking each type of changed data record in turn.

Figure 9-11 shows new incremental data for day 4 to be merged into the existing BDW for day 3.

Record 005 is added to the BDW. The start time is set to the current date and time (of which only the month and day are shown in the figure). The end time is set to the special value, indicated here by "#", to show that this is a currently valid record. The action flag is set to the value "A", found in the changed data and representing the action that took place in the operational system to generate this record, namely the addition of a new occurrence. For the BDW, a changed record of an "A" type indicates that this is a new occurrence of the business key and that no other record with a key of 005 should be found in the BDW. Indeed, this could be the basis of an integrity check. For new records, there is only one step in constructive merge, and the process for this record is complete.

Record 003 is inserted next, and the timestamps and flag are set as before. This record has an action flag value of "D", which indicates that the corresponding record in the operational system was deleted. Therefore, a record with this business key that has an end time set to "#" should still exist in the BDW. The second step of constructive merge then resets the end time for this previous occurrence, by setting it equal to the start time of the new 003 record. This indicates that the previous record is no longer valid.

Similarly, when record 004 is added, constructive merge recognizes it as an update to a previous occurrence of 004, because of the "C" action flag. The updated version is written with the current time as start time, and the end time of the previous version is also set to indicate it is no longer valid. Record 006 is a simple add, equivalent to the case for record 005.

The timestamp inserted in start time (and copied to the end time of a superseded record) may come from the operational system as part of the captured data. In this case, it preferably represents the valid business time or the timestamp of the operational transaction, as discussed in Section 8.4. However, this timestamp may not be available from

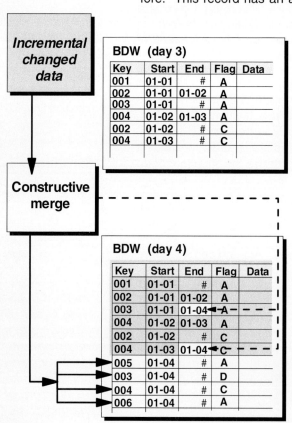

Figure 9-11: *Constructive merge—an example*

older operational systems, and the responsibility for creating it falls on the apply component. In this case, the timestamp represents the time when the record was added to the BDW. Whatever its source, the start time timestamp becomes an integral part of the key to that data.

Of the two distinct types of function involved in constructive merge, the first, identified in Figure 9-11 by the solid arrows, is a fairly straightforward insert of the changed data. It can be, and is, implemented through a simple SQL INSERT statement for all types of data—adds, changes, and deletes:

```
INSERT  INTO BDW_T
VALUES  (00n, current_time, ...)
```

The second type of function, shown by the dotted arrows, is far more complex, and operates only for changes and deletes. It requires an SQL statement of the following form:

```
UPDATE  BDW_T A
SET     (END) =
        (SELECT    MAX(START) FROM BDW_T B
         WHERE     B.END = '#'
         AND       A.KEY = B.KEY)
WHERE   A.START ¬ =
        (SELECT    MAX(START) FROM BDW_T C
         WHERE     C.KEY = A.KEY)
```

These two types of function may need to be performed in two separate steps to maintain data in the BDW. The first step is likely to be supported by a vendor product, while the IS shop might have to develop the second.

Data sources with very high change rates

We can see from the complexity of the processing above that constructive merge is most effective when the percentage of data changed is low. If the rate of change of the source data is particularly high, the percentage of data changed in a day may be higher than can be successfully handled by constructive merge. In this case, an approach to consider is to increase the frequency of replication runs from nightly to twice a day, four times a day, hourly, or even operating nearly continuously.

This approach spreads the processing load throughout the day and reduces the impact on the overnight batch-processing window. It also implies that the BDW will be changing during the business day. The potential need to adopt such an approach is another reason for not encouraging direct end-user access to the BDW.

Append

Append can also play a role in applying historical data changes to a target, but only under certain conditions. The discussion in the previous section on the two types of function included in constructive merge shows how. The simpler SQL INSERT function shown earlier is none other than append. The "magic" in constructive merge comes from the second step.

Thus we can see that only two situations allow the use of append to build periodic data in the BDW:

- when end time (or any other field that is changed in the superseded record) is *not* in use

- when the operational system adds only records with new business keys to the data

The most usual example of these two conditions is an event dataset.

An example is a set of transactions on a bank account, where a unique key identifies each transaction. It is a common practice in such operational systems to never change or delete a transaction, once it has been entered. If the transaction is later found to be in error, the operational system will enter a correction. This correction is a unique transaction in its own right. Therefore, all business transactions result in changed records with an "A" action flag. And therefore, append can be used to maintain a BDW table sourced from such an operational system.

In practice...
Append is the apply method to use when building a history of events in the BDW.

9.9   Refresh versus update of the BDW

Up to now, we have treated the capture and apply processes separately. This is because they are quite distinct functions that often operate in two different environments. Separate discussion allows a more detailed examination of the functionality and the strengths and weaknesses of each approach. However, they do have a shared purpose—to replicate data from source to target. In many discussions, these two components are treated together from the perspective of getting the data from source to target.

Viewing the process from this perspective leads to a very useful generalization—that there are broadly two ways of keeping a target database up to date. The first method is simply to write the target once and then rewrite it completely at intervals, an approach known as **refresh**. The second method, which assumes that the target has been written once in its entirety, is to write to the target only the changes in the source. This approach is called **update**.

Refresh

A replication mode based on bulk rewriting of the target data using static captured data.

Refresh mode replication can be described in the context of the previous sections as a combination of static capture and apply in load or append mode. Update mode replication is a combination of incremental capture and apply in merge or append mode.

Broadly speaking, we can think of refresh as a bulk data process, for use during the initial creation and ongoing maintenance of a target database. Update, on the other hand, is record oriented and can be used only during the ongoing maintenance phase.

A choice between refresh and update is therefore available for maintaining a target. It is possible, and useful, to compare refresh and update on the basis of a number of factors—most notably functionality, technical simplicity, and performance aspects—and to determine which is most appropriate in any particular instance.

In BDW population, however, the choice is very restricted. Unless the operational source data is periodic, maintenance of the BDW requires the use of update replication. This is the only approach capable of converting transient operational data into the periodic data required in the BDW. The considerations for replication from periodic operational data are the same as those for replication from the BDW to the BIWs. Section 11.4 discusses refresh and update in the context of BIW population.

> *Update*
>
> *A replication mode using captured change data to maintain the target data incrementally.*

9.10 Transformation—an introduction

The transformation component of data replication sits logically between capture and apply. It accepts data in the format of the source from the capture component and changes it to the format that apply will use in the target. In data warehousing, the changes in format required can range from the very simple to the highly complex. Consider the following examples:

> *Transformation*
>
> *A component of data replication that converts data between different logical or physical structures according to predefined rules.*

- An end user requires a complete copy of data stored in a mainframe-based, relational BIW for personal use in a PC.

  The transformation required is simply a technical one, taking into account different data representations on different platforms.

- Each branch of a bank needs to store a subset of the BDW locally, containing only certain information about its own customers. This is stored in an identical DBMS to the central BDW.

  The transformation needed in this case is to subset the source data along the attribute and occurrence dimensions.

- A company has historically developed a number of legacy systems containing uncoordinated data to manage different products. It needs to see a combined product view in the informational environment.

  The data in this example requires a number of transformations in addition to those described for the previous cases: integrating data from different sources, eliminating overlaps, aligning and reconciling data, converting to a common set of codes, among others.

- A multinational company requires a consolidated worldwide view of its business, eliminating any inconsistencies arising from the fact that it is operating across multiple time zones.

  In addition to the transformations already mentioned, an added requirement on the transformation component here is an ability to combine data arriving at different times. Transformation will therefore be a long-running process, rather than a single event.

The conclusion we can draw from these four examples is that transformation cannot be defined singly but must be described according to the type of function it provides. We should also note that the transformations required tend to decrease in complexity as we move from the operational systems toward the user: BDW population needs the most complex transformations, followed by BIW population, and finally extraction from a BIW to an end user's PC.

The next section describes how the transformation functions work, while Section 9.11 focuses on their use in BDW population.

Transformation functions

Transformation encompasses a wide and varied range of functionality. Ultimately, the function exists to meet a business need. However, distinguishing between different types of functionality requires descending to a more technical level of requirement definition. Classification of this functionality and assessment of its technical complexity depend on two factors:

- the relationship between the number of input and output records

- the type of computation applied at a field level within the records

From a consideration of this mix of business and technical requirements, six general transformation functions emerge:

1. selection

2. separation/concatenation

3. normalization/denormalization

4. aggregation

5. conversion

6. enrichment

The first four represent different ways in which input and output relate at a record level, while the last two operate at a field level.

Selection

Selection (or subsetting) is the process that partitions data according to predefined criteria. Selection is the simplest form of transformation, operating on one input record and generating at most one output record for each input record.

Selection is often included as part of the capture component. The different dimensions of selection—entity, attribute, and occurrence—were described earlier in Section 9.4. However, there are circumstances where selection may take place in a subsequent, separate step from capture. For instance, the technical structure of the source data may make it difficult to select the required subset. In this case, it may be more appropriate to capture all the data, convert it into a more useful format, and then select the subset required. Similarly, if a subset of the source data has been captured, and needs further subdivision in order to feed multiple targets with different subsets of the data, further selection is needed as part of the transformation phase.

Separation/concatenation

Separation splits the information relating to one business item into a number of separate records based on the business key. Subsetting is done to simplify an end user's view, to support different data uses, or for security reasons.

Separation seldom occurs in BDW population because it separates data logically belonging in the same entity, which is the opposite of what BDW population needs. However, separation does apply to BIW population.

Concatenation is the reverse of separation, joining information about the same item together. This function does play a role in BDW population.

The concatenation process allows an input record to be extended with more details about the primary subject. For example, different types of product information may be stored and maintained in different operational databases because they are the responsibility of different departments. Thus, packaging types and sizes for a product originate in the manufacturing systems, while prices come from the marketing systems. These are concatenated based on product number as the key in the BDW.

> **Selection**
>
> *A transformation function that selects all, part, or nothing of a single input record.*

> **Separation/ concatenation**
>
> *A transformation function that splits or joins data records while maintaining the original relationship to the primary record key.*

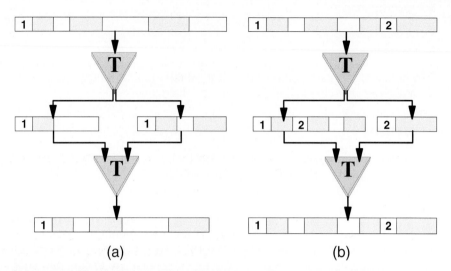

Figure 9-12: *Separation/concatenation and normalization/denormalization*

The overall characteristics of this type of transformation are that the relationship is one-to-many in both directions and all records are keyed on the same field. This is shown in Figure 9-12(a).

Normalization/denormalization

Normalization/ denormalization

A transformation function that splits or joins data records, while maintaining relationships between primary and secondary record keys.

Closely related to the previous category is normalization/denormalization. As with separation/concatenation, **normalization** involves splitting a single input record into multiple outputs, and **denormalization** is the reverse. However, as shown in Figure 9-12(b), the difference lies in the handling of record keys.

Consider an example of normalization. A product inventory record keyed on product number contains both a description of the product and details of where it is stocked. The normalization process splits this record into two parts, one containing the product data, keyed on product number, and the other containing data on stocking locations, keyed on location code. Clearly, to maintain the relationship between product and stocking location, one of the output records must contain the key of the other record (as a foreign key relationship) or else a third link record will be required.

The initial, denormalized structure, which stores related but logically distinct data in one record, is common in operational systems. This is particularly so where the system is file based or a hierarchical database. The approach is not confined to a single set of related data, but there may exist a number of sets of such data in a structure known as repeating groups. When replicating such data into the BDW, it is necessary to normalize the data.

As mentioned, the opposite of this is a denormalization process. For example, names and addresses from a customer file may be added to a sales record whose input contains only the customer number.

In general, while normalization is a common occurrence in BDW population, denormalization is usually found in the BIW population process.

Aggregation

Aggregation is the transformation process that takes data from a detailed to a summary level. Because data is stored in the BDW at a detailed level, the aggregation function is not applicable to BDW population. It does, however, have a significant role in business information warehouses as discussed in Chapter 11.

Conversion

Unlike the previous transformations, which operate at record level, ***conversion*** operates at a field level. Its function is to change data from one form to another. It is the simpler of the two field-level transformations because it operates within a single data element and each conversion is independent of all others. The process thus takes as input a single piece of data and applies a rule to transform it into another form, as shown in Figure 9-13(a). This rule may be an algorithm or a lookup table.

Conversion

A transformation function that converts the value in a single data field to some related form.

Algorithmic conversion

We can often describe the simplest types of conversion in mathematical form. In this case, all of the logic required can be included within the conversion process itself. Common examples are:

- converting mixed-case text to all uppercase or all lowercase

- converting between measurement systems, such as imperial to metric

- converting from codes to descriptions where the set of possible values is small and unchanging, such as "(m,f)" to "(male, female)"

Conversion by lookup

Conversions that cannot be expressed as a simple algorithm instead use a lookup table. This approach provides a greater level of flexibility in the relationship between input and output, particularly in its ability to easily extend the relationship over time. Examples are:

- ASCII to EBCDIC and similar code-page conversions

- converting from codes to descriptions with large or open-ended sets of code values, such as ISO (International Standardization Organization) country codes to country names

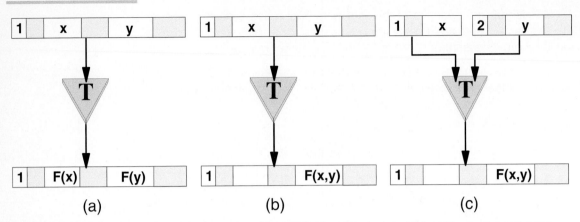

Figure 9-13: *Transformation by: (a) conversion, (b) multi-field enrichment and (c) multi-record enrichment*

Enrichment

Enrichment	Enrichment uses data in one or more input fields to improve the data available in an existing field or to create a new field or fields. Enrichment is an important type of transformation in the data warehouse, particularly in BDW population where it allows the creation of fields in the warehouse data that do not exist in the source.
A transformation function that combines data from two or more fields in one or more records to create a new field or fields in the output record.	It is important to note that in BDW population, unlike in BIW population, enrichment does not create new business data. The new fields created during enrichment in BDW population result from simplification, re-arrangement, or cleansing of existing operational data. In general, enrichment during BDW population tries to simplify the complexity of coding schemes used in operational data from legacy systems. Operational data from more modern systems usually has less need for this function.

Depending on the relative locations of the input fields, enrichment can range in technical complexity from being relatively straightforward, where the input is a single field in a record, to highly complex, where input is taken from multiple fields located across multiple records.

Single record enrichment

In **single record enrichment** all of the required input information comes from one record. This is technically the simplest type of enrichment because the input fields all come from the same source and are guaranteed to be available to the transformation component at the same time. We can divide single record enrichment into single-field and multi-field cases.

- **Single-field enrichment** uses as input a single field within the one record and creates one or more new fields that represent a different view of the same data. The new field can be a simplification of the data to align it with the EDM. For example, a single set of codes in one field of the operational data represents manufacturer and country of origin of a product. The BDW should store these facts in separate fields.

- *Multi-field enrichment*, shown in Figure 9-13(b), allows interaction between the fields within a single input record. The outcome may be the creation of a new field in the output record or the update of an existing field. Examples of this type of enrichment occur in places where original coding approaches "ran out of steam" as the business changed, and so were extended by creating new data fields. In these cases, the original and new fields logically comprise a single field but have been physically split. The task of enrichment is to restore the logical unity. This task is, of course, complicated by the fact that the original field now contains not only coded values related to the business, but also codes that indicate that further information may be found elsewhere in the record.

Multi-record enrichment

In *multi-record enrichment*, the input fields no longer need to come from the same record but may come from more than one such record. This obviously increases the technical complexity of the enrichment process. However, the underlying purpose is the same as for single-record multi-field enrichment—the reunification of logically single but physically separated information. The output of multi-record enrichment is always the creation of one or more new fields in the output.

Figure 9-13(c) shows multi-record enrichment. Examples of this type are often found in operational data, such as fixed-length record structures and some hierarchical databases, where it is difficult to extend a record after the initial structure has been laid down. New data needs are then supported by the creation of additional records, chained back to the original one.

Unfortunately, multi-record enrichment does not end there. In some cases, the operational environment evolved such that logically single pieces of data (as defined by the EDM) are distributed among different operational systems. In such cases, one cannot assume that the fields to be combined are even simultaneously available. At a technical level, this may simply be a result of the order in which capture jobs run against different source files in the batch-processing streams. Combining data from systems that run in different time zones also gives rise to this situation. At a business level, it may result from different accounting periods between different departments.

Whatever the reasons multi-record enrichment is used, the outcome is that this type of transformation is potentially the most complex type of all.

9.11 Transformation in BDW population

We can relate the transformation occurring during BDW population to one primary goal: the normalization and alignment of the incoming data to the EDM. In theory, normalization of the data from operational sources should be a simple process, depending solely on recognizing and matching the keys of records from different sources.

However, we see this ideal situation only where the operational systems have all been designed according to a single data model and implemented consistently across the whole organization. This situation rarely exists. The companies approaching it most closely are those that have extensively reengineered their operational systems, or those that have built their entire operational environment around one or two major packages.

In many organizations, where the operational environment has grown over many years, and where largely unmodeled legacy systems still run some of the core business processes, normalization is very complex. It is complicated by the existence of inconsistencies in the source data, the often complex and compacted design of the physical databases, and the lack of quality in the data gathered. It addition to these problems is a timing issue, which applies equally to legacy and modern systems: where the BDW must combine data from a number of operational systems, the source data is often not available simultaneously.

These considerations lead to significant requirements that transformation in BDW population must meet. The following sections describe the characteristics of operational data that the transformation functions must address before application of the data to the BDW can occur.

Characteristics of operational data

The diverse nature of operational data

Operational data exists in a variety of structures. These structures were designed (or evolved) for a number of reasons:

- to circumvent, or exploit, the technical limitations or advantages of various data storage methods

- to reflect application boundaries, organizational divisions, and geographical responsibilities

- to improve application performance

The result is that the structure of operational data differs significantly from data in the BDW, which derives from the EDM. Transformation from the variety of structures that exist in operational data to the normalized structure of the BDW requires extensive use of the record-oriented transformation functions:

- Selection allows unwanted records to be completely discarded, or subsets of fields to be discarded or retained.

- Concatenation is required to combine data from different sources about the same item into a single record.

- Normalization is required to restructure hierarchical structures, repeating groups, and other common operational data structures.

It is also worth noting that implicit data meaning drives some data transformations. For example, after a merger of two banks, two different operational systems continue to handle the loan accounts, at least for some period of time. Different algorithms calculate the account balances in the two systems, although similar records are passed to the transformation functions during BDW population. Different transformations must be applied to the two types of records, based on an implicit knowledge of their sources.

The lack of consistency of operational data

This characteristic stems from the original design paradigm of the operational environment. Operational applications are designed to a restricted set of user requirements and are usually confined to a particular business area. Because of this narrow scope, matching the record keys from different operational databases is seldom straightforward. Common problems include the following:

- **Mismatches and discontinuities between the key sets of the different sources**

  This problem often occurs in the processes and applications in which people or organizations have been assigned arbitrary key identifiers. While such identifiers are, by definition, unique within any one operational database, they are seldom unique across all the operational databases that serve as sources for this data.

  It is not unusual for the structure of keys to evolve as businesses change. A product numbering scheme based on five digits may need changing to a six-character structure as the products move from the custom market to the mass market.

  Company takeovers and mergers are another common cause of these discontinuities. Combination of data from the original operational sys-

**Data cleansing
or scrubbing**

*Statistical and
other techniques
used to eliminate
variations in data
content, to re-
duce redundancy,
and generally to
improve the con-
sistency and
usability of raw
data.*

tems of the once separate companies leads to situations in which different parts of the combined product line, customer base, and so on,
have distinctly different key structures.

- **Lack of a basis for resolving mismatches between key sets**

  When IS personnel attempt to resolve key mismatches, a problem they
  usually encounter is the almost endless variety of forms by which organizations and individuals are commonly known, and which are then
  entered into the databases. For example, the name of the company
  owning one of the most well-known brand names in the world is "The
  Coca-Cola Company". However, its name is likely to appear in customer record databases in a wide variety of different forms, such as
  "Coca-Cola", "Coca Cola", "TCCC", "Coca-Cola Co.", "The Coca-Cola
  Company, Limited", and so on.

  Issues of data definition often further complicate the problem of resolving mismatches between key sets. For example, the relationship
  between parent and subsidiary company names may be incorrectly
  defined or local distributors may be defined as customers.

Addressing these issues is often a complex process. The use of conversion or enrichment functions can directly address the simpler problems
such as conversion of a number of key sets to a common base by a simple
formula or lookup table.

More complex cases often require a staged approach. This could involve
the initial static capture of the data from all possible sources. This initial
set is subjected to **data cleansing** or **data scrubbing**—sophisticated
pattern-recognition and artificial intelligence analysis techniques—that resolve overlaps and other inconsistencies in the data. This data then becomes the starting dataset for the BDW. It is usual in this case to then
clean up the existing operational data. In order to ensure that updates and
additions to this data retain the new level of consistency, special transformations are included in the BDW population process. In cases where the
mismatch is severe, the IS shop may need to design new data entry procedures in the operational systems to eliminate the problem at source.

In addition, there is the aforementioned aspect of asynchronous availability
of data from different sources to be considered. In such cases, the chosen
transformation tool must allow staging of the input data.

The terseness of operational data

Because of the age of many operational systems, the data they contain is
often highly encoded. IS developers originally used such encoding to improve system performance or reduce the amount of disk space required.
These schemes were then further expanded and modified as business

In practice...

*When the trans-
formation step is
particularly com-
plex, BDW im-
plementation may
require a separate
independent
project focused
on the quality of
the source data.
This, in turn, is
likely to require
fundamental
changes in the
supporting busi-
ness processes.*

needs changed. Where all of these factors operated, coding schemes were ingenious but totally alien to end users. Warehouse developers must remove such IS-driven coding or, at the very least, substantially simplify it as data moves into the BDW, by utilizing a combination of conversion and enrichment functions.

Unfortunately, it is not uncommon to find that multiple levels of encoding have been imposed on the data as the operational application has evolved. Often, fields are reused for purposes for which they were never intended, or the coding introduces complex interdependencies. Following are some examples:

- A field originally used to record the date of manufacture when the company custom-built products is used to record the first date of production as the company moves to a mass-production environment.

- The IS department introduces a special customer number for internal orders within the company for its own products. As a result, certain discounting codes have different meanings than if the orders were external.

- Because of how a product line and its associated operational systems evolve, diverse characteristics that should be treated separately in the BDW get shoehorned into a single coded field. For example, "123" might represent "100 ml size, disposable, waxed-cardboard, boxed in 50s", while "124" represents "200 ml size, disposable, plastic bottle, boxed in 50s".

All of the above examples use a variety of transformation functions, but enrichment is the most commonly required.

The examples also clearly demonstrate that the data transformations required to populate the warehouse from legacy operational systems are usually complex and often unique to each company, reflecting the design and programming styles of the original creators of these systems. Given such a level of specificity, generic transformation functions are likely to provide only partial solutions to the needs of populating the BDW.

Therefore, a combination of generic function from product vendors and unique functionality developed internally may provide the best solution to the transformations required for BDW population.

> *In practice...*
>
> *Transformation in BDW population often requires custom code, and vendor-supplied function should support easy integration of such code.*

The dubious quality of operational data

In general, the quality of operational date determined mainly by its value to the part of the organization responsible for gathering it. Unfortunately, it is often the case that the data-gathering organization places a low value on some data that is very useful or important in other parts of the company [Van Alstyne *et al.* (1995)]. The outcome is that certain data, although ostensibly recorded in operational systems, is in fact so unreliable as to be useless. This conclusion is best illustrated by some examples:

- When a customer enters into an agreement with a bank, the bank often requests the customer's date of birth and saves it in the customer record system. This data is of little use or interest to the branch that gathers it and is not verified with the same dedication afforded to the data recorded on income and expenditure. Consequently, date-of-birth and similar data in banks usually contains a high proportion of errors. However, such data may be of significant interest to the marketing department of the bank, which can use it as a key part of their target marketing programs.

  On the other hand, date-of-birth data in insurance companies is of significantly better quality. This is a result of the key role that this data plays in the operational, day-to-day activities of the branches that gather this information.

- In one bank, a record field originally intended for holding a telephone number, and described in the data dictionary as such, was found to be used in the branches to store the interest rate! The branch managers justified this misuse of the field by weighing the relative importance of the two pieces of data, and taking action because the IS department would apparently take too long to provide the required upgrade to the operational application.

In such cases, the usefulness of the transformation processes may be rather limited. Setting the contents of the offending field to a warning that the data is unreliable, unavailable, or indecipherable may be all that is possible here.

Correcting erroneous data

The existence of erroneous data in the operational databases is, unfortunately, widespread and unlikely to be solved in the near future. It also evokes a particularly strong reaction from users, who (quite reasonably) demand that the data be fixed before reaching them. When the requester is the CEO, this demand is particularly difficult to dismiss.

However, where and how to correct erroneous data is a different matter. Doing so through the use of transformation functionality during BDW population, when this is possible, is strongly tempting, because it allows each individual problem to be solved with relative ease and speed—and who doesn't want to look good in the eyes of the CEO? On the other hand, it is widely recognized among warehouse developers that the correct place to fix the problem is at the source, in the operational systems.

As with many design questions in data warehousing, the decision as to the correct approach involves a tradeoff between an urgent problem needing a tactical solution and the requirements of data quality that drive a strategic solution. The decision is often to provide the tactical solution and require the operational system developers to fix the underlying problem in a subsequent release. However, we can define some guidelines based on the type of error involved:

- **Errors in data content**

  Errors in data content that are caused through data entry (such as misspelled names) and that can be corrected by a generalized process such as data cleansing are good candidates for fixing in the transformation phase. However, improved verification procedures in the data-entry phase can reduce or eliminate certain types of error, so this requirement should be placed on the operational systems developers.

- **Errors in data usage**

  Errors in data usage indicate a serious deficiency in the function provided by the operational system. The correction of such errors during transformation is not recommended, because it usually leads to the introduction of unique logic that is more complex than what would be required to fix the problem at the source.

- **Operational system design errors**

  Correction of operational system design errors should occur only in the most urgent situations. Not only does it involve complex and unique logic, but it often introduces further problems in the operational systems themselves.

Thus, we conclude that while the cleansing of data can be a part of the transformation process, correction should in general be avoided.

In the case of certain types of data, particularly nonvolatile data or data that is updated fairly infrequently, it is often worthwhile to consider doing a special, one-time cleanup during the first load of the BDW. This cleanup is usually applied to the data at the source in the operational systems databases and is followed by introducing improved data verification procedures for data entry. A common example of this approach occurs in the initial build of customer data in the warehouse, which subjects such data as already exists to analysis and scrubbing, in order to detect common errors such as impossible dates of birth and mismatched addresses and area codes. In one example, quoted by a major UK bank, this scrubbing turned up a customer on their files whose occupation was listed as "steward on the Titanic"!

9.12 BDW population—the overall process

From the individual components and functions, we can now turn to the entire process of BDW population. The key aspects relate to operational data and its diverse origins and evolution over the years. Let's review briefly the characteristics of operational data:

• Its structure is fundamentally different from that needed in the BDW.

• It is of very variable quality.

• It usually lacks history—thus it is transient or semi-periodic.

These factors have a significant influence on the way all three components of data replication —capture, transformation, and apply—are used.

In general, the source operational systems have existed for some time prior to introduction of the capture component. For this reason, the first population of the BDW has a number of unique characteristics. As shown in Figure 9-14, a point in time must be chosen as the starting point of the historical record. At this time a static capture of the operational data is performed, and the data is applied to the BDW. This may be the only time static capture and load apply are used. The transformation step may also apply special processing to cleanse the data if significant problems with

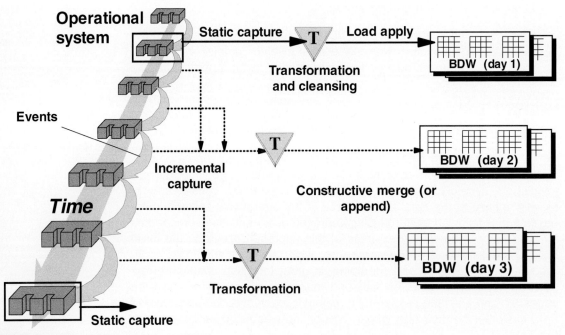

Figure 9-14: The BDW population process

the data content are known. The warehouse developer may also decide to extend the history back to some prior time by reading old log files, cleansing the data, and applying it in append mode to the BDW.

As business events occur over time, the capture component is responsible for incrementally gathering the changed data. These changes are then applied, often in batches, to the BDW. Each instance of BDW population invokes transformation, which may need to handle combinations of data from different sources asynchronously. Constructive merge is the apply mode most often used at this stage of the process. Append mode may also be used in certain circumstances, especially where the BDW table contains event data.

On occasions, it may be necessary to verify that the operational system and BDW are synchronized. And finally, it may be necessary (although, of course, we hope not!) to completely replace the contents of the BDW and start all over again. Such cases again require static capture.

9.13 Conclusions

The size of this chapter alone leads one to conclude that the work involved in populating the BDW is, indeed, significant, involving considerable technical challenges.

The approach taken here has been to split the function into three parts—capture, apply, and transformation. This approach allows the required underlying functionality to be more visible. In most cases, capture operates in one environment, apply in another, and transformation in either or both depending on resource availability. However, a close relationship exists among the three components, as is evident from the fact that vendors often combine all three functions in one product.

We can characterize both capture and apply firstly according to the type of data they produce or use. In refresh mode, they operate with static capture data, generally used only in the initial creation of the BDW. In update mode, they operate with incremental changed data. For BDW population, this is the usual way to maintain the BDW contents over time. This is because, in the vast majority of cases, BDW population involves the creation of an historical record of periodic data from transient or semi-periodic operational data.

The requirement to create periodic data leads directly to the need to capture data changes—preferably a complete set! The three methods of capturing a complete set of changes are application-assisted capture, triggered capture, and log capture. Each has its advantages, but, on balance, log capture provides the best support for capturing data from existing operational systems that use databases. For the application of changed data to the BDW, constructive merge provides the most complete support, although its complexity inhibits widespread acceptance.

If the use of complete incremental changed data in BDW population is not possible for technical reasons, then specific techniques of capture (timestamp-based and file comparison) and apply (append) can handle a potentially incomplete set of changed data. In many cases, this is an acceptable approximation to a full historical record, but of course, the business managers must agree to this.

The functions and techniques described in this chapter provide the basis for generic BDW population tools, often known as data replication tools. Such tools enable one of the key productivity advances needed in implementing a data warehouse—to move away from developing specific extraction applications for each kind of data needed from each operational system.

Transformation functions complete the set of functionality required. There are a number of generic transformation functions. Of these, selection, separation, and normalization are the basic functions required to restructure the diverse and dispersed operational data to the more generic structure demanded by the EDM. Conversion and enrichment address the need to cleanse and enhance the operational data at a field level. While all BDW implementations require common functions provided by vendor tools, many are likely to need substantial amounts of custom-built, handcrafted code. This is especially the case for older operational systems that have grown in an unplanned manner over the years.

Designing the BDW population approach, including the choice of replication tools, is one of the milestones in any data warehousing project. Warehouse developers cannot achieve this without knowing the technical environments of the operational systems and the relative importance of the different sources of data for the warehouse. It is also important to note that there is a strong interdependency between replication functionality and the level of normalization possible in the BDW.

The next logical task in building a data warehouse is to design and populate the business information warehouses, and it is to this topic we move in Part IV.

Part IV

Unlocking the data asset
for end users

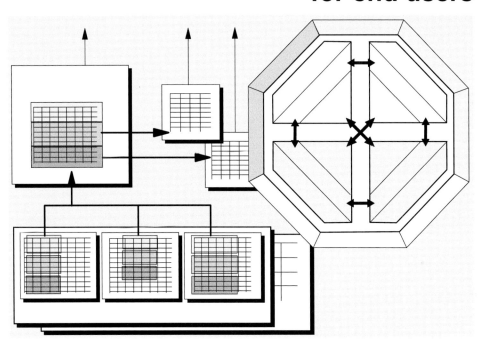

The use of business information

Chapter 10

Designing business information warehouses

In Part III, we focused on constructing the data asset of the enterprise. The purpose of Part IV is to show how the data warehouse makes that asset available to end users. This is where the business will realize the benefits through the use of business information warehouses (BIWs).

This chapter covers all aspects of the design of BIWs. As we move from the reconciled data layer to the derived data layer, a number of design differences are apparent. While the business data warehouse (BDW) is rigorously defined and largely centralized, BIWs are far more varied in their level of definition and are highly distributed. Because their usage is directed toward particular business needs, BIWs are designed more like traditional applications than is the BDW.

The chapter begins by defining in detail the two types of BIW—*staging BIWs* and *user BIWs*—and discussing their implications.

Section 10.2 describes the *modeling of BIWs* and how this establishes the relationship between data in the BDW and the BIW, particularly in the early stages of a data warehouse implementation.

We then consider *design and implementation* aspects of BIWs in Sections 10.3 and 10.4. BIWs are categorized according to their usage. The platforms on which each category can be implemented are discussed. Section 10.4 also briefly describes some of the *technological solutions* receiving significant attention in the industry at present—such as parallel databases, on-line analytical processing (OLAP) servers, multi-dimensional databases, and new indexing approaches. The implications of *historical data in BIWs* are shown in Section 10.5.

Finally, the chapter ends with a discussion of *archive and retrieval* of BIWs.

10.1 Types of business information warehouse

In the description of the logical data architecture of the warehouse given in Section 7.1, we optimized derived data by allowing the possibility of staging data between the BDW and the eventual application through which the user manipulated it. This led to the concepts of user BIWs and staging BIWs. The distinction between them is based solely on the level of control and management needed for each type. Both types reside in one layer of the conceptual architecture, because:

- Both types consist of derived data.

- Although data may flow through a staging BIW to a user BIW, it is also possible to source a user BIW directly from the BDW.

The characteristics of the two types of BIW are common in many areas. They are accessed directly by end users and are thus structured to facilitate this access. In comparison with the BDW, they address a relatively small area of the business. Either kind of BIW may contain detailed or summary data or a mixture of both. Either may be a snapshot of the business at a point in time, or a periodic, historical record of the business.

Their differences are also important, and the following sections describe both the differences and the similarities.

User BIWs

User BIW

A BIW that meets a specific user need but from which data is never further replicated within the data warehouse.

User BIWs are created to satisfy the business needs of an end user or a group of end users. Their contents are defined solely to meet the needs of those users, and when the users declare themselves to be finished with a user BIW, it can be discarded.

Figure 10-1 shows the population of a user BIW where data from three different BDW tables meets the user's business need. These tables are joined in the BIW population step. End users can then query this data, create views, and so on. In any case, there is no need to repeat the join process for any other user activity. The BIW thus both simplifies the user's view of the data and improves the overall efficiency of the data warehouse.

User BIWs can reside on any platform. User BIWs used by a group of end users can reside on a LAN server, a departmental machine, or a mainframe. They are often stored in relational databases, although some file-based systems do occur. An executive information system is an example of a group user BIW.

User BIWs created for individuals also exist. They often reside on the LAN or on an individual's own PC—in a spreadsheet, desktop database, or query tool. To qualify as a BIW, the data must be read-only once it is loaded into the BIW. If the user modifies the data contents after the population step, it becomes personal data and thus lies beyond the bounds of the warehouse.

The main characteristic that distinguishes a user BIW from a staging BIW is that data is never replicated further from a user BIW. This is the end of the chain of data within the warehouse. Any further copying or replication of the data occurs at the end user's sole discretion, and so is beyond the control of the data warehouse.

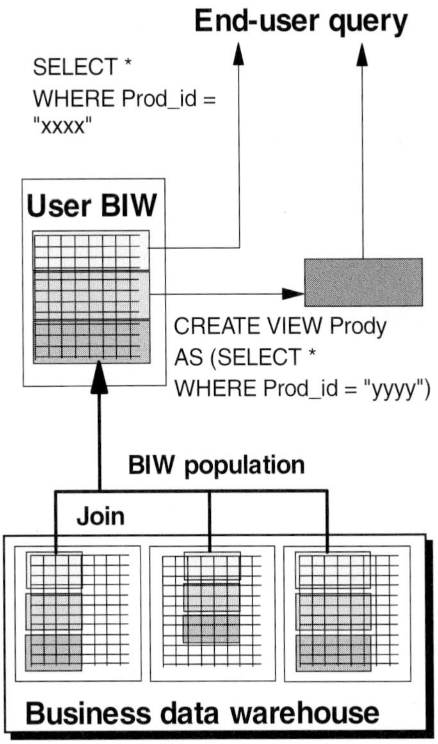

User BIWs represent the data boundaries of the warehouse. In a general text such as this, their definition (when is a user BIW not a user BIW?) is deliberately left a little vague. This is because there is no general answer as to which personal data should be included in or excluded from the data warehouse. In each warehouse implementation, however, the designers must carefully define the boundaries in consultation with the end users. How much personal data is included in the data warehouse varies by user type. For example, highly skilled business analysts require more freedom to manipulate personal data than senior management does. The business value of the data is another factor to consider. Thus, data summarized at the corporate balance-sheet level requires greater control than a departmental budget analysis.

Figure 10-1: Using the user BIW

Based on these considerations, we can draw a boundary to maximize data integrity and allow sufficient end-user freedom to use the data as needed. Once that boundary is drawn, a number of conclusions spring from it:

- Once data crosses outside the warehouse boundary, it can only reenter through a managed and controlled reconciliation process. Such data is thus analogous to external data as described in Chapter 7.

- Data in a user BIW cannot be used as a source for other BIWs within the warehouse. If a user BIW turns out to meet this business need, it must be redefined as a staging BIW and the appropriate controls on it put in place.

Thus, it should be clear the data warehouse architecture can define the borders of the data warehouse only in principle. They are policed by the end users themselves, who must be aware of the consequences of personally modifying data and reinserting it into the overall management information process.

Staging BIWs

Staging BIW

*A BIW provided
for a specific
business need
but which is
controlled and
managed to
ensure consistent
replication to
user BIWs in
addition to
direct use.*

The concept of a **staging BIW** can further optimize the overall performance of the data warehouse. As usual, optimization of performance comes at the expense of data volumes and requires added controls to ensure data quality. We can best understand the rationale by considering an example.

Referring back to Figure 10-1, let's assume that a number of end users in the sales analysis department do the same type of sales analysis but focus on different product lines. Each user, therefore, uses the same data structure but a different subset of the data records. Initially, they all use the same BIW, which is sourced from the BDW, by a join of the sales, customer, and product tables in the BDW. Each user then selects the required subset (based on product number) as part of each query. This approach works well but can have some drawbacks. Each query includes either an explicit or implicit selection statement. If explicit, then the user must repeat it in each query. An implicit statement (which is provided through a predefined view) improves the security and usability, although views may be subject to certain usage restrictions.

It may therefore be appropriate to provide each user with his or her own BIW. However, if all the BIWs are directly populated from the BDW, the three-table join mentioned above must be repeated to populate each BIW. This is not the most efficient approach. Introducing a staging BIW, shown in Figure 10-2, is the answer. The table join occurs once during its population, and then the product-based selections are made when populating the user BIWs from the staging BIW.

In practice...

*Introduce staging
BIWs only where
they will improve
the overall per-
formance of the
BIW population
step.*

Because a staging BIW is the data source for a number of user BIWs, it is subject to more control and management restrictions than is a user BIW. In particular, changing or deleting it will affect in some way all the user BIWs sourced from it. In general, the central or departmental IS function should control and manage staging BIWs, for the same reasons as they do the BDW. Creation of staging BIWs must be subject to strict controls. Once a staging BIW is created, it is difficult to delete later because of the possible effects on user BIWs sourced from it.

We should note some further characteristics of staging BIWs:

- Because they are a source for multiple user BIWs, staging BIWs are usually restricted to a standard relational database, residing on some common platform.

- BIW population may occur in two phases, the first populating the staging BIW, and a second, later phase that populates the user BIW.

- The transformations involved in populating a staging BIW from the BDW cover a wide set of functions. In the case of populating a user

BIW from a staging BIW, transformation is generally simpler; often it is restricted to selecting a subset of the data in the staging BIW.

- A staging BIW is often the optimal approach for supporting departmental needs, because it stores the set of data required by the department. This data is optimized for that department's informational needs, both by eliminating unneeded data and by denormalizing the required data.

- Where business needs demand that the data be physically partitioned for additional security, the staging BIW allows an extra level in the security hierarchy.

Sharing information

A group of end users working cooperatively often needs to share information within the group. A staging BIW can support this need. In this case, however, its data is sourced not from the BDW but rather from the individual user BIWs. Clearly, such sourcing contravenes the principle stated throughout this book that data should flow unidirectionally through the layers of the architecture. Nonetheless the need exists, and sharing the data by using the data warehouse emphasizes the role of the warehouse as the single source of information in the organization.

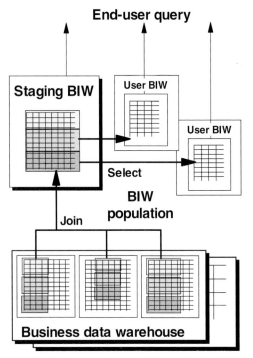

Figure 10-2: Using the staging BIW

Any staging BIW used to satisfy this need, should be treated differently from other staging BIWs, because in purely architectural terms it is not really a BIW. Thus, it should contain no data sourced directly from the BDW. It should also be clearly identified as a shared resource containing data that has not been subject to full quality control.

10.2 Modeling BIWs

When designing the BDW, the use of data modeling techniques is mandatory. Data modeling is also usual in the construction of modern operational applications. This is because application developers widely accept that the benefits accruing from the consistency of data meaning and usage across the user population for these systems outweighs the cost.

The situation for BIWs is less clear-cut. The principal reason for this ambiguity is the range of audience size for a BIW. At one extreme, the audience may be a single user; at the other extreme it may be a whole department, or everybody performing a similar function across the whole company. Where the audience of a BIW is small, the benefits of consistency in data usage and meaning diminish, and modeling is difficult to justify. However, there is significant value in a number of other ways, which will become apparent in the following sections. We also describe situations where modeling is either inappropriate or impossible.

Enterprise data modeling for BIWs

In a logical flow of the definition of a data warehouse, the final stage in the modeling process is building the model of the derived data that resides in the BIWs. The starting point, therefore, is the generic ERM and its physical implementation in the BDW.

Ideally, the business need identified for the BIW falls within the scope of the data that has already been modeled and implemented in the BDW. The objective then is to take a subset of that model, within the application scope, down through the logical application views and physical data design layers to achieve an agreed database design for the derived data in the BIW. Modeling at this level is essentially traditional application-level modeling where the scope of the model is limited to a particular set of business needs. Figure 10-3 shows this situation.

As the BDW progressively grows to cover the entire company, this ideal situation, where the data scope of the BIW model falls completely inside that of the BDW data model, becomes the norm. In the early stages of BDW implementation, however, a second situation often arises. This occurs when the data scope of the BIW model only partially overlaps with that of the BDW model, as shown in Figure 10-4.

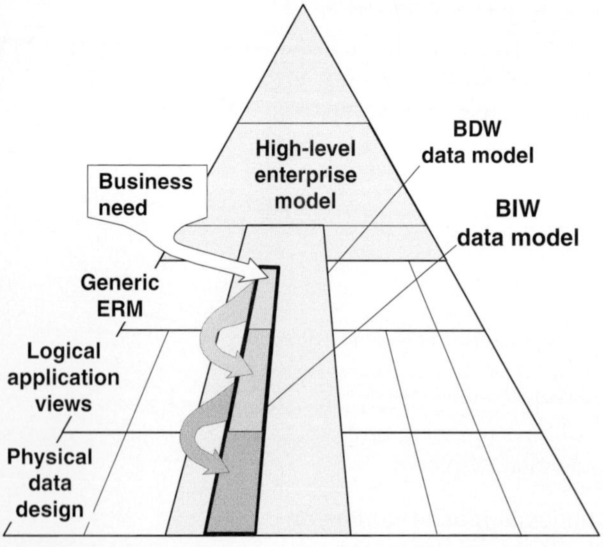

From a business point of view, what this represents is the case where the users' need is mainly in one subject area, but where one or two data items lie beyond that subject area. When only one or two segments of the generic ERM have been defined, and an even smaller subset physically realized in the BDW, it often happens that some of the data the end user requires is not available in the BDW.

While the purist might insist that such a BIW should not be built, the pragmatic view is that, if it is required by the business, especially if urgently, and if a possible source

Figure 10-3: *Modeling the BIW—the ideal situation*

exists in the real-time operational data, then it should be made available to the end users. And where the end users include the CEO, it is difficult to say no!

In modeling terms, this view leads to modeling some pieces of data that are not based on the generic ERM, but relate more closely to some existing models of the real-time data, as shown in Figure 10-4. (If the operational system is not modeled, there is an implicit data model, but it may have to be reverse-engineered from the code and data structures.) Because the generic ERM is not the source of these models, the designers must clearly identify definitions derived from them in order to highlight potential reconciliation difficulties. This annotation will also support the future update of these parts of the BIW model when the generic ERM expands to cover this area.

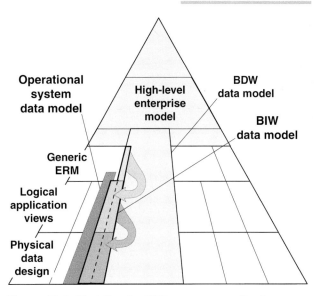

Figure 10-4: *Modeling the BIW—a common situation*

From the viewpoint of the physical implementation, these data elements come directly from the source operational applications rather than from the BDW. This type of sourcing leads to **warehouse bypasses** as shown in Figure 10-5. Because operational data is distributed over a variety of platforms that differ from those on which the BIWs are implemented, such bypasses may be difficult to design, implement, and maintain.

These bypasses amount to the old-fashioned, quick-and-dirty approach to providing data in the informational environment. While needed, particularly in the early phases of a warehouse implementation, developers should use them sparingly and replace them as soon as practicable.

Application-level modeling

Chapter 6 introduced application-level modeling. As was pointed out there, application-level modeling is not very useful in designing the BDW because of its enterprise-wide scope. However, BIWs have a narrower scope, and are often built to reflect a single business need or the needs of a single department or group of users. As a result, traditional application-level modeling approaches can be effective for implementing this layer of the architecture.

The process of modeling BIWs, like all other areas of the data warehouse, focuses on data rather than process aspects. It aims at identifying the data needed to perform some business analysis, and then determining the data source—normally the BDW.

Application-level modeling has an apparent advantage over enterprise-level modeling in this area of the warehouse. Because it does not demand as broad a scope, it is generally considered to be cheaper. However, because the data in the BIW must be sourced from the BDW (assuming the data exists there), a mapping between the BIW model and the BDW model is required in any case. The additional support that enterprise-level modeling provides in this area may outweigh the cost saving associated with the narrower scope of application-level modeling.

Benefits of data modeling for BIWs

Given that BIWs are for end users, and that end users are expected to develop their own BIWs, the question we may ask is whether BIWs should be modeled at all. As with many questions in the world of data warehousing, the answer is that it depends on the circumstances. Data modeling for BIWs shows a number of benefits:

- Modeling does, of course, provide a formal methodology for documenting users' data needs. This documentation is an important source of input to the data warehouse catalog (DWC).

- Along with the BIW design, modeling also provides the mapping (defining the physical data sources and the transformations needed in BIW population) between the BDW and BIW data models. This benefit accrues only where enterprise-level modeling is used.

- Finally, modeling provides a means for the identification and documentation of data that must be sourced from the operational environment rather than from the BDW during the initial growth of the data warehouse.

However, there may be occasions when modeling is inappropriate. The two types of BIW—user and staging—and the number of users provide a basis for deciding when to model BIWs. We can distinguish three cases:

- Staging BIWs are designed for common use by a group of users and as a source for user BIWs. Modeling of staging BIWs is vital to ensure consistent usage and understanding of the data.

- Some user BIWs are also designed with many users in mind. Examples include executive information systems (EIS) and other business analysis tools based on a common data store. Again, modeling is important for the same business reasons as for staging BIWs.

- Other user BIWs may be conceived with one or two users in mind. Such data may even be personal data

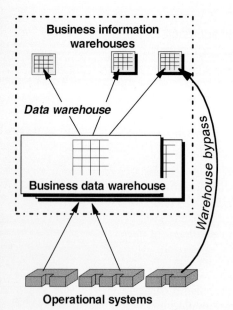

Figure 10-5: *The warehouse bypass*

used and controlled by a single end user. It is unlikely to be modeled. If this single-user data is considered to be potentially public data, there is a stronger case for modeling it, especially when the data has high intrinsic value to the business. However, modeling is still rare in this case.

10.3 Key influences on BIW design

Whereas the BDW design is highly normalized to align to the enterprise data model (EDM) and to provide the most general structure of data that is useful and common to the entire organization, BIWs are generally denormalized. This denormalization springs from two sources. One reason is to increase performance: the performance of queries on normalized data is rather poor because of the overhead of performing the same joins many times as a basis for many similar user queries. The second reason for denormalization of the BIW data structure is to reduce the complexity of the data from a user viewpoint. Any such complexity is often hidden today by more intuitive tools in the business information interface (BII), but as users attempt to use the data in new and innovative ways, the complexity cannot be entirely hidden by the end-user tools.

Beyond the statement that BIWs are usually denormalized, we must ask what type of denormalization is appropriate. The choice depends the users' data analysis needs. The remainder of this section describes these analysis needs, and allows us to categorize in Section 10.4 the types of BIW that exist and how they are commonly implemented today.

Analytic needs—from known to unknown

In the past, application developers have assumed that users' data analysis needs are well-defined and reasonably stable. Such an assumption leads to the conclusion that the developers can select and structure data in advance to meet this set of needs and that they can likewise build the required queries. This has resulted in the production of reports. Once upon a time, these consisted of tabular information, produced in vast quantities on green line-flow paper, and delivered at regular intervals to the user, who would scan them for the gems of information they contained. Nowadays, the report may be provided on a screen, with graphs of various types, and in a variety of fonts and colors. However, the basic assumption remains the same: the analysis need of the user can be determined in advance.

With the advent of decision support systems (DSS), another assumption became prevalent: user analysis needs are *not* known in advance, so the

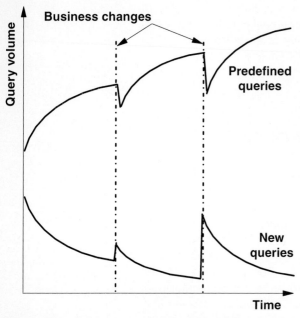

Figure 10-6: Query volume as a function of time

data required becomes all of the data, and the user is faced with the need to use sophisticated data analysis tools [Devlin and Murphy (1988)].

In fact, the reality lies in a combination of the two assumptions, and is dependent of the level of change taking place in the business itself, or in the environment external to the business. Figure 10-6 shows this by tracking against time the numbers of predefined queries (representing the known analysis needs) and new queries (the unpredicted analysis needs).

After any change that affects the business, the number of new queries shows a sharp rise as users try new ways of looking at the business. At the same time, the use of predefined queries shows an immediate decline because the previous ways of analyzing business performance are no longer useful. The size of the change in usage of both query types reflects how much the change in environment has affected the business. A relatively small change, such as introducing a new product line, results in relatively minor blips in the lines. A merger or a major external event such as deregulation of the market has a significant effect on the query volumes. Note also that technical changes (such as moving to a new query environment) also have a similar impact on the two curves.

A closer analysis of what happens between the discontinuities in the graphs leads to an important conclusion. As new queries are defined and executed after the business change, some will turn out to provide information likely to be useful on a regular basis. Such queries rapidly become the new generation of predefined queries. Other queries do not make the transition, as they are found to provide no useful information, or are rather exotic in business terms or difficult in technical terms. Such query development is always taking place and continues even in periods when there is no major business change. This latter type of activity is now generally described as data mining and gives rise to a particular type of BIW discussed in Section 10.4.

Over the years, developers have found that the queries end users most commonly use tend to revolve around analyzing business events along relatively few dimensions. For example, marketing analysis of sales data compares data from such categories as different time periods, different geographical regions, or different product types. Data is then aggregated along these dimensions to see major trends, and "drilled down" along the dimensions to understand the trends. Havelka and Khazanchi (1994) give a description of this process and its implications on information value for accounting data.

As we focus in on a specific business need, we reduce the scope of the required data by selecting a subset of the data, by reducing the number of dimensions along which it can be analyzed, and by restricting the level of detail stored through an aggregation process. For example, middle management may need to see sales summaries by country and district on a weekly basis as a predefined report. Such needs are supported by single-purpose BIWs, described further in Section 10.4.

An important trend, however, is away from generating reports at fixed intervals and toward producing reports only when particular events occur. This requires the existence of intelligent agents—software capable of understanding and detecting such events and initiating the required actions.

Between the two extremes of data-mining and single-purpose BIWs lies the general-purpose BIW. This type of BIW supports the most likely analysis dimensions, often by structuring the data according to a star schema, as described in Section 10.4.

> *In practice...*
>
> *Standard reports do not disappear with the introduction of the data warehouse—rather the warehouse becomes a new and more flexible source for them, freeing the developers of the operational systems of this responsibility.*

Time dependence

The analysis of business data concerns two different types of time dependence—snapshot and periodic.

The simpler case is where the user simply wants to see a snapshot of the business at some point in time. In this case, the underlying time dependence of the business data is ignored. The user needs a stable view of some aspect of the data as it existed at some moment in the past, or as it is predicted to be at some time in the future. Such snapshots can be used singly to answer specific questions about the state of the business, or they can be used in groups to discover trends.

Basing trend analysis on snapshots is not always sufficient. This is because peaks or troughs in the data, which may occur between the snapshots, are not visible. To see such detail requires a continuous view of the data as it changes over time—periodic data. As previously mentioned, any snapshot can be derived from a set of periodic data.

The implication for BIW designers is that there is usually a need for BIWs that contain only snapshots and for BIWs that contain both snapshots and periodic data. Managers and executives mainly use the former to follow the macro-trends in the business, while planners responsible for analyzing the business in detail need the latter.

Aggregation

Business data is aggregated on a number of dimensions, such as time, geographical or organizational unit, and a variety of categorizations of customer and product. Data aggregates (or summaries) play an important role in BIWs. They form the starting point for most users in understanding how the business is performing. This is because they have a higher information value density than sets of detailed data.

However, aggregates of data are less useful in understanding the reasons why the business has performed in a certain way. It is often necessary to carry the analysis from summary to detailed level in specific areas—known as drilling down—to gain this type of information. For this reason, aggregates on their own have limited business use.

Aggregation is an irreversible process. It takes detailed data as input and builds summaries, removing the detailed information *en route*. It is thus vital that the link back to the detailed data (either in the BIW or BDW) is maintained through the data warehouse catalog. This allows the user to drill down to the required level in the data.

Aggregation can be, and often is, performed as a part of an end-user query on the detailed data. However, BIWs can also store particular predefined aggregates. The decision whether or not to store any particular aggregate represents the usual tradeoff between processing and storage cost. If a particular type or level of aggregation is commonly used throughout the organization, it is worthwhile building it once and storing it.

Because aggregation is clearly a data transformation, we return to the subject in more detail in Section 11.5.

10.4 BIW implementation

The discussion in the previous section introduced three different categories of BIW, defined according to the type of data analysis required. In descending order of specificity of use, these are:

- single-purpose BIWs
- general-purpose BIWs
- data-mining BIWs

In each of these three categories one or more implementation approaches are possible. The choice of approach depends on the number of users to be supported, the volume of data stored, and the specific type of analysis required.

Single-purpose BIWs

Each **single-purpose BIW** is usually used by one individual or by a small group with a very narrow view of the business. In reporting terms, they correspond to a summary view of the business or a detailed report on a very specific area of the business. Today, they are usually implemented in spreadsheets, desktop relational databases, and report generation tools.

Design of a single-purpose BIW is usually straightforward. In reality, many such systems are not designed through any formal approach, but are built using the interfaces provided by the spreadsheet or other tool. This leads to an iterative, prototyping method of delivery. Such an approach is quite acceptable given the generally restricted audience. Performance is seldom a significant issue, and there is little need to enter the normalization/denormalization debate.

Note that the vast majority of spreadsheets fall outside the scope of the data warehouse because they contain personal data. Recall that the warehouse boundary drawn in Figure 4-1 places most personal data outside the scope of the warehouse.

> **Single-purpose BIW**
>
> *A user BIW designed to address a narrow, well-defined set of business needs.*

General-purpose BIWs

The **general-purpose BIW** is a database used by a number of users with similar data analysis needs, that has been denormalized to support these needs efficiently, and that can be queried in a reasonably general way. Examples include general management information systems (MIS), executive information systems (EIS), and market analysis applications.

Marketing analysis applications attract much attention today. In fact, in some cases, these general-purpose BIWs are mistaken for BDWs. The reason for this is probably their large size. In many cases, the marketing analysis application is the component of the warehouse that directly addresses the business requirement for which data warehousing was first introduced into the organization. However, the BDW and the general-purpose BIW do have different characteristics:

> **General-purpose BIW**
>
> *A user or staging BIW designed to meet the common needs of a group of users for ad hoc and pre-defined queries of a generally well-defined structure.*

- The BDW spans the enterprise, while the general-purpose BIW usually has a significantly narrower scope.

- The BDW contains only detailed data, while the BIW may contain both detailed and summarized data.

- The BDW is normalized for generality, while the BIW is denormalized to improve query performance and usability.

General-purpose BIWs are often implemented in relational databases, or in relational-like structures such as multi-dimensional databases. Depending on the data volumes, parallel databases may be required.

Users usually access general-purpose BIWs through a user-friendly interface, but may require some knowledge of data structures and usage in order to make full use of the potential and power of these BIWs. At the other end of the scale, EIS tools emphasize ease-of-use. However, such ease-of-use is obtained by limiting access to the data in novel or unplanned ways.

The more general systems are usually implemented on large relational databases that are centralized at either a company or departmental level. They almost always start out as user BIWs, accessed directly by a number of users. However, they tend to turn into staging BIWs, feeding multiple user BIWs, as end users demand specialized subsets of the data within them, or as users need specialized tools that require data to be stored in a particular structure. Direct usage of the data then decreases, and is eventually limited to specialists needing access to the full depth and breadth of the data.

Designers of these general-purpose BIWs, especially the larger ones used for marketing data analysis and similar applications, have to take into account the fact that they cannot know in advance the precise nature of each user query. However, the observation mentioned previously—that the majority of analysis takes place along a relatively small set of dimensions—allows developers to optimize a design for query along these dimensions. This design—the star schema—is an important aspect of BIW design.

The star schema

The name *star schema* reflects the appearance of a database designed according to this approach. It consists of one or more fact tables, around which a set of dimension tables cluster.

Star schema

A database design, particularly suitable for ad hoc queries, in which dimensional data (describing how data is commonly aggregated) is separated from fact or event data (describing individual transactions in the business).

Fact tables contain the basic transaction-level information of the business that is of interest to a particular application. In marketing analysis, for example, this is the basic sales transaction data. However, before this transaction data is placed in a fact table, any field that is regularly used as an analysis dimension for this data is replaced or supplemented by a reference (via a foreign key relationship) to the appropriate dimension tables. Fact tables are large, often holding millions of rows, and mainly numerical.

Dimension tables, on the other hand, are usually small in comparison to fact tables and contain more descriptive information. Dimension tables contain the data needed to place transactions along a particular dimension. In a marketing analysis application, for example, typical dimension tables include time period, marketing region, product type, and so on.

Figure 10-7 shows an example of a simple star schema consisting of a fact table of sales and three dimension tables of product type, time period, and market. The primary key of the fact table consists of product code, period

Period code	Year	Quarter	Month
002	1996	1	February
003	1996	1	March
...			
012	1996	4	December

Dimension table: time period

Market code	Country	Region	Outlet
1004	England	London	ASD
...			
1045	France	Paris	QWE
...			
2105	France	Cannes	ZXC

Dimension table: market

Dimension table: product

Product code	Brand	Package type	Description
14003	Rsx	Plastic	1" widget
...			
15125	Kph	Paper	2" gizmo
...			
15435	Kph	Can	1" widget
...			

Product code	Period code	Market code	Units sold	Sell price
14003	012	1004	3	7.40
15125	002	2105	5	10.25
15435	003	1045	5	3.56
10631	002	2003	6	3.45
42310	004	1041	4	6.55
20498	025	1004	11	11.25
34129	003	1314	5	5.43
21435	004	2423	8	5.67
63474	016	1567	2	8.12

Fact table

Figure 10-7: *A simple star schema*

code, and market code, each of which is also a foreign key linking to its respective dimension table. In this example, the key is not unique, because more than one sale of the same product can occur in the same time period, in the same outlet. In this schema, there exists a one-to-many relationship between a row in a dimension table and rows in the fact table.

A number of extensions of this approach also exist, and Poe (1996) covers these in some detail.

The major advantage of the star schema is the variety of queries that it can handle in an efficient way. In the example shown in Figure 10-7, analyzing the sales data by year, quarter, or month is possible on the time dimension without resorting to a table scan. Similar varieties of analysis are possible on the other two dimensions. A second point in favor of the star schema is that it matches well to the way end users perceive and use the data, thus making it more intuitively understood.

On the other hand, this design does make some assumptions about the behavior of users that may or may not be borne out in practice. For example, in Figure 10-7, the time dimension includes neither week nor day. This is a design-time decision. If, however, users need to analyze data at a weekly or daily level at some later date, problems will occur. If the fact table contains the actual sales date (as well as a reference to the time-

In practice...

Don't use a star schema for the BDW, because it is not general enough; however, it is ideal for BIWs.

period dimension table), the analysis will be possible but inefficient. If the fact table does not contain the actual sales date, the BIW will need substantial rebuilding to add the additional entries to the dimension table and to rebuild the index on the fact table. However, when the base information exists in the BDW, this task is much simpler than if the database were sourced directly from a number of operational systems.

This type of problem emphasizes again why this schema is appropriate for the BIW level, which can be specifically tuned for good query performance, but is not suitable for the BDW level, where completeness and generality of use are the primary drivers.

Data-mining BIWs

Data-mining BIW

A user BIW designed to meet the needs of data-mining tools, and generally very large in volume.

In terms of specificity of usage, a **data-mining BIW** is, of course, the least specific. Obviously, if you knew specifically what you wanted to find, never mind how to find it, you wouldn't be data mining! **Data mining** is a method of searching data for unexpected patterns or relationships using a variety of tools and algorithms.

The most basic requirements for data that will be mined are that it be cleansed and that it be as complete as possible. Because the BDW is the first place in the three-layer architecture where this requirement is fulfilled, it is the logically correct level at which to undertake data mining. However, its physical implementation may not make it suitable. This is particularly the case when the data in the BDW is archived after the shortest possible time due to storage-volume considerations. Also, some data-mining tools work only with particular types of database or file, which may differ from the kind used in the BDW.

For both these reasons, the better approach is to build a data mining BIW, populated from the BDW. This allows the warehouse developers to perform any further transformations required, in terms of either logical content or physical structure, before making the data available to the data-mining tools. Needless to say, data-mining BIWs are by nature very large, and it is likely that when finished with, they will be erased as soon as possible.

It is not the intention of this text to describe data-mining techniques. For a full description of such techniques, as well as the rationale for using them, see Adriaans and Zantinge (1996).

Some technology considerations

Parallel databases

In general-purpose and data-mining BIWs, parallel databases play a significant role today. This is due to the ability of such databases to efficiently handle *ad hoc* queries on large tables without the need for predefined indexes on every possible search key. The underlying implementation of the parallel database—in terms of its partitioning scheme for data and even at a physical hardware level—provides different advantages for differing usage types.

Some of the factors affecting the use of parallel technology in the BDW, outlined in Chapter 8, are also relevant for BIWs. There are two main differences:

- BIWs may be subject to substantial levels of *ad hoc* queries.

- BIW population (discussed in Chapter 11) is less likely to require the complex constructive merge technique needed in BDW population.

As a result, parallel databases optimized for query at the expense of update pose less of a problem at the BIW level than they do in the BDW.

Tuning parallel databases in BIWs is somewhat easier than in the case of the BDW. This is because BIW usage, although still very unpredictable, is often restricted by its focus on a particular division of the organization or set of business problems. Thus, while tuning the BDW has to take into account sales, production, and personnel data, a marketing analysis BIW only has to deal with sales data.

Physical design, principally the choices of how to partition the data and how to balance data across partitions, is the key to the efficient performance of BIWs using parallel databases [Ferguson (1995)]. The initial design of these BIWs is simplified because of the prior existence of the data in the BDW and the possibility of analyzing value distribution patterns there. Indeed, because the data already exists in a cleansed and easily accessed form, the opportunity exists to test a number of partitioning approaches.

Bit-mapped indexing

Traditionally, relational databases use B+ tree indexing techniques to provide indexes on those columns likely to be used as search keys. Further explanation can be found in Date (1995). While such indexes are efficient in the type of processing found in operational systems, some vendors promote an alternative approach called bit-mapped indexing for querying data [French (1995)].

A *bit-mapped index* contains a bit array for each possible value of the indexed field. Each bit is set on or off depending on whether the corresponding row contains the value associated with that array. The size of each array in bytes is clearly the number of rows in the table divided by 8. Thus, for an 8-million-row table indexed on the field representing the U.S. state where a customer resides, the index consists of 50 arrays, each of 1 megabyte (MB).

The approach dates back to the 1960s and was considered suitable only for indexes built on columns of low cardinality (where the set of possible values that the data can take is small). Recent advances have increased the cardinality supported, giving the approach a new lease of life. Reports suggest significant query performance gains for certain types of query, coupled with smaller index sizes. Index build time is reported to be longer than for traditional B+ trees. Although too early to draw firm conclusions, the characteristics just mentioned closely match the requirements of the BIW layer of the data warehouse.

OLAP and multi-dimensional databases

The term *On-Line Analytical Processing (OLAP)* has been invented in recent years to represent the opposite of *On-Line Transaction Processing (OLTP)*. In many ways this is simply a restatement of the old distinction between informational and operational systems described in Chapter 2, but with added emphasis on some special characteristics of the usage of such data. Key characteristics include:

- large data volumes, potentially in sparsely populated arrays

- consolidation upward and drill down along many dimensions

- dynamic viewing and analysis of the data from a wide variety of perspectives and through complex formulae

The underlying rationale is that users often view and analyze data multi-dimensionally, using hierarchical segmentation along each dimension. Thus, a user may analyze sales along the time dimension (such as months within quarters within years), along the geographical dimension (cities within regions within countries), and along the organizational dimension (salespersons within branches within territories). We can conceptualize this approach as a cube, or even a hyper-cube that has more than three dimensions of analysis.

While well accepted as a description of a valid and important user requirement, there is much debate about how best to implement it.

On one side of the debate, the vendors of OLAP servers and multi-dimensional databases—software specifically designed to address the above requirements—argue that relational databases are incapable of efficiently meeting these needs and propose specially optimized software.

On the other side of the debate, vendors of relational databases and decision support tools that operate against such databases point to star schemas, parallel processing, and improved indexing technologies, which allow relational databases to handle such data efficiently while allowing the front-end tool to provide the multi-dimensional view.

While the performance aspect is important, technology can readily help in both approaches to address the need. At any one time, either approach may be favored on performance grounds, but technological advances usually result in passing that advantage back and forth between the competing approaches.

Of more importance is the management and maintenance of the environment. In this area, relational databases, given their longer history and wider acceptance, have some clear advantages. We can see this by evaluating how each method—OLAP and relational databases—handles the following issues:

- What systems management facilities (such as archive and retrieval, security, and performance tuning) does each method support?

- How do they maintain the data—through refresh or update mode?

- How open are the interfaces, allowing access and use through multiple different tools?

- What support does each method provide for linkage to an EDM?

- How easy is it to change the underlying dimensional structure to accommodate business changes?

A final point to consider is how an OLAP server or multi-dimensional database fits into the three-layer architecture of a data warehouse. The positioning proposed here is as a BIW, sourced from the BDW. Some vendor approaches suggest that the OLAP server can obtain its data from a wide variety of sources, including flat files, hierarchical databases, and so on—basically the operational systems. Such an approach, while technically feasible, runs counter to the whole intent of data warehousing, because it ignores the inherent lack of data consistency between such sources.

10.5 Historical data in BIWs

Analysis of historical data is one of the key needs supported by data warehousing. The BDW is where a definitive set of historical data is first built, and may appear, at first sight, to be the ideal place to satisfy this need. However, its enterprise-wide scope as well as usage and access considerations tend to mitigate against this. Historical data could also be stored in BIWs since this is the correct level in the architecture for user tasks such as analysis of past business performance and for all types of trend analysis. The outcome is that historical data may exist in both layers of the data warehouse. However, the volumes of data involved require developers to give special consideration to both storage and performance.

In order to minimize the amount of data stored, we could envisage storing the one and only copy of historical data in the BDW. However, as previously described, the normalized design of the BDW can lead to excessive table joins, which impacts performance and increases the complexity of query design.

At the other extreme, an approach that optimizes performance aspects would be to use the BIWs as the main store for historical data. Each BIW is designed for the best query performance, but the data may be duplicated in a number of BIWs. In this approach, the BDW simply becomes a staging area for historical data while it is combined and cleansed before moving to the derived data layer: little or no historical data is stored on a long-term basis in the BDW. As well as the potential problem of data volumes, this approach has the added restriction that the single, definitive source for historical data needed to support new historical analysis is generally archived and perhaps less readily accessible.

Because BIWs are populated for the specific needs of individual users or groups of users, historical data at this level is potentially transient. Sets of historical data are generated as required for particular analysis needs and retained only for the required periods of time.

In practice, a compromise between these two approaches is the most likely choice. This solution is further supported by considerations of archive storage, as Figure 10-8 shows. We can summarize this compromise approach as follows:

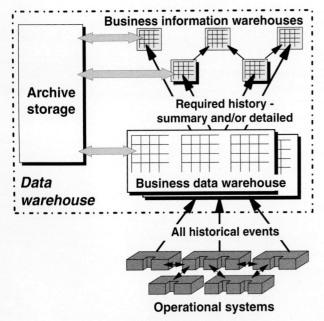

Figure 10-8: Historical data in the warehouse

- Business needs for historical data are analyzed, and the most common needs are supported through one or a small number of historical BIWs, each containing data that has been structured for optimal query performance. These are general-purpose BIWs.

- Such BIWs are available to a number of business functions and are expected to meet the majority of business needs for historical analysis. Depending on business needs, organizational structure, and technical limitations, historical BIWs may be either user or staging BIWs. Given their size, the latter is more common.

- Historical data pertaining to many years (likely more than 10) is stored on-line in these BIWs and may then be archived, maintaining its current structure.

- The data stored in the historical BIWs is built in the normal way from the reconciled data in the BDW, which is in turn sourced from the operational applications.

- The BDW stores historical data on-line for a shorter time period than do the historical BIWs. Typically this might be in the order of 1 to 3 years, but of course, this depends on business needs. Older data is available in the archive in its normalized form.

- The purpose of the historical data maintained in the BDW and its archive is to support unanticipated business needs that cannot be immediately supported in the historical BIWs. Performance of new queries on the BDW is likely to be a problem. If the new need is seen as recurring, the IS department may update the structure and contents of the historical BIWs to support this new requirement, or define a new historical BIW if necessary.

  If the structure of the historical BIW is changed to accommodate new business needs, the IS department may have to rebuild the archive of the historical BIW from that of the BDW.

Because of the longevity of historical data in the reconciled data layer, particularly when archived, it must be assumed that changes in the EDM will take place between the time the data is stored and when it is used. When this happens, it is necessary to map the old model to the new model. The most likely requirement will be to use the historical data according to the current data model. The mapping required here is precisely analogous to the mapping between operational and reconciled data, and the archived data can be treated as another operational data source. In fact, it is a relatively clean operational data source, because it has previously been reconciled against the old EDM. If the requirement is to use the new data according to the old EDM, the analogy also applies, but now the current reconciled data in the BDW is treated as the operational data source that must be reconciled with the old EDM.

The IS department should consider the output of this reconciliation to be a BIW rather than a part of the BDW. This is because in a formal sense, the outcome is not a valid representation of the business, either as it existed at the time when the archived data was originally captured, or at the present time.

In either case, the old EDM should also be archived when it is replaced by a new version. With current modeling techniques, this process must be performed manually as part of the warehouse maintenance processes.

10.6 Archive and retrieval in BIWs

Chapter 8 discusses archive and retrieval in general, along with its application to the BDW. Similar considerations apply to its use at the BIW level, and ideally the functionality should be identical in both cases. Figure 10-9 shows this relationship.

Data in the BIWs can be archived either at creation or deletion time. The choice depends on how the BIW will be used. For staging BIWs and those containing historical data—BIWs that are used widely in the organization and contain significant volumes of detailed data—a likely choice is to archive at creation time. Locally used, small, or summary BIWs are likely to be archived, if at all, before being deleted.

While archival is a mandatory process at the BDW level, warehouse implementers have considerably more freedom when dealing with the BIW level. Because all data is archived at creation time in the BDW, it follows that a BIW can be created or re-created at any time from a combination of data in the BDW and its archive. The decision, therefore, revolves around an assessment of the relative costs of building and maintaining separate archives, of retrieving from the BDW archive, and reprocessing the data through the required transformation routines. In most cases, the decision is to rely on the BDW archive.

As it does for the BDW, metadata plays an important role in the archive and retrieval processes for BIWs. It is the source of information used to

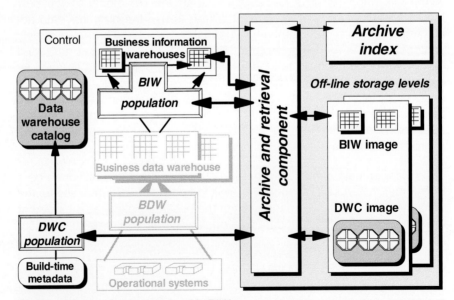

Figure 10-9: *Archive and retrieval in BIWs*

control the process. In addition, historical versions of metadata allow users to make full and consistent use of retrieved data.

10.7 Conclusions

Business information warehouses are the basic structures through which users gain access to the data warehouse. The vast majority of user access is likely to occur at this level, so developers structure BIWs to enable this access as far as possible. BIWs are the last stage in the chain that provides information to end users. The continuity and integrity of this chain is ensured primarily through the data modeling process. Where possible, even BIWs should be modeled, both as a formal mechanism for ensuring the completeness and quality of the user requirements, and as a means of defining the mapping required for their population.

We can distinguish two broad categories of BIW, staging and user BIWs, although both are formally part of the same layer of the three-layer data architecture. They allow an extra level of staging and permit common execution of transformation processes. This separation can have significant performance benefits and align with the organizational structure of many large companies.

The design of BIWs is more akin to that of traditional applications than is the design of the BDW. This is because BIWs have the narrow scope common to traditional applications. However, the similarity ends there, because BIW usage by end users is difficult to predict in advance. Designs that provide good performance over a range of the most likely ways of accessing the data in the BIW are therefore favored. In general, BIWs are substantially denormalized relative to the BDW.

BIWs exist in a range of sizes and for a variety of uses. In this sense, they represent the most variable component in the data warehouse. At one extreme, we may consider a single-user spreadsheet to be a BIW if it contains public data. At the other extreme of size and number of users, an historical marketing analysis database is also a BIW.

This range of size and uses leads to a variety of technical implementations. At the low end, spreadsheets are the most common implementation, along with PC- and LAN-based databases. As we move to larger and more general-purpose BIWs, relational databases become the norm. There also exist more specialized implementations to support particular data analysis or manipulation needs.

At the high end, a number of technological advances in the recent past have provided significant performance boosts to the type of processing common in BIWs. These include parallel databases and star schemas.

Other advances, such as bit-mapped indexing and multi-dimensional data-bases, also look promising.

Because of their position in the architecture, and indeed, because they are seen as the responsibility of user departments in many cases, archiving and retrieval is not mandatory. All BIWs can be re-created if required from the BDW and its archive. Except for the largest historical BIWs, which would take considerable effort to rebuild from the BDW archive, a separate archive is seldom necessary.

Chapter 11

Populating business information warehouses

The population of business information warehouses (BIWs) is relatively straightforward in comparison to the previous step of populating the business data warehouse (BDW). However, the techniques used are almost identical, so you should read this chapter in conjunction with Chapter 9, which explains most of the underlying concepts and terminology. The first section of this chapter explains how BIW population differs from BDW population.

As in populating the BDW, ***data replication*** is the generic function used to populate BIWs. This chapter discusses the BIW population process in the three steps previously identified:

- ***Capture*** of data from the BDW

- ***Apply*** of data to the BIWs

- ***Transformation*** of the data between the two environments

Defining which data to capture, how to transform it, and where to apply it is the responsibility of the administration component of data replication, which is discussed in Chapter 19.

11.1 BIW population—an introduction

The factors determining the approach to replication at the derived-data level of the architecture are rather different from those that drive BDW population:

1. The source data in the BDW is based on the EDM, and has been highly normalized, reconciled, and cleansed.

2. BIWs—containing the target data—are individually designed and de-normalized to meet the business needs of a specific sets of users.

3. The BDW resides in a relational database on one hardware/software platform, and usually in one or a small number of physical locations.

4. The target BIWs may reside on a variety of platforms, and in structure are usually highly distributed but relational or relational-like.

5. The source data in the BDW is periodic in nature and contains a complete record of the historical events that describe the business.

6. The BIW target data is either a snapshot of the source at a point in time or retains the periodic structure of the BDW.

This combination of factors generally allows both greater flexibility and simplicity in BIW population than is possible in BDW population. In fact, flexibility and simplicity are important aspects of any approach to BIW population. There is a wide variety of BIW platforms, the choice of which often lies with the business departments themselves. BIW population must therefore be capable of supporting these different targets without necessitating a complex and interdependent environment. Some of the responsibility for its definition and use may then be delegated to the business departments which define the data needs and may choose the BIW tools to be used.

BDW population is a closely integrated set of steps, both in design and implementation. In order to ensure the consistency and integrity of the BDW, the population processes from the various operational systems must work in harmony. BDW population is a ***push*** process where the operational data is "driven into" the BDW as it becomes available.

On the other hand, BIW population is largely independent for each BIW, and the characteristics of that BIW—size, type, and ownership—dictate how the population of each BIW is achieved. BIW population is likely to be a ***pull*** process for user BIWs, where each BIW determines how and when it will receive the data it requires. It is a push process for staging BIWs for the same control and management reasons as BDW population does.

11.2 Capture from the BDW

Section 9.4 defined six capture modes, which we review here. The following mode ignores any time dependence in the source data:

1. **Static capture**—a method capturing a static, time-independent view of all or a subset of the data in a source dataset

The next three modes—forms of immediate capture—result in a complete capture of changes in the source data if it is periodic, or an incomplete capture if the source is transient:

2. **Application-assisted capture**—depends on the application that changes the source data to also store the changed data in a more permanent manner

3. **Triggered capture**—depends on the database manager to store the changed data in a more permanent manner

4. **Log capture**—depends on the database manager's log as a more permanent store of the changed data

The last two modes—forms of delayed capture—ensure that all changes in a time-dependent source are captured, irrespective of whether the source data is transient or periodic:

5. **Timestamp-based capture**—selects data that has changed based on timestamps provided by the application maintaining the data

6. **File comparison**—compares versions of the data to detect changes

While all capture types play a role in BDW population, the situation in BIW population is considerably simpler.

File comparison is not needed because the BDW is a relational database.

The three methods that capture data as it is applied to the BDW—application-assisted, triggered, and log capture—are all possible but have limited use. The reason for this lies in the temporal reconciliation that is often needed as data arrives in the BDW. As described in Section 8.4, the complete population of a row in a BDW table may occur in stages, as data arrives from different operational systems due to operational, technical, or geographical constraints. The intermediate states in the population process are seldom, if ever, required in a BIW. All three immediate-capture modes thus require special processing to identify these intermediate states and ensure that they are not passed to the BIW.

In reality, the situation is made more difficult by the fact that most BIWs comprise data from more than one BDW table. Synchronization between these source BDW tables is also required before populating the BIW. We conclude, therefore, that these modes of capture are only useful where all columns in all the BDW tables that feed into the required BIW are updated completely and simultaneously.

Fortunately, the fact that the BDW consists of complete, periodic, time-stamped data means that these three modes of capture are seldom, if ever, required. Timestamp-based capture, and the occasional use of static capture, can do the job. In fact, this is a very positive conclusion, because these two modes, being straightforward SQL SELECT statements, are the simplest capture modes and should present little problem to even the most basic BIW population tools. However, it is still necessary to distinguish complete and incomplete records in the BDW from one another.

Of the two types of time dependence required, as identified in Section 10.3, the required data can be captured in the BDW as follows, using the start time and end time timestamp fields described in Section 8.4:

- **Snapshots**

  All or a subset of the columns of the BDW table is selected where the start time is prior to the time for which the snapshot is required and is the maximum for that business key. To obtain a snapshot of the current situation, the end time can be used instead of the maximum of start time for improved performance.

- **Periodic views**

  All or a subset of the columns of the BDW table is selected where the start time is prior to the time for which the view is required. Where the BIW is to contain a subset of the data in the BDW up to the present time, static capture can be used.

The above algorithms provide for full refresh of the resulting BIW. Enabling updates of the BIW is also straightforward. The algorithms are simply extended to capture only those rows that have a start time later than the last time the capture component was run.

11.3 Apply to the BIW

Chapter 9 identified four apply modes, which we review briefly here:

1. **Load**—the target dataset is loaded or reloaded, and any existing target data is completely replaced by the incoming captured data.

2. **Append**—incoming captured data is unconditionally appended to the existing target data. The existing data is preserved, but, depending on

the contents of the captured data and on the target DBMS, new records may duplicate existing ones or may be rejected.

3. **Destructive merge**—incoming captured data is merged into the existing target data. The keys of the existing target data are examined, and, where keys match between the existing and incoming data, existing data is updated accordingly. Otherwise, new records are added.

4. **Constructive merge**—similar to destructive merge but with one important difference. Where keys match, existing data is marked as superseded rather than being overwritten. Incoming records are therefore always added to the target.

Unfortunately, the choice of apply mode here is not as obvious as that for capture in the previous section. This is because the time dependence in BIWs can be either snapshot or periodic. In fact, all four modes of apply can be used, depending on the circumstances. For further details on load, append, and constructive merge modes, see Chapter 9, which describes their use in creating and maintaining the BDW. Destructive merge has been reserved to the present chapter, because it plays a role only in applying data to BIWs.

Snapshot data in BIWs

The creation of snapshot data in a BIW is straightforward. Load is the mode used to apply the initial data captured from the BDW to the BIW. Existing data, if there is any, is replaced in its entirety.

Load can also be used to maintain snapshot data in a BIW. This is the usual approach for a number of reasons:

- Many BIWs have proprietary data formats that require a specific population tool. In many cases, the tool does not support update or it must rebuild the file structure each time new data is added.

- Snapshot datasets are, by their nature, relatively small. Thus, the added complexity of update is seldom justified, even when possible.

- Update is based on the assumption that the target data has not changed since the previous time the replication tool ran. This is necessary because this mode captures only data changed in the source since the last run. Many BIWs, especially those containing only snapshot data, are directly under the control of end users, where it is difficult to guarantee that they have remained unchanged.

Clearly, snapshot data in BIWs may need updating in circumstances opposite to those listed above. Update replication should be considered only where the snapshot is large and resides in a controlled environment capa-

Destructive merge

A method of applying captured changed data to a target dataset that maintains an exact copy of the source data at the time of capture.

ble of being updated. This often equates to a relational database. Update is performed in this case using destructive merge.

Destructive merge

Destructive merge is so named because of its effect on records in the target BIW when new records arrive with the same keys as existing records. This apply mode physically applies updates and deletes to the corresponding records in the target in order to mirror the actions that occurred in the source. Records with new keys are, of course, appended to the target in the normal way.

Figure 11-1 shows a simple BIW table. Users of this BIW are interested only in the current product list, and not in the history of products that the company has offered in the past. The requirement, therefore, is to generate a snapshot in the BIW from the periodic data in the BDW.

Referring to the figure, we can see that on Sept. 2, four changed data records are merged into the existing data. Records 007 and 008 are new records and are simply appended to the target. In business terms, these are new products. Record 003 is an update of an existing record—an existing product has been changed—and the changed data replaces the corresponding fields in the target. Record 006 is deleted as a result of applying the changed data, because the company no longer offers this product. We can see that this update approach destroys the previous contents of data in fields, and indeed, entire records.

However, the outcome of capture followed by destructive merge is that the target becomes an exact copy of the source (or a subset of the source) at the time of capture. This does, of course, assume that the source and target were identical to start with and that all net changes in the source have been captured. This is precisely the effect needed to maintain a snapshot BIW of data in the BDW.

The advantage of this approach over a simple load is that it is likely to significantly reduce the volumes of data transferred between environments.

However, this approach has several disadvantages. First of all it adds complexity to the processing. Moreover, ensuring the integrity of the data is more difficult because it requires the

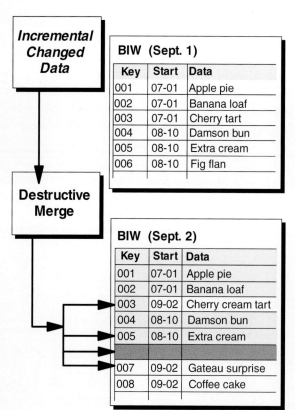

Figure 11-1: Destructive merge

complete and sequential application of all the changed data. In addition, while all types of physical BIW implementation can be refreshed using load apply, the use of destructive merge is confined mainly to BIWs implemented in relational databases. Other implementations, such as spreadsheets, multi-dimensional databases, and so on, are often quite limited in the apply modes they support.

In summary, destructive merge is used most often to maintain staging BIWs, which are large enough and suitably managed to benefit from this approach.

Periodic data in BIWs

BIWs containing periodic data are structurally identical to the BDW. Therefore, apply in this instance follows the pattern already described for BDW population in Chapter 9, to which you should refer for the details. This section describes how populating BIWs containing periodic data differs from BDW population.

BIW definition is not as closely linked to the enterprise modeling process as is the case for BDW definition. However, for larger staging BIWs and BIWs containing historical data, enterprise data modeling is highly recommended.

Initial population is carried out through the load and append modes of apply, as with initial BDW population.

When it comes to maintaining these BIWs, constructive merge is again a candidate. However, destructive merge can also be used, because both the source and the target are periodic. This means that an identical copy of the historical view in the BDW (including timestamps) can be maintained in the BIW, simply by copying across all changes. In fact, destructive merge is the preferred approach because it is technically simpler than constructive merge. Again, we must take into account the restricted use of update with non-relational database targets. The ability to use refresh mode only is a substantial drawback, because periodic datasets tend to be rather large.

As in the case of maintaining periodic data in the BDW, append can also be used for BIWs. As before, it is restricted to the situation where an end time field is not being used in the BIW. Whether this is a reasonable restriction on the design depends on how the BIW will be used. As discussed previously, end time is particularly useful in queries that must determine the time span for which a particular record is valid. If the BIW is used principally for trend analysis or is an events database, the end time timestamp can be omitted and append mode can be used.

11.4 Comparing the performance of update and refresh modes of replication

Update mode is often proposed as the most appropriate mode for data replication in the data warehouse. This approach does indeed have a number of advantages, but there are some instances, as already described, where the technically simpler refresh modes are a better choice. However, in BDW population only update mode is capable of creating the periodic data in the BDW from transient operational data. As a result, we compare these two modes of replication only in the context of populating BIWs.

Other than the ability to create periodic data, which is not needed in BIW population, the major benefit claimed on behalf of the update mode of replication is performance. This stems from the fact that update mode works only on changed records, the volume of which is usually considerably less than the volume of the full dataset in data warehousing applications. The proportion of data that is changed in the target in any particular replication run is determined by the rate of change of the source data and the time interval between incremental capture runs.

In many instances, the combination of the above two factors results in a percentage change in the target of less than 10% of the total number of records. The reduction in volume of data—to be captured, transformed, transferred, and applied—leads to both lower operating costs and a more even use of resources. Where replication occurs during a restricted batch window, these advantages can outweigh all other considerations.

However, at a record level, the update mode of replication is more costly per record processed than refresh mode is because:

- Incremental capture usually involves more processing than static capture, especially for triggered and application-assisted capture.

- Row sizes are slightly increased by timestamps.

- Apply has to identify corresponding rows in the existing target data and update them in both constructive and destructive merge.

In addition to the mechanics of capture and apply, the mix of record types within the set of changed data is also a major influence on the overall performance of update mode. Given the complexity of processing required in constructive merge for record changes and deletes shown in Section 9.8, we can see that the higher the percentage of simple adds there are in the changed data, the faster the overall update will be.

As a result of the number and type of factors involved, it is impossible to predict in any given situation whether refresh or update mode is more appropriate. Thus, it may be necessary to perform trial comparisons of the different approaches to ascertain how to achieve the best results.

However, one relationship, seen in a few cases, is a useful starting point for such trial comparisons. This relationship is between the overall processing cost and the percentage of source records that have changed since the most recent run of the capture component.

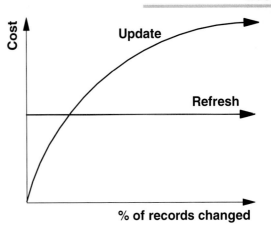

Figure 11-2 shows that the cost of refresh mode is independent of the percentage of records changed. This is due to the fact that the whole target is rewritten in any case. The relationship for update mode, however, turns out to be non-linear because of the differing costs of capture

Figure 11-2: *Performance of update and refresh modes as functions of data change rate*

and apply at varying dataset sizes. The shape of the curve and its eventual height in comparison to the refresh line is dependent on the numbers of deletes or updates to existing records relative to the number of records added into the target data set.

In any case, the conclusion is clear. At low percentages, update mode is an effective approach as a result of the smaller volume of records processed. This advantage over refresh mode quickly disappears, however, due to the higher cost per record of update. The percentage where the crossover occurs varies, but tends to be in the range of 10% to 25%.

11.5 Transformation

In comparison with the transformation required in the BDW population process, transformation between BDW and BIW is cleaner and can be described in a more formal way. This is a direct result of the three-layer architecture, which separates reconciliation from derivation. Because the data in the operational systems is often poorly modeled and inconsistent, transformation in BDW population is difficult. However, because the BDW is modeled and internally consistent, we can often easily describe in formal modeling terms the transformation of data from that structure to BIW structures that satisfy individual business needs.

Furthermore, BDW population often leads to the creation of data elements that are very difficult to obtain from the source operational data, because of timing or semantic mismatches between the operational systems. On the other hand, BIW population leads to the creation of data elements that are easier to calculate than those in the BDW. From a technical viewpoint, a further simplification arises from the fact that the source is relational and the target is either relational or relational-like in structure.

Transformation functions

Chapter 9 has already described the transformation functions. Most of the functions described there are also used in BIW population. The underlying purpose for each of these functions is the same—to make it easier for the end user to use and understand the data.

Selection

Selection is obviously necessary to reduce the number of records and fields moving from the BDW to the BIW. This function occurs as part of the capture process, selecting subsets of data from BDW tables on either the attribute or occurrence dimensions.

Selection of a set of fields excluding the key field of the record—a special case of subsetting on the attribute dimension—is useful in BIW population. This leads to the generation of classification categories of the input data. For example, a delivery record containing, among other fields, names, addresses, cities, and countries of the receivers of the deliveries could be subsetted to produce output records containing only the fields city and country. The result would be a list (following elimination of duplicates) of all cities and countries delivered to and only those.

Separation/concatenation

Separation is used in BIW population to subset data in the BDW for multiple targets in different BIWs. An example of separation is as follows. A complete customer record in the BDW contains details of name, addresses (legal, delivery, billing, etc.), and credit rating. For decision support purposes, the shipping department needs to analyze customers only by delivery address, while the credit control department is interested only in credit ratings. Separation provides two or more output records, each containing the key but with different non-key fields for each input record.

BIW population rarely uses concatenation because of the high level of normalization of the data in the BDW.

Normalization/denormalization

Normalization is not required in BIW population because the source (the BDW) is already normalized.

Denormalization *is* required because the highly normalized data in the BDW must be transformed into denormalized BIW data in order to be both easy to use and perform well. This is a many-to-one record transformation, taking a number of records from two or more normalized tables in the BDW and joining them on the basis of their keys into one, denormalized table in the BIW.

The process involves joining tables based on primary and foreign keys. Thus the customer and orders tables that exist separately in the BDW may be combined in a BIW using the foreign key "Customer" contained in the orders table. The result is that each order record in the BIW contains customer details.

Aggregation

This is one of the most prevalent and important transformation functions occurring in BIW population, but is not used in the BDW population step at all. It is used to build summaries, averages, totals, etc.

Aggregation is an important process in increasing the informational density of data. This implies that a given volume of summarized data is of greater informational value to the organization than the same quantity of detailed data, and is thus more useful at a management or executive level.

Mathematically, aggregation consists of grouping the data according to some criterion and totaling, averaging, or applying some other statistical method to the resultant set of data. This process is technically rather simple and is well supported by relational databases. Examples include:

- summaries of sales by time period, such as daily, weekly, or monthly

- summaries of expenses by geographical area

- averages of productivity by organizational unit or other grouping

The aggregation function is significantly different from the previously described transformation functions. It can operate only on sets of identically structured records. For each set of detailed input records, the output is a smaller set of summary records where significant amounts of detail have been removed. In fact, the act of aggregation leads to a loss of data content and is irreversible [Havelka and Khazanchi (1994)].

> **Aggregation**
>
> *A transformation function that groups and mathematically combines data from a set of detailed records.*

Conversion

Conversion provides data that is more usable in the BIW by translating individual fields into more user-friendly terms.

The examples of conversion shown for BDW population in Section 9.10 are also applicable to BIW population. In addition, the conversion of codes into business terms is a common requirement for BIW population.

Enrichment

Enrichment is used to generate fields that are commonly required in the BIW, but would need to be calculated from two or more fields at the BDW level. As in BDW population, we can identify single-field, multi-field, and multi-record cases.

Single-field enrichment uses as input a single field within one record and creates a new field that represents a different view of the same data. We could argue that this new view of the data is entirely redundant, since users could deduce it at any later time provided that the input field used as the basis for the enrichment also exists in the BIW. However, we can also view the new field as a simplification of the data, which may be more useful to the target audience than the base data itself, or as a categorization of the data according to a rule defined and set by personnel outside the target audience. The following examples clarify this point:

- setting a credit-worthiness field to "good" or "bad", depending on the value found in the account-balance field

- allocating a sales total to one of a variable set of organizational units, based on the geographical region in which the sales occurred

- creating a categorization of accounts based on age of customer, postal code, or other characteristic

Multi-field enrichment allows interaction between the fields within a single input record. The outcome may be the creation of a new field in the BIW output record or the update of an existing field. Examples are:

- creation of a field containing a demographic category, where this category depends on a combination of the age, sex, and income

- extension of a product description field to include attributes such as weight, color, or size, which are to be found in separate input fields

In multi-record enrichment, the input fields are no longer restricted to the same source record, but may come from more than one record. This obviously increases the technical complexity of the process but leads to a higher value output. Although the argument about data redundancy is quite strong in the case of single-record enrichment, it loses much of its weight in the multi-record situation. The redundancy, of course, still logically exists. However, it would be unreasonable to expect any BIW user to be capable of combining the required data at a later stage.

The output of multi-record enrichment is always the creation of one or more new fields in the output. In some cases, the new field represents business information that previously did not exist. An example is creating a sales analysis code that represents the success of selling different product types into different market segments, requiring a logical combination of product sales numbers and customer market segmentation data.

Relating transformation to the data model

Of the preceding transformation functions, denormalization and aggregation are both well supported by SQL, as are the more straightforward types of conversion using lookup tables. Furthermore, we can formally relate these operations back to the data models of the source (BDW) and target (BIW) datasets and the mapping between them. As a result, it is possible to consider a scenario in which the transformation required is automatically generated by the tools on behalf of the user who has defined the BIW, without intervention by the highly skilled (and expensive!) analysts and programmers of the IS department.

This scenario is seldom possible to realize with today's transformation tools, because they have a limited user interface, and because they base their mapping definitions on physical database structures rather than on the business definitions of the data model, as discussed in Chapter 6.

11.6 BIW population—implementation aspects

Bear in mind that BIWs are often implemented outside the control of the IS department, which is responsible for the data warehouse as a whole and for the BDW in particular. Assigning responsibility for many BIWs to business departments, groups, or even individuals is a quite deliberate decision, empowering the business organization to use their data when they need it and in the manner they require.

One implication of this decision is that BIWs are quite varied—as has already been described in Chapter 10. Another implication is that BIW population tools are equally as varied, and the extent to which these tools can be aligned to the capture, transformation, and apply components described above (and to the administration component covered in Chapter 19) is limited by the functions provided by the vendors of these BIWs.

The only area where it is reasonable for the IS department to expect to retain some level of control is in the population of staging BIWs. These BIWs are a shared resource, and so should be subject to common IS standards. As pointed out in Section 10.1, these BIWs are most likely to be implemented in relational databases, and for many reasons might well be implemented on the same hardware and software platform as the BDW. Such a choice is also of great benefit in BIW population, because it means that the infrastructure built to support the BDW will also be capable of supporting the staging BIWs.

For user BIWs, the lack of integration in their design and population with the wider data warehouse environment can be addressed through the data warehouse catalog and its user interface, the business information guide. The requirement is to provide a comprehensive definition of both the business meaning and implementation of the data in the BDW, so that the designer of these BIWs can input the definition into the tools provided by the BIW vendor for building the BIW and defining how to populate it. This process is, of course, considerably aided by cooperation between vendors to enable sharing and reuse of this metadata.

A further aspect that requires careful consideration in BIW population is the potentially highly distributed nature of this environment. This is described further in Chapter 18.

11.7 Conclusions

In terms of the underlying functions required, BIW population has much in common with BDW population. Both processes consist of capture, transformation, and apply components, and Chapter 9 has a detailed discussion of much of the underlying functionality.

In terms of replication function required, BIW population is simpler than BDW population. This is a direct result of the work that has been put into the design of the BDW. The high level of semantic, temporal, and technical integration and consistency achieved in the BDW allows the designer of the BIW population step to focus on the business content and meaning of the data. Capture components have only to operate on a single environment, and usually on a small number of physical platforms. Transformations are limited to those that can be achieved mainly through the use of standard SQL.

At an implementation level, BIW population is complicated by two factors: the variety of BIW types, and the limited functionality provided in the tools used today to populate BIWs. Examples of such limitations are an inability to use the update mode of replication, and the lack of a link to the enterprise data modeling environment.

The simplicity of BIW population is important for two reasons. First, it reduces the development effort in implementing BIWs—and if the data warehouse is successful, there should be a great number of such implementations. Second, it holds out the promise that users (albeit reasonably skilled users) can define the population step themselves, and through the use of replication tools significantly reduce the need to involve IS personnel in the process.

Chapter 12

User access to information

It may seem ironic that, for an architecture whose primary *raison d'être* is to support end users, we have had to wait until now to discuss end-user access to the data in the warehouse. However, it should not be surprising. The key purpose identified earlier for the warehouse is the need to provide consistent, understandable, and usable data. These goals can only be achieved by implementing the architecture described over the preceding chapters. Once that is done, end users are free to use the data in whatever way is necessary to achieve their business needs.

The goal of this chapter is not to describe the applications that can be built to support these business needs. Such applications are specific to different industries and to different functions within each business. However, all such applications and their users require a set of generic support functions. This chapter discusses this support functionality, which divides logically into two distinct areas—the transformation of business data into information, and the technical aspects of accessing the underlying data.

Any application that allows a user to access and manipulate business data in the warehouse contains elements of a *business information interface* **(BII)**. The BII provides the function needed to select data, perform any required analysis, store the results (both final and intermediate), and produce reports in any required format. This process transforms data finally into information. The BII also provides the ability to define, store, and manage procedures for some or all of this functionality.

Before data can be transformed into information, it must be physically retrieved from wherever it is stored. Because today's environment is increasingly distributed, it makes sense to separate out a *data access* component, which logically lies beneath the BII and which the BII and other components can invoke as required. Data access is the second component described in this chapter.

12.1 The business information interface

*Business
information
interface*

*The user's means
of selecting, ma-
nipulating, and
displaying data in
business termi-
nology, both ini-
tially and for later
reuse across the
organization.*

In any application, from the simplest BASIC program to the most complex business system, data acquires meaning only at the stage where it is presented to the user. For example, generating the most basic report consists of manipulating, structuring, and describing rows and columns of data in a way that is meaningful to an end user. The data in the underlying application is stored in a structure entirely different from the form the end user sees, and is separated from its descriptions. It is data and no more than data. However, by the time it reaches the user, through the medium of the report, it has been transformed into information.

The same applies to the warehouse. The transformation of data stored in the data warehouse into useful and usable information takes place in the final stages of the process and is mainly the responsibility of the *business information interface (BII)*.

Transforming data into information

Creating information—the basic process

The high-level stages in the transformation of data into information are:

1. **Defining the business need in data-related rules**

    The business need must first be translated into a set of rules, expressed in IS terms, that allows execution of the subsequent selection and manipulation steps.

2. **Selecting a subset of the data**

    The relevant data is gathered according to the rules defined in step 1.

3. **Manipulating the data**

    The selected data is complemented with additional calculated data—such as totals or averages—and transformed if appropriate, for example, by translating codes into meaningful terms.

4. **Associating the resulting data with its meaning**

    The resulting data is reunited with the metadata, so that, for example, we now know that we are talking about length in centimeters rather than the herd size of elephants.

5. **Structuring the information so that it is useful to the end user**

    The structure of the information presented may range from simple tables to complex graphical representations, and everything in between.

6. **Presenting the structured information**

This takes a variety of forms, from paper-based to electronic.

This set of steps, shown in Figure 12-1, is followed every time a user builds a query, and is present in every software tool that delivers information to end users, although with varying degrees of emphasis on the different steps. For example, basic spreadsheets and report generators focus on steps 5 and 6. Basic query or decision support tools emphasize steps 1, 2, and 3, although the level of support for step 1 varies enormously. However, today's tools cover all the steps to some extent [Walker (1994)].

Beyond the individual user

In addition, we must recognize that not all transformations from data to information are unique. Different people may perform identical sequences many times on different sets of data.

Thus, an end user, faced with the need for a set of business information, follows the steps outlined above and produces a report. In the interests of efficiency, this procedure should be repeatable, perhaps allowing for small variations in data or conditions. In the normal course of business, the company may find this procedure to be useful in other departments or even at a business-wide level. We therefore need a means to promote this procedure from the level of personal use to departmental or enterprise-wide use. In this way, the company as a whole can gain from the experience of each individual end user. Figure 12-1 shows the reuse of the process once it has been built.

In an environment of rapidly changing management information needs, this osmotic process—by which new procedures spread and become common

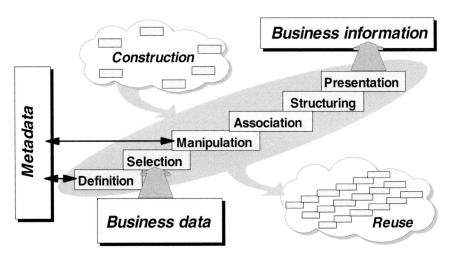

Figure 12-1: *The process of transforming data into information*

In practice...

The early growth and success of a data warehouse depends on its adoption by end users. A formal support structure enabling sharing and reuse of queries will speed user acceptance.

before being replaced by newer updated versions or entirely different procedures—is important. It is productive and allows for rapid change. It is also widely, if informally, used today.

There is a requirement, therefore, to provide an environment that encourages the management of the process, and prevents the spread of inconsistency in reporting—clearly a risk in such a scenario.

Creating information in the context of the warehouse

We can relate the six-step process outlined above to the three layers of the data architecture and to the data warehouse catalog (DWC). The process of populating BIWs addresses steps 2 and 3 and to some extent step 5. This is consistent with the definition of BIWs: given the size and scope of the data in the warehouse, it is reasonable to subject it to an initial selection and structuring process to provide a more manageable and understandable set for any end user.

Similarly, we can view BDW population as beginning the process of transforming data into information, although at this level, the transformation mainly involves reconciling inconsistent data and structuring the data in line with the EDM.

Step 4—associating the data with its meaning—deserves special focus in the warehouse context. The data architecture has defined the DWC as the repository for this metadata. It is the need for access to metadata that drives the close linkage between the BII and the business information guide (BIG), described in the next chapter.

However, prime responsibility for this process does lie with the BII, and it is within the BII that the major portion of the transformation of data into information takes place.

Requirements for the BII

The discussion in the previous section leads to a set of generic, high-level requirements for the BII:

1. The BII should be an intuitive and easy-to-use interface supporting the expression of any business need.

2. The BII must convert this need into a set of formal rules for selecting, manipulating, and transforming data into the required information.

3. The BII should include a means of storing the rules for future use.

4. It should be able to locate and use existing business needs or rules.

5. It should provide end users with an easy-to-use interface in order to modify existing rules.

6.   The BII should link to data storage in order to select the required data.

7.   It must have a set of data transformation and manipulation tools.

8.   The BII should have the ability to obtain definition and explanatory information (or metadata) and link it with both the data used and the business information produced.

9.   The BII should be able to format and structure information output in a variety of ways, both textual and graphical.

10. It should have the ability to pass the information output to other processes, such as electronic mail, charting programs, and so forth.

11. It should include a means of building a procedure consisting of all the steps needed and storing the resulting procedure.

12. The BII should have a procedure management facility to make existing procedures available and usable throughout the organization.

The structure of the BII

The requirements described above lead to a logical structure for the BII. This structure, shown in Figure 12-2, is intended to place the requirements in relation to one another and to position the BII relative to other functional components in the architecture of the data warehouse.

Within the BII, the **user interface** is the main source of control information to the other functions. Its primary interactions are with:

- the definition and association function, through which the business request is translated into data-oriented terms

- the structuring and presentation function, through which the business information is finally returned

- the procedure management function, through which new procedures are stored and existing ones retrieved

The **definition and association function** is the main control point for all aspects of query building and transformation specification. A variety of techniques—graphical, natural language, artificial intelligence, and so on—can, and probably will be required to, support different user aptitudes. This function also supports reuse of existing queries and parameterization of queries—allowing users to easily adjust selection or manipulation conditions by setting query parameters at runtime.

The overall aim is to isolate the user as far as possible from the IS view of the data and to focus on the business definition of the need. Such a representation of the required business analysis is often referred to as a

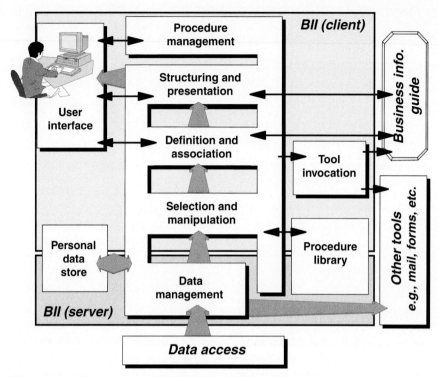

Figure 12-2: *The structure of the business information interface*

model in the DSS literature [Kaula (1994)]. Such models are process, rather than data, models and are stored in the data warehouse catalog (DWC) and accessed through the business information guide (BIG).

Definition and association uses the *selection and manipulation function* to build the query on the data. This function generates SQL or another data manipulation language that selects the appropriate data under a defined set of conditions (WHERE clauses) and sorts the result as required.

The definition and association function is also responsible for the subsequent association of business meaning with the returned data. In all these tasks, the metadata required is obtained through the BIG.

The *data management function* is responsible for all access to data. Such data may reside in personal storage or in the data warehouse. Data in personal storage is the sole responsibility of data management. As shown, personal storage is used in read/write mode. Data can be stored there for personal use by the user or by functions in the BII. However, once stored there, the data is effectively outside the bounds of the data warehouse, and its management is the responsibility of the end user. Data management supports this responsibility by providing information about versioning or time currency of data as appropriate. It is here, also, that data is prepared for export to other external tools.

The data management function relies on the data access component, described in Section 12.2, for all data retrieval from the warehouse. This ensures that data can be retrieved from any physical location or format.

The **structuring and presentation function** transforms returned information into the required format for use. This format ranges from simple textual reports, destined for printing, to complex graphical, multi-dimensional structures that the end user can view and directly manipulate.

Procedure management is responsible for constructing procedures involving functions supplied at all the lower levels and for the storage of such procedures in the procedure library. Procedures vary enormously in complexity. At its simplest, a procedure may be no more than an SQL query. At its most complex, it may contain a number of interlinked SQL queries on different databases, substantial analysis of the data returned, complex formatting and charting of the results, followed by their distribution to interested parties via electronic mail.

Procedure management also supports a number of ways to invoke procedures automatically. Some users need to know only about exceptional situations in the data. This need is supported by procedures that are automatically triggered when certain events or conditions occur. It is procedure management that controls such alerts or notifications. Some users require that their view of the data be updated at regular intervals. This requirement is met through the use of subscriptions, which are simply procedures that run at set intervals and dispatch a set of data or a report to the user. Procedure management is responsible for invoking subscriptions when needed.

Information about stored procedures is required in the DWC. Procedure management passes such information to the BIG for subsequent storage.

The BII is a client/server type of application. Substantial parts of the function related to query definition and the manipulation and presentation of the data are clearly best performed in the end user's workstation. However, other functions can have a distributed aspect. In particular, the procedure library is likely to be distributed over the local workstation and a commonly accessible server. This enables promotion of more widely useful procedures to a wider audience in the company. There are also reasons (such as data size) for cases in which the personal data store may partially reside on a server, complementing local storage.

Although the principal user of the BII is the end user, part of the procedure management function is clearly aimed at the administrator of stored procedures available in the warehouse.

In line with the main principles of data warehousing, the function of the BII described above focuses on read-only access to the data in the warehouse, particularly that residing in the BIW. In practice, the BII is a component of a larger process, requiring access to real-time data in both read-only and read/write modes. This is because the BII function is generally common to both personal data and the data in the warehouse.

Implementing BII functionality

A wide variety of tools exist today that provide the functionality described in the previous section. Unfortunately, most tools focus on particular aspects of this functionality, and effectively ignore the rest.

In terms of the business function supported, the tools fall into two broad areas: query-and-reporting tools and data analysis-and-prediction tools. Like all categorizations in a rapidly changing marketplace, some tools can be placed in either category or both. The purpose of the categorization is to simplify the process of evaluating and choosing appropriate tools.

We should also note that current research on the role of decision support systems (DSS) in organizational decision making clearly indicates that functionality from both categories is needed in all organizations [Winograd and Flores (1986), Wilson and Wilson (1994)]. Such variety ensures that the end users' view of data is not limited by traditional ways of analyzing it.

Query-and-reporting tools

Query-and-reporting tool

An end-user tool designed to support the definition of queries and reports where the analysis need is well understood in business terms.

Query-and-reporting tools are based on the premise that there is a single, definitive subset or summary of the data that will meet a particular business need.

These tools have evolved from the original need to put a more understandable face on the "bare-bones" data access language—typically SQL—through which programmers access data in databases. Closely following this need was the requirement to translate the output into a report format that could be easily related to traditional reports. As a result, such tools put a strong focus on the selecting, manipulating, structuring, and presenting functions of the BII.

While the user interface of such tools has greatly improved over the years, especially with the advent of windows-based front ends, these tools are usually more appropriate to users who are data-literate. This is because these tools had to retain the power and flexibility of the underlying data selection and manipulation features of SQL, and because they lacked any real links to the business meaning of the data involved.

These limitations led to the emergence of a more specialized category of the tools—executive information systems (EIS). The characteristic feature of EIS was the restriction of access to the underlying SQL and an emphasis on predefined queries. The procedure management function was thus more strongly developed. In addition, the user interface was made more friendly, and it often had tighter links to other tools, such as electronic mail, for tighter integration of the executive's desktop view. This focus often led to defining specialized data structures, with little thought of how they might be populated.

Today, query-and-reporting tools are focusing on addressing their weaknesses. In particular, user interfaces are now standardized to a large extent, and data management function based on SQL allows access to most data sources.

The key functional aspects that continue to be poorly supported are:

- **Linkage to business meaning for both definition of queries and use of results**

  Many tools are beginning to support a more business-oriented view of the data. However, the support is often internalized within and specific to the tool itself. This leads to considerable difficulty in supporting multiple tools, and may require the user to manually transfer metadata between tools.

- **Management of procedures**

  Most query-and-reporting tools focus strongly on the process of building the query or procedure for the individual user. Management of completed procedures, particularly support for the enterprise-wide re-use of procedures, is generally weak. While tools from an EIS background provide more support in this area, they are often limited by proprietary structures for procedures, which restricts their widespread use.

  In a mature data warehouse environment, re-use of existing queries is the norm, and needs to be actively facilitated and encouraged to reduce the proliferation of similar queries. Such multiple copies of queries are difficult to manage, and they lead to inconsistency in reporting.

Data analysis and prediction tools

Whereas query-and-reporting tools aim at producing a single answer, *data analysis-and-prediction tools* are more concerned with viewing the total dataset in a variety of ways and drawing conclusions based on these differing views.

Data analysis-and-prediction tools come in two distinct varieties. The first consists of statistical packages, which are based on traditional statistical data analyses—means, averages, standard deviations, curve fitting, and so on—that can be performed on a set of data. These tools emphasize the structuring and presentation function of the BII. The second set of

> *In practice...*
>
> *Many tools have equally good user interfaces today, but support for query sharing and management across the enterprise continues to be a key differentiation factor.*

> *Data analysis-and-prediction tool*
>
> *An end-user tool that provides an end user with a variety of ways of looking at data with a view to finding the right questions to ask.*

In practice...

*How spread-
sheets integrate
and use metadata
from the data
warehouse is one
of the most im-
portant factors in
evaluating them
because they are
historically weak
at these tasks.*

tools consists of the now ubiquitous spreadsheets, which also focus on the structuring and presentation function of the BII.

Spreadsheets originated in the stand-alone PC world, and statistical packages came from a somewhat specialized mathematical discipline. As a result, both were originally characterized by their use of specialized data stores and structures, and both assumed a small user set (equal to 1 in the case of spreadsheets). As a result the data management, selection, and manipulation functions were of little relevance, as was procedure management. Similarly, linkage to the business meaning was assumed to be in the user's head—consider the difficulty of knowing the meaning of cell J12 in any spreadsheet!

The two types of data analysis-and-prediction tool are converging, driven by the popularity of the spreadsheet interface. A recent outgrowth of the spreadsheet paradigm is the concept of multi-dimensional analysis, allowing a whole new category of manipulations of the data view. The volumes of data, especially in multi-dimensional analysis, and the need to share common data sources has led to greater emphasis recently on the data management, selection, and manipulation functions.

However, the major areas of missing or weak functionality among this category of tools are the same as for query-and-reporting tools—linkage to business meaning, and procedure management.

12.2 Data access

Data access

*The function re-
quired to support
read-only queries
to transparently
access and com-
bine data that re-
sides in a variety
of locations, in
various formats,
and on differing
hardware and
software plat-
forms.*

A *data access* component is required as part of a warehouse because the information needed by an end user may reside in any location and on any platform within the IS environment of the enterprise. With the growth in end-user tools on distributed, PC-based platforms, summary data has tended to move toward those platforms. However, much of the detailed data remains departmentally or centrally based. This is because volumes are large, and data integrity and security are of prime importance.

As previously described, the vast majority of the data used by end users resides in BIWs. These BIWs are relational or relational-like. Physically, they tend to be located as near to the end user as possible, for reasons of availability, ownership, and improved performance. However, they may reside on the end user's PC, on the LAN server, on a departmental machine, or centrally.

Depending on the type of user, the culture of the organization, and the technical characteristics of the BDW (such as size or update frequency), end users may occasionally be given access to the BDW itself. Even when permitted, such usage is small relative to that found at the BIW level. The BDW is centrally located, perhaps distributed over a small number of databases, and exists in relational format.

Finally, under special circumstances, end users may require direct access to data in the operational systems. The dangers and difficulties associated with such access have already been described. They revolve around the semantic and temporal inconsistencies found in operational systems. However, where it is allowed, such access usually significantly expands the range of formats and physical platforms on which data must be accessed to include non-relational databases and flat files.

Therefore, users need to be able to access data on many platforms.

Requirements for data access

The above considerations lead to a set of requirements for the data access component, prioritized here in descending order:

1. **A common language for data access**

   Because of the variety of end-user tools and the data formats that may have to be supported, the data access component needs a single language to express inquiries, combine them where required, and return the results.

2. **Read-only access to distributed, relational data**

   The physical location of relational data is irrelevant to the end user, so she/he should not be required to know where the data resides in order to use it. Where remote access significantly increases response time, the system should warn the user.

3. **Read-only access to distributed, relational-like data**

   The same considerations apply here as for relational data (item 2).

4. **Joining data from different locations**

   Where inquiries require data joins, the underlying data may reside in different locations, either local to or remote from the original source of the query.

5. **Joining data from relational and relational-like platforms**

   In addition to residing in different locations, the required data may reside in different formats or structures on different hardware or software platforms.

6. **Read-only access to distributed, non-relational data**

   This requirement expands the access scope to non-relational data. The same considerations apply as for relational data (item 2).

7. **Joining data from non-relational and relational platforms**

   This requirement expands the requirement for joining data from different locations and platforms (items 4 and 5).

A structure for data access

In the past few years, SQL has become the *de facto* standard for database access. Like most standards, of course, there are many varieties. However, SQL does provide a good basis for a common language for data access. This is illustrated in Figure 12-3, where the first step in the data access component is to translate the query from the language used by the end-user tool to SQL. If required, the query is then split into parts applicable to different locations and/or platforms. The next step is to translate each sub-query to the language required by the receiving DBMS.

The process of returning the response to the user (the bottom half of Figure 12-2) is a mirror image of sending the inquiry. Various databases return the answer sets to the data access component, which translates them to a common relational format and combines them into a single response. The final step is to translate this response into a format appropriate for the end-user tool and pass it back to the user.

A control-and-administration function defines data locations and formats or allows their capture from other sources of metadata. In its fullest form, this function is similar in scope and functionality to the administration component of data replication, described in Chapter 19.

On both the inquiry and response paths, data access invokes data transfer function (also described in Chapter 19), where needed. On the inquiry path, the data being transferred consists of short messages, while on the response path, data sizes are significantly larger. Because the end user is awaiting the result of his/her query, data access requires that data transfer operate at synchronous or near real-time asynchronous speeds.

Figure 12-3 also shows an inquiry-and-response path around the outside of the data access component. This represents the situation where the end-user tool provides direct access to data stored in a format that is immediately usable by that tool. While many tools provide such direct-access facilities, access is usually local and limited to a small subset of the potential data in the data warehouse. As a result, end-user tools that link into the more generic data access component (within the shaded box in Figure 12-3) provide better coverage of the data warehouse environment.

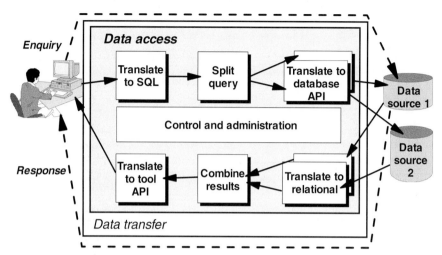

Figure 12-3: *The structure of the data access component*

However, such access does have an associated cost. Translating between different formats, splitting queries, and combining result sets all take time and require CPU resources. Delays in data transfer across the network add to the response time that the end user experiences. In cases where the query is unique or unusual, such delays may be acceptable, but, in general, trying to satisfy everyday queries by this route is unlikely to be successful.

Key to the overall performance of the data access component is the physical location on the network of the function that combines the results. In many cases, the output of the combination step is significantly smaller than the total volume of data in the inputs. This is because many split inquiries use the data coming from one source to further qualify the result dataset coming from another. Added to this, if the result set coming from one source is substantially larger than that coming from another, then it is more efficient to place the combination function close to the source of the larger result dataset.

Vendors have constructed comprehensive solutions to the above problems by using artificial intelligence techniques to analyze queries, predict sizes of result datasets, and so on, and thereby provide optimum performance. However, within the data warehouse, careful data modeling of end-user needs generally allows the construction of BIWs that minimize the need to regularly access data located on multiple platforms. The strength of a data access component in the warehouse lies in its ability to service the more unusual needs for data and particular data combinations, as well as to detect when such unpredicted needs become part of common usage. This latter aspect then allows the creation of new BIWs to serve these needs.

In practice...

Some vendors promote a data warehouse architecture based on data access. Note that the underlying assumption—that the operational data is consistent across the enterprise—must be true if this approach is to produce a true data warehouse. Ongoing performance tuning and maintenance costs as the operational systems change usually offset the faster initial startup of warehouses based on data access.

12.3 Conclusions

The BII focuses on the transformation of business data into real business information and provides the user with the means to analyze, report on, and draw conclusions from the data in a business context. It is only in these activities, and in the applications built around them, that the business obtains real value from the investment in a data warehouse.

At a functional level, the BII supports querying, manipulating, and reporting on data. As importantly, but often overlooked, it also provides the means for saving and reusing them, not just by their creators but by suitably qualified people throughout the organization.

In support of the BII, as well as other components of the warehouse, data access provides the underlying function required to retrieve data from a variety of platforms and locations.

We can see the BII as being independent of the principal task of the data warehouse—the imposition of order on the current chaos of data stored in the organization. However, the BIG also plays a key role here, and it is to this subject that we now move to address the final stage of this transformation.

Chapter 13

Information—data in context

The previous chapter concentrated on describing the task of providing users with a usable and useful view on the data in the warehouse through the business information interface (BII). While the BII is ultimately responsible for conveying the information to users, it requires the assistance of a second component.

This second component, the **business information guide** (BIG), which focuses not on business data, but on the metadata, is the subject of this chapter. It supports the user in finding relevant data and understanding its meaning. In principle, the BIG provides the same set of functionality for metadata that the BII provides for business data. However, because of the more specific nature of metadata and the way it is used, this functionality is more limited in scope. The purpose of the BIG is to support the use of the data in a business context, using the metadata stored in the data warehouse catalog (DWC).

This chapter first describes the requirements for access to and use of metadata and illustrates these requirements through an extensive user scenario. We define the audiences for the BIG, and then outline a structure that delivers the required functionality. Finally, we deal with the question of how the DWC is populated with the required metadata; this last point is one the major difficulties associated with metadata.

It is through the BII and the BIG that users perceive, and indeed obtain, value from the data. These two components provide the link between the underlying data stored and managed in the warehouse, and the information required by the end user. Together they place the data in a business context—they transform data into information.

13.1 The business information guide—an introduction

For end users, access to all of the data in the company is useless if they have no way of understanding what is being provided. In fact, because the data warehouse gives access to a vast amount of data, we might argue that users are in a more difficult and dangerous situation than when their access to data is limited. We can simply state the problems as follows:

- The more data that is available, the longer it takes to find something useful.

- The more data that is available, the smaller is the percentage that any individual user understands.

The consequences are that users are both less productive and more likely to be mistaken in their decision making. Put more graphically, as more data is poured onto the desktop, the user may drown in it.

Business information guide

The end user's sole means of accessing the contents of the data warehouse catalog, providing the business context for the data stored anywhere in the warehouse.

The solution to this problem has been mentioned many times in this text, most recently in the previous chapter. Data must be transformed into information by placing it in the context of the business. The process of transforming data into information is the responsibility of the BII. However, the BII must rely on a second component—the **business information guide**—for access to and use of the information (or metadata) that describes the data in a business context.

Basically, then, the BIG is the component of the warehouse through which users access and use the metadata residing in the data warehouse catalog. We might ask what is special about it, and in particular, why it is separated from the BII. This chapter answers these questions, first by examining the business requirements, and then by presenting a scenario set in a company in which the data warehouse is in full production and a BIG supports users in their daily business tasks.

It must be emphasized that the users of the BIG are business people, not IS staff. However, the availability of such functionality can be of great benefit to IS personnel. This is because the BIG presents users with both the business meaning of the data (that is, how data is understood by the business analysts) and the IS interpretation of that business meaning. Either or both views may be in error. The BIG provides a means of addressing such errors.

The BIG allows users to explore the meaning of data, refine their understanding of how it is or could be used, and feed back information on mismatches or errors to the owners of the data and to the IS department. It can therefore play a key role in driving improvements in the quality of data in the organization. This aspect is discussed further in Chapter 15.

Because the BIG has such a central role in the data warehouse [Haisten (1995c)] and many of the requirements on it are unique, we describe them in some detail. The next section examines the needs of users as they use the metadata, while Section 13.3 concentrates on the structural needs that such use implies.

13.2 Requirements for the BIG

We can divide the use of the BIG into the four areas shown in Figure 13-1 and deal with the requirements for each in turn.

First, there is a distinct division between the overall business view represented by the top half of the octagon, and the IS world of the lower half. Each half is further divided in two. In the business level view, we can clearly distinguish between the business functionality itself and the organization that performs the functions. In the IS world, the split is between the underlying data and the functions that create or use that data.

Another dimension of characterization is also evident. In each area, there is a trend from the generic to the specific as one moves from the center to the edges of the octagon. Thus, the **business processes** consist of tasks and the organizational units of individuals. Similarly, the **data groupings** such as table or file consist of columns or fields (or elements in general), and functional applications or procedures contain queries or reports.

We now describe the requirements for each quadrant in the following sections. Note, however, that the structure is strongly interconnected, and thus many of the metadata elements and their uses are related to the connections between the different quadrants. For simplicity, rather than discuss this type of relationship information as new categories, it is placed with one of the two related quadrants where the choice of quadrant is based primarily on a logical order of description.

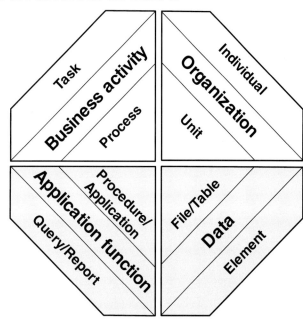

Figure 13-1: *The usage quadrants of the business information guide*

Business activity

The business quadrant represents the understanding that a business user may have of the business and its activities. It is likely that the user's view will be specific to that part of the organization for which he or she works but is influenced by other parts with which the user has dealt.

Required metadata

1. **Definitions of business terms and their relationships to data, function, and so on**

   Business terminology varies considerably throughout the organization. There is extensive use of synonyms (different terms having the same meaning) and homonyms (different meanings for the same term).

   Business terminology is a living language, so tracking its evolution requires ongoing effort. However, such terminology is a key entry point for end users into the BIG and the value of the BIG is significantly reduced if the terminology is not kept up to date.

2. **Definitions of business processes, tasks, and their relationships**

   Business activity consists of a series of tasks, automated and manual, that link together into processes. Processes are triggered by external or internal events and may span departments or divisions.

   The work of documenting such processes is often initiated as a result of total quality management studies and may lead to introducing workflow technology and/or simplifying the existing processes. Such activity usually occurs outside the scope of the warehouse project.

3. **Relationships of business processes, tasks, and terms to the organization, application functions, and data**

   Part of the value of having documented business processes, tasks, and terms in the DWC comes from the links that designers can build to the IS world of applications and data. Business processes and tasks are related to application function, while business terms may link to any of the quadrants. These relationships, like all others in the BIG, are two-way and may be used in either direction.

Usage

1. **Inquire about the meaning of business terms, tasks, and processes.**

   This is the primary entry point for users undertaking new or unfamiliar activities. Such activities are described in common or department-specific business terminology, which may be unfamiliar or not defined precisely enough to allow the user to undertake the required activity.

2. **Inquire about related application function or data.**

   The previous entry point of inquiry about meaning generally leads to inquiries about which applications already exist to perform the required activity, or which data is available that is related to it.

3. **Inquire about the business context of applications or data.**

   Such inquiries originate from work already done in the IS portion of the BIG. In this case, data or application function has been discovered, and the question is: What is the business context? Such inquiries are often used to qualify previously found definitions for data elements, values, and so on.

4. **Update business terms.**

   Because business terminology is rather informal and evolves over time, it is important to capture the changes that occur. The most useful way of capturing this information is from the end users themselves, through a tool, such as the BIG, which they use regularly.

   Data administrators are likely to be the only personnel allowed to update business terms that are generally available throughout the organization. The BIG must, therefore, provide a feedback mechanism for end users to submit changes to the data administration staff.

> *In practice...*
>
> *There is often a temptation to include process documentation within the data warehouse project. This is unwise, because it would be likely to overextend the project scope.*

Organization

The organization quadrant represents the organizational structure. We might argue that this is business data rather than metadata, and for the personnel department, particularly, there is indeed overlap. However, some of the information here, such as who has responsibilities for which data or applications, may not be stored or managed elsewhere and is a key driver for data quality.

Required metadata

1. **Definitions of organizational structure and individuals' roles**

   Although not extensively used directly in the BIG, this information about organizational structure is required to trace responsibility within the organization.

2. **Organizational or individual responsibility for function and data**

   Different types of responsibility can and should be tracked:

In practice...

Many companies have already assigned ownership for applications and processes. However, ownership of data is particularly important in the data warehouse and should be assigned independently of any application ownership already assigned.

- **ownership**—the organizational unit that has accepted ultimate responsibility for the data or function
- **stewardship**—the individual who is responsible for the quality of the business definition and the contents of the data or function on an ongoing basis
- **responsibility for delivery**—the unit within the IS department responsible for physically delivering data or function to the end users
- **responsibility for access**— the individual who authorizes access to the data

There may be a debate about whether stewardship and responsibility for access should be associated with a role or with the individual performing that role at a given time. While there are maintenance problems with assigning these responsibilities to individuals who often change roles, general experience suggests that assigning the responsibility at an individual level is more effective in ensuring data quality.

These responsibilities apply to data at a variety of levels of aggregation, and to functionality such as queries, procedures, applications, subscriptions, and so on.

Usage

1. Notify or send action request to person responsible.

The most common use of the organization quadrant is to enable an end user to contact an individual responsible for some aspect of the data or applications of the warehouse. This contact can be:

- a request for permission to access a particular set of data
- a request to cancel a subscription to a set of data
- a notification of a data problem, such as an error in definition or content, or the unavailability of data having the required currency

Electronic forms or mail applications accessed by the BIG are likely to provide most of the functionality. The BIG passes appropriate information, such as sender and receiver identification and the names of data fields or applications, to this component.

2. Inquire about data or application responsibility.

This inquiry usually precedes a notification or request for action. Its purpose is to identify the potential receiver of the request.

3. Update individual responsibilities for data or application function.

Arguably this function should be provided by a dedicated application, that tracks the individuals responsible for different data or functions in the organization. This type of information is difficult to maintain, principally because it falls entirely to the end user. Given the everyday use of the BIG by many end users, functionality provided here is both easily accessible and in a familiar environment, and therefore more likely to be used.

While procedures for allocating responsibility are generally well used, those for relinquishing responsibility often fail because of the normal human desire to focus on a new role rather than tidying up after finishing the old one. However, a user who has moved to a new responsibility is likely to be constantly reminded of the old role by user requests driven by the BIG. This behavior reinforces the central role of the BIG in handling such information.

Application function

The application function quadrant represents how the IS department has implemented the business processes over the years. Because implementation has been fragmented, and because the business process changes rather rapidly, the business view of the functions required to run and manage the business at any time may significantly differ from the way the IS shop currently implements them.

Required metadata

1. **Definitions of applications and procedures**

    This is mainly textual information describing applications and procedures. There is only a little distinction between the two: applications are often operational in nature, while procedures are more often informational. Both consist of an associated group of programs, queries, reports, and tools, either formally interrelated in their development or data, or informally interrelated in users' minds.

2. **Definitions of queries and reports, and their relationship to applications and processes**

    These definitions comprise the component level of the application function quadrant. As for the group definition level described above, the descriptions are mainly textual. Information relating this component level to the group level of definition is, of course, also needed.

3. **Linkages to query or report "code"**

    The most comprehensive description of a query or report is, in fact, the source code defining it. Such detail is likely to be of interest to sophisticated users, who are building their own queries or reports, or modifying existing ones.

4. **Listings of query definitions, parameters, and allowed values**

    A specific area of query or report modification function that is usable by end users in general is parameterization. The BIG lists parameters of the query or report, together with their meanings and allowed values. This supports users as they begin to customize queries.

5. **Data used or produced by applications, procedures, queries, and reports**

    This linkage information between application function and data is important because it allows users to explore the data in the warehouse and understand how it is used.

Usage

Metadata about queries and procedures developed in support of informational needs is of greater interest and is more frequently used than metadata describing the formally developed operational applications.

1. **Search for existing application function.**

    This is a free-format search for application function, based on the user's description of what the application does. The objective of this search is to avoid re-creating queries or procedures that already exist.

    Note that this functionality is aimed not at application developers but at end users. While it could be an initial starting point for analysis of a business area when defining a new application, developers need a more formal methodology, such as that provided by CASE tools.

    This entry point is closely related to business terminology and to the link, defined in the business activity metadata (item 3) above, between business term or activity and application function.

2. **Discover which data and applications are related together.**

    A complete understanding of application function is often difficult to obtain without knowing the data the application uses or produces. Therefore, starting from the application quadrant, this query clarifies the user's understanding of what a query or application does.

    Discovery of data/application relationships is also very useful when initiated from the data quadrant. Again, it provides clarification of data meaning. However, beyond this, it provides:

    *   a view of which data is often related and how it is used together
    *   a means of discovering existing queries that use or produce data of interest. Such queries could then be used as templates for developing new queries on the same data

3. **Document the application function descriptions and parameter information.**

   End users who develop their own reports and queries must be able to document this new functionality, first for themselves and possibly for use by others. The application function quadrant must support this documentation.

   For formal (usually operational) application development in the IS shop, this documentation takes place through CASE tools. Indeed, we could argue that a similar approach should be used for less formal informational application development, and that query and reporting tools should provide this documentation functionality. Those tools that do not support this approach need an alternative method—provided by the BIG—of entering the required information.

4. **Support basic query/report customization.**

   Where end-user tools allow query and report customization through the use of parameters, users need access to parameter names, descriptions, and allowed values to enable them to use these facilities efficiently.

5. **Initiate a query or procedure.**

   Last, but perhaps most obviously, when an end user has discovered the required query or report, he or she should be able simply to start it up and run it directly from the BIG, implicitly invoking the appropriate tool and passing the query/report name to it.

Data

The data quadrant of the BIG represents the descriptive information required for the business data. This information includes both business-oriented meanings and definitions, and IS-related information such as data type and structure. These two views are kept together because the end user, in general, expects a close correspondence between the two. In addition, the IS shop has usually maintained a close relationship between them.

Required metadata

1. **Business descriptions of data groupings and elements**

   The business-oriented descriptions of data groupings correspond to the definitions of data entities at the logical level of the EDM. These are set in the context of the higher levels of the model, such as subject areas and business data classifications.

Business descriptions of data elements in the BIG derive from the attribute definitions of the logical level of the EDM. The data quadrant also documents the relationship between attributes and entities.

2. Technical descriptions of data groupings and elements

Data entities at the logical or business level translate into files, tables, views, and other structures at the physical level. Information stored includes name and alternate names, location, storage and access modes, and size. The linkage between business and technical descriptions—or in modeling terms, the relationship between the logical and physical levels of the data model—is also important information.

Taking attributes to the physical level results in columns in tables or fields in records. Information stored includes name and alternate names, data type, field length, allowed or possible values, and so on. As with item 2 above, the linkage between the logical and physical levels of the model is required.

3. Relationships between data groupings and elements

At both business and technical levels, the relationships between data groupings and elements are stored. This shows the entity/attribute relationship in logical terms and the column/table or field/file relationships at a physical level. Another important aspect of the relationship is the identification of keys and indexes in tables and files, as well as the foreign key relationships that exist between tables and/or files.

4. Translations of encoded fields

Tables of coded fields and their corresponding values allow translation between them. Such tables may be considered either business data or metadata, and, in fact, the distinction is difficult to draw. It is most likely to be defined on the basis of common usage. Thus, the table of U.S. states and their two-letter abbreviations is used everywhere and changes very rarely, and so is clearly metadata. On the other hand, a table of product status codes and their names (for example, On order, Delivered, In transit) is localized in usage and may change. It may therefore be more appropriate to treat such a table as business data.

5. Derivation rules

In the informational environment, data is derived according to particular rules. These can vary in complexity from simple summaries or aggregations, to complex combinations of data from different sources and over specific time periods to produce some high-level business measurements. The exact nature of the derivation may be vital to an understanding of the correct usage of the resulting data element, and for this reason derivation rules are made available through the BIG.

For most end users, a textual description is sufficient. Sophisticated power users may need a more formal representation, perhaps even given in design-level pseudo-code.

6. **Data currency and scheduling information**

Schedule information describes how often or when updating of the data in question is planned. Currency gives the status of the update—when the data was actually updated. Together these two pieces of information allow the user to judge the value of the data as a basis for making particular time-dependent decisions.

Such information is often summarized to a data grouping level in the metadata for ease of use. Of course, the user can also find the currency of individual records from the timestamps in the data warehouse.

7. **Data utilization statistics**

This information, used mainly by administrators, allows an understanding of how and when information is used. End users may access it occasionally when defining new queries, as a basis for choosing appropriate information. For reasons of privacy, the BIG may confine end-user access to only summarized, statistical utilization metadata.

8. **Data quality information**

The BIG stores annotations on known quality problems concerning particular data items, such structure or content errors under investigation, and data that has not been updated according to its schedule. This information allows users to avoid making decisions based on such data.

Usage

1. **Understand the data meaning.**

As data becomes more widely used throughout the organization, users must have access to a single, consistent description of the meaning of data in a business context. This function allows the user to recognize similar and conflicting meanings ascribed to data throughout the organization, and promotes communication between the different parts of the company.

2. **Locate the appropriate data.**

Having defined data needs for a particular task, a user often finds it worth asking whether this data has been generated previously, and if so, how to obtain it. Not only does this choice reduce development effort; it also reduces needless duplication of data—a benefit from the viewpoints of both storage costs and data management.

3. **Decide on the appropriate usage of data.**

Appropriate usage of data is necessary in order to obtain valid results. The user must understand the meaning, currency, and derivation of the data before using it in a new way.

4. **Support the development of new queries.**

Steps 2 through 4 are prerequisites to defining a new query. However, the BIG can provide further support in the development phase. This support stems from its knowledge of the relationships that exist within the data. For example, tables can be joined sensibly only via foreign keys. Only certain fields are appropriate for use in grouping clauses. Using this information, the BIG can aid the user in developing queries that are reasonable in the context of the data structure. The result is a business-driven query generator [Stecher and Hellemaa (1986)].

5. **Understand the data presented in reports.**

When queries have been generated by users who are familiar with the business, or by IS staff who are familiar with the data, the resulting re-ports often use terminology without explanation. Such information without its context is confusing and misleading.

A prime example of IS terminology is the use of database column names as headers in reports. Similarly, abbreviated business terms may be used in column headings where space is at a premium. In both cases, the general user often requires a more complete descrip-tion that can be called up directly from the report viewer.

6. **Obtain meaningful translations of encoded fields.**

In a manner similar to that of item 5 above, coded fields used for brev-ity in a report or query result often beg an explanation in "real English" (actually the user's native language)—at least when the user first en-counters them.

7. **Obtain information on data quality.**

When a user accesses data with known or suspected quality prob-lems, the BIG should automatically warn the user. This requires that data administrators set up alerts or triggers in the DWC for specific items of business data when quality issues arise.

Overall structural requirements

Assigning requirements supported by the BIG to the four quadrants puts order on their diversity. However, it also obscures the unifying principles that unite these different areas of need.

The overall structural requirements define how the individual elements within the BIG interact with one another as well as the interaction of the BIG with its users and with other components in the data warehouse. Figure 13-2 shows how these requirements extend the octagon drawn in Figure 13-1.

From the user's point of view, the BIG is optimized to support the questions they might ask about the business and its use of data, applications, and so on. Figure 13-2 show these questions in abbreviated form around the edges of the octagon. Examples are:

- What does that term mean?
- Where can I find that information?
- When was it last updated?
- How was it calculated?

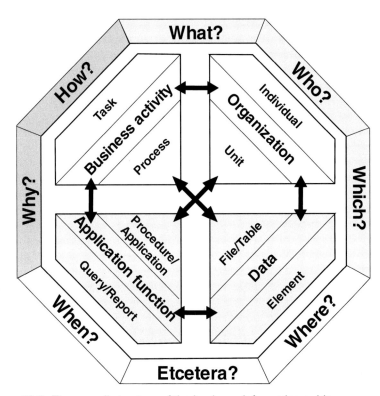

Figure 13-2: *The overall structure of the business information guide*

- Why is it different from the information found in another field?
- Who is responsible for its quality?
- To which business process does that application belong?
- Was this question already answered?

Internally, delivering answers to these questions requires a set of linkages between and within the different quadrants of the octagon, shown by the layering within the quadrants and the arrows between them. These linkages represent the variety of ways in which the user can navigate around the metadata areas and functions of the BIG.

The following set of requirements draws these elements together:

1. Universal user access to metadata

In principle, all metadata should be accessible to all users. As with all principles, this one requires some clarification.

Access to business data is authorized according to business need, in order to protect the assets of the organization, individual privacy, and so on. Therefore, the default access level to business data is typically "no access", and higher levels of access must be specifically granted.

Read access to metadata, on the other hand, must be open to all users, in order to promote awareness of the value and potential uses of the data asset, to facilitate communication in the organization, and to support openness and teamwork. Therefore, the default read access level to metadata is "public", and more restricted levels of access to particular metadata elements must be specifically granted.

Security considerations may be cited as a reason for denying public access to certain aspects of the metadata. While there may be extreme examples where this is justifiable, in normal business pursuits, security risks are unlikely to outweigh the benefits of understanding the meaning of the data stored by the company. Some people cite reducing confusion in end users' minds as a reason for limiting access to metadata. Thus, some might argue that a specific set of data should only be used in a particular department and that making the metadata available publicly is unnecessary and counterproductive. In certain cases, this may be true. However, such islands of totally isolated data run counter to a key objective of the warehouse, which is to promote effective and consistent use of data throughout the organization.

Write access to certain areas of the metadata may be public, although mediated through some data administration function. Most metadata in the warehouse is sourced from build-time metadata tools, such as CASE tools and systems administration functions. This metadata can be written only through these interfaces.

In practice...

Metadata should be implemented as a public resource containing all descriptive information. As with a telephone directory, the impact of omitted or erroneous information is greater than the area covered by that information; it diminishes the perceived usefulness and value of the total resource.

A personal level of access to metadata is also required to enable documentation of personal usage of data, providing the end user with a permanent means of storing such important information—rather than the traditional method of scribbling on a scrap of paper and pinning it to the wall behind the desk! This level of access also supports the development of metadata that is tried and tested personally before being promoting to the public-access level.

2. Support for historical metadata

When dealing with historical data, the structure of which changes over time, end users must be provided with the metadata that is relevant to the historical structures they are using.

There is an important additional requirement. When the required business data spans a long period of time over which the data structures have changed, the metadata must inform the users of this and support them in choosing a single structure for all the data. A common example is trend analysis of business performance of different organizational units. Because the organizational structure often changes, the user should decide whether to:

- perform the analysis using today's structure (converting previous results to this structure)
- perform the analysis using some previous structure (again, with relevant conversions)
- simply note that there are some discontinuities in the data where comparison is not valid

3. Entry to the BIG from any starting point

The starting point of an end user in his or her search for information is variable. He or she may approach a topic from business terms, from known data or application function, through a knowledge of the organization, or simply from a keyword without context. The BIG inquiry may result from a query on the business data that has delivered poorly documented data. The user may undertake the inquiry before even trying to approach the business data.

4. Navigation of the BIG via any route

Once the user has entered into the BIG, the path he or she follows is also variable. The usage of the BIG is more like that of hypertext linkages on the World Wide Web than of a structured drill-down through information.

For example, an inquiry on the use of a particular data field and the applications that produce it may lead from there to related applications, to other data fields produced by the same application, or to questions about ownership and authorization for access.

5. **Exit from the BIG to any process or application**

    When the user has found the necessary information, the most likely next step is to want to use it!

    If the user has found a previously built application, the requirement is often to start it up, passing parameters to it, if appropriate. If the end point of an inquiry in the BIG is the identification of an owner of some data that is in error, the user may want to e-mail the owner directly—to send a note, including the addressee name and user ID, the data element and table in error, and so on, without having to manually enter this information.

6. **Close coupling with the business information interface**

    Requirements 3 to 5 clearly indicate the need for a high degree of co-operation between the BIG and the BII. Users invariably need to enter the BIG from the BII and *vice versa* as they perform business tasks. The BII also depends on the BIG to support its functioning, particularly in query construction and report generation.

    These two components, then, are very closely linked and require a substantial and well-structured set of interfaces. It is possible to combine the two functions into a single component, as some end-user products do today. This is a restrictive approach, however, because one BII tool is unlikely to supply the variety in function required across the organization. Close integration of the BIG function into individual BII tools would probably lead to multiple, inconsistent approaches to providing BIG function, because they were potentially based on separate and conflicting metadata stores.

    The arguments that lead to a single, consistent set of business data apply even more strongly to metadata, and any approach that tends toward multiple and potentially inconsistent metadata stores must be avoided [Herget (1994)].

7. **Support for the creation and maintenance of metadata**

    As described in Chapter 5, metadata is created and maintained by the build-time components, of which CASE tools are common examples. However, the BIG is required to provide build-time function in a number of areas:

    *   business terminology
    *   responsibility for data or function, particularly at an individual level
    *   documentation of application function and data usage in personally developed queries

---

> ***In practice...***
>
> *Unless there will never be more than one end-user tool used throughout the organization, a BIG separate and independent from the end-user tool ensures more consistent definition and use of metadata.*

While each of these areas could be supported by an application in its own right, each is rather small and used mainly by end users as an aside to their real business activities. Placing this function within the scope of the BIG is therefore reasonable in development terms and logical for end users. If the functionality to create and maintain this metadata exists elsewhere in the organization, then the BIG should not, of course, duplicate it.

A model of the metadata

We can bring together all these requirements in a data model that describes the metadata. This model is almost completely generic, because the requirements described vary little from company to company or from industry to industry. As a result, the definition of a **metadata model** is seldom the responsibility of an IS department but correctly belongs to the vendors who deliver such tools. The metadata model underpins any implementation of a data warehouse catalog and business information guide. Therefore, the quality and usefulness of such products depend strongly on the depth and breadth of the underlying model.

The metadata model is sometimes described as a metamodel—that is, a model of the model of the business. For example, the entities in a business data model are objects of interest to the business, such as customers and products. However, the entities in a metamodel are business terms and processes; organizational structures and entities at the logical level; and tables, data elements, and applications at the physical level. While this additional level of abstraction is confusing at first sight, it has an important purpose: to formally describe the structure required to allow users to understand and explore the activities of the business and how they are represented in the IS terms of data and application function. Brackett (1994) provides an extensive discussion on the various aspects of metadata representation and the use of models.

13.3 The naïve and sentimental user[1]

The scope of requirements listed in Section 13.2 may be somewhat daunting, so the following example illustrates how the metadata and the functionality around it supports a typical end user.

Jane is on her first week in headquarters after a number of years in a customer-facing role in a major bank. Her new manager, who is, as usual, too busy to explain how, has just asked Jane to prepare a report on the

[1] With apologies to John Le Carré

average profitability of the long-term loan products offered to class AAA corporate customers.

The request presents a number of problems:

- What is average product profitability?
- Which long-term loan products are offered to these customers?
- Do figures already exist, or must they be calculated?
- If they must be calculated, how to do so?

Jane begins her search for answers in the company's BIG.

Figure 13-3 shows the BIG in simplified form with steps numbered to match Jane's progress. The obvious entry point [1] in this case is the business quadrant, because what Jane has been given is clearly a business task, with an associated set of terminology.

In this scenario, let's assume that Jane's manager has not defined a new way of looking at the business, and that the terms "product profitability", "long-term loan product", and "AAA corporate customer" are known business terms previously defined in the DWC.

The definitions Jane finds there give rise to some additional questions:

- Over what variable is the profitability averaged?
- Could it be time, customer segment, geographical area, and so on?
- If it is time, what are the averaging periods—monthly or quarterly?

Following the trail of product profitability [2], Jane can see that there are a number of alternative meanings, each of which relates to its usage in the business processes of different parts of the organization. From this information, Jane makes an informed judgment [3] that her manager meant "average product profitability over time by month". (It is a well-known fact that managers are rarely around when you need them to clarify exactly what they meant!)

From the fully qualified business term definition, it is an easy step [4] to the IS definition, where it becomes clear that this data item is not permanently stored but is calculated using a predefined procedure. It is also worth noting that the procedure—an IS construct—is related to a business task, and that Jane could equally have arrived directly at the procedure and data from the business quadrant in the first step and later checked their ownership in the organization quadrant.

Having defined the procedure, Jane follows the trail [5] to its associated data. She can now determine that the existing procedure applies to all products for all customers. Therefore, she has the choice of running this query as it already exists, or of further qualifying the conditions to restrict the customer and product sets. It is also clear [6], however, that the procedure and data are subject to access restrictions and that Jane's manager is responsible for granting access. Jane requests access to the data, and awaits her manager's return from that long business lunch.

In this process, the BIG has supported Jane in discovering:

- the meaning of the business terms and their relationship to the overall process
- the organizational distinctions in meaning
- the ownership of the data and applications
- the available data and how it is calculated
- the available procedures, how they use data, and how they can be modified to support a specific data need

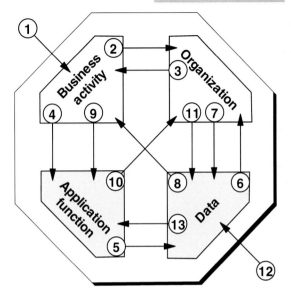

Figure 13-3: *Using the business information guide*

However, this is only the first step in understanding the meaning and use of the data in the warehouse. The BIG provides the means of utilizing the data in new and imaginative ways.

While Jane is awaiting her manager's return, she looks again [7] at the set of columns that comprise the product cost table, which is a major component of the calculation of product profitability. (Note that Jane can continue her investigation, even though she has not yet obtained authority to access the business data itself.) She notices that it contains a data element described in business terms [8] as "estimated sales cost allocation", and she begins to trace how this is calculated, where it comes from, and so on [9]. It strikes Jane, from her previous role in the branch, that a new workflow process recently introduced in the branches will provide a more reliable calculation of this cost. Finding the ownership of the existing application and data from the BIG [10], she contacts the right person at the first attempt and makes her proposal for improving the process.

The added value of the BIG is in providing a means to:

- explore the data in a business context
- apply existing knowledge to expand or improve the process or even to initiate the correction of data errors
- easily trace responsibility for data and process in order to support process improvement

With the return of Jane's manager to the office, and his belated authorization [11] of Jane to use the required data, the production of the report can begin. The initial response, provided through a traditional query-and-reporting tool, betrays the IS background of the person who originally built it. Jane finds a number of column headings defined according to a familiar formula—remove all vowels, replace spaces with underscores, use only uppercase, and make sure the whole thing fits in six characters.

Again, using the BIG, this time starting from the data quadrant [12], Jane can trace back to the correct business meaning, choose a short name in business terms, and replace the column headings with the appropriate business language. She can further make an explicit association [13] in the DWC so that each time a user runs the report, or translates the results into a graphical format such as a bar chart, whatever BII tool is in use can automatically access and use meaningful business terms.

The BIG, therefore, supports the transformation of data into information, by providing for:

- attachment of the business meaning to the data

- access to business context information from the BII

- the construction of a common pool of business knowledge that can be reused by future end users

At this stage, we leave Jane using the BIG not only as a means of understanding the data available in the warehouse, but also as a tool to further explore its relationships and improve its quality. (Unfortunately, the BIG is unlikely to improve the quality of the relationship between Jane and her manager—who has just defined the next mission impossible!)

13.4 Users of the BIG

The foregoing discussion views the BIG exclusively from the viewpoint of the end user. Given the role of the data warehouse as the single supplier of data to end users and their tools, this focus is entirely correct.

However, the metadata stored in the DWC is clearly valuable to audiences besides the end user. In particular, the BIG can support the administrative functions of the warehouse and its models and databases. Supporting such users entails additional function, as Figure 13-4 shows.

The types of administration the BIG can support and the functions it needs to do so are:

- **Data administration**

  As the link between the business processes, their data needs, and the IS definition of data, data administrators are responsible, on behalf of the business owners of the data, for mapping the business meaning to its IS implementation.

Data administrators' needs are adequately supported by the metadata already described. Functionally, there is an additional requirement to link more closely to the metadata build-time tools, particularly the enterprise modeling tools used to define the business/IS relationship.

- **Database administration**

  The database administrator is also supported by the metadata and functionality already defined. The added value to the database administrator is the company-wide metadata about which databases already exist and how they are used. Such information enables administrators to make better decisions about whether requested new BIWs are truly needed, and when to build a new staging or user BIW before performance becomes degraded. Conversely, the metadata allows administrators to decide whether a BIW should be maintained at all if usage has diminished—an often neglected function in IS departments. It also provides a means for understanding and redressing past design tradeoffs.

- **Utilization tracking**

  Given the size and potential growth rate of a data warehouse, understanding which data is underutilized or where access bottlenecks exist is vital to its smooth running. Utilization information stored in the DWC supports the administration of performance and tuning of the data warehouse. In particular, the link to organization in the BIG provides administrators with a valuable context for analyzing utilization and determining sensible responses to demands for additional resources.

By now, it should be obvious that the discussion has omitted consideration of whether the designers and developers of both operational applications and of the warehouse and all its components are potential users of the BIG. This omission is intentional.

While we might argue that giving these groups access to the BIG would be useful in general, there is little doubt that such designers and developers require a more structured and formal approach to the definition, use, and reuse of data and function. Such a formal and structured approach is already provided through metadata build components such as modeling and CASE tools, supported by traditional data dictionaries.

> *In practice...*
>
> *A successful warehouse tends to grow and grow! The IS staff must put procedures in place to delete unused BIWs and to archive seldom-used BDW data.*

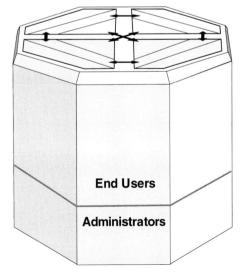

Figure 13-4: Expanding the BIG's user set

In practice...

In evaluating vendors' BIG tools, we should focus solely on the way they support the end user. Although, support for other user types may be a bonus, it may also indicate a tool designed for developers, and thus, not be wholly adapted to end-users' needs.

The BIG can play a significant role in supporting the end users who are involved in defining and verifying requirements at the early stages of the development process for both operational and informational applications. The BIG provides them with descriptions of existing data and function in a known business context, thus reducing the effort involved in defining the current situation and providing a common language for users and IS staff.

Therefore, the reason for omitting application designers and developers is not because they would derive no benefit from the BIG. It is simply to focus sorely needed attention on the requirements of end users rather than on those of application developers, who are usually better supported.

13.5 Structure of the BIG

As mentioned earlier, there is a great deal of similarity between the BII and the BIG in that the former provides the means of accessing the business data, while the latter addresses metadata. Essentially, the BIG is a very specialized form of BII, optimized for use with metadata. The implication of this relationship is that the structures of the BIG and BII are very similar, as a comparison of Figures 12-2 and 13-5 shows.

At the heart of the BIG is a set of functions comprising query definition and association, manipulation and selection, metadata management, procedure management, and report structuring and presentation. In general, these functions are simpler and more specific than those required in the BII, but their roles are identical. A description of these functions in the BII is given in Section 12-1. The simplifications in the BIG are as follows:

- The vast majority of useful queries on the metadata can be defined in advance and stored as procedures. Therefore, the BIG has minimal need for the kind of query building support provided in the BII.

- The structure (or model) of the metadata is known and is more stable than that of the business data. As a result, the definition and association component need handle only this one structure.

- The association function of the BII requires access to the BIG to link IS and business-oriented names and information. The association function in the BIG is, of course, self-contained.

- Structuring and presentation of the result of a metadata query are usually textual. The only other type of result of general interest is a graphical representation of the relationships in the business data.

- Statistical analysis functions and presentation techniques support utilization tracking. However, because of the limited audience for this function, other tools may be more appropriate for providing it.

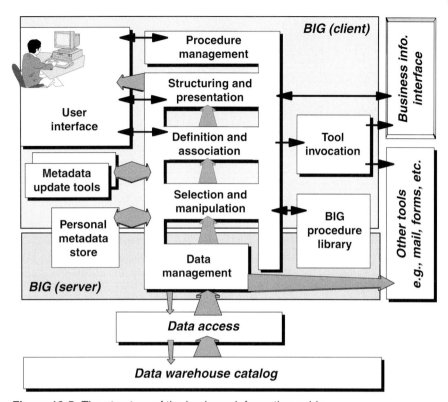

Figure 13-5: *The structure of the business information guide*

- The result of a query on metadata is seldom an end in itself. Rather, the user will take this information and use it to run a query on the business data or as input to a form or note to someone else in the organization. Therefore, the tool invocation function must provide close integration between the BIG, the metadata it is passing, and the external tool or function being invoked.

The only functionality in the BIG additional to that in the BII lies in the area of metadata update tools. As previously mentioned, these tools are somewhat peripheral to the basic function of the BIG and could be provided elsewhere if required.

13.6 DWC population

The BIG provides a means of creating and maintaining some specific pieces of metadata in the DWC. However, the majority of DWC metadata is sourced from build-time metadata components. CASE tools or their common repository, database catalogs, and so on, are common sources of metadata. Just as the business data warehouse (BDW) is populated from operational systems, the DWC is populated from build-time metadata. See Chapter 9 for a full description of population components. The following specific comments also apply.

Metadata volumes are small, and the rate of change is low. Therefore, the choice of capture and apply approaches is simple: static capture combined with load apply (refresh mode replication) is sufficient.

The high-volume, rapidly changing component of metadata—the currency metadata—is summarized as a separate store in the DWC. This step is similar to BIW population. However, as described in Chapter 5, the detail-level currency metadata remains with the business data records in the reconciled layer—the BDW. The BDW and BIW population steps are important users and suppliers of detailed currency metadata.

The transformations from build-time metadata into the appropriate structure for the DWC are similar to those for BDW population. The main work here is in selecting the appropriate metadata from the variety of sources and transforming the metadata into a structure suitable for end users.

If vendors cooperate successfully in such activities as the Metadata Council, established by vendors in late 1995, then much of the function required should become available in vendor tools within a year or two of this effort.

Although DWC population is technically less difficult than BDW population, the logistical and organizational effort to acquire and maintain the required metadata is considerable. Because there are differences in the business value associated with different types of metadata and also differing degrees of difficulty in gathering them, it is worthwhile prioritizing the required metadata described in Section 13.2. This is shown in Table 13-1.

Notice that the basic metadata describing the meaning, structure, and relationships of business data has the highest priority. This ranking stems from the urgent needs expressed by users and the relative ease of gathering and maintaining it. This metadata is a prime candidate for an initial BIG implementation. At the other end of the scale, metadata that has less immediate pay-backs and is more difficult to manage, such as, organizational metadata, can often be addressed later in the implementation cycle.

13.7 Conclusions

From the end user's viewpoint, there is little doubt that the business information guide is a pivotal element in the data warehouse. Users have become increasingly used to the user-friendly functionality provided by BIIs today. They are also becoming increasingly sophisticated in their needs for and use of data. Without a comprehensive, user-oriented set of func-

Table 13-1: *Prioritized requirements for metadata*

Quadrant		Metadata	Priority
Business activity	1.	Definitions of business terms and their relationships to data, function, and so on	Medium
	2.	Definitions of business processes, tasks, and their relationships	Low
	3.	Relationships of business processes, tasks, and terms to organization, application functions, and data	Low
Organization	1.	Definitions of organizational structure and individuals' roles	Low
	2.	Organizational and individual responsibility for function and data	Low
Application function	1.	Definitions of applications and procedures	Medium
	2.	Definitions of queries and reports, and their relationship to applications and processes	Medium
	3.	Linkages to query or report "code"	Low
	4.	Listings of query definitions, parameters, and allowed values	Low
	5.	Data used or produced by applications, procedures, queries, and reports	Low
Data	1.	Business descriptions of data groupings and elements	**High**
	2.	Technical descriptions of data groupings and elements	**High**
	3.	Relationships between data groupings and elements	**High**
	4.	Translations of encoded fields	Medium
	5.	Derivation rules	Medium
	6.	Data currency and scheduling information	Medium
	7.	Data utilization statistics	Low
	8.	Data quality information	Medium

tions to provide them with relevant metadata, users cannot productively use the warehouse.

The role of the BIG is simply and solely to satisfy that need. Although the BIG could be described simply as a user interface to metadata (just as the BII is a user interface to business data), it warrants special treatment in the data warehouse. It is separated from the BII for two primary reasons:

1. It has previously been neglected and requires special focus.

2. It should be common to all users, irrespective of the type of BIW or BII they are using.

A successful BIG implementation will rapidly become an integral part of the end users' common tool set, allowing them both to understand the business data they use and to explore the data they might use.

An interesting and important side effect is also to be expected. The BIG increases end-user involvement in the definition and verification of the business meaning and value of data provided by the IS department. This strengthens the feedback loop between the business and IS organizations and leads to significant improvements in the quality of information available.

Part V

Implementing the data warehouse

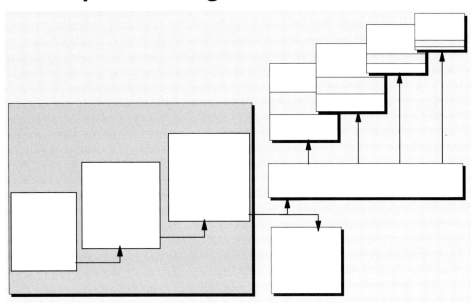

Managing the project and environment

Chapter 14

Obstacles to implementation

There is little doubt among those who try to build a data warehouse that it is a project quite unlike any IS project they have previously undertaken. Of course, some of the problems encountered are the same as those found in any application development project. However, there are a number of obstacles in the path of the data warehouse implementer that are unique— and the nature of these obstacles is such that data warehouse projects are often undertaken with some reluctance.

The purpose of this chapter is to introduce the key problem areas:

- *the size and scope of the data warehouse*

- *justifying the investment in a data warehouse*

- *organizational issues*

- *placement of the BDW and BIWs in the enterprise*

- *ongoing administration*

The following chapters show how to overcome these obstacles.

14.1 The size and scope of the warehouse

The architecture of the data warehouse described in Parts II to IV is explicit. A true data warehouse is enterprise-wide. The reasons for this are many. Some can be seen in the difficulties previously encountered in building compartmentalized decision support environments, as Chapters 2 and 3 describe. Others relate to the business needs a warehouse tries to satisfy, which Chapter 16 describes. Once you accept these reasons, the scope of the data warehouse *must* be enterprise-wide.

Furthermore, a data warehouse is also clearly historical in nature. In decision support and management information applications today, users often demand detailed data over time periods of 5 to 10 years. The historical nature of the warehouse, combined with its enterprise-wide scope, defines the size of the data warehouse. It is big—very big!

Project managers know from bitter experience that this combination of factors is potentially disastrous. These factors typically result in projects that overrun both budget and schedule. They sometimes end in project cancellation rather than completion.

As if these factors were not enough, data warehouses—like all projects in the informational rather than the operational environment—suffer from the fuzziness of user requirements for both data and functionality. Prioritizing needs in such circumstances is extremely difficult.

And so, you may be tempted to conclude—"nice architecture, shame about the implementation".

Fortunately, however, a project plan can be devised that circumvents all of the above problems. The approach described here has evolved from much experience with data warehouse projects—some successful, some less so—over the past few years.

The secret lies, of course, in dividing the overall implementation into achievable pieces that can be implemented in a staged process. The approach, described in Chapter 15, depends on achieving a careful balance between business needs and the planned growth of the data warehouse infrastructure. The result is an implementation process that spans a number of years but delivers business value in 6- to 12-month cycles, in parallel with the progressive, staged implementation of the data warehouse architecture.

14.2 Justifying investment in a data warehouse

Although linked in many ways with the size and scope problems already mentioned, justifying a data warehouse is a big enough issue to warrant special treatment—and thus a whole chapter (Chapter 16).

Little financial training is necessary to perceive that the scope and size of the data warehouse and an implementation process spanning a number of years requires a significant investment. The IS shop can easily calculate data volumes and estimate CPU requirements for satisfactory performance. The effort needed to understand legacy data stores and to implement ways of extracting the data from them can be determined from previous experience. The cost in terms of additional hardware, software and development effort often runs to millions of dollars for larger companies and hundreds of thousands of dollars for smaller companies.

The benefits side of the equation is, unfortunately, more vague. As we will see in Chapter 16, the traditional approach of calculating cost savings is usually not sufficient to offset the implementation expense. Other, and indeed more important, benefit areas must be included in the calculation. However, these benefits are often difficult to predict in advance of implementing the warehouse.

The bottom line is seldom as obvious in dollar terms as is the case for traditional operational applications, although data warehouse proponents may predict it to be an order of magnitude greater. Because of the expenditure involved and the difficulty in predicting the exact return on investment, committing to a warehouse implementation is often an act of faith for the company. And naturally, this decision must involve senior management, both business and IS, in the organization.

14.3 Organizational issues

We cannot expect a data warehouse to be organizationally neutral. From the decision process to build one, through its design and implementation, and on to its use in the enterprise, a data warehouse demands new levels of cooperation. The results of its use should include new business opportunities and changed ways of working. Both of these require that the organization adapt to the new circumstances.

The previous section has already mentioned the first organizational issue to address: the need to make an act of faith during the justification process requires a considerable level of trust between business managers and the IS department. Building such trust in the earliest stages of the process is essential to ensure that the first project is initiated.

In the planning and design phases of building the data warehouse, openness and cooperation are vital. Business departments that previously competed for IS support must now work together. IS developers of different systems must also cooperate to provide data to one another. In some organizations, the developers of operational and informational applications must learn to cooperate in ways they have not previously attempted.

All of these activities require the willingness to cede power and control of information. Warehouse implementers must convince the owners of existing decision support systems (DSS) that the warehouse will be of more benefit to the company than their existing DSS. The prize for these concessions is an information-driven enterprise that works from integrated and consistent data. The price is a diminution of individual or divisional control.

As the implementation the data warehouse proceeds, responsibility for decision making in the organization changes. The data warehouse, because it frees previously inaccessible data, is probably one of the most powerful tools available for empowering staff and creating a team-based environment. The result, of course, is the ability to do without layers of middle management.

Chapter 17 considers the organizational issues to address in the planning and implementation stages of a data warehouse.

14.4 Placement of the BDW and BIWs in the enterprise

The logical architecture described in Parts II to IV defines the roles and relationships of the business data warehouse (BDW) and the business information warehouses (BIWs) in a general way. This description is relatively straightforward, emphasizing the different types of data that exist and the different functions needed to transform raw data into useful information.

However, there is another design stage—sometimes called the physical architecture—required before implementation. In data warehousing, this stage deals mainly with the physical placement of the BDW and BIWs. The main issue to consider is whether to make the implementation centralized or decentralized with respect to:

- the organizational structure of the company
- the geographical structure of the company
- the physical platforms used by the company

This stage is highly dependent on the environment of the enterprise so we cannot easily generalize it. However, because it is an area of some considerable concern, Chapter 18 provides the background for making decisions on the physical architecture.

14.5 Ongoing administration

The final set of issues to resolve before first putting the data warehouse into production revolves around the ongoing administration of the warehouse. Chapter 19 does not, however, attempt to cover all areas of administration. Many of these topics are common to all data processing and particularly database implementations. Such topics are well addressed in other textbooks.

The most obvious area where data warehousing is unique is in the setup and administration of data replication between the layers of the architecture. The text has already shown the value of a model-driven approach to defining how data is replicated. However, the tools available today only partially meet this requirement. Chapter 19 discusses how to implement and administer replication in this situation.

Other topics include the functionality underlying the principal data warehouse components. This functionality—which includes process management and data transfer—is likely to be common to both the data warehouse and other applications.

14.6 Conclusions

Although there exist some considerable challenges to the implementation of a data warehouse, remember that it *has* been done before. With the appropriate internal IS organization, support from business management and often consultancy from vendors or independent experts, a successful implementation is certainly possible.

The topics covered over the remaining chapters cover the key problem areas that previous implementations have uncovered.

The earlier chapters of this book proposed the architecture of the data warehouse. It is, I believe, the only architecture capable of addressing the underlying issues of data consistency and integrity inherent in many companies today. In the implementation aspects that remain to be covered, there are many "right" answers. The approach that suits one company could be a disaster in another.

For that reason, read Part V not as a recipe or formula, but as a background discussion for the types of questions and decisions that the company and the warehouse designers and implementers must typically face in implementing a warehouse. It is a generalization of the implementations with which I have worked—an amalgam of the starting points and successful situations I have seen. However, it is most unlikely to correspond exactly to any particular data warehouse implementation.

Chapter 15

Planning your implementation

The approach to data warehouse implementation shown in this chapter springs from two diametrically opposed requirements. On the one hand, a data warehouse must address the need to provide a new and extensive infrastructure to ensure information quality. On the other hand, every project today—even one as worthy as a warehouse—must deliver some visible and significant business benefit in a reasonable timeframe that, at least, justifies its continuation.

The approach, therefore, is to define a process that delivers the required infrastructure in stages, while ensuring that each stage delivers visible business value. This chapter shows this process.

First, we show an approach to **segmenting the data warehouse** into sections that can be delivered reasonably independently. This approach brings us back to the enterprise data model (EDM), which is one of the founding principles of the data warehouse.

From there, we introduce the concept of the planned, organic growth of the warehouse. This **staged implementation** provides the basis for planning the individual projects in the overall data warehouse delivery process. Each project is designed to stand on its own merits from the point of view of the business benefit it delivers. However, in terms of costs and technical implementation, each project is built on the steps that preceded it and serves as the foundation for those that follow.

Putting such a planned organic growth process in place is, in itself, a challenge. The next topic we cover, therefore, is the planning and implementation of the first step in this process—**the data warehouse initiation project**. This project has a number of key outputs, or deliverables, which we describe in some detail. This leads into a discussion of **the ongoing implementation process**. We describe the role of a project office, which is responsible for ensuring the planned, organic growth of the warehouse.

Finally, we list the **critical success factors** for the overall process.

15.1   Segmenting the data warehouse

It is probably no surprise that the EDM is the basis for segmenting the data warehouse, and thus a means for separating out reasonably independent projects for implementation. The structure of an EDM itself shows a progressively greater segmentation down through the layers. The use of that model first in the business data warehouse (BDW) and then in the business information warehouses (BIWs) also depends on this progressive segmentation. This chapter now brings together these concepts, described separately in Chapters 6, 8, and 10, in order to show the overall implementation approach from the perspective of the EDM.

The outcome provides the basis for staging the data warehouse implementation. This is a result of the progressive narrowing of scope of the model as it drives toward more detailed levels. Figure 15-1 shows this progression, where the numbers correspond to the steps in the process.

- **Step 1, defining the high-level enterprise model,** is at most a 1- to 2-month exercise, as previously described. In any warehousing approach that aims, even long term, to become enterprise-wide, skipping this step adds significant risk to the overall consistency of the model. This first step is carried out only once, except for future realignments, which become necessary only if the business changes substantially enough to affect the overall model. Therefore, the cost of step 1 is borne only during the first stage of warehouse implementation.

- **Step 2, modeling a subset of the BDW,** which involves defining both its structure and its relationship to the operational applications that are the source of its data, is by far the most complex step. Realistically, one can expect this step to take 6 to 9 months, depending on the scope of the BDW subset and the difficulty encountered in sourcing the required data.

- **Step 3, modeling the first BIW,** which involves defining both its structure and its relationship to the BDW, is a relatively straightforward task and could be accomplished in 4 to 6 weeks. Step 3 usually overlaps with the latter parts of step 2.

It is important to understand the difference between steps 2 and 3, also shown in Figure 15-1. Step 2 is driven mainly by an understanding of the generic business needs. Step 3, on the other hand, is driven by the specific data needed to achieve a known business objective. Step 2, therefore, is a step toward the generic model infrastructure that the total warehouse needs, while step 3 is a specific application implementation. Section 15.2 discusses in detail how these two steps relate to one another in project terms.

The iterative modeling steps 3A, 2A, and 3B follow from, and are of similar size to, their precursors. We can see two distinctly different situations here. In the first, represented by 3A, a new BIW is built on the basis of an existing BDW. Step 3A, and further steps like it, can be—and usually should be—delegated to the department or user group requiring this BIW. Step 3A is not formally part of the process of building the data warehouse, because it does not contribute to the warehouse infrastructure.

Steps 2A and 3B, on the other hand, are equivalent to steps 2 and 3. Step 2A is an expansion of the warehouse model, and step 3B delivers associated business value. These two steps together form the next stage of the overall data warehouse implementation process.

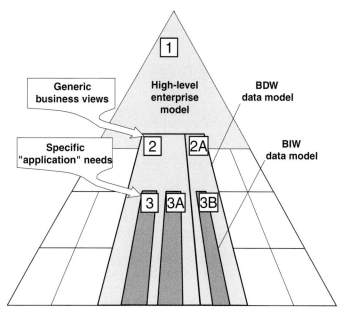

Figure 15-1: Segmenting the data warehouse implementation

15.2 Staging the warehouse implementation

Beyond the use of an enterprise data model, the key to the whole implementation process lies in aligning infrastructure delivery with real, visible business value [Fairhead (1995)]. This requires a **staged data warehouse implementation**, for three very pragmatic reasons:

- The successful staged delivery of visible business value is a powerful argument for continuing the funding of any IS project—especially one that contains a substantial element of the dreaded infrastructure cost!

- The inclusion of specific application needs ensures that the relevant business need will not be met through a competitive development elsewhere in the business, which only delays the achievement of that key goal of data consistency and integrity.

  As a result, the IS shop can now apply the resources that would have been directed at that local project to building the data warehouse.

- Finally, experience has shown that having a real application need against which to define and test the generic business view for the BDW significantly eases and improves the definition.

Staged data warehouse implementation

A process for implementing the warehouse that stages the delivery of the required infrastructure to ensure maximum reuse and in close association with specific, prioritized informational applications.

Defining the project stages that make up the overall implementation process such that each stage contains both aspects—delivery of infrastructure and business value—ensures that these two elements are closely interlinked. Each project thus contains generic modeling of a subset of the BDW and specific application modeling of a BIW that is based on the generic model. Other infrastructural activities are then aligned with these modeling stages.

A staged implementation approach

Figure 15-2 depicts the first four project stages of a data warehouse implementation. Each stage combines tasks relating to both the generic infrastructure and the specific business applications. There are three major components:

1. **Infrastructure development**

    The infrastructure components that will be used broadly throughout the data warehouse are implemented in stages in this part of the project. The implementation may consist of the choice and installation of appropriate tools or the internal development of the required functionality. The principal infrastructure areas that normally occur are:

    - database management system (DBMS) implementation
    - BDW population
    - BIW population
    - data warehouse catalog (DWC) and business information guide (BIG)
    - administration components

2. **Enterprise modeling**

    This part of the project involves generic enterprise-level modeling from the logical to physical level of a bounded area of the business. This corresponds to step 2 of the process shown in Figure 15-1.

3. **Business application**

    The business application part of the project consists of any work that must be done solely to support the specific business requirements of the users. This normally consists of:

    - gathering specific business requirements for information usage
    - modeling the BIW (step 3 in Figure 15-1) at both logical and physical levels
    - documenting business terms, data definitions, and so on, for subsequent capture and use in the DWC

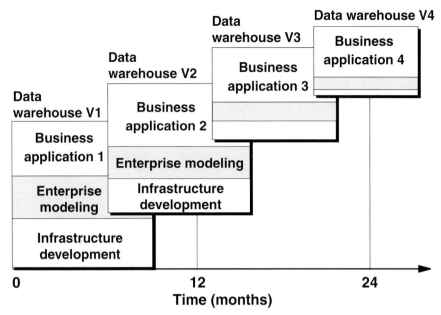

Figure 15-2: *A staged implementation approach*

- designing and developing any specific routines needed for population of this BIW
- designing and developing or acquiring new business information interface (BII) tools, if required
- designing and developing queries, procedures, and so forth

Figure 15-2 represents the effort involved in the projects by the size of the relevant rectangle. We can draw a number of broad conclusions regarding project size from this figure. If the business application parts of the projects are reasonably consistent in size, overall project size decreases from iteration to iteration. This is because the effort spent on new infrastructure and enterprise modeling decreases at each stage, as each new development builds on the achievements of the previous stage.

The implementation schedule

Figure 15-2 also gives an indication of the duration for each project step. There are a number of considerations that influence duration.

The most predictable consideration derives from the effort involved in modeling, as already discussed. This leads to an outlook for initial delivery of business value from the data warehouse in some 9 to 12 months, with iterations following at 6 to 9 month intervals for each extension of the BDW. Note also that the delivery time for new BIWs (sourced from an existing BDW segment) should be about 1 to 2 months.

The business application and infrastructure development components run in parallel with the modeling component. However, the size of each of these must be evaluated at an individual project level. For example, installing a new DBMS on a new parallel processing platform as part of the infrastructure project will obviously increase the size of this component considerably. Similarly, the effort required to deliver the business application component can vary enormously.

The version 1 project builds the initial piece of an enterprise-wide infrastructure for the provision of management information. Therefore, a 9- to 12-month time span for the delivery of the first business value is not unreasonable. However, business managers often ask the question, Can that delivery period be shortened? We must approach the answer from two directions—political and technical.

From a political perspective, it is important to understand that a data warehouse will have profound implications for the political and organizational structures of the company, because it provides significantly expanded access to data and enables data-based decision making in areas of the organization that were previously unsupported. The warehouse enables a shift in power both within the business organization and from the IS shop to the business departments. Obtaining approval and support for such changes is a long process, and the delivery of the first business value may depend on such changes. Earlier delivery may even be counterproductive.

From a technical point of view, the major inhibitor to faster delivery of the first BIW is the time taken to model, design, and populate the BDW—a prerequisite to delivering the first BIW. There is one approach that under certain circumstances reduces the delivery time for the first BIW, although it requires great care in its use. This approach, called a seed pilot, initially combines the BDW and BIW, and is described in Section 15.3.

In practice...

Examine closely any implementation approaches promising shorter delivery times than stated here to understand whether they are building a true data warehouse or simply a large, but traditional, MIS system.

The answer to the question asked earlier, therefore, is that while it may be technically possible to somewhat shorten this first stage of the development, organizational and technical issues may not make it worthwhile.

Another key consideration that limits the size of the project stages shown in Figure 15-2 is the political climate for IS development within the company. Business managers have an increasing impatience with the IS department, and projects longer than 9 to 12 months are exceedingly difficult to sell to management. In some cases, the threshold has dropped to 6 to 9 months. Such timeframes are not incompatible with the figures shown earlier. However, a 6-month timeframe for an initial production version of the data warehouse is unrealistic, given the amount of political activity and the high-level modeling involved.

The aim then, as shown in Figure 15-2, is to deliver the first version of the data warehouse in around a 9- to 12-month period, with subsequent deliveries gradually increasing in frequency to 6-month periods. Depending on the state of the existing operational systems, after three or four iterations over 2 years, we might expect 70% to 80% of the EDM to be completed and 80% to 90% of the warehouse infrastructure to be in place.

How long will it take to build the complete warehouse? The only fully correct answer is that it will never be finished, because the business will always be changing, and the EDM and therefore the warehouse must reflect this. However, to all intents and purposes, after the first six to eight iterations, there will be few, if any, new areas of the business to support, and reworking the existing implementation will be the main activity. Thus a time span of 3 to 5 years is the most common answer to the question about duration.

Planning for organic growth

Figure 15-2 shows a process that clearly requires careful planning, because each stage is limited by a number of factors.

Most importantly, of course, there is the business need to address. As with any other project, each stage in the warehouse implementation needs justification. A real and substantial business benefit *must* be provided at each stage.

However, unlike all other areas of IS development, prioritizing business factors is not sufficient in planning the order of stages in implementing the warehouse. There are two other factors to include:

1. The relationship between the BDW and the EDM is vital. When the first segment of the EDM has been implemented in version 1 of the BDW, the second segment to be implemented must relate closely to the first. When the second segment has been implemented, the third segment must relate closely to either of the first two; and so on. There are two reasons for this interrelationship:

    *   The existence of a close relationship allows each project to benefit from modeling work that has been previously done—thus reducing the incremental cost of each step.
    *   If the warehouse is allowed to grow from separate segments of the EDM, there is a danger of ending up, in the worst case, with two or more independent data warehouses or, at best, with a significant reconciliation effort later on.

2. There is a need to build on existing infrastructure in two ways:

    *   The existing operational systems infrastructure must continue to run and support the business. The new informational infrastructure must accommodate this mandatory requirement.

- New components of the informational infrastructure should, as far as possible, be built on those provided in previous phases. The reason again is to reduce the incremental cost of each step. However, in this case, the danger of disconnected development of pieces of infrastructure is less significant than in the case of the EDM.

In practice...

Planning the roll-out of the data warehouse is a joint activity among all business areas and the IS shop.

The outcome of the above factors is that the growth pattern of the data warehouse must be planned on the basis of business need, enterprise modeling considerations, and infrastructure limitations. Planning this way is a novel situation for most companies: the prioritization of IS projects is usually solely (and in other areas of development, correctly) the prerogative of the business community. Planning the implementation, or roll-out, of the warehouse, however, is a joint business and IS responsibility.

Last but not least, the data warehouse requires that the different parts of the business organization be involved in a formal process of cross-organizational prioritization of business needs. The data warehouse as an enterprise-wide support tool needs an enterprise-wide prioritization of business requirements as input to its planning process. In many companies, where divisional or other structuring is deeply embedded, such prioritization is difficult to achieve.

These factors lead to the need for new organizational structures to handle prioritization, both at a business level and at the level of combined business and technical needs. These are discussed in Chapter 17.

The complexities listed above led the lead designer of Blue Cross/Blue Shield NCA's data warehouse to describe the process as being similar to swapping out the engine of a jumbo jet in flight [I/S Analyzer (1994)].

15.3 Kick-starting the implementation process

The roll-out just described is rather complex and the different components strongly interdependent. Obtaining commitment to it and putting in place the structures required to make it happen is, in itself, a substantial exercise. Among the activities needed before the roll-out can happen are the following:

- The promoter of the data warehouse must often gain acceptance of the overall business justification for the entire approach.

- If this is the company's first use of enterprise modeling, establishing a support structure for this activity may be necessary.

- A new approach to the justification and prioritization of IS development must be established to enable subsequent steps.

- New organizational structures to promote cooperation between different areas of the business may need to be established.

And, on top of all that, the teams—two or more of them—responsible for implementing the first step need education and training.

This preparatory work comprises the data warehouse initiation project.

The data warehouse initiation project

The **data warehouse initiation project** is not a development project—it does not deliver any code, and design work is confined strictly to architecture and high-level design. Rather, it is a preparatory project designed to define the structure of the warehouse in the organization, to plan for its implementation, and to set up the correct organizational infrastructure needed to enable its development.

As Figure 15-3 shows, we can view this project as having three main phases that precede the development of version 1 of the data warehouse.

> **Data warehouse initiation project**
>
> *A preparatory project that establishes the structure and roll-out of the data warehouse.*

Phase 1: initial education and orientation

In the past, this phase has tended to be a rather long, drawn-out process involving the part-time efforts of the person in the company who first discovered the phrase "data warehousing" to understand the concept and obtain management approval to proceed. This often took 12 months or more. Today this stage should take no longer than a month given the interest in data warehousing.

Typically, phase 1 consists of the following activities:

- **Initial exploration of and education on data warehousing**

  This could be done through reading the literature; attending conferences; or holding discussions with vendors, consultants and other companies that are building a warehouse. Probably the most important outcome today is an ability to distinguish between a real data warehouse and the approaches being promoted as a single answer to every problem.

- **Obtaining the necessary management approval to proceed**

  This approval is for the data warehouse initiation project—the purpose of this phase is *not* to obtain approval for a data warehouse. Such approval requires substantial preparatory work—undertaken during the data warehouse initiation project itself.

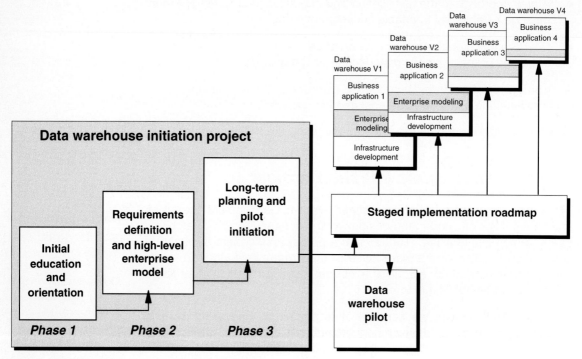

Figure 15-3: *The data warehouse initiation project*

- **Building and educating the teams responsible for this project**

    Two key teams are often identified: the initiation team and the extended team. Chapter 17 describes these teams in greater detail.

Phase 2: requirements definition and high-level enterprise model

Phase 2 is designed to discover and document the broad business requirements that will drive the implementation process. This stage must focus on the business as a whole and on the general issues regarding access to and use of data within the enterprise rather than on the specific problems in particular areas (although, of course, these specific problems will serve as illustrations of the general problem).

There are two parts to phase 2, usually carried out in parallel:

- **Requirements definition**

    This involves an investigation of existing business strategies and their information needs. This information may already be documented. Interviews with senior management are advisable to verify this strategy and to understand how a data warehouse approach could support it.

It is important to emphasize the need for leadership and vision in this activity. The business executives and managers involved must be able to envisage what the company could achieve with enterprise-wide access to consistent, business-driven information.

- **High-level enterprise model**

  This second, and more formal, activity is the high-level enterprise data modeling exercise previously discussed.

The duration of phase 2 is highly dependent on the prior existence of an enterprise-level data model. If such a model exists, either as a generic industry model or from prior work within the company, phase 2 can be completed within 4 to 6 weeks. In the absence of such a model, this phase will take longer, although the aim is to complete it within 2 months.

Phase 3: long-term planning and pilot initiation

The objective of phase 3 is to gain business approval for and commitment to the data warehousing implementation process and to prove that this process can deliver both business value and data warehouse infrastructure. By the end of this stage, the initiation team has completed its job and is seeking executive approval for the roll-out process to begin.

Phase 3 has three major deliverables:

- **Customized data warehouse architecture**

  This is a customized version of the generic data and function architecture described in Parts II to IV of this book, adapted to the specific environment of the company. It also identifies the tools or development needed to build it.

- **Staged implementation roadmap (SIR)**

  This document outlines the overall shape of the warehouse and the major implementation steps. This document is the basis for executive approval of the roll-out. It also provides for each area of the business an initial view of how and when the warehouse will meet their particular needs.

- **Pilot data warehouse plan and high-level design**

  The data warehouse pilot proves the ability of the IS shop to deliver a data warehouse. It can focus on a number of objectives, such as demonstrating some business value or testing some of the technology. The pilot itself is developed as a separate project by a different team but under the direction of the initiation team. This third deliverable is a plan and high-level design for the pilot.

This phase can be completed in less than 3 months in many cases.

The staged implementation roadmap

Staged implementation roadmap (SIR)

A high-level design and roll-out plan produced by the data warehouse initiation project to sell the warehouse to the whole company, and in particular to business management.

The staged implementation roadmap should not be confused with a traditional project plan. Although it must contain some outline implementation plan, it is not a committed plan either in detailed deliverables or schedule, with one exception, noted below.

The purpose of the SIR is to provide the entire enterprise with a view of what the data warehouse is, what benefits it could bring, how it would affect the organization in general, and a flavor of how it could be delivered. If successful, the SIR will convince management that a data warehouse is essential and will gain their support for its implementation.

In many respects, the SIR is an internal marketing brochure that provides a vision of the data warehouse to be implemented and an assurance that it can be delivered. Unlike many documents produced by the IS organization, the SIR should receive close attention to production issues such as readability, layout, use of color, understandable diagrams, and so on. In general, it should be less than 50 pages, and a senior manager should want and be able to read it over a glass or two of wine!

The audience of the SIR is primarily the executive board, the heads of the various business units, and their IS managers. Depending on the culture of the organization, the senior business planners and IS architects should also be included among the approvers, or at least receive copies.

The key elements of the SIR are:

1. **Executive summary**

   As with all executive summaries, this should be brief and to the point, summarizing the main business reasons for the data warehouse and its conceptual design.

2. **Business strategy overview**

   Based on previous strategy work in the company and the executive level interviews carried out during the initiation project, there may not be much new information in this section. However, it should focus specifically on the information-related aspects of the strategy and key areas that could benefit from the availability of consistent information across the company.

3. **Statement of the existing situation**

   This provides a summary of the problems encountered today in achieving the business strategy or, indeed, in meeting current business needs for information. It should, of course, avoid any allocation of blame.

4. **Outline of the data warehouse architecture**

   The purpose of this section is to describe the three-layer data and function architecture at a high level and to show how it applies within the organization.

5. **Implications for existing and new systems**

   This section allows the owners of existing systems to see how the warehouse will affect them and what areas will need investment in application changes or new infrastructure.

6. **Potential areas of benefit and possible cost**

   Note that this section is *not* a cost/benefit analysis. Although the costs could be estimated to a reasonable level of certainty at this stage, benefits are far more difficult to estimate with any degree of accuracy. We return to this topic in Chapter 16.

7. **Summary of the data warehouse roll-out**

   This is the key section of the SIR. It shows, in broad terms, the staging of the data warehouse delivery. It gives a view of which stage of the roll-out will include which data, and when each part of the organization will benefit from the data warehouse. As a consequence, it also shows when each part of the organization will have to invest in the data warehouse in order to gain this benefit.

   A number of points are worth noting:

   - Preparing this section is a delicate political process, involving negotiations with all areas of the business.
   - This section is likely to be subject to ongoing change as business needs change and evolve.
   - This section will become the initial version of a larger and more comprehensive plan that guides the overall implementation process of the data warehouse over the following 3 to 5 years.
   - This summary is *not* a commitment-level plan, but rather a statement of intent, as this section must make clear.
   - The summary should contain a minimum of detail.

8. **Proposed organizational structure**

   This section shows the organization needed to drive the data warehouse implementation process forward over the following 3 to 5 years. It covers both the central IS organization—technical and user involvement—and the contributions to come from business units within the organization.

9. Outline of pilot project scope, deliverables and timeframe

This section summarizes the plan for the pilot project. Unlike section 7, this plan *is* making statements at a commitment level. As a result, it must estimate costs with some level of certainty and show any benefits accruing from the pilot.

10. Sign-off

The SIR is not a "for your information" document. The business management and IS departments are expected to accept the direction and buy into it. This final section is for signing in blood, and to mix metaphors, may be used later in evidence!

The data warehouse pilot

Data warehouse pilot

The first development project of the warehouse implementation process, designed to prove the viability of the overall approach.

There are four main variations on the theme of a *data warehouse pilot*. Each one has its own principal purpose but suffers from some disadvantages. In practice, of course, a real pilot will often contain a little of each purpose and may not fall neatly into any one of the four categories. However, for clarity, the following sections describe each category of pilot independently.

The technology pilot

In many respects, a *technology pilot* is the simplest type of pilot and also the least useful in moving the data warehouse forward. Its purpose is to allow the IS shop to prove the technical viability of the tools to be used in the production warehouse. These tools may be vendor supplied or developed internally.

Common technology pilots include:

* introduction of a new parallel processing and/or UNIX-based environment in which the data warehouse will be implemented

* installation and testing of one or more data replication tools

* initial use of an enterprise data modeling approach

The strength of the technology pilot lies in its ability to focus on a particular aspect of the data warehouse implementation. It proves the ability of IS personnel to deliver in this area or tests the claims of a vendor for its particular tool. On the negative side, such pilots are of little use in proving that all the parts of the data warehouse can work together, and because they deliver no business value, technology pilots cannot provide a rationale for introducing the warehouse into the business community.

The business pilot

At the other extreme from the technology pilot, the ***business pilot*** approach focuses on delivering specific business value, usually at the expense of some aspect of the strategic data warehouse infrastructure.

The driver for a business pilot[1] is an urgent need for the delivery of a particular management information or decision support application. As a result, the requirements are reasonably well defined, the users are already supportive, and a successful data warehouse pilot will deliver real business value. As any project manager knows, these conditions significantly increase the probability of success and are thus strongly positive factors.

On the negative side, because the data scope is well defined in advance, a business pilot may conflict with enterprise modeling considerations. In particular, it may span a wider segment of the model than can be reasonably defined in the required timeframe. This may require compromises in the completeness of modeling performed in some areas of the project.

Related also to the data scope is the fact that the sources for this data may be multiple and varied. This leads to a potentially more complex initial BDW population project than would be ideal. This is the most technically complex aspect of any data warehouse implementation, and the complexity increases dramatically with increasing numbers and types of operational sources of data. Again, the initial population project will often need compromises. This may involve postponing the introduction of new data replication tools (with their associated learning curves and testing periods) in favor of reusing some of the older data extraction applications in the initial build. This latter choice speeds up the first delivery, but at the cost of later migrating to newer data replication tools.

Finally, such business pilots are often subject to severe delivery pressure, because the company has identified the business need before agreeing on the scope of the data warehousing pilot project.

We might conclude from the above discussion that a business pilot is a bad choice. On the contrary, it is the one most likely to cement the success of the data warehouse approach—provided the pilot itself is successful! The difficulties can be overcome through a combination of strong project management and good cooperation between the business and IS organizations. A company that successfully implemented a business pilot—Lands' End Inc., a U.S. catalog marketer of clothing—is described in Bustamente and Sorenson (1994).

---

[1] Note that, in the context of Figure 15-3, a business pilot and version 1 of the data warehouse are essentially equivalent. This implies a faster delivery of business value in the whole process than the technology or user-oriented pilot can deliver.

The user-oriented pilot

The focus of the **user-oriented pilot** is on what the eventual end user of the data warehouse will see. The aspects included in this pilot are usually:

- a new end-user tool set for the BII
- the BIG

This type of pilot makes an assumption about the data sourcing issues. It assumes either that the sourcing is adequate as it is, or that any problems of quality or timeliness can be ignored for the duration of the pilot. Of course, this is, in many cases, simply postponing the problem.

However, the introduction of a new end-user tool set is often valuable in selling the concept of a data warehouse to a suspicious business community where the tools currently available to end users are particularly poor or significantly out of date. In such cases, the introduction of the data warehouse is linked in users' minds to this new (and exciting) technology.

There are a number of negative aspects to bear in mind. The end-user tool set is likely to vary from area to area within the business, and is often the subject of considerable debate. These factors mean that success in such a pilot may be hard-won, and may not be of great value in the roll-out process to other areas of the business.

In addition, the lack of focus on data, and in particular on integrity and sourcing issues means that the quality of the data in the pilot is potentially rather low. The business value of the user-oriented pilot is thus debatable.

Focusing on the BIG adds considerably to the business value. Including the BIG addresses data meanings and drives improvements in data quality. It also brings this aspect of data warehousing to users' attention, and associates the work needed with improvements in data quality rather than simply the introduction of new technology.

In general, however, the user-oriented pilot is of value only in some rather limited circumstances, and is not often the recommended choice.

The seed pilot

This final pilot approach is attractive in many instances. The underlying rationale of a **seed pilot** is to try to simplify all of the technically difficult areas of the data warehouse implementation, and to deliver a useful, although limited-scope, data warehouse.

Notice from Figure 15-1, that we could reduce the scope of the initial BDW until it corresponds exactly to the scope of the first BIW. The advantage is twofold. First, it eliminates the additional modeling effort required for the BDW, since the BDW and BIW models are essentially equivalent. Second, for the initial implementation, the BDW and BIW can be collapsed into one physical database layer. However, it is important to note some key restrictions on this approach:

- It is only appropriate for the first implementation in any business area.

  Using this shortcut to deliver subsequent segments of the data warehouse would lead inevitably to the original data reconciliation problems that the warehouse approach was designed to avoid.

- The structure of the resulting combined BDW/BIW should not be too highly optimized for performance of the business application.

  Although this restriction sounds ridiculous, it is necessary to allow for the eventual separation of the two layers when new BIWs are added in the same business area. The optimization is made possible if the user set of the pilot is small in number and lacking the expertise to seriously stretch the performance of the system.

- The company must develop and approve a plan to migrate to a full three-layer approach even before delivery of the pilot.

  The business must recognize and agree in advance that it will need a piece of infrastructure work, which in itself delivers no extra business function, to enable further expansion of the data warehouse.

The use of an "all-in-one" data warehouse package further supports the delivery of such a pilot implementation. These tools support the pilot approach by allowing the warehouse development team to postpone the initial learning curve associated with the use of full-function modeling or population tools for the warehouse. Deferring this learning curve until after delivery of the first business function allows the faster delivery of initial, although limited, business value.

Although it is always attractive to deliver business value as early as possible, two powerful considerations, already mooted, limit enthusiasm for this seed approach: have all the political hurdles been cleared? and has everyone agreed on the migration path to the full architecture? If either of these tests fail, the seed pilot will simply become another component in an ever expanding set of disparate applications delivering conflicting data to end users.

Choosing a pilot approach

As already stated, the pilot eventually defined may well combine aspects of all of the above types. However, the major direction of any pilot usually corresponds to one of the above approaches.

The choice of pilot approach depends mainly on the existing business and technical environment into which the data warehouse is being introduced. The following factors influence the choice:

- If the initiative for data warehousing is driven primarily from the IS department, a user-oriented pilot can increase business awareness and support, but must be followed directly by a business pilot to ensure further expansion.

- If there is an extensive, existing decision support environment, together with a well-defined business need for integrated data, a business pilot is the only option. This is the most common case today.

- Where the data warehouse involves a major change in the technical architecture and business needs are only vaguely defined, a technology pilot can be used to prove the doability of the approach. However, there is a strong need for the business to work in parallel with the technology project, to identify a business need for a subsequent business-oriented version 1 project.

- Where minimal or no decision support environment exists, a seed pilot is often the best choice to introduce data warehousing concepts to both business users and IS staff simultaneously. This approach is also valid where an existing decision support environment is confined to a particular business area or is not widely trusted.

Given a choice, the order of preference for data warehouse pilots is thus:

1. business pilot
2. seed pilot
3. user-oriented pilot
4. technology pilot

The sequence relates primarily to the perceived business value of the pilot.

The choice of initial warehouse segment

The choice of an initial warehouse segment to implement in a business or seed pilot has significant consequences for the overall success of the data warehouse implementation process. Assuming that specific and predetermined business needs do not entirely dictate which data to put in the data warehouse first, choosing which segment to build first can be a difficult decision. A careful balance must be struck among the following:

1. Position in the EDM

The first data warehouse implementations must come from a segment of the EDM that is central to the model. This is necessary to ensure that the implementation is clearly extensible. If the first segment implemented is on the periphery of the model, with few links to other areas, implementation of the second segment is likely to gain little benefit from implementation of the first.

Needless to say, a multiplicity of poorly defined links between a chosen central segment and its neighbors is likely to lead to disaster, with subsequent steps in the process causing considerable reworking of the initial segment of the model. Therefore, the segment chosen should be well bounded, with clearly defined links to other segments of the enterprise model.

2. Importance or value to the business as a whole

The value provided by the initial data warehouse project must be clearly visible. It is usually not sufficient that the sponsoring business area alone receives benefit from the implementation. Rather, a number of business areas should gain some small benefit, or at least see potential benefit from the next stage in the process.

However, an executive information system (EIS) is not a good choice as a first BIW. It is probably too visible, but more importantly, it is likely to require data from too many sources.

3. Support from a particular business area

The department or user group with which the initial BIW is built stands to gain most from the first stage in the data warehouse implementation process. This business area should understand and agree to a number of requirements placed on it:

- This business area must commit to investment in the project, both in the construction of its own BIW and in cooperating closely in the design and construction of the BDW.
- It must be willing to compromise on the time scale for delivering some of its needs when these are incompatible with delivery of a warehouse that is more widely useful in the business.

  A BIW that can allow no flexibility in its delivery schedule, especially if it must be delivered in less than 6 months, is *not* the BIW with which to start.
- This business area must serve as an ambassador throughout the business for the data warehouse, both during and after completion of the pilot project.

4. Size

Size can be measured in many directions, but in a first data warehouse project, limiting the size of the undertaking is important. This may be done in a variety of ways:

- limiting the number of operational sources of data
- restricting the volumes of data in the first data warehouse
- avoiding the use of too many new tools
- limiting the audience at first to a subset of the full audience

> *In practice...*
>
> *Keeping the number of operational data sources small is the key factor in the success of the initial warehouse project. Given a choice, limiting the number of sources to two is ideal—one legacy system and one modern, modeled system.*

5. Likelihood of success

If there is a choice of which business need to provide for first through the warehouse, a degree of pragmatism is wise. A small but visibly successful first project is a much better first step than a larger one that overruns on budget and delivers only part of what has been promised.

Note that these considerations lead to an initial project quite unlike the typical IS pilot project. In contrast to those typical pilots, the data warehouse pilot is in a central area of the business activity, has high visibility, and delivers business value. The implication is that any doubts about the suitability of a particular tool or environment, or any of the other topics of a typical pilot project, should be addressed before starting the pilot.

A starting point for infrastructure

Of the topics listed earlier for possible inclusion in a technology pilot, two occur most often as the initial area for implementing infrastructure.

The first is the use of data replication tools for BDW population. As has been stated many times already, this area is the most technically challenging of the data warehouse implementation [Chowdary (1995)]. An early start is thus appropriate. In addition, the productivity payback for the IS department can be large enough to allow it to redirect resources to other areas of infrastructure at a later stage. In general, the use of data replication tools is the area of infrastructure that warehouse developers should indeed address first.

The second common starting point for infrastructure is the adoption of a new technology for data storage in the warehouse. This usually involves a move to parallel processing hardware and software. Although this may be necessary in the longer term, there are a number of arguments against doing this in the pilot or even in an early version. These include a potentially steep learning curve, the tuning issues often associated with parallel implementations, and the relatively minor benefit when pilot data volumes are likely to be small.

A third broad area where a pilot can focus initial infrastructure development relates to metadata—its definition, storage, and availability to users. The example of Whirlpool Corporation in the following box shows how powerful this approach can be. However, addressing metadata is often left to later in the implementation process. Indeed, this postponement can be logically justified—because the warehouse has an urgent mandate to provide clean business data, and because the initial users are often using data with which they are already familiar.

The above considerations relate entirely to the infrastructure required to run the data warehouse. In addition, infrastructure is also required to

---

Real-life example: Whirlpool Corporation (USA)

Whirlpool Corporation was an early proponent of the power and usefulness of metadata. In 1991, when planning its first data warehouse, a key concern was the ability of end users to effectively use the data provided. These users previously had only minimal exposure to the data stored in IS, and then only in the context of specific applications.

Whirlpool looked at the IS data dictionary as a possible source of metadata about data meaning and usage. Like many companies, it found that source to be less than adequate. Ownership of data was another key user requirement but was hardly supported at all.

The capture of ownership metadata is notoriously difficult. It is seldom assigned in the business. In addition, changing roles and responsibilities make it difficult to maintain. Whirlpool's solution was simple but effective: data could not enter the warehouse unless a business manager (acting as a data steward) was willing to publicly admit responsibility for the data.

The outcome observed probably exceeded the company's expectations:

- *Data quality was improved because owners felt responsible for the correctness of their data and because users now had a businessperson to go to when they found problems with the content or currency of the data.*

- *For metadata quality the results were even better, because for almost the first time, the business users actively contributed to documenting data meaning.*

The early success at Whirlpool in implementing a data warehouse is largely attributable to this simple method of ensuring the documentation of data ownership. Their experience shows that the quality, integrity, and consistency of both business data and metadata are important to end users. With these aspects assured, Whirlpool found that use of the warehouse grew rapidly, and managers trusted the output because of their role as data stewards.

---

support the design and development phase the warehouse implementation. We may assume that suitable compilers, debuggers, and so on are already in place in the IS shop. However, a key element that the company may have to acquire and commission is the tool set to build and manage the enterprise model. This effort, if required, should not be overlooked.

15.4 Coordinating the data warehouse implementation process

There are two characteristics of the data warehouse implementation process that together make it rather unusual. Both have already been mentioned, but each requires some further consideration. First, the overall process requires a significant level of coordination. This can be achieved through a project office approach, described here. The second characteristic of the process is that the individual project steps must simultaneously address both specific and generic business needs as well as technology needs. This aspect of a typical data warehouse project, described in Section 15.2, must also be considered by the project office.

*Staged
implementation
plan (SIP)*

*The detailed,
evolving plan for
the overall data
warehouse im-
plementation
process, devel-
oped and used by
the project office
to manage that
process.*

The staged implementation roadmap (SIR) is the starting point for coordination of the implementation process. Once the business and IS community have agreed and signed off on the SIR, it becomes the basis for a more detailed **staged implementation plan (SIP)**, as Figure 15-4 shows.

The SIP is not static. Defining and managing it is an ongoing activity. From its first definition, it is the definitive plan of how to roll out the data warehouse. Like all plans, it must be subject to a change management process as business circumstances and technical factors evolve. Responsibility for this type of activity typically rests with a **project office**.

In defining the SIP, the project office needs business guidance on the strategy of the organization and on the priority the business puts on different informational activities. The source of such input is the business itself, typically a cross-enterprise steering committee. Chapter 17 discusses the steering committee and project office in the context of project organization.

Based on the SIP, the project office is responsible for defining and initiating the individual data warehouse projects. In this process, the project office needs input about specific requirements from appropriate areas of the business. The project office ensures the correct balance in each project between the effort expended on the generic elements (the enterprise modeling and infrastructure development) and on the specific business needs supported. Once the project office has produced a high-level definition of the project, it is passed to an implementation team.

The division of responsibility outlined above is different from that found in most projects, and is important. It is necessary to ensure that the individual projects each contribute to the organic growth of the data warehouse, as well as support a particular business need. Only the project office has a broad enough view of the generic needs to make this happen.

As each project proceeds, the implementation team must liaise closely with the project office through regular reviews. This leads to a two-way information flow. The progress (or lack thereof!) of the individual projects influences the SIP, which is regularly updated to reflect what has been achieved and what is now possible in the next phase. The project office participates in the change management process for each project, supporting prioritization of project change requests and in some circumstances raising such requests itself.

The responsibility of the project office is to manage the overall roll-out of the data warehouse. We can see from Figure 15-4 that this is an iterative

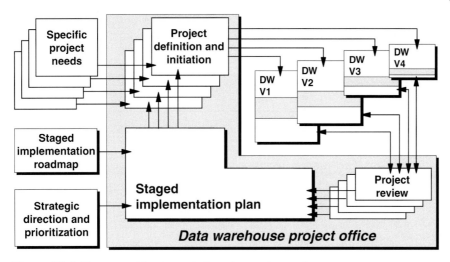

Figure 15-4: *The staged implementation plan and overall process*

process containing a strong feedback loop. Within this loop, the staged implementation plan influences each project, which in turn contributes to the development of the plan.

The implementation plan in Section 15.2 described a roll-out with deliverables eventually at 6-month intervals. Given a number of implementation teams and a sufficiently strong project office, there is no reason why a number of implementation projects could not proceed in parallel. This would, of course, speed up the delivery of the whole data warehouse. Realistically, parallel implementation can occur only after the major segments of the enterprise model are well defined, in order to reduce project interdependencies when two or more projects are involved in defining the same area of the model. The switch-over point between serial and parallel project initiation could occur around version 3 of the data warehouse, or some 12 to 18 months after beginning the process.

> *In practice...*
>
> *Undertake implementation projects in parallel only after all the key, central segments of the enterprise model are well defined.*

15.5 Critical success factors

The foregoing discussions enable us to define some factors that are vital to the success of the overall process:

- **Long-term, committed business executive involvement**

  This is the most critical success factor of all—committed and active executive sponsorship of the data warehouse implementation process is the one factor common to all successful data warehouses.

  It is driven by the organizational implications of the warehouse. The organizational impact of the data warehouse is widespread and difficult

In practice...

When a data warehouse has been strongly promoted, especially by the IS shop, the start of the pilot project is a good time to begin managing users' expectations. Continuing to promote the concept while developing the pilot may require a damage limitation exercise at a later date! A successful pilot will be sufficient advertisement for the process.

to manage. It generates fear and resistance as power shifts within the organization. Not only is such change needed to build the warehouse, but it is an inevitable outcome of a successful implementation. The IS department cannot effectively drive changes of this nature. They require support and direction from the highest levels of the business organization.

At a practical level, this involvement supports and drives prioritization of business function and resolution of debates on requirements.

- **A pragmatic, staged implementation plan**

  The staged implementation plan defines the process. It must, of course, define the vision of where the data warehouse is going. But most importantly, it must define the steps for getting there, recognizing the current business and technical realities.

- **Well-defined and agreed business needs for individual projects**

  The individual projects must deliver real business value in order to prove that the data warehouse is worth doing, and worth doing well.

- **Managed expectations**

  The process described above will clearly not deliver instant gratification to all areas of the business. An important point in the initiation process occurs when managing the users' expectations for the delivery of real business applications must replace the objective of selling the concept of a data warehouse.

A word of warning, however, is appropriate. Do not confuse committed and active executive sponsorship with day-to-day executive involvement in the implementation process. The latter type of "sponsorship" can be extremely damaging to the delicate balance that must be maintained between business and technical factors throughout the implementation process. Experience suggests that the intimate involvement of a business executive in this process often results in over-emphasizing the short-term business benefits at the expense of building a solid foundation for future growth.

15.6 Conclusions

We may baldly state that defining a practical approach to implementing the warehouse is more important than choosing an architecture. Of course, it is true that implementation cannot proceed without an architecture. However, more data warehouses fail through a badly planned implementation approach than for architectural reasons.

The most important fact to bear in mind when planning your implementation is that the process must carefully blend together business value and infrastructure delivery. The outcome is a series of projects, each delivering business value and infrastructure in a staged and controlled manner.

Prioritizing the sequence of deliverables in this process is, unlike most IS projects, determined by a combination of business needs and technical aspects. The most important influence is the EDM. Its segmentation provides a view of which business areas need early support in the data warehouse and supports the definition of a staged delivery. The resulting staged implementation process must be managed carefully. This is achieved using a staged implementation plan.

The first implementation project is usually treated as a pilot. Although we can envisage a variety of pilot approaches, one that involves both business value and technical infrastructure aspects is preferable. This balance provides the best and fastest approach to overcoming the initial learning curve associated with the data warehouse implementation.

In building a data warehouse, a wide variety of business, technical, and organizational issues will arise. The business issues are similar to those encountered in most IS projects. Today, improved tools help to overcome the technical issues. The organizational issues often prove the most intractable. The active support of an executive business sponsor is the most effective way to deal with organizational problems.

This chapter is prescriptive—it describes a particular implementation approach. Other, similar approaches exist, examples of which are described in Walker (1994) and Haisten (1995a,b). I have chosen a commonly encountered set of circumstances on which to base the description of the methodology. However, your starting point is likely to be different from the one shown here. You must therefore be pragmatic in adapting this approach to your circumstances. Trying to change the existing circumstances to allow the unswerving use of this approach is, of course, a nonstarter!

Chapter 16

Justifying the warehouse

Justifying the implementation of a data warehouse differs significantly from the process of justifying traditional applications. It is often considered to be a difficult, even well-nigh impossible, process. In reality, it requires a combination of approaches, some well-known from traditional development as well as others requiring an innovative view of the business. This innovation is particularly required in areas where the actual benefits of the data warehouse cannot be specifically predicted in advance.

Another obstacle to overcome stems from the duration of the implementation process. As the previous chapter shows, this can take from 3 to 5 years. Few, if any, IS departments have a planning process that allows commitment to such long-term investment in advance. The data warehouse implementation process must therefore contend with the reality that funding priorities may change over its lifetime.

This chapter addresses the justification of the data warehouse from a number of viewpoints.

First, there are the aspects of the data warehouse that are capable of *justification in the traditional manner*. This means that both cost and benefit can be estimated with some degree of certainty, and a "standard" business case can be developed.

Second, we look *beyond cost avoidance* to benefits that cannot be quantified in advance. In truth, these are usually the most significant advantages expected for the data warehouse. It has been said that they require an act of faith by the business to accept them. This chapter describes how current experiences with warehousing and an understanding of how the business environment is changing can assist in making this leap of faith.

Finally, a brief examination of the *costs of a data warehouse* is appropriate. We show where the major costs are incurred and give some guidance on how to allocate them.

16.1   The traditional justification approach

This approach to project justification revolves around cost savings. The formula amounts to an estimate of the costs that could be avoided by automating a particular process. In the extreme, the company may achieve savings by eliminating jobs and reducing staff as a result of this automation.

Introducing a data warehouse seldom eliminates jobs. There is an emphasis on the elimination or simplification of particular tasks, with a resultant increase in the productivity of the people involved. We could argue that this allows a reduction in staffing. However, the more usual end result is a re-deployment of effort that allows the support of many of the new or underutilized areas of management information.

The second area where a company can achieve productivity improvements is in IS. The provision of data to the informational environment is recognized today as an inefficient process. The application of new tools in this area can improve the efficiency of the IS department in providing such data. Again, a reduction in IS resources as a result of implementing a warehouse is an unlikely outcome, at least in the short term. The expectation is that resources freed in this area will allow IS staff to focus on data meaning and quality, and to expand rapidly the scope of management information available to the business.

Improving the productivity of end users

While the business focus on and justification for decision support have continued to grow at a rapid pace, end-user productivity and, indeed, satisfaction have tended to remain low. Users point to a number of problems that prevent efficient exploitation of the data in the business. Many of these problems are a result of the way informational systems have evolved, as described in Part I and summarized here.

The key complaint relates to the difficulty end users experience in finding and accessing the data they require for a particular process. Users typically go from system to system gathering the data they need, signing on and off multiple times, and using different tools and user interfaces. Most surveys suggest that users spend three to four times as long locating and gathering data as they do actually using it.

The technical and geographical diversity of the required data is only one aspect of the problem. In many organizations, the documentation of data meanings and locations ranges from minimal to nonexistent. IS departments have seldom had the time or resources to document the data content of applications under development. Only the more recent application development efforts have used CASE tools to capture and maintain the data definitions, which provide a level of data description that is useful to end users. In companies that have consistently used data dictionaries in their application development shops, users find that the available data descriptions are expressed only in non-business terms. Indeed, users often have great difficulty in relating data as stored and described by the IS shop to the business view that they need.

Beyond internal data, end users have an increased ability to obtain data from sources outside the company's systems. Typically, this means accessing or acquiring data from market data providers such as Dow Jones or Dun and Bradstreet through on-line service connections. Matching such information with internal data poses significant problems.

Even when the relevant data is discovered and made available, further pitfalls await the unwary. Multiple copies of apparently the same data turn out on further analysis to be subtly different. Data with different names is discovered to be identical. Some data is valid as of today, other data from last month, while even more data has no indication of its period of validity.

And finally, even when the user has identified the correct data source, ascertained its meaning, and incorporated the data into the decision-making process, the providers of the base data are unlikely to guarantee its quality. The quality, accuracy, and consistency of data in operational applications has been a long-term problem for IS departments, especially where these applications have been incrementally changed and upgraded over the years.

Today, IS departments are generally more aware of end users' needs and are making much more data available to them. Nonetheless, users continue to complain that they need more data.

Despite the apparent variety of these complaints, there is an underlying common cause, which can be summarized simply: users are being presented with data—the IS view—as opposed to information—the business view. And improving the productivity of end users is contingent on making the transition from data to information.

Figure 16-1 provides a view of the relative costs and benefits of the various stages in the decision-making process as supported by decision support systems (DSS) in many companies today. Although significant cost is associated with the early stages of the process, the business value accrues from the later stages. We can deduce from this

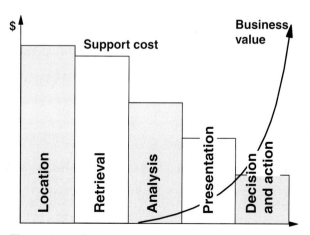

Figure 16-1: Cost and value trends in the decision-making process

figure that companies can improve the return on investment in DSS principally by reducing the costs of the early stages of the process, particularly the location and retrieval steps.

The case for the business information guide

While all of the data warehouse environment is involved in this transition from data to information, the business information guide (BIG) and its underlying metadata store, the data warehouse catalog (DWC), play a pivotal role. These components have their greatest impact in the highest-cost areas—location and retrieval—of the graph shown in Figure 16-1. We can develop a very traditional cost-reduction justification, as follows:

1. First we analyze the productivity of end users, focusing on the proportion of their time used in analyzing data and making business decisions based on such information. Typical figures that emerge are:

    •   50% of end users' time is spent working with information.

    •   Of this, 80% is spent searching for, acquiring, and understanding the data available. This amounts to 40% of the total end-user resources used in the business.

    •   The remaining 20% of this time is used in the real work of analysis and decision making. This amounts to 10% of the total end-user resources applied to the business.

2. One measurable value of the BIG and the DWC lies in the reduced time end users spend in the search, acquisition, and understanding phases of their job. Potential improvements in productivity range from 10% to 40% depending on the complexity of the task and the facilities offered by the BIG.

    •   As a mean, we assume a 25% improvement in productivity here. (This figure also simplifies the mathematics!)

    •   Applying this figure to the 40% of total end-user resources expended in the business in searching for, acquiring, and understanding the data results in a total saving of 10% of the end-user resources. Note that this figure is equal to the resources currently used in the analysis and decision-making phase.

    •   This percentage could mean savings of $10,000 per user per year.

This amount is a significant and quantifiable saving in itself. However, in addition there are the intangible benefits described earlier: improved quality of information provides a better basis for informed decision making.

The associated hardware and software costs are largely well identified and easy to calculate. The only major area of difficulty is in determining the initial and ongoing costs associated with documenting data ownership.

Improving the productivity of IS

Part I of this book has already identified the major problems associated with delivering data from the operational to the informational environment. From the point of view of IS, these problems amount to significant costs in the development and ongoing maintenance of the applications used to extract data from the operational systems.

Replacing these applications with modern data replication tools has two benefits. The first is that it lowers the initial development cost for new data extracts. Savings are similar to those accruing from the use of other fourth-generation languages for application development.

The second and longer-term benefit is more significant. This derives from a simpler and more efficient maintenance process. The costs of the current situation are evident in the backlog of user requests for data, which result because the majority of management information IS resources are committed to maintenance efforts. Such maintenance is the result of real business needs at the operational level, leading to changes in the operational systems that supply the data to the informational environment. By using a model-driven approach to replication, the IS shop can divert a significant percentage of these maintenance resources to addressing new management information needs.

Increases in IS productivity are more difficult to predict generically than savings in user productivity. This is because the inefficiencies of the current approach are extremely variable. Where the existing environment is based on completely stand-alone extract programs, productivity improvements could result in a doubling or tripling of the current productivity levels in maintaining the informational support environment.

There may be further potential savings in disk space and/or processing power. The traditional approach leads to substantial, and often unrecognized, duplication of data. This data is generated and stored a number of times. Elimination of such duplication may lower costs, and such cost reduction can be an element in justifying the data warehouse. In practice, however, many IS shops offset these lower duplication costs against the additional cost of storing increased volumes of historical data.

> *In practice...*
>
> *Using increased IS productivity as a major factor in the initial justification of a data warehouse is risky. It begs a rather awkward question: who was responsible for the current nonproductive situation?*

16.2 Beyond cost avoidance

In general, the cost-avoidance approach described above does not provide sufficient savings to justify the investment required to implement the architecture depicted in Parts II to IV. Rather, it is necessary to focus on the changed ways of doing business that the warehouse enables and the benefits that accrue from them, in order to justify the implementation cost.

The difficulty is that estimating the size of these expected benefits is not an exact science, by any stretch of the imagination. First, one must predict what end users can discover through the data warehouse; then one must estimate the impact of such discoveries. This is followed by an analysis of how the organization must change to utilize this new information. Finally, one can calculate the benefits and the cost of change.

In such a scenario, no formulaic approach can give an answer applicable to all situations [Brown (1994)]. However, examining the areas where data warehousing projects have already yielded benefits provides guidance on where to look for benefits and what can be achieved. These benefits derive directly from new uses of existing information or from the availability of information that differs in substance, quality, or detail from that currently used. It is from such new information that competitive advantage flows [Porter (1985)].

Successful businesses today are, in general, characterized by their management's ability to take a view of the business as a whole and to base future directions on this knowledge. This broad view is reflected in the way managers can transform data about the detailed operation of the business into information about its overall performance and prospects. It further relies on the availability of real and detailed data about the marketplace that management can compare realistically with internal data.

These novel uses of information, and the benefits they provide, can be divided into three areas:

1. supporting new ways of competing

2. changing the business management environment

3. automating marketing

The following sections deal with each of these topics in detail.

16.3   A new basis for competitiveness

The expanding scope of decision support

The initial justification for introducing data processing into business was to gain competitiveness by automating the repetitive day-to-day tasks needed to run the business. Because such processes usually operate at a departmental level, the focus of this automation has remained within a departmental scope. As already described, automating these processes leads to operational systems. A key characteristic of these applications, driven by the departmental scope of the operational processes, is their very narrow business view.

Data processing support for decision making has also followed these traditional boundaries. There are two principal reasons. The first is simply organizational: the need for reporting and tracking is often first recognized within the confines of each department. The second reason is pragmatic: because companies initially directed their reporting and decision making toward monitoring operations, these operational applications are the most obvious source for the basic data required.

Over the past 30 years of such automation, businesses have benefited considerably from this approach and have used the resulting process improvements and productivity gains to successfully compete with one another. Since businesses today are almost fully automated and largely optimized at a departmental level, they can only gain competitive advantage by moving to a new level of automation [Manheim (1992)].

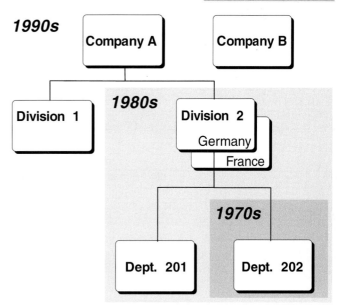

Figure 16-2: *The expanding scope of decision support systems*

Figure 16-2 shows how the required view of business information has expanded over the last 20 years. In the late 1970s, businesses could gain advantage through better use of information at a departmental level. During the course of the next decade, they had to raise the level of automation to address cross-departmental needs in order to maintain competitive advantage. Today, companies in many industries need an enterprise-wide view to compete successfully. In most cases, even this is insufficient—there is a further need to include data originating from other businesses.

This is particularly the case when an industry is undergoing major changes such as deregulation, major technological innovation, and commoditization, or when it is feeling the effects of major political or environmental upheavals. In these instances, the companies that survive and prosper are those that most fully understand the changes taking place both internally and externally and that can react with appropriate and timely measures.

We can see these phenomena in many different industries. The telecommunications industry, for example, has undergone substantial deregulation. Companies competing in this industry have been forced to broaden the scope of their information analysis processes to gain competitive advantage. The European telecommunications industry (see the following box) provides an example of this. The airline industry is currently undergoing a similar transformation.

Real-life example: the European telecommunications industry

Up to the mid-1980s the European telecommunications industry was geographically localized, regulated, and operated in a monopoly situation. Within each company, management focused on distinct and disparate views of the business at the level of departments, lines of business, geographical regions, or individual business processes. Each distinct area ran and managed its own business and reported only at some consolidated level to corporate management. This business model aligned well with the traditional data-processing approach— which also dealt with distinct and disparate subsets of the business data.

As competition entered this environment, companies found that they couldn't compare different aspects of their business—is the cellular-phone business more profitable than the residential line rental business? What is the return on investment in one region compared with another? This level of analysis was needed to enable these established companies to compete effectively against new niche competitors.

The 1990s has seen the emergence of cross-border competition in this industry along with the possibility of mergers and acquisitions. And companies have realized that to compete internationally (and in some cases to survive) requires yet another, broader view—not only of their own businesses, but also of competing companies.

As one CEO has commented, a single wrong decision in setting tariff structures could spell the end of the company. It follows that almost any cost is justified if it provides the right information as a basis for making the right decision.

Another industry that has undergone substantial changes in the last decade is the insurance industry. These changes result, in part, from new competition emerging from other financial institutions. Another factor, however, has been a series of natural disasters that have substantially eroded the financial reserves of the companies. The result has been a new focus on the overall structure of the business, in an attempt to gain a deeper understanding of its dynamics. Such analysis can only occur across the totality of the business.

Current trends in the manufacturing and retailing sectors show that they require an even broader view of the business to compete. Here, manufacturers can compete against one another in the major retailers only if they can take on some or all of the stock management functions once handled solely by the retailers themselves. The business factors driving this shift are increased speed of goods to market and reduced reaction time to changes in market trends. The introduction of electronic data interchange (EDI) over the last few years has technically enabled the change. However, the consequence in data-processing terms is that manufacturers now have to handle and understand a significant class of data whose structure and content is totally outside their own control.

The common thread in all of these examples is a need for information spanning a far broader scope than previously available. Such information, combined from both internal and external sources, enables companies to manage their business, making decisions based on real information, rather than on guesses and estimates as previously done.

The value of information-based management

The actual added business value of decisions based on better information is difficult to predict in advance. However, a number of trends become apparent when decision making is mapped onto the traditional organizational hierarchy shown in Figure 16-3. This hierarchy consists of horizontal layers of management responsibility and vertical segments representing the different divisional and functional areas of the business.

With each higher level in the organization, the value of a single decision increases. For example, at a professional level, the value of a single decision may be on the order of thousands of dollars, while the value at the executive level is likely to extend up to the value of the company. The consequences of a single error similarly scale upward.

Clearly, therefore, the requirement for accuracy and consistency of the data used in decision making also increases. Unfortunately, the underlying diversity of the data-processing base becomes more apparent as more data is brought together from different parts of the organization. The ability of the data warehouse to overcome these problems and improve the accuracy and consistency of data therefore gives the most value at the executive level and at other high levels of management in the company.

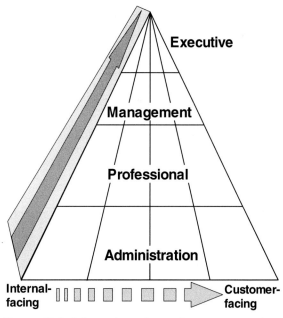

The value of data in decision making also varies across the functional areas of the organization. For internally facing functions such as finance, broader, more consistent data does, of course, contribute to a better understanding of the business. However, such data provides its most significant value when applied to customer-facing functions such as marketing. This is because of a difference in focus. It is through better support of marketing that the business can grow, whereas better data for finance at best allows better management of costs. Section 16.5 discusses this point in further detail.

Figure 16-3: Information value and usage across the organization

16.4   Changing management structures

The structures of business organizations are changing at a rapid pace. New management theories emphasize flexibility and empowerment rather than structured flows of information and chains of command [Peters and Waterman (1982), Drucker (1988), Hammer (1993)].

Figure 16-4 again shows the rather rigid structure of the traditional organization. Within such a structure, we can identify different requirements for data processing that correspond to the different layers and segments. As we move upward through the layers, for example, the level of detail required of data decreases. Executives use highly summarized information, while line managers work at a detailed level. We can also make functional distinctions between the different levels. Administrative workers need to create and maintain individual data items such as orders or customer records. Professional workers and line managers require statistical analysis tools. Executives require systems that highlight anomalies or graphically show key indicators, and allow drill-down in problem areas.

Within this traditional structure, decision support has developed and prospered in the highly localized manner shown in Figure 16-4. Different segments of the company choose different tools in the various layers to analyze data of the required level of detail. The scope of data addressed by each of these systems has been limited to a narrow segment of the business.

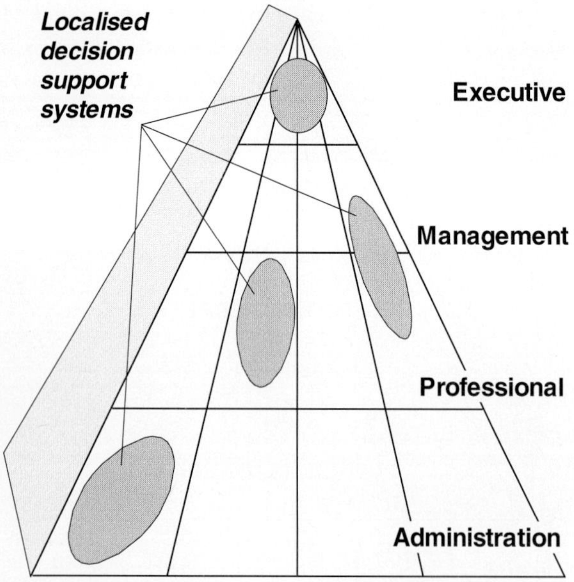

An exception to this vertical specialization is, of course, the executive information systems (EIS) provided in the upper layer of Figure 16-4. The relative lack of success of these systems is well known. One reason for this is the difficulty already described of combining the data flowing upward from the diverse systems in the lower layers of the structure.

Today, the drive in business is toward a structure that is more fluid. Many businesses have dramatically decreased the number of layers of management responsibility. They are breaking and remaking divisional and functional boundaries at regular intervals and adopting team-based approaches to give new vitality to their business and to increase the speed of reaction to market changes. In terms of the organizational structures described by Mintzberg

Localised decision support systems

Executive

Management

Professional

Administration

Figure 16-4: Decision support in the traditional organizational hierarchy

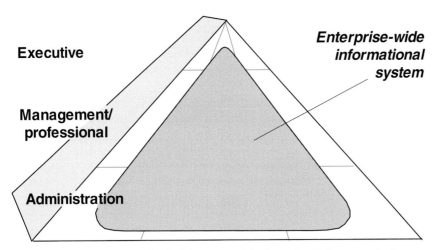

Executive

Enterprise-wide
informational
system

Management/
professional

Administration

Figure 16-5: *Enterprise-wide decision support for broader, flatter organizations*

(1979), this is a move from a bureaucracy to an "adhocracy". In this environment, a team may require data of a variety of types and levels of detail, together with diverse functions to use the data, to operate together, and to communicate with other teams in the business.

What businesses require, therefore, is an environment that combines both data coherence and functional integration, enabling users to achieve their business goals. This is depicted in Figure 16-5.

Supporting this change in the way the business is managed is a vital requirement for the IS department [Jordan (1994)]. Data warehousing provides the only reasonable solution to this need because it does not require a complete reconstruction of the existing operational systems.

16.5 The automation of marketing

In the past, financial and administrative departments have been prime candidates for the initial introduction of decision support into companies, because they had previously automated their base data and their users already had some exposure to computing. Today, the main target for decision support is increasingly becoming marketing, because it is here that companies are most likely to gain competitive advantage. (Or it may be that there are no other departments left on which to inflict decision support!)

However, it is also the case that the type of information required here is significantly different from that required previously. Whereas financial and administrative departments' needs are mostly confined to structured, formatted, and mainly numerical data, marketing requires significantly more

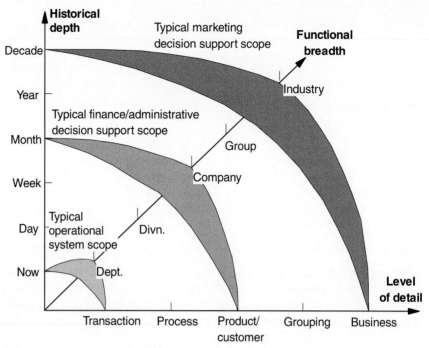

Figure 16-6: *The expanded data scope needed by marketing*

unstructured, unformatted, textual, and other data types such as pictorial and multimedia data. These differences in information type, while important from the technical point of view of storage and access, are overshadowed by a more subtle distinction in the way the two groups use data.

Marketing processes use data in broader and more unpredictable ways than financial and administrative functions do. Where the financial analyst works at a product and customer level, the marketer analyzes data at the level of product groupings and customer categories. While the administrative department may look at the business on a month-by-month basis, marketing may look for trends over years.

And although marketing may require data at less detailed levels, the types of aggregation required are very variable. This unpredictability leads to the need to store more and more detailed data to allow for all potential aggregations. As a result, the potential scope of data required by the marketing function is an order of magnitude greater than that used in the traditional decision support areas.

This combination of characteristics, shown in Figure 16-6, leads directly to the use of data warehousing as the main delivery vehicle for marketing analysis applications. The justification for such applications, and therefore for the warehouse to support them, comes directly from the business case developed by the marketing department for them [Verity (1995)].

16.6   Data warehouse costs

In comparison with calculating the benefit of the warehouse, finding the cost is straightforward. In fact, it is so similar to costing for other IS projects that this text will not cover the topic in any detail. Rather, we will consider the differences between data warehouse construction costs and those for typical applications.

Data storage cost

Data storage is probably the most obvious cost associated with the warehouse and is mainly a function of the historical period and level of detail required. This may run to hundreds of gigabytes, and its cost is easily calculated. However, recall that, in all mature informational environments not built according to the data warehouse architecture, there is considerable duplication of data—much of which is undocumented. When implementing a warehouse, the IS shop can locate and free up this storage for reuse and partially avoid the cost of the new storage for historical data.

Processing cost

Again, in most mature informational environments, there is considerable duplication of extract processing. Eliminating multiple extracts of the same operational data is a key technical rationale for the warehouse—so, expect a net saving in this area, unless the warehouse addresses substantial new areas of data for the first time.

As discussed in Chapter 11, the use of update mode of replication rather than refresh can be an important factor in reducing processing costs.

Development costs

Development costs for a data warehouse are very variable. They depend particularly on the state of the existing operational systems and whether the development entails the introduction of an entirely new hardware and/or software environment.

At one extreme, if the existing operational systems are unmodeled and implemented on a file system, development costs will be high. Two principal development costs are the analysis of existing systems, and the development or modification of methods for extracting data from the operational systems, cleansing it, and populating the warehouse with it. Today's data replication tools may be of limited value in this type of environment.

In practice...

Bitter experience shows that development costs are typically under-estimated by a factor of at least 2 in many warehouse implementations. Build this contingency into your plans.

At the other extreme, if the existing operational environment is relatively modern—based on a relational database—and the warehouse is to be built in the same physical environment, the development cost is relatively small. This is because populating both the BDW and the BIWs is straightforward and can be achieved entirely using data replication tools.

Experience in many large warehouse implementations shows that populating the BDW accounts for the major share of the development costs. The development or customization of the EDM, including the physical design of the BDW, is usually the next most expensive area.

In fact, in most cases, the development costs exceed the total hardware and software costs by a considerable amount.

Cost allocation

Section 15.2 described a staged implementation approach where each stage consisted of three areas of effort:

- infrastructure development

- enterprise modeling

- business application

The development costs associated directly with the business application can clearly be allocated to the business function that is benefiting from that application. However, the other two components are less easily allocated.

One approach is to fund both infrastructure development and enterprise modeling from the corporate IS budget. The advantage is that it enables the IS department to plan and deliver the required infrastructure and model relatively independently of the budgetary constraints of the business departments that gain the early benefit of the warehouse. Unfortunately, large infrastructure budgets in IS shops have a habit of attracting the CFO's attention—with predictable results!

The alternative approach is to allocate these costs to the business areas that benefit from the development. There are two problems:

- The aim of the business departments is usually to obtain their specific needs at the lowest possible cost. For any individual business need taken in isolation, the data warehouse is not the cheapest approach.

- Business departments that get early benefit from the warehouse pay the lion's share of the infrastructure costs, because, as we can see in Figure 15-2, infrastructure and modeling costs decrease dramatically after the first couple of iterations of the staged approach.

In spite of these difficulties, this model of cost allocation is generally more likely to succeed than the previous approach of allocating all costs directly to the IS department. This is because the various business departments have a stake in the infrastructure and therefore feel more in control of what is happening. In the face of proposed cost-cutting measures, these departments are also more likely to defend the project. Companies do need to address the problem of inequitable distribution of costs, which can usually be done with the support of their financial departments.

16.7 Conclusions

The detailed justification for a data warehouse is a task unique to each organization that undertakes it. This is not because the benefits are unique to each company—rather, each company starts from a different position. It is this position—comprising the industry situation, the company's position in the market, its product maturity, its organization, and its existing IS infrastructure—that makes the benefits and costs unique.

Data warehouse justification is further complicated by the fact that many of the benefits are difficult to quantify in advance and may take years to achieve.

In general, the key to justifying the warehouse lies in establishing the link between specific business advantages and the more generic concept of data integrity and consistency. Quality data forms the basis of a number of substantial changes in the way a company behaves. It allows better evaluation of competitive advantage and improves marketing effectiveness. It enables more flexible management approaches, and it underlies all attempts to move from traditional mass production to the new world of mass customization [Kelly (1994)].

As has been shown, some justifications based on traditional cost saving apply to data warehousing. However, they are usually too small to offset the cost of implementation. In addition, they tend to focus on fixing what the IS department has done wrong in the past, rather than looking to the future. As a result, companies should confine such arguments to the detailed business cases of specific projects, rather than for justifying the overall approach.

Because of the qualitative nature of the major potential benefits of the data warehouse, most organizations today attempt to base an estimate of their own benefits on reports of what previous implementers have achieved. This can be useful in many circumstances, and a substantial body of evidence now exists. For example, a recent study [IDC (1996)] shows significant quantitative benefits across all industries and describes a number of qualitative gains.

However, one fact remains constant. At a certain stage in the justification process, the business must make an act of faith that the investment will show return. The real challenge is to ensure that such return occurs incrementally, in line with the expenditure.

Chapter 17

Organizational implications of data warehousing

As has been pointed out several times throughout this book, there are a number of organizational issues a company must address when implementing a data warehouse. These arise during two main stages in the timetable for implementation.

During the initial planning stage, the first task is to establish the project teams that will be involved in implementing the warehouse. The team with prime responsibility is the *initiation team*, which defines the overall architecture and implementation process. Also during this phase, it is advisable to establish an *extended team* of people from the areas of the organization—both business and IS—whose support and advice will be crucial over the duration of the implementation process.

Also during the initial planning stage, the proponents of the warehouse must obtain *approval and sponsorship* for the overall approach. This activity is vital to the long-term success of the warehouse, but is often overlooked in the effort to establish the initiation project.

The second major stage when companies should address organizational issues occurs soon after completing the pilot implementation. At this stage, a structure must be established that plans the roll-out of the warehouse. Key to this activity is a *project office* that develops and monitors the roll-out plan. At an executive level, the company should establish a formal process, or *steering committee*, to address prioritization of requirements across the entire business. Last but not least, broad organizational responsibilities and roles need to be aligned with the goal of delivering consistent information throughout the company.

Because organizations differ in their cultures and structures, you should view the approach described in this chapter more as a guideline than an answer. It must be adapted to the specific organization of your company before use.

17.1 From planning to pilot

Section 15.3 describes the typical progression from the initial thinking about a data warehouse through to the completion of the pilot implementation. This phase defines the architecture of the data warehouse and maps out the implementation approach.

While this phase demands significant amounts of technical education and decision making, the company must also address organizational issues. These issues are as important as the technical ones, but often receive far less attention. In fact, it is widely accepted in the industry that most data warehouse projects fail not for technical reasons but as a result of organizational shortcomings [Adelman (1995)]. We can trace many of these back to the planning phase. You may ask, therefore, why so little of this book is devoted to these organizational considerations. The answer is that organizational considerations are straightforward to describe. The difficulty lies in putting them into practice in a specific organization. This is a topic that lies beyond the scope of any book, depending as it does on the organization culture and individuals involved.

Team structure for the initiation project

Two teams—the initiation team and the extended team—play key roles in the data warehouse initiation project. This section now defines the roles and composition of these two teams.

The initiation team

The **initiation team** is responsible for gaining acceptance of the overall data warehousing approach, defining the technical architecture and approach for the warehouse, defining a high-level roll-out roadmap, and initiating the first pilot warehouse project. The principal roles are described below. Chowdary (1995) also provides a useful list of roles and responsibilities.

Ideally, a different person should fill each of the key roles described below. However, in smaller projects, as few as two people could divide these roles between them.

> **Initiation team**
>
> *The team responsible for defining the overall technical approach and roll-out plan for the warehouse and for ensuring its widespread acceptance.*

- **Data warehouse promoter**

  This person is responsible for the progress and overall success of the initiation process. Likely to be a manager, he or she should have good contacts and relationships throughout the business and in the IS organization in particular. This is probably a part-time role. This may well be the person who introduced data warehousing to the company.

- **Initiation team leader**

  This person is responsible for the day-to-day progress and success of the initiation team, and should be someone quite senior, capable of taking a broad view, and willing to make decisions that balance the technical and business aspects of the warehouse. Given the project scope, this is unlikely to be a first-time or second-time project leader.

- **Architect**

  This is the key technical person on the team, and should have a good understanding of databases, data management, and application development. The architect needs good communications skills, including the ability to present and write clearly on technical matters in a business context.

- **Business analyst**

  This person provides the business input; she or he should have a broad business background and an understanding of current and strategic business issues. A familiarity with data modeling concepts and some basic knowledge of technology would be very useful.

The extended team

The **extended team** is the sounding board for the initiation team. This is the first place the initiation team brings its proposals for review and comment. The extended team is a key source of information and advice for the initiation team in areas where the latter has no prior knowledge. Although the extended team is often engaged in the initiation project on an informal basis, the project teams should schedule formal progress review meetings at regular intervals, probably as often as once a month.

The composition of the extended team will vary considerably from company to company, depending on business, political, organizational, technical, and other factors. It is likely to number between 5 and 10 people and consist of both business and IS participants. When the initiation team has identified a particular business area for the pilot warehouse, the extended team should include key people from this area. People capable of bridging the gap between business and IS are prime candidates. Typical participants may include:

> *Extended team*
>
> *A representative group of senior business and technical people who guide and review the work of the initiation team.*

- **Manager(s) responsible for key business area(s)**

  They provide a view of the business priorities in different areas.

- **Senior business analyst(s)**

  Such analysts bring their detailed knowledge of the business operations at a day-to-day level to the data warehouse process.

- **Data administrator(s)**

  Data administrators provide information on how the business actually uses data and how it is stored.

- **Manager(s) responsible for IS support and development—usually operational—in key business area(s)**

  These managers are responsible for ensuring that required data in the operational systems is available to the data warehouse and that resources are made available to support this process if required.

- **IS architect(s)**

  The IS architects bring a detailed knowledge of existing and planned applications and infrastructure tools to the design process.

The role of external consultants

In practice...

Using consultants in the early stages of development can speed delivery and increase the likelihood of success. However, your business obtains real value only if the consultants are willing and able to educate your staff at the same time.

The data warehouse initiation project is quite unlike any other project the IS shop has previously undertaken. It requires a combination of organizational and technical skills that are seldom brought together in the company.

In this situation, external consultants who have experience of the process can support a rapid startup and help avoid known pitfalls. However, it is not advisable to hand over the entire process to external consultants. They would need to spend significant time getting to know your existing organization and infrastructure in the absence of someone who already has this knowledge. In addition, as outsiders, they are unlikely to fit easily into the politics and culture of your organization.

The ideal roles for consultants in the initiation project are as follows:

- education of the internal team at the early stages of the project

- investigation and proposal of architectural and technical solutions

- moderation and guidance of requirements definition and modeling

- ongoing review and input to the project, for example, as a key member of the extended team

- justification of the warehouse approach to senior management by reference to other experiences in the industry

Approval and sponsorship

Obtaining business commitment to the data warehousing approach is a vital activity during the data warehouse initiation project. This commitment must be obtained at the right time and at the right level in the organization.

Almost every analysis of the success or failure of a data warehouse implementation has placed executive sponsorship as the single most important factor in determining the outcome of the process.

Successful implementations are almost always associated with companies in which a business executive initiated the approach. In these cases, it is not sufficient that the sponsoring executive have a clearly defined business need that cannot be solved by existing methods. In addition, he or she must understand enough about how data is created and distributed in the company to appreciate that this need can best (or only) be satisfied through a new structure such as a data warehouse. Unfortunately, such visionary business executives are the exception rather than the rule.

Today, given the mass popularity of warehousing, one of two starting points usually drives initiation of the warehouse. The first, and still the most common one, is the IS department. The second possible initiator is a business executive who has heard the popular descriptions of a data warehouse. These focus on the potential benefits but tend to underplay the costs. In both cases, the question of approval and sponsorship of the data warehouse requires careful consideration, but from different directions. The third starting point for a warehouse—the previously mentioned visionary business executive—can be safely ignored in this discussion, since sponsorship in this case is a foregone conclusion.

The IS-initiated warehouse

In general, the IS department initiates a data warehousing approach because it recognizes the problems inherent in the current approach to delivering data to informational applications. These problems have already been described:

- excessive maintenance costs and lengthy backlogs

- high management, storage, and processing costs associated with multiple extracts of the same data

- a lack of data integrity and quality in the informational environment

Such problems lead to a focus on architectural and infrastructural issues in the project. The absence of a well-defined business need leads to difficulties in prioritizing development. In addition, since the business does not have any real understanding of the benefits beyond the IS department, funding is difficult to obtain and maintain. Ultimately, most such projects fail unless a "real" business need can be grafted onto the IS rationale.

It is therefore essential that the IS manager responsible for the warehouse is well-respected in the business side of the organization and is capable of convincing business executives of the business benefits of the project. This IS manager must achieve a delicate balance between underselling the concept and overselling it. In the former case, the business will not buy into the warehouse; in the latter case, the business has impossible expectations and will not wait for the warehouse to deliver.

The business-initiated warehouse

In many ways, the problems encountered here are the exact opposite of those described the IS-initiated warehouse. Often a business executive decides that a data warehouse is the answer to a known business need, decides that the IS shop cannot support this need, and adopts a do-it-yourself approach.

The outcome is at best a data mart as described in Chapter 5. In other words, it leads to a system that has no more structure than any other traditional MIS application. Because an enterprise-wide view is lacking in the early design stages, it is difficult to expand. Larger organizations often have a number of these data marts, each serving a small population and all containing similar and overlapping data.

Some vendors and consultants encourage this approach. They focus on the speed of delivery of specific business results. This is done at the expense of structure capable of addressing future expansion and overall data quality and integrity issues. This clearly leads to significant suboptimization in the delivery of information to the business.

Experience has shown that once such data marts are established, it is very difficult either to expand them to an enterprise-wide view or to replace them with a new enterprise-wide data warehouse. The IS organization must therefore address this issue at the beginning of the process. This is most effectively done by quickly researching and documenting multiple uses for the same data throughout the business, and enlisting the business executives' support to argue against a suboptimized solution. This is, of course, only effective where the business itself operates as a whole, rather than each division having total control of its own targets and budget.

The role of the business sponsor

It will be clear from the foregoing sections that an effective sponsor of the data warehouse can reside only at the highest levels of the organization. It is only at such levels that the required cross-divisional and longer-term investment views are possible. Indeed, market conditions or current business plans may dictate that a data warehouse is not the highest priority at this time! The roles of a business sponsor are to:

- build and ensure cross-enterprise support for the data warehouse

- allocate long-term budget provision for the warehouse

- sign off on costs versus benefits for the overall process

- set up and chair a steering committee to prioritize needs

- resolve conflicts until the steering committee is set up

Organization at the pilot project stage

By the time the data warehouse pilot has been initiated, there will be a number of significant efforts underway. These are all interrelated and must operate together effectively, as Figure 17-1 shows.

The data warehouse sponsor is directly responsible for two projects: the data warehouse initiation project and the pilot. He or she may also have an involvement in other projects in the organization. This is particularly the case where there are existing informational systems. In addition, the enterprise data model (EDM), if it is introduced initially in support of the warehouse, may also become the responsibility of the data warehouse sponsor.

The data warehouse initiation project defines the scope and shape of the pilot. It is supported in this by the extended team. As the pilot progresses, the lessons learned are communicated back to the initiation team and used in refining the staged implementation roadmap (SIR).

The enterprise data modeling projects do, of course, influence the definition of the SIR. In addition, data modeling within the pilot must at least be aligned with the enterprise-wide efforts. Ideally, these data modeling efforts are so closely related that the boundary between them is invisible.

Do not underestimate the influence of other projects on both the pilot and the initiation project at this time. The development of new operational or informational systems or the reengineering of old operational or informational systems will certainly influence the SIR, and may also have a substantial impact on the pilot, depending on the type of pilot and its positioning in the business.

The following situation is typical of many organizations attempting to introduce a

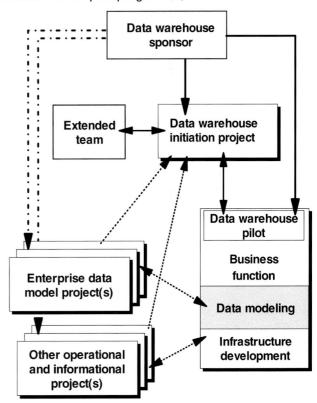

Figure 17-1: Project organization

data warehouse. In parallel with—but independent of—the data warehousing effort, a company is reengineering one of its major operational systems. Where the pilot data warehouse requires data from this system, the timing of its upgrading determines whether the pilot should reuse an old extract application to obtain this data or shift immediately to a new replication tool. Similarly, where the data warehouse pilot is to replace existing informational systems, new requirements arising for these systems will require careful analysis to see whether they will significantly impact the development of the pilot.

17.2 From initiation to roll-out

As the pilot project comes to a—hopefully successful—conclusion, the company must put in place the organization required to support the ongoing roll-out. A steering committee and project office are the two key elements of this organization.

Steering committee

While it is usually sufficient to have a single project sponsor in the initiation and pilot phases of warehouse development, the decision making and support required during the roll-out phases are usually beyond the scope of a single sponsor.

Interdivisional prioritization of requirements becomes a more complex task. There is more likely to be conflict between the different parts of the organization about the importance of their requirements once it becomes clear that the data warehouse is providing substantial benefit. Timing and order of delivery of particular functionality or data must be carefully evaluated to ensure that the company as a whole achieves the maximum business benefit. The implementation must also accommodate the IS goal of organic growth of the warehouse.

Steering committee

An executive group, drawn from all parts of the business, responsible for prioritizing projects in the data warehouse.

The introduction of a **steering committee** at this stage is almost inevitable, in order to ensure political acceptance of the decisions taken. The original sponsor often becomes the chairperson of this committee. And it becomes increasingly clear why the sponsor should be a member of the executive board of the company.

The steering committee takes over the responsibilities previously vested solely in the business sponsor at this stage. In addition, one of the most important roles of the steering committee is to manage the expectations of the different divisions of the organization as to what benefits they can obtain from the data warehouse and when they might expect to see them.

Project office

The steering committee, as an executive function, requires a staff to support their decision making. This is the responsibility of the project office.

As described in Section 15.4, the project office is responsible for defining and maintaining the staged implementation plan (SIP), and ensuring that projects are initiated in accordance with it. Thus, the project office must be staffed with senior professionals from a number of backgrounds. The skills that are particularly appropriate for the project office are:

Project office

A small team of professionals, directed by the steering committee, who define and maintain the SIP and ensure that it is used to initiate and monitor all warehouse implementation projects.

- **Project management**

  Because of the role of the project office in initiating and reviewing the staged projects that implement the data warehouse, project management experience is particularly useful.

- **High-level business knowledge**

  Project office members are likely to be closely involved in debates about prioritization of business needs when initiating data warehouse projects. While the ultimate decisions on prioritization lie with the steering committee, their decisions are accelerated and simplified if the project office eliminates options that are not practical and recommends appropriate priorities.

- **Strong but broad technical knowledge**

  The project office must always balance the business needs with the data warehousing need for organic growth of the environment. This requires a knowledge of product capabilities, in order to support project teams in making choices about the technical environment for new projects. A knowledge of the existing technical environment is also vital, as there are considerable tradeoffs to make in this area, particularly in the early stages of data warehouse development.

Many organizations see project offices as a rather expensive overhead. However, this investment is almost mandatory in building a data warehouse, because of the level of interdependence among the different projects. In general, the size of the project office depends mostly on the number of projects that are part of the overall data warehouse implementation, and on the number of different parts of the organization that are involved or want to be involved in the roll-out.

Usually, the initiation team described earlier becomes the project office. As the project roll-out becomes more "business as usual", project office staffing is likely to drop to one or two key project managers, supported on a part-time basis by some business and technical experts.

Project organization during roll-out

While project organization is, of course, very specific to each company, a number of questions often arise in this area:

- **Splitting projects into operational and informational parts**

    If not already done, one possibility a data warehouse provides is to remove all responsibility for management reporting from the individual operational systems. The resources thus freed can support the data warehousing effort in two ways:

    1. They transfer responsibility for the delivery of the data and metadata from that operational system to the data warehouse population tools. These skills remain part of the operational project team.

    2. The resources that were devoted to report structuring can become part of the overall data warehousing effort. These skills are vital to the company-wide effort to rationalize management reporting.

- **Control of legacy informational systems**

    If the data warehouse is to grow and prosper, there must be a policy in place to phase out existing MIS. These can be both substantial and pervasive throughout the organization. Clearly, from a functional point of view, the data warehouse must provide at least equivalent, and preferably improved, facilities over those previously available to encourage users to move. Such support can be additional data, better functionality, or increased ease-of-use.

    More importantly, however, is the more political side of the migration. Here we must recognize that the organization currently providing this support for users will be giving up power when the data warehouse is in place. The company must address this problem at an early stage.

    It is usually advisable to bring existing project teams and their deliverables under the control of the data warehouse steering committee and project office before making any attempt to bring the users of these legacy informational systems into the warehouse. This ensures that the developers give highest priority to delivering new and improved functionality through the warehouse, and that the legacy environment delivers new functionality only if it is absolutely essential and cannot be delivered early enough through the strategic data warehouse.

- **Positioning the enterprise data modeling project**

    If an enterprise data modeling project predates the data warehouse implementation and is progressing well, clearly no organizational changes are required. The data warehouse project simply becomes

---

In practice...

Be aware that where legacy informational systems exist, there is likely to be a large and un-documented body of user-defined and -built queries. Migrating these queries to the new environment will require careful planning.

another customer of the modeling project. If, on the other hand, no enterprise data modeling project previously exists or is not progressing well, a good approach may be to bring this project under the data warehouse steering committee and project office. This allows the modeling project to align closely with the needs of the warehouse and to follow the same stages. This provides a more focused model development and increases the probability of a successful project.

- **Data administration**

  Data administration is a vital process in the data warehouse because of the importance placed on data meaning and usage there. Brackett (1994) provides a comprehensive treatment of the topic. A strong data administration function can contribute substantially to the eventual success of the data warehouse. In the early stages of the roll-out, the IS shop tends to be the primary driver for data administration. This is a result of the focus on existing, legacy data sources and the need to understand their meaning. However, as the focus shifts to consolidation and integration of data from different business areas, the IS flavor of data administration diminishes. At this stage, the principal value of data administration lies in its cross-divisional role in the business.

  Data consistency and cross-divisional usage are vital in the overall business context as organizational structures change at the high rates currently occurring [Weldon and Plagman (1994), English (1996)]. A data warehouse supports this trend but must be integrated in a wider view of data administration.

- **Changing management priorities during the roll-out**

  During any 3- to 5-year planning period, business priorities will inevitably change. A changing economic climate can threaten the roll-out of the data warehouse. It is therefore important that a warehouse begun in good times can adapt to business needs in bad times, and *vice versa*. The data warehouse can support either. However, the SIP must be flexible enough to allow a change of direction when required. In times of growth, the needs of the marketing and development divisions should take precedence. In leaner times, finance and risk management should get preference.

  While it is important to be able to switch between these directions, bear in mind that ongoing projects must be allowed to produce some deliverable of business value before being redirected.

- **Managing expectations**

  In the early stages of a data warehouse roll-out it is often necessary to sell the concept to the business side of the company. This must be done with some care, so that management doesn't obtain unrealistic expectations. In particular, underestimating the time scale for delivering certain information is guaranteed to alienate the business.

Where particular business needs are very urgent and will probably take a considerable time to satisfy through the warehouse, it is often better to admit this and seek a short-term workaround than to impose the strain of excessive promises on the warehouse process. Such short-term solutions must, of course, be noted and a migration plan defined for a later date.

17.3 Conclusions

While most data warehouse experts agree that organizational issues are the most common cause of failure of a data warehousing project, there are no guaranteed answers to many of these issues. Organizations are sufficiently different in both structure and culture that what works in one may be a disaster in another.

Tasks that the initial planning stage of the data warehouse must address include obtaining the correct level of sponsorship, structuring an initiation team capable of delivering both an architecture and a roll-out plan, and ensuring a visible and accepted means of involving all areas of the company—both business and IS—in the warehouse plan.

As the roll-out proceeds, another set of implications—organizational in nature—need attention. In particular, the company requires a structure that allows the prioritization of business needs across the whole organization. This structure must be combined with a mechanism for balancing the immediate needs of the business against the long-term goal of building a warehouse—to provide easy, enterprise-wide access to consistent and meaningful information.

In the longer term, it may also be useful for the enterprise as a whole to consider the overall organizational implications of using a data warehouse. Essentially, the question is whether the new ways of using information in the business necessitate a new organizational structure. Indeed, we could argue that the data warehouse has not achieved enough if such a reorganization is not required! But that, as they say, is another day's work.

Chapter 18

Physical structure of the data warehouse

The aspects of data architecture and enterprise modeling discussed in Parts II through IV are all very well in theory, but at the end of the day, they must enable the practical implementation of the data warehouse. In particular, they must be adaptable to the characteristics of an individual organization. There are a number of aspects of organizational structure that determine how the data warehouse will be implemented.

The most obvious factor is the **geographical structure** of the organization. At one extreme, a company may be multinational, with aspects of its business located throughout the world. At the other extreme a company may operate from a single location. Where a particular organization lies on this spectrum strongly influences the physical implementation of the data warehouse.

In a similar manner, the **reporting structure** of a company must be taken into account when defining the physical implementation. This structure, like the geographical structure, determines where data comes from and where it is used.

This chapter discusses the influence of both geographical and reporting structures on the data warehouse implementation.

In general then, the data warehouse implementation must take into account the fact that the information required to run and manage the company comes from and is used in many locations. This inevitably leads to a discussion of the relative merits of **centralization and distribution** of data in the warehouse. Because this topic is crucial to the implementation decision process, we discuss it first in this chapter.

18.1 The data warehouse environment— centralized versus distributed

In recent years, many people have characterized the distinction between centralization and distribution (or decentralization) of computing resources, particularly data, as a battle between mainframes and client/server implementations. This view of the world, while fascinating as a marketing debate, has little to do with reality.

Figure 18-1 shows another view. Most computing functionality can benefit from an initial centralized implementation, for several reasons:

- New function requires close monitoring to ensure that it works.
- Centralized data allows for simpler management and security.
- In a centralized approach, synchronization of data is easier.

However, as users better understand the functionality and data, they increasingly need greater flexibility in using them. This need, as well as a general shift toward more departmental empowerment, drives the distribution of functionality and data, both operational and informational.

It is not the intention to debate here the rationale for decentralizing operational systems. Rather, we accept it as a fact of life, and consider its impact on the informational environment and the factors that favor centralization or distribution.

In the mid-1980s, there was very little choice in the implementation approach for warehouses. Data was collected from a variety of mainframe- or minicomputer-based operational applications. For mainly technical reasons, the reconciled data layer was implemented in a mainframe relational database, and the derived data was generally implemented in the same environment. Today there is a full range of choices, from entirely centralized to highly distributed.

The following sections examine how the warehouse architecture applies at both extremes. On one side is the implementation of a warehouse in a traditional computing environment, controlled by the IS shop. This contrasts with the more informal computing environment that grows around PCs and the client/server approach. Finally, we describe the reality found in most medium-sized to large companies today: a mixture of both approaches.

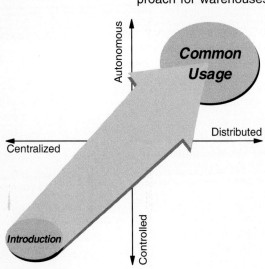

Figure 18-1: Trends in application availability

The centralized environment

The traditional approach to management information systems (MIS) implementation begins with the need to make existing data from the operational systems available to end users in a more understandable and usable way. The left-hand side of Figure 18-2 shows this copying (and cleansing) of data from the legacy databases and files into the relational database.

This implementation shows a number of the aspects that have been discussed earlier. There is a clear distinction between operational and informational applications (represented in this and later figures by O/A and I/A respectively). This is true even to the extent that they may run on physically separate and distinct machines. In this environment, we can also readily distinguish between real-time and derived data, often stored on different machines in different formats.

Users may access data from dumb terminals or from PCs. In the case of PCs, end users copy data (often at their own risk) down to local storage.

Data and function can also be "centralized" at a departmental level. This occurs in autonomous departmental systems, both operational and informational, often implemented on minicomputers, also shown in Figure 18-2. These departmental systems also usually separate real-time and derived data. However, control tends to be less strict than in the mainframe environment, for a combination of organizational and technical reasons. Thus, for example, the figure shows a PC-based informational application accessing real-time data.

From a warehousing point of view, the most significant aspect of departmental systems is the increase in the number of data sources that it implies. For simplicity, the figure shows only one departmental system, but in reality there may exist a number of such systems in most large companies. However, the structure is still highly centralized, in terms of both physical location and control.

Figure 18-3 introduces a reconciled data layer (business data warehouse, or BDW). In such an environment, there is little debate but that the BDW should also be highly centralized, since this is where the vast majority of data and processing power already resides.

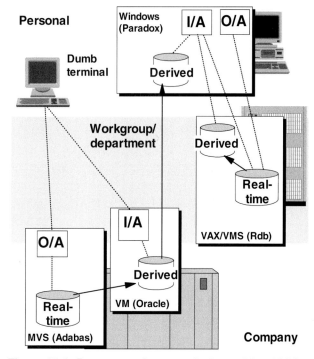

Figure 18-2: Departmental systems in the traditional MIS environment

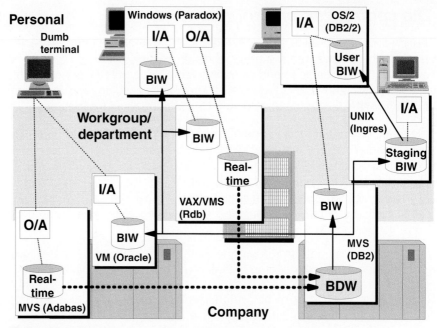

Figure 18-3: *The three-layer data architecture in a centralized environment*

One of the most important—although often unconscious—factors in this decision is the recognition that the reconciled data layer requires significant control and management. Integrity can be ensured only if data is carefully verified on acceptance and entry into the BDW. Security must be tight because the BDW represents the most comprehensive information asset in the organization. These factors are, of course, those that argue for the centralization of any application.

On the other hand, derived data (business information warehouses, or BIWs) exists in many locations and on many levels—company-wide, departmental, and personal. This also corresponds to the needs of users to have local access to and control of data. The right-hand side of Figure 18-3 shows the use of a staging BIW to support the need for departmental data that is derived according to departmental needs and then further subsetted or derived for individual end users accessing user BIWs.

Clearly, then, we can directly and easily map the three-layer architecture onto a centralized data warehouse implementation.

The distributed environment

The distributed data warehouse implementation has its origins in the single-user PC or LAN-attached environment shown in Figure 18-4. In such an environment, users are often largely self-sufficient in many data needs. Their needs are satisfied through the use of spreadsheets such as Lotus

1-2-3 or of functionality built on PC databases such as DBase. In satisfying these stand-alone needs, users do not distinguish between operational and informational usage, and they see all data as essentially the same.

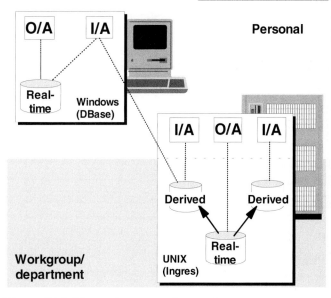

Resources, including data, are shared through LANs, eventually allowing the deployment of shared workgroup or departmental applications. In this environment, some separation between operational and informational data may appear. This situation closely parallels the two-layer data architecture, with operational applications responsible for maintaining the real-time data, and separate, often distributed, informational applications accessing derived data that is stored on the same server

Figure 18-4: *The workgroup environment*

but in different databases. A characteristic of this environment is that there is often little or no formal IS support organization, and so no imposed direction toward standardization of data or application environments between the different single users or servers.

Figure 18-4 doesn't show the full complexity of the environment. In addition to the existence of multiple data stores at the personal level, the LAN approach is such that there will also be multiple servers and data stores at the workgroup level, each supporting its own set of users. The inevitable outcome of this structure is the promotion of uncontrolled data duplication. This duplication exists among the workstations at the personal level, among servers at the workgroup level, and between the workstations and servers.

This situation is further complicated when a backbone network linking servers is introduced at a company level, to provide new "super-servers" supporting company-wide data sharing or applications. This step, on its own, cannot address the issues of data consistency and duplication.

From a structural point of view, this duplication occurs first in the real-time data when different, and in many cases overlapping, subsets of the enterprise model are implemented multiple times. This is not a technical issue; rather it is a technical consequence of an organizational fact. The fact is that different parts of the company need to use data in different ways. They see no need, or cannot wait, for the IS shop to design and develop a fully modeled and integrated data store. In the real-time data of a physically distributed environment, duplication and inconsistency are natural

In practice...

In a distributed environment, organizational factors cause duplication in real-time data. The company must address this problem before the IS shop can introduce a pervasive reconciled data layer.

consequences of the dynamic nature of the organization, not easily tackled by a technological approach.

On the other hand, in the derived data, duplication and inconsistency are mainly technical problems caused by the lack of any reconciliation as data moves out of the real-time layer. The solution to this problem clearly lies in adopting of the three-layer data architecture.

Figure 18-5 shows the three-layer architecture in a distributed environment. This structure involves bringing data together for reconciliation from the dispersed real-time data sources before distributing the derived data to locations that use it. In contrast to the situation using a centralized structure, the distributed environment requires designers to consider a number of aspects:

- In some cases, although both real-time and derived data need to reside on the same physical server, the distributed approach may require that the data passing between them go to another server holding the reconciled data layer before returning to the first server. Such cases have obvious consequences for the network load.

- The figure shows data from the personal level being input to the reconciled data layer. The extent to which this occurs depends on how much different groups of users need to share this data, as well as on how valuable the company at large perceives this data to be to its decision-making processes. If the data is widely shared and of significant importance to the company, then the reconciled data layer must include it to ensure its quality and consistency with other decision support data. The decision to input such personal data to the BDW leads to inevitable restrictions on what the end user can do with the structure and contents of the real-time data. As a consequence, the IS department may conclude that this real-time data needs to reside on a server where it can exercise a higher degree of control.

- In this example, the reconciled data has been split over two environments. This decision has some immediately obvious consequences: First, it reduces network traffic between these two machines in both the reconciliation and derivation steps. Second, and more important, a bidirectional data flow between the two machines becomes necessary in order to synchronize the two sets of reconciled data.

The placement and number of reconciled data sets are influenced by the enterprise data model (EDM) and by the physical environment, as follows:

- The EDM suggests the maximum number of subsets possible for the reconciled data. Each subset must be capable of internal reconciliation without the need for more than a minimal level of data

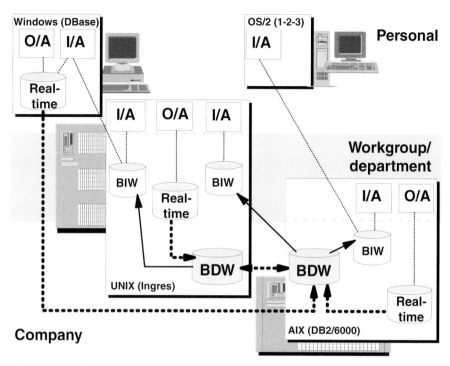

Figure 18-5: *The three-layer architecture in a distributed environment*

from other subsets. Enterprise models usually show only a small number of independent subsets, and any subsetting of the reconciled layer between servers often leads to significant data transfer between them.

- The physical system configuration determines the actual number of subsets implemented and their placement. While the processing power and disk capacity of the individual servers must be considered, network capacity is often more important.

- End-user access to reconciled data is rare, and the networking aspects are therefore related to the bulk transfer of data from real-time to reconciled layer (or BDW), between the various subsets of the data in the reconciled layer and from reconciled to derived layer (or BIWs).

The situation depicted in Figure 18-4 required no central IS involvement. However, once the need for reconciliation becomes clear, an IS role becomes mandatory. This is driven by the need to define and enforce the required levels of standardization in gathering real-time data and to manage the reconciled data layer. This further leads to requirements on systems management tools to support these activities.

In practice...

An enterprise-wide three-layer architecture can be fully deployed only by a central IS department.

The mixed environment

The above two examples, taken from either end of the spectrum of distributed versus centralized environments, show how the concept of the data warehouse and reconciled data support the business need for consistent, widely available data.

What may perhaps be unexpected is that the solution turns out to be the same in both cases, despite the radically different physical environments. The reason for this similarity in solution is that the underlying problem is the same—multiple different data sources that have led to:

• widely dispersed data that is difficult to find and use

• uncontrolled duplication of data into the informational environment

• a significant decline in the quality and usability of the data

It is clear that the physical implementation of the data warehouse can take a number of different forms. End-user access to data may take place from any platform, and data may reside on any platform. In this sense, the implementation of a data warehouse approach is independent of the level of data distribution adopted in the organization and of any debates over downsizing or right-sizing.

However, very few companies exist at either of these two extremes. More mature companies, in particular, although coming from a highly centralized environment, face the problem of a mixed environment. On the one hand, the central IS organization has been expanding support for end-user assess to data and sees the environment broadly as shown in Figure 18-2. On the other hand, users themselves have installed spreadsheets and databases on their PCs independently of the IS shop. Some companies have installed departmental LANs, thus creating in these areas an environment similar to that depicted in Figure 18-4.

From an architectural point of view, this mixed environment is identical to the extreme cases combined to make it. However, organizationally, it presents a more difficult problem to solve, because of the conflict it tends to create between the end users and the IS department. The solution—the introduction of a reconciled data layer—is the cause of this conflict.

Because of the data volumes involved, and because the IS shop already has an existing environment, as well as the skills to manage it, the reconciled data is likely to be placed on one large, centrally owned server (or at most, a few of them). End users see this as a major reduction in the independence and autonomy that they have so recently gained. Introducing a warehouse in this environment will succeed only if the end user community benefits significantly from it [Van Alstyne *et al.* (1995)].

18.2 Aligning the data warehouse with the organizational structure

Bearing in mind that the BDW is largely centralized, both in control and location, and the BIWs are largely distributed, we can now consider how the organizational structure influences the physical implementation of the warehouse.

Dealing with reporting structures

Throughout this book, we have considered the data warehouse within an enterprise-wide scope, for two reasons:

- It is a valid and common requirement in data warehousing to view the enterprise as a whole in an integrated and consistent manner.

- This is the widest scope applicable to a data warehouse today.

However, it is possible to address the warehouse at a lower level in the organization and still achieve significant benefits. This might be done as part of a staged implementation, or as a longer-term solution that derives from the reporting structure of the organization.

In one common organizational structure, the divisions of the company operating in different markets are essentially independent and autonomous, and report to corporate or headquarters management only at a summary level. This structure also applies, of course, to a holding company and its individual subsidiaries.

A company like this can structure a data warehouse in a number of ways. This section discusses two of the most common approaches using the example of a bank with two distinct areas of business—the personal and corporate finance markets.

Headquarters-level reconciliation

As we can see in Figure 18-6, both personal and corporate divisions are responsible for their own operational systems, through which they each run their individual businesses. Divisional management needs to monitor and control this business. Headquarters requires a summary

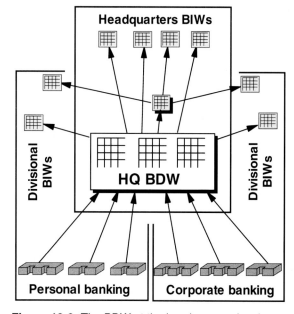

Figure 18-6: *The BDW at the headquarters level*

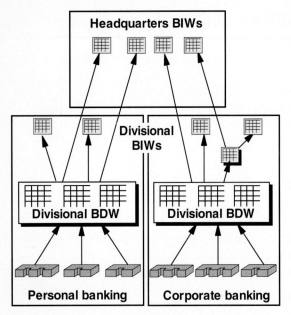

Figure 18-7: *Divisional BDWs*

view of the overall business status and is also responsible for preparing financial statements for the entire business as required by law. In terms of the data warehouse architecture, specific BIWs meet all of these business needs.

The next question in such a situation is where should the BDW be placed?

Figure 18-6 shows an approach that positions the BDW as a reconciliation point for data from all operational systems, irrespective of their ownership at the divisional level.

A major advantage of this approach is that it allows for correlation of personal and corporate business, at both the divisional and the headquarters levels. The personal banking division can thus offer its personal customers special treatment if they also handle their business banking through the corporate banking division. This service may provide the bank with considerable competitive advantage. The figure also shows the use of a staging BIW. This allows, for example, the production of a fully consistent set of month-end reports based on a single BDW derivation.

Division-level reconciliation

However, there is a cost involved in reconciling data from the two divisions. Their respective operational systems may be based on substantially different data structures or platforms. If the overlap between the two businesses is small, the costs of consolidation may outweigh the benefits.

An alternative approach is to treat each division essentially as an individual business and to reconcile at a divisional level as Figure 18-7 shows. The advantage of this approach is, of course, that it eliminates the need to tackle cross-divisional reconciliation issues such as different data structures. It also prevents the political difficulties associated with losing control at a divisional level, which is inherent in the headquarters BDW approach.

Unfortunately, eliminating these problems also eliminates the potential competitive advantage of having a single, consolidated view of the complete customer base. Note that this approach allows staging BIWs to be shared within a division or between a division and headquarters, but not between divisions. The reason for the latter is that no reconciliation has taken place between the data from the different divisions. For the same reason, each headquarters BIW can be sourced only from the BDW of a single division.

In practice...

Reconciliation of data across the entire organization offers the largest potential benefits, but incurs the highest cost. You must understand the strategic business directions in order to make this tradeoff.

Adding geographical considerations

The previous example focused on the reporting structure of the company. In many cases, an additional complexity is introduced by considering the geographical topology of the organization.

The following example is typical of a multinational manufacturing company, whose structure is shown in Figure 18-8. The company has local autonomous organizations responsible for all activities in each country. Each organization runs operational applications in-country to support its local business and reports its overall summary position to headquarters.

In addition there are two operational areas that operate on an international basis. The production facilities are managed at a detailed level by the production headquarters group. In addition, the local production groups report their summary positions to the local country headquarters. The market planning group is a headquarters group that feeds information into each of the country operations.

The initial data warehouse focuses on a company-wide view of data, leading to an implementation aligned closely with the logical data architecture. As Figure 18-9 shows, real-time data from each country's operational systems is reconciled into a BDW in headquarters. The BDW in turn provides derived data to a BIW running within each country headquarters.

This structure supports the internationally based operations in exactly the same way. Production data is gathered from the countries into the same BDW, as is market planning data from the headquarters group. All this

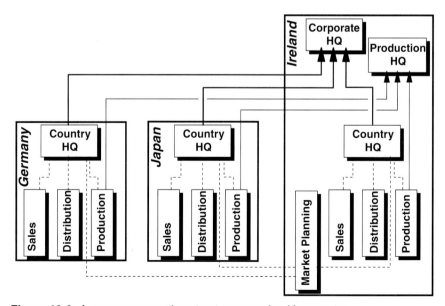

Figure 18-8: *A company reporting structure organized by country*

data is then made available as needed to country headquarters BIWs as well as to corporate and production headquarters BIWs.

In addition (although not shown in the diagram for the sake of clarity), each country sales or distribution organization can also have one or more BIWs to support its local management information needs. Each of these BIWs is sourced from the corporate BDW, through staging BIWs as needed.

We can easily see the strength of this approach—in which data quality is controlled by reconciling all of the company's data in the hands of a central IS function. However, the weakness of this approach is also clear: it requires moving a substantial volume of data around the network to populate the BDW and then sending derived data back to the country BIWs. The challenge, therefore, is to reduce the network loads by distributing the BDW, while at the same time maintaining control of the data management aspects. This task can be divided into two parts:

1. understanding the use made of the data in the various locations, and as a result, the volumes of data that need to move between locations

2. matching these requirements to the structure of the EDM and allowing the definition of sensible subsets of the data

We can make the following assumptions about usage, location, and volumes of data:

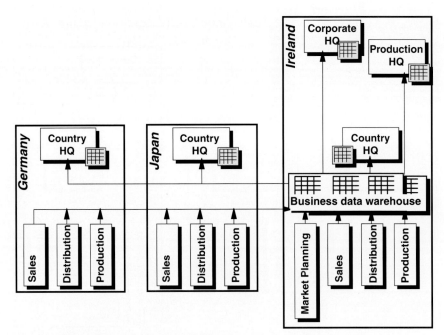

Figure 18-9: *Using a single physical BDW for the country reporting structure*

- Corporate headquarters is interested primarily in summary information from all of the countries, and the volumes of data required on a regular basis are small. There may be an occasional, exceptional need for analysis at a detailed level to solve some problem.

- Production headquarters is interested in the detailed manufacturing results from each production site. In this example, the company is not in a high-volume production business, so the volumes of data required are medium.

- Each country headquarters is responsible for the detailed management of its local sales and distribution operations and therefore require both detailed and summary information. Volumes of data are relatively large, since individual sales and invoices may need to be tracked at the level of individual events.

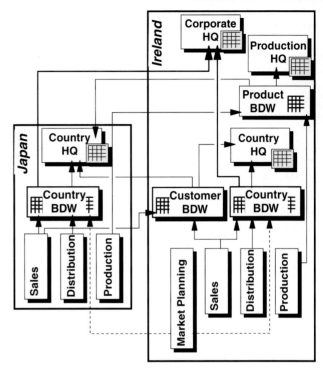

Figure 18-10: *Using a distributed BDW for the country reporting structure*

- Country headquarters requires only low-volume summary data from the production units located in its country.

- Market planning feeds low volumes of data to country headquarters at quarterly intervals.

Figure 18-10 shows the result. There are five separate subsets of the BDW, located over three sites. (One of these subsets is in the German operation which is omitted for clarity.)

The sales and distribution data is reconciled at a country level, because this data can be uniquely partitioned into country-specific subsets. This structure is valid for all of this data, with the exception of the customer entity. In this business, customers operate internationally and therefore cannot be assigned to any country.

The production data is relatively separate in the EDM from the sales and distribution data and is also used in a central manner. Therefore, the company uses a separate BDW for reconciling this data. The market planning data is small in volume and can be readily distributed to the country BDWs, to which data it logically relates.

<table>
<tr><td>

In practice...

The BDW can be subsetted for geographical distribution, but only based on the EDM and an understanding of data usage by location and data distribution costs.

</td><td>

Each country has its own country-based, general-purpose BDW, which focuses on the sales and distribution data and includes market planning information. In addition, each country contributes to a common reconciled base of customer information, which is stored centrally. The product data is also reconciled centrally.

Note that this arrangement leads to some redundancy between the customer and country BDWs, because the sales and distribution data stored in the country BDWs clearly also contains some customer information. The reconciliation step for customer information must take this into account.

Depending on the exact shape of the EDM, each country BDW may also require some degree of cross-reconciliation with the product BDW. Figure 18-10 omits these data flows for clarity.

</td></tr>
</table>

Supporting sales analysis databases

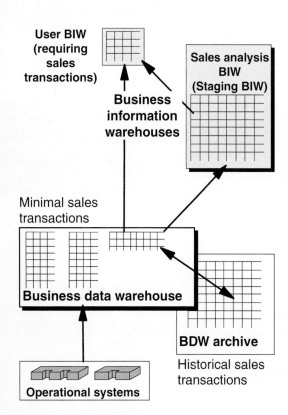

Figure 18-11: Supporting market and sales analysis

A common reason why a company opts for a data warehouse is to allow detailed analysis of its sales or market data. This need can be satisfied only by gathering detailed sales transaction data over a period of time, which leads to a substantial volume of data. For example, Wal-Mart, a major retailer in the United States, commonly quotes volumes of data on the order of 6 terabytes of such information.

In architectural terms, this data clearly resides in a BIW because it is specifically defined to meet a particular business need. However, an historical record of sales transaction data is also a basic element of the BDW. The architecture therefore suggests that this data be stored at least twice— once in the BDW and also in the required number of BIWs. (Given the data volumes involved, this is a solution that would appeal only to the vendors of large disk drives!)

In fact, there exist two alternatives to this suggestion. The first approach is to accept that this example is an exception to the architecture and to allow the market and sales analysts direct access to the BDW. While probably the simplest solution, it does have some inherent drawbacks. The structure of the data in the BDW is largely normalized according to the EDM. This may be unsuitable for sales analysis in terms of understanding or performance, unless the business centers entirely or mainly on the sales cycle, and the EDM reflects this to the virtual exclusion of other business needs.

The second approach, shown in Figure 18-11, is more generically applicable. Here, the sales analysis application remains a BIW and is sourced from the enterprise BDW. However, because this BIW maintains a substantial historical record of the sales transactions on-line, there is little need to also keep an historical record of the sales transactions on-line in the BDW. Therefore, the sales transactions pass through the BDW, are stored there on-line only as long as they are needed for reconciliation purposes, and are then archived.

Provided that other business needs for sales transaction data are small and can be satisfied from the sales analysis BIW, the result is that this BIW becomes a staging BIW, used principally by the sales and market analysts and structured according to their needs. Given the size and importance of this staging BIW, it is likely to be stored centrally and controlled by the IS department.

> **In practice...**
>
> *A market analysis database is a BIW and, in spite of its size, should not be mistaken for the BDW.*

18.3 Subsetting the BDW

Generalizing from the discussion in the previous sections, we can see that there are two ways to divide the BDW into subsets, as Figure 18-12 shows.

1. **Segmenting the BDW**

   The first approach is to segment the BDW into sets of closely related tables, where each set corresponds to an area of the data model that shows many internal relationships but few external ones. The resulting segments will, in general, correspond to functional areas of the business, and often correspond to different organizations in the company.

2. **Partitioning the BDW**

   The second approach, which can be taken within a segment, is to partition the data in the segment according to the value sets of the data. The re-

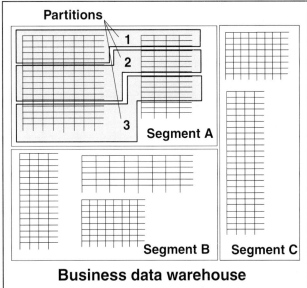

Figure 18-12: BDW segments and partitions

sulting partitions can reflect any chosen grouping of data. The example shown in Figure 18-10 divided the sales information by geographical area. Another example would be to partition product data by different categories of product. At the highest level, such categories could correspond to different business areas. For example, in the insurance industry, product data could be partitioned into "life", "motor", and "household" categories, corresponding to three independent business areas. At the lowest level, such partitioning may often be a matter of performance [Bustamente and Sorenson (1994)].

Noted that segmentation of the BDW relates more directly to the underlying characteristics of the data than partitioning does. This is because segmentation is based on the EDM, which is less liable to change and is thus a more stable basis for subsetting the BDW. Partitioning, as we can see from the above examples, is subject to change as the business undergoes management reorganizations—a not infrequent occurrence in many companies.

18.4 Conclusions

The logical design of the three-layer data architecture set out in Parts II through IV leads to a very flexible and powerful set of options for the physical design of the data warehouse. These options range from a design based on a centralized implementation to a fully distributed approach based on a mixture of different size platforms.

By considering data modeling, data usage requirements and constraints, and network traffic, warehouse designers can determine an optimal physical arrangement of data. With careful design, the tradeoff between these various options can lead to a data warehouse implementation that supports the IS need for control and management of the company's data as well as allowing end users flexible access to that data in a way that meets their expectations for both performance and quality.

Chapter 19

Data warehouse management

This chapter brings together the main aspects involved in the management and underlying operation of the data warehouse. The intention is to focus on those aspects that are unique to data warehousing, rather than to provide complete coverage of all of the general aspects of systems management required.

Of all the components of warehouse administration, one in particular requires special attention. This is **replication administration**, used to define how the data replication function operates. This component addresses two distinct groups of users:

- It supports the IS department in populating the BDW.
- It supports users and IS staff in populating the BIWs.

The diverse audience and their different skill sets pose significant challenges for this component.

There are two other components used in support of the major activities of creating, maintaining, and using the warehouse:

- **Process management** is the component responsible for coordinating functions that operate across environments and whose actions must occur in a particular sequence.

- **Data transfer** is responsible for the movement of data at all levels of granularity, from a single record to a complete file, between physically separate systems.

Finally, in implementing any software system, providing a way to manage and administer database usage and security is a key requirement. The data warehouse is no exception. However, the requirements here differ only minimally, if at all, from those of other database systems. This chapter ends with a brief overview of the requirements in these two areas; for further details refer to standard texts.

19.1 Replication administration

Replication administration

A component of data replication that maintains the metadata—source, target, and mapping definitions—required for data replication.

The runtime functionality required for data replication in populating both the business data warehouse (BDW) and the business information warehouses (BIWs) has been described at length in Chapters 9 and 11. Chapter 6 introduced the concept of model-driven mapping, as the means of linking the definition of data replication and population to the underlying business meaning of the data. Based on the functionality described in these chapters, we can deduce the requirements for administering such an environment. As Figure 19-1 shows, *replication administration* concentrates on managing the definitions of data sources and targets and the mappings between them.

Although the administration component may run only once for every hundred invocations of the runtime components, this does not imply that administration is less important. In fact, the availability of high-quality definitions is a prerequisite to any use of the runtime components. Thus, the performance aspects of administration are of little consequence. However, its usability and consistency, and its ability to access and use a diverse set of existing definition information are all vital to the implementation of a high-quality data replication environment. The usability of the administration function is a particularly important consideration in BIW population, because of the expectation that users, rather than IS personnel, will be increasingly defining and managing BIWs.

The administration component supports the definition and maintenance of information (or metadata) in five main areas:

- definition of the source data
- definition of the target data
- mapping between the source and target data
- assignment of replication mode
- assignment of replication schedule

The following sections describe these areas along with the structure and audience of replication administration.

Source data definitions

In most types of application development, defining the structure and contents of the data sources is a fundamental design step. Data replication, on the other hand, starts from the premise that the source data already exists. Therefore, its structure and contents are already defined.

The function of administration in this area, therefore, is not to create source definitions, but rather to capture the required definitions from existing metadata stores. These definitions encompass both logical, business-related meanings of the data and physical location and structural aspects. Ideally, these definitions should be sourced from a common model base for both source and target. However, administration must also deal with the current reality, where such a complete model seldom exists.

Because operational systems as a data source in BDW population have different characteristics from the BDW as a data source for BIW population, we will consider administration for these two areas separately.

Source data definition for BDW population

In the ideal case the operational system is a modern system, developed using a computer-aided software engineering (CASE) tool, and based on a data model that has been defined from the logical business requirements on down to the physical database design. In this case, the source of the data definitions should be the repository of the CASE tool. This source provides information about both the physical data structure and the business meaning of the data.

Older systems—those developed without CASE technology—require a number of approaches, some pursued in parallel, others independently:

- Where the source data exists in a database, the most obvious source of the definition information is the catalog of the database itself. In this case, replication administration must access and extract the contents of the catalog and make it available to the user.

- Where the source data is file based, obtaining the definition information presents more of a challenge. One approach is to go to the data defini-tion sections in the source code of the applications that create and maintain the data files of interest. In general, this makes it more difficult to obtain the required metadata, and the quality of the resulting metadata is lower than in the previous in-stance.

- CASE tools that analyze programs, files, and databases and reengineer a data model from their existing structures are also potentially useful in replication administration. The output of such tools, stored in the

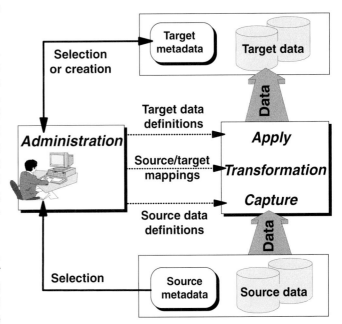

Figure 19-1: Administration overview

same repository as the business-level model, is often more usable than the descriptions or catalogs mentioned above. However, a method is needed to ensure that the repository also reflects any further maintenance of the operational system.

- In all cases, the link back to the business meaning of the data must be manually generated. Data dictionaries of operational systems should provide this information, but they are notoriously unreliable. Documenting this information may require a specific project, involving the designers (if they are still around!) and users of the legacy systems.

Because population of the BDW must handle many data sources in different locations and on different hardware and software platforms, it is best to bring together the metadata describing these sources and store it in a common format. This approach improves the design and use of the administration component, by providing:

- improved performance—because the metadata store is local

- better availability—because the administration component is no longer dependent on real-time links to the sources of metadata

- better support for ongoing maintenance of the source definitions by the users of the administration component—because the metadata used for replication administration is isolated from any changes in the underlying source metadata

This last item describes the maintenance needs of data replication—that is, new requirements for data in the warehouse cause BDW designers to select different data from the operational system. However, there is another parallel stream of change: the maintenance of the metadata of the operational system. This reflects the data needs of the users of the operational systems themselves. While some of these changes have no impact on existing data replication source definitions, others—changes to or deletions from existing structures—clearly do.

Source data definition for BIW population

In contrast to the situation for BDW population, defining the data sources for BIW population is rather simple. The source in this case is, of course, the BDW. By definition, the BDW is modeled, and the definitions of both business meaning and physical implementation are stored in the repository of the CASE or modeling tool used. As mentioned in Chapter 13, this information is also copied into the data warehouse catalog (DWC), which physically resides in the same environment as the BDW.

In this case, therefore, administration has two possible sources of the information required to define the data sources for replication:

1. The DWC, since it already resides in the same environment as the BDW, is the obvious choice as the source of this information.

2. The build-time metadata for the definition and maintenance of the BDW, since it is the original source of this information, is also a possible source.

Building the source data definition

Having obtained the basic metadata describing the structure and contents of the source data, the role of administration is to present it to the user in an understandable format and record which data is selected for replication. The information recorded in the source data definition includes:

- location
- format
- access method
- key fields
- other fields

The business-level metadata is conspicuous by its absence from the resulting source data definition. This is because the only further role of the source data definition is to tell the data replication runtime components which data to capture. The role of the business-level metadata in this process is to allow the user to understand the source data in a business context. As replication administration moves toward full support of model-driven replication, the user could expect to select data at the business level and to allow the administration component to look after the physical details of location, format, and so on. This ideal is still far from being achieved in today's replication tools. This facility is of much greater importance in BIW population, where the users of the administration tool are likely to be closer to end users, than in BDW population, where the users are IS staff.

Target data definitions

Many of the considerations just described for source data definitions apply equally to the creation and maintenance of target data definitions. However, there are again differences between BDW and BIW population.

Target data definition for BDW population

Where the BDW is the target, the model definition at the logical level should exist before any attempt is made to populate it. It is also expected that an initial physical definition of the BDW database structure will exist. However, as Chapter 8 shows, this initial physical design involves a significant level of compromise due to source data availability and the ability of the data replication tools to populate the required structure.

The result is that defining the initial target data for BDW population is a highly iterative process, which is likely to be carried out partially in the modeling tool used to design the BDW, and partially in the replication administration tool. This is a complex project environment, but, until a single tool can support both processes, there is little choice but to grin and bear it. Today's replication administration tools do not extend all the way up to enterprise data modeling, nor do modeling tools integrate well with replication administration.

Nevertheless, from a conceptual point of view, it is clear that the data model of the BDW is the ultimate source of target data definitions in BDW population. It follows, therefore, that target data definition for the BDW involves selecting existing fields as targets, rather than defining new ones.

Target data definition for BIW population

Target data definition for BIWs is complicated by the different types of BIW that exist. A number of options therefore exist:

- Staging BIWs, widely used BIWs, and complex BIWs all require a formal design phase that involves the use of CASE tools to model the data from the logical level down to the physical level. In such cases, this model is the source of the target data definition.

- User BIWs and simple BIWs are likely to be designed in the same step that defines the required population approach. The result is that the definition of the structure and contents of the target database potentially derive from the replication administration component. This can simplify the task of the administration component in this area, if it can be assured that some independent mechanism will not subsequently change the target database structure.

- Certain types of BIW are defined through a stand-alone process that is unrelated to data modeling or replication in any direct way. An example is a spreadsheet, where the design usually evolves through prototyping. In such cases, there is often no obvious metadata to provide target data definitions to the administration component, and the user is forced to reenter this information.

   As an added complication, end-user tools such as spreadsheets and OLAP tools often provide their own extract mechanisms, which are independent of any broader data replication environment. As a result, the user defining the target data is unlikely to have any access to the business definitions to aid her or his understanding of data usage.

Building the target data definition

From the viewpoint of the user, the requirement is clear. If the target database structure already exists, replication administration should present it to her or him. At most, the user will simply exclude any fields in the target that are not being filled or changed by this replication process. (Of course, some other replication process must maintain such fields.) If a target database definition does not exist, the user must be presented with a means of defining it. The most obvious, and basic, approach in this case is simply to present a default definition equal to the subset of the source data the user has previously selected.

The information recorded in the target data definition is similar to that recorded for the source definition, and includes:

- location
- format
- access method
- key fields
- other fields

As for source data definition, the business-level metadata is absent. This is because the only further role of the target data definition is to tell the data replication runtime components where to apply the data. Again, the role of the business-level metadata in this process is to allow the user to understand the target data in a business context. The implications are identical to those for source data definition previously described.

All of the information needed as the basis for the next step—the source/target mapping—is now available, and is described next.

Source/target mappings

The source/target mapping step defines the relationship that exists between the fields of the source and those of the target and must support a range of relationships from the simple to the rather complex.

At its most basic, a mapping is a statement that the contents of a single field in the source should be stored in a particular field in the target. In addition, the mapping may specify a transformation that should take place—for example, converting from EBCDIC to ASCII, or converting from a variety of codes to a self-consistent set. At the other end of the scale, a mapping may have to bring together fields from a number of sources and combine them according to some rules into one or more fields in the target. In short, mapping must reflect the full range of complexity in transformation. It follows that the administration component must support the definition of source/target mappings that include:

- simple source/target field pairings
- conversion routines
- lookup tables
- aggregations
- references to company-unique transformation routines or "user exits"

Replication administration stores the resulting map for future use by the runtime components of data replication.

Assignment of replication mode

As Chapters 9 and 11 describe, the combination of capture and apply functions involved define which replication mode—refresh or update—is being used. Because of the variety of capture and apply techniques available, the number of possible combinations is quite large. In some specific cases, where the technical requirement is especially restrictive, it may be necessary to specify precisely which capture and apply functions to use for a particular replication. However, this is rather unusual, and the more general need is to specify the replication mode required. A combination of business and technical considerations determine the choice of mode.

The business requirements that affect the choice are the temporal structure of the source data and the type of time dependency needed in the target data. Both aspects fall into the three categories of data defined in Chapter 6: transient, periodic, and snapshot. However, the set of valid choices is reduced by the fact that the BDW contains only periodic data, operational data is never snapshot, and BIWs never contain transient data.

The technical considerations are data volumes and rate of change of source data.

Table 19-1: Replication mode—refresh versus update

Source and structure	Target and structure	Data volumes		Rate of change	
		Large	Small	High	Low
Operational	*BDW*				
Transient	*Periodic*	**Update**	**Update**	**Update**	**Update**
Periodic	*Periodic*	**Update**	Refresh	**Update**	Refresh
BDW	*BIW*				
Periodic	*Periodic*	**Update**	Refresh	**Update**	Refresh
Periodic	*Snapshot*	Refresh	Refresh	Refresh	Refresh

Table 19-1 shows how these factors interrelate to suggest which replication mode to use. These choices, in general, represent a recommendation based on good practice rather than a definitive answer. In some cases, there is no choice—for example, periodic target data can be produced from transient source data only through the update mode of replication.

The result of this definition, in common with all of the other outputs described above, forms a part of the metadata needed by data replication. Therefore, the replication administration component stores and manages this definition, both for use by the runtime components and for further use by the users of the administration tools. However, much of it is of potential interest to end users and so is also made available in the DWC.

Assignment of replication schedule

Although there are some cases in which the data replication process must be performed immediately after it has been defined, perhaps as a one time event, this is not the norm. More generally, the requirement is to perform the replication process a number of times, at regular intervals and when predefined conditions have been met. Data replication is therefore a scheduled process, and its execution must be controlled and managed by some process management techniques.

Section 19.3 describes the process management function as used in data warehouse management. The user sees the administration of schedules for data replication logically as part of the process of administering data replication, but physically it is part of the process management component. Therefore, the metadata produced by this step is stored together with other process management control information, rather than in the data replication component itself. However, like other metadata of interest to end users, it should also be available in the DWC.

Structure of the administration component

Figure 19-2 shows the structure of replication administration.

The ***internal metadata copy store*** supports continuous availability of source and target definitions for users. This necessitates a function to manage versioning—the ***external metadata manager***—which ensures ongoing synchronization of data between the internal and external stores. External stores of metadata include database catalogs, file structure definitions in programs, and data models in CASE tools. A second function of the external metadata manager is to translate metadata into a common, easily understood format. This is particularly necessary for metadata from hierarchical databases such as IMS or IDMS.

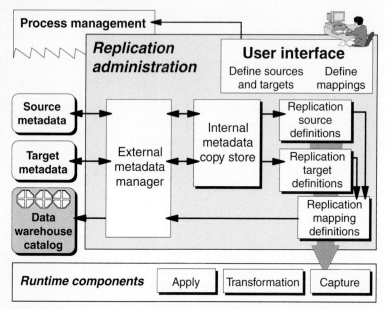

Figure 19-2: *The structure of the replication administration component*

In certain circumstances, it may be possible to dispense with both the internal metadata copy store and the external metadata manager. This is the case if all sources and targets exist in the same database format and reside on machines that are continuously connected.

The user interface provides the function to define and store the definitions of the sources, targets, and mapping rules related to each instance of replication. It also provides a link to the user interface of process management where the user defines the actual replication schedule.

Of course, the runtime components use the replication definitions, as do the end users of the data warehouse through the DWC. Section 19.2 discusses how the runtime components use the replication definitions.

Users of the administration component

The users of the replication administration component fall into two main categories: IS personnel and end users.

The designers of the BDW, and therefore the people responsible for defining the mapping from operational systems to the BDW, are from the IS department. The complexity of the source data structures and the resulting mappings make this necessary. In contrast, mapping from BDW to BIW is generally a simpler step because it can be logically defined; therefore, end users may undertake this step. However, even in this case, it is likely that only the more advanced and "IS-aware" end users will undertake this task. Often, such users are nominated to do this on behalf of a department or other grouping of users.

In the short to medium term, the task of defining data replication mappings, whether into the BDW or into the BIW, is likely to remain an IS responsibility. Two factors influence this. The first factor is the current state of administration components themselves, which are generally difficult to use and are closely tied to physical data definitions, without good links to the logical business data model. The second factor relates to the state of maturity of data warehousing in general. Because most warehouses today are in an early stage of evolution, there is seldom a critical mass of advanced users available for any particular warehouse who can take on the role of defining the BIW population step, so this responsibility falls to IS.

However, enabling users (even those in the advanced category) to undertake the definition of BIWs and the mappings needed to populate them is an important factor in achieving one of the key goals of data warehousing—to give users control over management information. This goal emphasizes the need for continuous improvement in the user interface for data replication and a closer linkage to business data modeling. Since end-user departments are all too often over worked and under staffed, they need every possible encouragement to assume this responsibility, which their desire to control their own data rightly entails.

19.2 From administration to runtime

Having defined the set of runtime functions that can be used, and the approach to mapping from source to target data, the next question clearly is how to tie these together into one or more population components in the warehouse. The aim, of course, is generally to use off-the-shelf tools provided by software vendors as a means of reducing development and ongoing maintenance costs. Such generic tools fall into two broad categories as the next section describes. However, a company may also need functionality that is specific to its own environment, a topic that the following section covers.

Generic data replication tools

Generic data replication tools provide more flexibility and generality than simply designing and coding the required function specifically for each source/target combination. All generic tools use one or another of two distinct approaches. The distinction between the methods is characterized by the way each uses the definitions and mappings after administration has completed its role.

- **Data replication by code generation**

  In the code-generation approach, the definitions and mappings are input to a specialized CASE tool that generates the capture, transformation, and apply code appropriate to the sources and targets and to the types of transformation required. In general, this method uses a building-block approach—providing a library of functions, and plugging the required modules into an overall framework. The generated code is compiled and/or linked and then moved into production in the runtime data warehouse environment.

- **Data replication engines**

  In the case of a data replication engine, the definitions and mappings are used at runtime by a table-driven engine. The engine contains all the function required to capture, transform, and apply the replicated data and the choice of function to be used is a runtime decision.

Comparison of approaches

Each of these approaches has its advantages and disadvantages. The main difference between them is the time when integration of the required functions occurs. In the code-generation approach, this integration occurs at build time, while in the engine approach, it occurs at runtime. Therefore, the basic technical difference is in the size of the resultant run-time code, which tends to be smaller in the case of the code-generation approach.

The strengths of the code-generation approach stem from the early integration of required function and the early disposal of unneeded function:

- One tool can support a wider variety of sources and targets.

- One tool can support a larger set of transformation functions.

- Inclusion of new sources and targets is simplified.

- Expansion of the range of transformations supported is reasonably straightforward, including integration of the transformation function that is specific to a unique need of a particular company.

The weaknesses of this approach are a result of the early stage in the overall process at which the definitions and mappings are "fixed" into code:

- Because runtime code is specifically generated for each requirement, each component must be individually, and often manually, promoted into the production environment, which lessens IS productivity.

- Changes in replication needs can be handled either by going back to the code-generation component, or by directly updating the previously generated code, leading to potential maintenance problems.

The strengths and weaknesses of the engine approach are the exact mirror image of those described for code generation. In particular, the engine approach ties the build-time and runtime environments closely together and thus enables improved IS productivity and better-controlled maintenance of the replication environment than code generation does.

However, the engine approach does not lend itself to supporting a wide variety of sources or targets in the one tool because of the growth in the size and internal complexity of the engine. Nonetheless, within a smaller set of source/target combinations, an engine can be closely tuned to meet the needs of that particular environment. Similarly, expanding the set of transformation functions beyond those originally provided by the engine is often more difficult than in the code-generation approach, because the engine has a more integrated design. This, however, can be readily overcome by using an engine design that is modular.

The advantage of the code-generation approach clearly lies in its ability to cater to a wide variety of sources and targets. However, this is offset by potential problems in productivity and maintenance. On the other hand, the engine approach provides strong support for IS productivity and control of maintenance in a more limited source/target set.

While some argue that the runtime performance is better for the code-generation approach than for an engine, little theoretical reasoning supports this contention, other than the probably small overhead of a larger code size inherent in the engine. However, because the engine approach supports a smaller set of sources and targets, with good design, it allows for greater optimization, which in turn is likely to offset this overhead.

> *In practice...*
>
> *Support of BDW population from older operational systems often needs custom-built functionality. From the start, it should be designed to be reusable for many sources, and to be easily integrated with the chosen vendor tools.*

Do-it-yourself data replication

The structure and functionality for data replication described thus far makes it clear that there should be little or no role in the data warehouse for separately developed extract programs addressing specific sets of data. However, there are two areas where organizations building their own data warehouses often have to provide functionality. These are:

- **Unique transformation function**

  In the BDW population component, it is not unusual for a company to need a particular type of transformation unique to that organization. This is particularly the case where the operational systems are designed around flat files. Such functions often involve the normalization or combination of data from different data files, rationalization of record keys, and other structural cleansing.

- **Unusual data sources or targets**

  Although becoming less of an issue as vendors extend the reach of their replication tools, there are still a few file or database structures that are unsupported.

In both cases, it is the responsibility of the organization's IS shop to address the need by developing a piece of code. The most important criterion for this development is that it must be well integrated into the wider data replication tool set. To accomplish this, the IS department must ensure that the administration component of this function is integrated with that of the generic tools. It also requires that the generic tools provide the ability to invoke an external function and pass data to and from it—the traditional "user exit".

When a company requires such company-specific capture, transformation, or apply function, it should, of course, be built in the most generic way possible. Although this will add to the initial development cost, later savings from reusing this function for other data needs and as data needs change will usually offset any such increased initial costs.

19.3 Process management

Process management

A set of functions supporting the definition of inter-related process steps and the management of their execution across a variety of hardware and software platforms; used mainly by data replication.

A *process management* component is required in many areas beyond the data warehouse, as a means for sequencing and interlinking the individual steps in a larger process. Within the warehouse, its main role is to support data replication. The data replication process, with its numerous functions and the possibility of spanning several systems, requires the underlying support of a process manager to support the definition and management of its rather complex processes.

Support of data replication

Process management supports data replication in a number of ways:

- definition of replication processes

- sequencing and initiation of the components needed

- initiation of alternative actions in the event that errors occur

- communication between the different components

Traditional process management consists of a number of tasks connected in a network that describes the events triggering each task, the communication between the tasks, and the outcomes resulting from each task. Tasks in this approach may relate directly to human tasks or may be carried out entirely by software programs. The responsibility for managing the task network lies with the process management component.

An example of a process that could be managed in this way is the insurance claims process. This consists of a number of steps or tasks carried out in many different locations throughout the company, often as part of different applications. In the manual process, a number of people physically move the claim from desk to desk and from department to department, accumulating a file of attachments such as investigation reports, approvals, evidence of premium payment, and so forth. Well-known problems associated with this environment, include:

- It is difficult to know where the file is at any given time.

- Ensuring that each step of the process is triggered by the previous one and that unusual situations are correctly and speedily handled incurs significant overhead.

When an electronic environment replaces the paper-based system, a computer-based process manager takes on the responsibility of tracking progress, ensuring efficient and timely handovers from one step to the next, and performing other assorted actions required to run the process.

The data replication process has many similarities:

- Actions are required in many different locations.

- Some actions must be initiated according to a schedule.

- Other actions are required in the event of some unusual occurrence.

- Some actions can occur only when one or more previous actions have successfully completed.

- The outcome of these actions, whether successful or not, may need communication to other components or to some human operator.

The outcome is a network of decisions and actions, a simplified example of which is shown in Figure 19-3.

Requirements for process management

Figure 19-3 also demonstrates the type and extent of the functional requirements that data replication places on process management:

- **Process schedule**

  The process schedule is the master list of data replication processes that are needed to populate the data warehouse. A process consists of a network of tasks and decision points. It may be initiated repeatedly or just once; at regular intervals (such as daily, weekly, etc.) or at particular days, dates, or times. It may include BDW and/or BIW population steps. The administration component creates and maintains the schedule entries.

- **Process map definition**

  The network of tasks and decision points that make up a process must be defined and maintained. For complex, repeatedly used processes, process map definition requires a fairly sophisticated, probably graphical tool that is an integral part of the process management component. For simpler or single-occurrence processes, process map definition

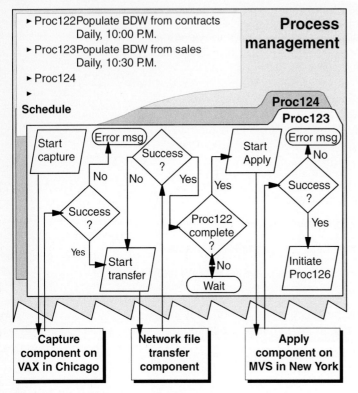

Figure 19-3: *Process management in data replication—an example*

reduces to the type of function traditionally found in batch control programs.

- **Task initiation**

  Initiating tasks on all of the hardware and software platforms in the entire environment in which the data warehouse operates, including those in the operational environment, requires support.

- **Status information inquiry**

  In addition to the ability to initiate tasks on multiple platforms, process management must also be able to inquire about the status of components that are running on all platforms.

The extent to which any component, such as capture or data transfer, manages its own error handling, rather than allowing process management to take care of it, is an implementation decision. Broadly speaking, each component should be as independent as possible. In Figure 19-3, for example, capture is shown as a single task; the process, Proc123, defines only one response to an error condition—generate an error message and give up. This response implies that the capture component has exhausted all internal possibilities for error handling, which could include multiple retries or attempts to use different capture techniques. As described in Chapter 9, the capture technique used will influence which apply techniques are suitable, and therefore this is part of the information that must be stored and passed on by process management.

19.4 Data transfer

As in the case of process management, ***data transfer*** is required in the warehouse mainly to support data replication and only when the source and target data reside on different physical platforms. In addition, data transfer functionality is required to pass status or information messages between the various components of the data warehouse.

Data replication and the messaging needs of this and other components place certain requirements on data transfer. The technical implementation of the data transfer function is less important than the extent to which the requirements are met.

Requirements for data transfer

The requirements placed on data transfer are listed below:

- **Support for all required hardware and software platforms as source and target**

  The general requirement is, of course, to support all platforms as both source and target. However, this is a difficult goal and within any individual data warehouse implementation, only a certain subset of platforms needs support as either sources and/or targets. This implies that the sending and receiving functions of data transfer often operate on different platforms.

- **Asynchronous data transfer**

  As previously described, the data warehouse is not expected to be exactly synchronized with its underlying operational data sources. Therefore, asynchronous capture and apply of data is the norm, leading to the requirement for asynchronous data transfer.

  This type of data transfer is generally regarded as synonymous with "file transfer", and indeed, from a physical viewpoint we can view it as such even for data replication. However, you should recall that in many cases the file being transferred consists of one or more changes captured in the update mode of replication. File sizes, therefore, tend to be small, and the sequence in which they are applied to the target is of vital importance. In addition, of course, large files must be supported for refresh mode replication.

  Asynchronous transfer also supports situations where the link between the source and target systems is not always available. Staging of the data is thus required at the sending side of the transfer component.

- **Synchronous data transfer**

  This mode of data transfer is required to support data access, as Chapter 12 describes.

- **Transparency to the underlying transfer mechanism**

  As with all transport protocols, the replication or other calling function need not worry about how data transfer gets data from source to target. In theory, the transfer mechanism could span the entire spectrum

Data transfer

The data transport function, that underlies data replication and data access, and is responsible for transferring data —ranging from messages to complete files— between data warehouse components in any combination of locations, hardware, or software.

of media—from the physical transport of a tape, to the establishment and use of a synchronous connection from source to target.

- **Transparent support of local and remote data transfer**

  As the data warehousing environment grows over time, the locations of source and target for data replication are likely to change. An initial implementation, for example, might place both the BDW and the first BIWs on the same machine, before BIWs are distributed to departmental platforms for improved response time. The data transfer function can support these configuration options by recognizing source and target locations as either local or remote, initiating a physical data transport mechanism only in the remote case.

- **Optional support for guaranteed delivery times**

  There may be instances that require a guaranteed delivery time particularly when the data warehouse becomes heavily used.

- **Sequencing transferred data**

  Transformation involving multi-record enrichment, especially when using update mode replication, places very stringent requirements on the sequence and timing for applying data to the target. Most of the responsibility for ensuring the correct outcome of replication in these situations lies with the transformation and apply functions themselves. However, at a minimum, the data transfer component should guarantee the correct ordering of "files" that are passed through it. This need implies a staging area at the receiving side.

- **Full error recovery**

  Where possible, the data transfer component should handle internally all breakdowns or errors in the transfer mechanism. Only complete failure should require operator intervention.

- **Support for initiation as part of an overall process**

  Occasionally it may be necessary, both within and outside of the data warehouse approach, to initiate data transfer manually. For the most part, however, data transfer needs to be part of an automated process, controlled and managed externally to the data transfer function itself. Process management supplies this automation, and data transfer should be capable of being integrated in any managed process.

- **Support of status notification and status inquiry**

  Whether as a result of an error condition, or in response to a status inquiry, the data transfer component should report on the status of the file transfer completed, in progress, or pending. Such reporting will normally be to the process management component, but it may also result from direct operator intervention.

Data transfer structure

The structure of data transfer is less important than its ability to satisfy the requirements listed in the previous section. Such a structure is shown in Figure 19-4. The component is divided into send and receive portions, which can run on different physical platforms. When running across platforms, a network transport function is needed. The staging function, accessible from both sender and receiver, resides on both platforms. When send and receive run on a single platform, no network transport function is required and staging is confined to the one platform. The components can be initiated and queried from process management.

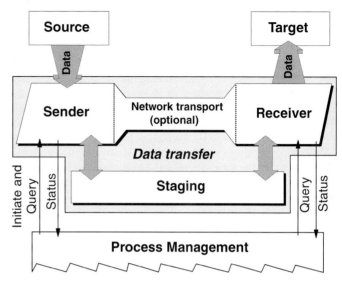

Figure 19-4: *The structure of the data transfer component*

In the data warehouse, the source for replication (see Figure 19-4) can be either the capture or transformation function, while the target can be either the transformation or apply function. Therefore, transformation may physically reside on the same platform as either the capture or apply functions, or may even reside on its own separate platform. If capture, apply, and transformation all reside on the same platform, data transfer provides only staging functionality.

Message-queuing techniques provide an approach to data transfer that is particularly suited to the data warehouse environment. This is because message queuing is fully scalable—from passing individual messages or change records to entire refresh files in support of data replication. The approach also provides the level of management and control needed to ensure the overall integrity of the data warehouse.

19.5 Other database support functions

This text treats both security and database management only briefly. Although important topics in their own right, the needs of data warehousing in regard to them are largely identical to the needs of the IS environment in general.

Security

The security needs of the warehouse are functionally the same as any database environment. The key requirements arising from the three-layer structuring are:

1. The definition of security requirements for data is the responsibility of the data owners. The owners of the physical storage media are responsible for implementing the required level of access control.

2. The most strict access control to the data in the warehouse is usually in the BDW because the total data asset of the organization resides here. It is confined to read-only access, and restricted to database administrators and a small handful of business users with a demonstrable need for detailed data from across the business as a whole.

3. Access control to the contents of the BIWs is highly dependent on the data they contain:

    *   Summarized data showing or predicting the performance of the complete business is highly confidential and secured accordingly.

    *   Staging BIWs, because of their shared nature, also deserve special security arrangements.

    *   Access to BIWs—wherever they reside—is read-only. For user BIWs, distributed to LANs or PCs, this restriction may simply be a convention rather than enforced by software, because of the freedom users have on their own machines.

4. The DWC is generally accessible in read-only mode to all.

5. Write access to the warehouse is confined to the population components.

6. Access control is best done by views, which may range in scope from a subset of rows and columns in a table to a set of complete tables.

7. Given the breadth of usage of the data warehouse, access rules must be defined in a hierarchical structure, with users inheriting the access authorizations of their group, department, and division. On top of this, unique privileges may be granted to access particular sets of data.

8. As data replication tools advance and allow users to easily define and populate BIWs, the definition of security and authorization rules for these BIWs also requires automating.

For further discussion of these topics, see Date (1995) and references therein.

Database management

The ongoing management and administration of a database as used in a warehouse environment is a topic that lies beyond the scope of this book. In general, the fact that the system is used as a data warehouse introduces no new complexities into the subject. In fact, some aspects are simpler: Data in the warehouse consists of periodic data and snapshots, and is thus persistent in nature. In addition, the clear separation of update and access activities, which often occur during different time periods, allows optimizing of these activities relatively independently.

Database management, particularly in a client/server environment, is described in Zantinge and Adriaans (1996).

19.6 Conclusions

In many ways, managing a data warehouse is no different from managing any other large, mission-critical application and data system. Undoubtedly, new problems of scale of the warehouse and the scope of its interactions with other systems arise as the warehouse grows to its full extent. However, in general, no new principles are involved.

The exception lies in the area of data replication. The general use of tools to populate the warehouse—in particular the BIWs of the future—requires a close examination of how to empower users to satisfy their own data needs without compromising the overall integrity of the company's data asset.

The approach to replication administration described here addresses these diverse needs by using, as far as possible, model-driven replication. This ensures that definitions built through modeling tools are available and used at the time of definition of the replication mappings. There are, however, restrictions due to the current state of the technology:

- Modeling and replication tools seldom effectively exchange the required metadata today.

- Popular tools for implementing BIWs usually provide no means of using external modeling tools to define their data: they instead insist on using a stand-alone population mechanism.

Nonetheless, companies can apply the approach shown here in a limited way even while awaiting improvements in metadata integration from vendors.

The areas of process management and data transfer have seen substantial advances in the recent past. These functions are key components underlying data replication. Although the IS infrastructure requires them outside the data warehouse as well, the needs of the warehouse raise substantial requirements in both areas. After introducing and implementing the data warehouse, the IS department may therefore need to revisit the company's existing decisions on what products to use to support process management and data transfer.

Chapter 20

Looking to the future

At this stage in any book, it is appropriate to review the key conclusions and to emphasize the major messages.

Data warehousing has been around for 10 years. In spite of this fact, it is still a relatively immature topic. Tools that were envisaged 10 years ago have only matured sufficiently in the last 12 to 24 months to enable their widespread use. Architectures and methodologies for implementation are at a similar stage.

The approach taken in this final chapter is, therefore, to review the conclusions and messages in the context of their applicability today and the likely directions for the near- to medium-term future. Section 2.4 introduced five key themes:

1. The data warehouse is the single information source for the enterprise.

2. It promotes the widespread, distributed availability of information.

3. It provides end users with information in a business context.

4. The delivery of information throughout the business is automated.

5. It allows end users to be confident of the quality of information they use and to take the ownership of business information that is rightly theirs.

These messages form the basis of this chapter's review of data warehousing today and into the future.

Needless to say, predicting the future is a risky business. And if there is one prediction of which we can be assured, it is that looking back on these predictions at the turn of the millennium will provide considerable amusement for those involved!

20.1 A single information source

The business data warehouse (BDW) has been defined as the logically single, ultimate source for all information. Its key characteristic is its universality in the enterprise, coupled with a structure designed to store only one copy of each piece of relevant information.

Today's situation

While in principle the BDW can exist in a physically distributed environment, circumstances today tend to minimize the level of such distribution:

- Advances in hardware and database technology make it conceivable for even the largest companies to implement a BDW over one or only a few physical databases.

- Limitations in the management functions of distributed databases and systems make the synchronization of highly distributed databases a complex task.

While beginning to expand, the scope of the data in the warehouse remains largely confined to structured, public business data and metadata, as shown in Figure 4-1.

Enterprise data modeling is the basis for defining the contents and structure of the BDW. With the availability of generic industry data models, the task of building enterprise data models is considerably simplified and more cost-effective. However, today's modeling tools lack the functionality to cope effectively with versioning of models and historical data. Usually, IS personnel have to add these aspects manually onto the generated model.

Directions

An expanding data scope

The scope of data in the warehouse is clearly set to expand over the next few years. One of the most likely areas is that of unstructured business data. Such data represents a significant proportion of the marketing data of many companies. When combined with the structured data already in the warehouse, it allows companies to perform new types of analyses. In addition, the quantities of unstructured business data being digitally stored continue to increase exponentially with the inclusion of voice and image data. This leads to demands for new ways to use and analyze such data. Schlatter *et al.* (1994) provide a description of the benefits of such integration and the requirements it drives, as well as an example of how to address many of these needs with today's tools.

In companies that fully adopt data warehousing, the proportion of personal data, both structured and unstructured, is likely to decrease. This is because companies will increasingly recognize that such data is of interest and value to a wider audience within the organization, and so needs to be reclassified as public data and treated accordingly. Thus, the size of the warehouse will grow not because its scope is expanding to include personal data as such, but because personal data is moving into the data warehouse, being transformed by this process into public data.

As Section 4.4 describes, data as a product lies outside the scope of the warehouse, and this business distinction will remain.

Finally, there is the perennial debate about the distinction between informational and operational data, and whether it will ever disappear. Although most observers focus on the technological reasons these two categories of data exist, the reasons relating to business usage and organization, described in Chapter 4, are far more significant. While the technological rationale for maintaining the separation between the two types has diminished and is likely to do so further, the usage and organizational rationale will remain and will ensure continued separation of the two data types.

These same arguments equally justify maintaining the existence of reconciled and derived layers of data within the informational environment.

Inter-enterprise data warehouses

The distinction made today between internal and external data is likely to undergo some change. In today's situation, described in Chapter 7, data crosses company boundaries through interfaces in and out of the data warehouse. As data warehouses become more widely used, the opportunity exists to treat internal BDWs and those in other companies as peers. In this case, the "receiving" company, rather than repeatedly modeling and reconciling external data from the "sending" company, depends on the modeling and reconciliation carried out by the "sending" company. This allows the creation of ***inter-enterprise data warehouses*** which span a number of companies.

> **Inter-enterprise data warehouse**
>
> A data warehouse used as a shared resource between two or more companies.

Of course, such warehouses have significant legal and competitive considerations. In addition, the data in the different parts of the warehouse must have a common model, or there must exist a defined and automated transformation process between the different parts. These issues suggest that inter-enterprise data warehouses will be relatively uncommon, except between those companies who share a substantial and long-term cooperative business arrangement.

Enterprise data modeling

The requirements placed by the data warehouse on enterprise data models and on the modeling tools themselves are growing. In the short term, it is vital that vendors in these areas respond to these needs. The modeling process for a data warehouse is complex, and many companies find that the effort involved here far exceeds expectations.

Of these requirements, support for historical (or temporal) data is the subject of the most active research [Dey *et al.* (1995)]. The incorporation of events into the traditional entity relationship modeling approach allows a more formal representation of time dependence in databases that is likely to have important consequences in data warehouse design in the future.

The broad area of conceptual data modeling, especially at the enterprise-wide level, is the topic of some research [Ba *et al.* (1995), Batra and Marakas (1995)], but there is little evidence of the type of advance needed to significantly ease its adoption.

Object-oriented modeling is currently a hot topic in research as well as among the vendors of modeling tools. This approach ties process and data more closely and directly together than the traditional entity relationship method. This linkage suggests that object-oriented modeling is less appropriate for use in the design of the BDW and the business information warehouses (BIWs), which focus almost entirely on the data rather than on the process.

20.2 Distributed information availability

The needs of end users for independent access to distributed information are addressed by BIWs. BIWs provide their users with independent data stores designed and structured according to their needs, but sourced only from the single, unequivocal BDW.

Today's situation

To a greater or lesser extent we can map almost any decision support or data analysis tool onto the concept of a BIW. Today's tools achieve a high degree of user-friendliness and actively promote the use of real information. However, because these tools focus on the end user, and because many of them have PC origins, they tend to de-emphasize the need for commonality of data usage and understanding across an organization. In addition, many of these tools, especially PC-based spreadsheets and query tools, allow the user full freedom to manipulate the data without maintaining the original data or clearly separating the changed data from the original.

Directions

The Internet

The success of the Internet as a means of making information available to end users suggests a number of potential impacts in data warehousing:

- The ability in the future to use functions directly from the Internet or from an intranet (an internal company network based on Internet technology) is being promoted as a way of reducing or eliminating the need for multiple copies of applications residing on users' PCs. This would solve issues of multiple unsupported user tools and differing versions of code that currently plague many IS organizations.

- The further possibility of eliminating all PC-based storage for personal data is more problematical. There are two options here:

  1. The complete elimination of user-controlled storage would be counterproductive in data warehousing, because it would prevent users from performing long-running what-if types of analyses.

  2. Replacing PC-based storage for personal data with storage located on the network provides relief from the systems management problems associated today with backing up PC-based data, but is otherwise no different from the current situation.

Mobile computing

The increasing prevalence of mobile computing has implications for distributed data management, in both the operational and informational spheres. In general, these implications relate to the way in which data on the mobile machine can be synchronized with that in the home base.

In comparison with the operational environment, the issues are simpler in the data warehouse because of the unidirectional flow of data to the BIWs. The requirement is to ensure that, when BIWs at the home base are updated, the next time the mobile machine connects, its copy of the BIW either is automatically updated or is given the opportunity to do so.

This requirement is almost identical to that for PCs that store BIWs but are not always powered on. As a result, the solution involving notifications and subscriptions, discussed in Chapter 12 for the latter case, is needed for mobile computing as well. The business information interface (BII) also needs to be aware of whether the mobile user is connected to the home base or not. If the user is connected, then additional facilities are available that should automatically show in the user's view.

As the volume of available information grows, there is an increasing need for tools that automatically filter the required information to reduce the volume that each individual user sees. Key enablers in this area are intelligent agents, whose development promises to improve user productivity. They must, however, be closely tied to advances in decision theory, modeling, and optimization [Radermacher (1994)].

20.3 Information in a business context

Based mainly on the metadata generated and stored through enterprise data modeling, the data warehouse catalog (DWC) and business information guide (BIG) combine in the data warehouse environment to provide the business context for information.

Today's situation

While clearly recognized by all data warehouse vendors as a key requirement, fully functional DWC and BIG implementations are a rare commodity. This is due to a combination of metadata and functional limitations:

- Sources of accurate and relatively complete metadata are rare today.

- Much of today's BIG function is based on IS-oriented data dictionary tools, and so focus on physical rather than business characteristics.

- There tends to be too great an assumption that the user is knowledgeable about data (an IS concept) rather than information.

Directions

In the short term, we can expect current vendor initiatives to address some of the function lacking in BIG implementations. This will result in functions more appropriate to true (naïve) end users than to the more IS-aware variety. Functionality currently available in, and being considered for Internet browsers, based on hypertext links and other types of search technologies are further prime candidates for BIG function. Fully distributed functionality in both the DWC and BIG is also recognized as an important requirement, and vendors are likely to address this area in the near future.

With respect to the actual metadata content, efforts to consolidate metadata from multiple sources will continue for the foreseeable future. The variety of tools that generate and store metadata is a major obstacle to attempts to standardize on a particular structure and content. In the longer term, the next major steps in this area are likely to require substantial advances in the conceptual modeling process that allow more intuitive descriptions of the meaning and usage of data.

The management of metadata lends itself to an object-oriented approach, and Jarke *et al.* (1995) describes some of the research directions in deductive object bases that could have a significant influence on the evolution of BIG functionality.

20.4 Automated information delivery

Data replication functionality is the underlying basis for the BDW, BIW, and DWC population components. It provides for the automated delivery of data and information to the physical location where it is required. In combination with an administrative approach that is substantially model driven, these functions can be made available beyond the IS department, thus empowering the business to build the information sets as and when they are needed.

Today's situation

Data replication tools have made major advances over the past few years. In fact, the current popularity of data warehousing stems, at least in part, from the expanded functionality and usability of these tools. Coverage of source and target databases in refresh mode is quite good, although update mode is less well supported. Most commonly needed transformations are available in one tool or another.

The weakest area remains the administrative function. Because it focuses on physical data mapping between source and target, only IS staff can use it. While this is a reasonable restriction for BDW population, BIW population should be increasingly defined by the user community.

The use of generic data replication tools in BIW population is also hampered by the fact that end-user tools often provide their own proprietary population function, sometimes to the exclusion of any other method.

Directions

In the short term, vendors are likely to concentrate on additional source/target combinations and transformation function and on providing update function from previously unsupported sources. This focus is very reasonable, given the current state of the market.

The complexity of reconciliation in BDW population, especially in the case of asynchronous update from multiple sources, has been mentioned in Chapters 8 and 9. Further fundamental research in this and related areas is needed to solve some of the underlying problems [Widom (1995)].

However, it is in the administrative area that the next major advances are likely to be made. These administrative requirements are complex, and need a more standardized approach to data modeling and the use of data dictionaries. The current lack of standards is likely to slow progress in this area.

20.5 Information quality and ownership

In many ways, information quality and ownership are the consequences of the previous four items.

As a company moves to establish a single information source, it must address the issues of information ownership in the BDW in order to ensure the quality and usefulness of the data being stored and subsequently made generally available. Defining the business context of the information also drives the resolution of quality and ownership issues.

As most IS departments and data administrators will readily admit, today's situation is less than satisfactory. Data quality is mixed. Information quality is generally poor. Businesses rarely take information ownership seriously. Indeed, given the data environment that exists, it is difficult to see how the situation could be different.

The technological advances envisaged in the Sections 20.1 to 20.4 are not, in themselves, sufficient to ensure information quality and ownership in the future. However, each can and will contribute to these goals.

Advances in data modeling will allow a closer and more clearly defined linkage between the real business world and the formality of IS. Improvements in the function of the BIG will enable users to actively participate in the evolution of data structures as business needs for information change. Tying the administration of data replication back to the underlying data models will empower end users to define and obtain the data they need, when they need it. Simplifying the maintenance of BDW population will free IS resources to support the end users more proactively. Ultimately this will ease the migration of the current unstructured operational environment to a more consistent, integrated approach [English (1996)].

With a focus on information quality and ownership comes the possibility of —and indeed the need for—changes throughout the organization. The IS department must adopt new development approaches. Power and control of information will move from computer-literate support staff to real end users. Such changes, together with the technical items already mentioned, will have significant impacts on organizations. Academic research in these areas is still in its infancy [McFadden (1996)].

20.6 Concluding remarks

Part I of this book outlined the evolution of data warehousing and asserted that we are now entering an era of information-based management. This era is characterized by decision making based on the reality of the business environment, captured in quality-assured information. In such an environment, successful businesses will be those at the forefront of data warehouse implementation.

As we progressed in the text through examinations of the architecture and design of the warehouse and finally to its implementation, a number of messages have been clear.

An architecture built around information and data is the essential foundation of the warehouse. It can and indeed must ensure that the data stored accurately reflects the information needed and generated by the business. It must ensure enterprise-wide consistency of the time-variant data that describes a business. The three-layer data architecture is the only approach capable of reaching these goals from today's starting point.

From the three-layer architecture springs the technology needed to relate data to information, to extract and reconcile it from the disparate systems of the operational environment, and to distribute it to the end users in a business context. The technology now available has simplified the task of building a warehouse, but it is by no means complete. The data warehouse builder must also construct a sometimes substantial piece of the infrastructure. In fact, it may be argued that, given the diversity and constant evolution of IS environments, this will always be the case.

Implementing the technology of a data warehouse is no guarantee of success. Building a data warehouse is a substantial political undertaking that will result in new organizational structures, new responsibilities, and new ways of doing business. Unless the organization is ready and willing to undergo such change, building a warehouse will be a waste of time and money. However, given the right political environment, a warehouse can be a catalyst for change in the business. It is this possibility that sets data warehousing apart from the majority of other IS initiatives.

The benefits of a warehouse are not easily quantified in advance. However, the success of an implemented warehouse is easy to see. It relates directly to the growth rate of its usage. It relates even more closely to the types of users it attracts. A data warehouse that continuously attracts new users and encourages the uninformed to sit down and work with it is a success.

Today's data, because it lacks business context, is the preserve of the few in most organizations. Management depends on the computer literate to

> *In practice...*
>
> *Three main tasks challenge a warehouse builder today:*
>
> *1. identifying an executive business sponsor with the vision and power to change the organization*
>
> *2. modeling the data warehouse at an enterprise-wide level in realistic steps*
>
> *3. mapping and populating the BDW from existing legacy systems*

prepare and massage this data before it can be effectively used. Information, on the other hand, is understandable by all. From an IS perspective, a data warehouse represents the automation of that preparatory stage.

Simply put, a data warehouse transforms disparate data into information that is consistent across the whole organization, that represents a complete history of the business, and that is valued as a shared asset of the enterprise. A data warehouse unlocks the value of data and makes usable information available to all.

From a business perspective, this is the basis for reinventing the business. In today's rapidly changing and highly competitive business environment, only those businesses that clearly understand themselves and their markets will survive. And only those that constantly seek change in response to or in advance of the market will prosper. For these companies, a data warehouse is the instrument of change.

References

Adelman, S., "Exploring the Data Warehouse's Organizational and Cultural Issues: People-Oriented Issues", *Database Programming and Design*, 25–27 (June 1995).

Adriaans, P. W. and Zantinge, R., *Data Mining*, Addison Wesley Longman, Reading, MA (1996).

Aggarwal, A. K. and Rollier, B., "Issues in Enterprise-Wide Data Modeling", *1994 Proc. Annual Conf. of the International Association for Computer Information Systems* (1994), pp. 192–197.

Ba, S., Whinston, A. B., and Lang, K. R., "An Enterprise Modeling Approach to Organizational Decision Support", *Proc. 28th Hawaii International Conf. on System Sciences*, **3**, IEEE Computing Society Press (1995), pp. 312–320.

Bair, J., "It's about Time! Supporting Temporal Data in a Warehouse", *InfoDB*, **10**, No. 1, 1–7 (1996).

Batra, D. and Marakas, G. M., "Conceptual Data Modeling in Theory and Practice", *European J. of Information Systems*, **4**, No. 3, 185–193 (1995).

Bontempo, C. J. and Saracco, C. M., *Database Management: Principles and Products*, Prentice-Hall PTR, Englewood Cliffs, NJ (1995).

Brackett, M. H., *Data Sharing Using a Common Data Architecture*, Wiley, New York (1994).

Brancheau, J. C., Vogel, D. R. and Wetherbe, J. C., "An Investigation of the Information Center from the User's Perspective", *Data Base*, **17**, No. 1, 4–15 (1985).

Brown, A., "Appraising Intangible Benefits from Information Technology Investment", *Proc. 1st. European Conf. on IT Investment Evaluation*, Operations Research Society (1994), pp. 187–199.

Burk, C. F. and Horton, F. W., *InfoMap: A Complete Guide to Discovering Corporate Information Resources*, Prentice-Hall, Englewood Cliffs, NJ (1988).

Bustamente, G. G. and Sorenson, K., "Decision Support at Lands' End— An Evolution", *IBM Systems Journal*, **33**, No. 2, 228–238 (1994).

Chen, P., "The Entity-Relationship Model—Towards a Unified View of Data", *ACM Transactions on Database Systems*, **1**, 9–36 (1976).

Chowdary, S., "Redeeming Information Systems with Data Warehouses", *American Programmer*, **8**, No. 5, 27–33 (1995).

Codd, E. F., "A Relational Model for Large Shared Data Banks", *Communications of the ACM*, **13**, No. 6, 370–387 (1970).

Date, C. J., *An Introduction to Database Systems*, Addison-Wesley, Reading, MA (1995).

Devlin, B., "Data Warehouse Implementation Experience in IBM Europe", *Proc. SHARE 1991 Spring Conf.*, SHARE Europe, Geneva (1991), pp. 231–247.

Devlin, B. and Murphy, P. T., "An Architecture for a Business and Information System", *IBM Systems Journal*, **27**, No. 1, 60–80 (1988).

Dey, D., Barron, T. M., and Storey, V. C., "A Conceptual Model for the Logical Design of Temporal Databases", *Decision Support Systems* (Netherlands), **15**, No. 4, 305–321 (1995).

Dolk, D. R. and Kirsch, R. A., "A Relational Information Resource Dictionary System", *Communications of the ACM*, **30**, 48–61(1987).

Drucker, P., "The Coming of the New Organization", *Harvard Business Review* (Jan./Feb. 1988).

English, L. P., "Turning Information Management into an Effective Business Enabler", *Information Strategy: The Executive's Journal*, **12**, No. 2, 16–27 (1996).

Evernden, R., "The Information FrameWork", *IBM Systems Journal*, **35**, No. 1, 37–68 (1996).

Fairhead, N., "Data Warehouses: Increasing the Value of your Decision Makers", *Business Quarterly*, **60**, No. 2, 89–94 (1995).

Ferguson, M., "Parallel Computing and the Data Warehouse: Status Report", *InfoDB*, **9**, No. 5, 11–16 (1995).

French, C. D., "'One Size Fits All' Database Architectures do not Work for DSS", *Proc. 1995 ACM SIGMOD, International Conf. on Management of Data* (M. Carey and D. Schneider, Editors.), SIGMOD Record, **24** No. 2 (1995), pp. 449–450.

Goldring, R., "Update Replication: What Every Designer Should Know", *InfoDB*, **9**, No. 2, 17–24 (1995).

Goodhue, D. L., Wybo, M. D. and Kirsch, L. J., "The Impact of Data Integration on the Costs and Benefits of Information Systems", *MIS Quarterly* (Sept. 1992).

Haisten, M., "Planning for a Data Warehouse", *InfoDB*, **9**, No. 1, 12–20 (1995).

Haisten, M., "Designing a Data Warehouse", *InfoDB*, **9**, No. 2, 2–9 (1995).

Haisten, M., "Information Discovery in the Data Warehouse", *InfoDB*, **9**, No. 6, 14–24 (1995).

Hammer, M., *Reengineering the Corporation: A Manifest for Business Revolution*, Harper Business, New York (1993).

Hammond, L. W., "Management Considerations for an Information Center", *IBM Systems Journal*, **21**, No. 2, 131–161 (1982).

Havelka, D. and Khazanchi, D., "An 'Events' Model for Information Aggregation", *J. of Computer Information Systems*, **35**, No. 2, 72–81 (1994).

Herget, J., "Meta Information Systems: How can they Support Corporate Information Management?", *Information Services and Use*, **14**, No. 4, 315–324 (1994).

I/S Analyzer, "How Blue Cross / Blue Shield NCA Designed and Modeled a Data Warehouse", *I/S Analyzer*, **33**, No. 11, 2–6 (1994).

IBM, "Information Warehouse: An Introduction", *GC26-4876-00*, IBM Corporation (1991).

IBM, "Information Warehouse Architecture I", *SC26-324-00*, IBM Corporation (1993).

IBM, "IFW Financial Services Data Model Description", *IFW03101*, IBM Corporation (1994).

IDC, "The Foundations of Wisdom: A Study of the Financial Impact of Data Warehousing", International Data Corporation, Toronto (1996).

Inmon, W. H., *Building the Data Warehouse*, QED Information Sciences, Wellesley, MA (1992).

Inmon, W. H. and Hackathorn, R. D., *Using the Data Warehouse*, Wiley, New York (1994).

Jarke, M., Gallersdorfer, R. and Jeusfeld, R., "ConceptBase—A Deductive Object Base for Meta Data Management", *J. of Intelligent Information Systems* (Netherlands), **3**, No. 2, 167–192 (1995).

Jordan, E., "Information Strategy and Organization Structure", *Info. Systems J.*, **4**, No. 4, 253–270 (1994).

Kalakota, R. and Whinston, A., *Frontiers of Electronic Commerce*, Addison Wesley Longman, Reading, MA (1996).

Kaula, R., "Integrating Decision Support Systems in Organizations: A Three-level Framework", *Industrial Management & Data Systems*, (UK), **94**, No. 4, 8–14 (1994).

Kelly, S., *Data Warehousing: The Route to Mass Customization*, Wiley, New York (1994).

Kerr, J. M., *The IRM Imperative: Strategies for Managing Information Resources*, Wiley, New York (1991).

Manheim, M. L., "Global Information Technology: Issues and Strategic Opportunities", *International Information Systems*, (UK), **1**, No. 1, 38–67 (1992).

Martin, J., *Information Engineering*, Prentice-Hall PTR, Englewood Cliffs, NJ (1990).

McFadden, F. R., "Data Warehouse for EIS: Some Issues and Impacts", *Proc. 29th Annual Hawaii International Conf. on System Sciences*, **2**, IEEE Computer Society Press (1996), pp. 120–129.

McFadden, F. R. and Hoffer, J. A., *Database Management*, Benjamin/Cummings, Redwood City, CA (1994).

Mintzberg, H., *The Structuring of Organizations: A Synthesis of the Research*, Prentice-Hall PTR, Englewood Cliffs, NJ (1979).

Orr, K., "Understanding Data Warehousing", *American Programmer*, **8**, No. 5, 2–7 (1995).

Peters, T. J. and Waterman, R. H., *In Search of Excellence*, Harper & Row, New York (1982).

Poe, V., *Building a Data Warehouse for Decision Support*, Prentice Hall PTR, NJ (1996).

Porter, M. E., *Competitive Advantage: Creating and Sustaining Superior Performance*, Free Press, New York (1985).

Radermacher, F. J., "Decision Support Systems: Scope and Potential", *Decision Support Systems*, **12**, No. 4, 257–265 (1994).

Scheer, A.-W. and Hars, A., "Extending Data Modeling to Cover the Whole Enterprise", *Communications of the ACM*, 166–171 (1992).

Schlatter, M., Furegati, R., Jeger, F., Schneider, H., and Streckeisen, H., "The Business Object Management System", *IBM Systems Journal*, **33**, No. 2, 239–263 (1994).

Soukeras, S. and King, P. J. H., "Temporal Databases: An Event Oriented Approach", *Proc. Directions in Databases, 12th British National Conf. on Databases*, Springer-Verlag (1994) pp. 38–54.

Stecher, P. and Hellemaa, P., "An 'Intelligent' Extraction and Aggregation Tool for Company Data Bases", *Decision Support Systems*, **2**, No. 2, 145–158 (1986).

Tauzovich, B., "Towards Temporal Extensions to the Entity Relationship Model", *Proc. 10th International Conf. on Entity Relationship Approach*, T.J. Teorey (Ed.), San Mateo, CA (1991), pp. 163–179.

Teorey, T. J., *Database Modeling and Design: The Entity-Relationship Approach*, Morgan Kaufmann, New York (1990).

Teorey, T. J., Yang, D. and Fry, J. P., "A Logical Design Methodology for Relational Databases Using the Extended Entity-Relationship Model", *ACM Computing Surveys*, **18**, No. 2, 197–222 (1986).

M. Van Alstyne, E. Brynjolfsson and S. Madnick, "Why Not One Big Database? Principles for Data Ownership", *Decision Support Systems*, **15**, No. 4, 267–284 (1995).

Verity, J. W., "A Trillion-Byte Weapon", *Business Week*, 80–81 (July 31, 1995).

Walker, W. E., "Organizational Decision Support Systems: Centralized Support for Decentralized Organizations", *Annals of Operations Research*, **51**, 283–298 (1994).

Weldon, J. L. and Plagman, B., "Can Data Administration Survive the '90s?", *InfoDB*, **8**, No. 2, 2–9 (1994).

White, C., "A Technical Architecture for Data Warehousing", *InfoDB*, **9**, No. 1, 5–11 (1995).

White, C., "Data Warehousing: The Role of the Information Directory", *InfoDB*, **9**, No. 2, 10–16 (1995).

White, C. E. and Christy, D. P., "The Information Center Concept: A Normative Model and a Study of Six Installations", *MIS Quarterly*, **11**, No. 4, 451–458 (1987).

Widom, J., "Research Problems in Data Warehousing", *Proc. 1995 ACM CIKM International Conference on Information and Knowledge Management*, ACM Press, New York (1995), pp. 25–30.

Wilson, F. A. and Wilson, J. N., "The Role of Computer Systems in Organizational Decision Making", *The Information Society* (UK), **10**, No. 3, 173–180 (1994).

Winograd, T. and Flores, F., *Understanding Computers and Cognition: A New Foundation for Design*, Ablex, Norwood, New York (1986).

Zachman, J. A., "A Framework of Information Systems Architecture", *IBM Systems Journal*, **26**, No. 3, 276–292 (1987).

Zantinge, R. and Adriaans, P. W., *Managing Client/Server*, Addison Wesley Longman, Reading, MA (1996).

Boldface page numbers indicate definition boxes.
Page numbers in *italics* indicate "in practice…" tips.